KV-540-752

EDUCATION
AND CULTURE

EURYDICE

eurostat

Key data
on education
in Europe

WITHDRAWN

EUROPEAN
COMMISSION

A great deal of additional information on the European Union is available on the Internet. It can be accessed through the Europa server (http://europa.eu.int).

Luxembourg: Office for Official Publications of the European Communities, 2000

ISBN 92-828-8537-2

© ECSC-EC-EAEC, Brussels • Luxembourg, 2000

Reproduction is authorized, except for commercial purposes, provided the source is acknowledged.

Printed in Italy

PREFACE

The quality of education and lifelong learning are at the heart of debate in the Community and constitute one of the priorities for action by the European Union on behalf of European citizens. At the outset of the third millennium, education and training are destined to become an essential investment for the future of societies and a key area of cooperation between European countries. The European Commission firmly believes that, if this cooperation is to be intensified and enriched, the availability of a basic set of different kinds of reliable, readily comparable indicators on education systems is an important requirement.

Since 1994, the report Key Data on Education in Europe has offered European citizens information on the current working of the various levels of education, and on developmental trends in recent years from the demographic standpoint but also as regards the transition to the labour market. It provides a comparative view of the effort invested in education in Europe both quantitatively and qualitatively.

This fourth edition is especially noteworthy. In terms of the number of European countries now covered, it testifies to the positive development of cooperation in Europe in its extension to the pre-accession countries. Furthermore, the book has been enriched by the inclusion of many new indicators reflecting the wide variety of common interests that bind Europe together. For example, an entire chapter is devoted to information and communication technology in education systems. This new source of information on a highly topical subject will undoubtedly fuel the debate on lifelong learning and the need to ensure that all citizens are able to use the technology effectively, now that it is vital for successful social and occupational integration.

The present report is the outcome of close collaboration between Eurydice, the information network on education in Europe, and Eurostat. We hope that it will contribute to discussion and debate, at national and European level, on the current position of education systems in Europe and their prospects for the future.

Viviane Reding
Commissioner
Education & Culture

Pedro Solbes Mira
Commissioner
Economic & Monetary Affairs

CONTENTS

Preface

Contents   III

Introduction   V

Key data in brief   A reader's guide to interpreting the data   IX

Glossary   XXIII

     Country codes and abbreviations   XXIII
     Definitions of statistical tools   XXVI

Chapter A — Context   1

Chapter B — Structures and establishments   17

Chapter C — Pre-primary education   43

Chapter D — Primary education   65

Chapter E — Secondary education   77

Chapter F — Tertiary education   103

Chapter G — Teachers   123

Chapter H — Special education   139

Chapter I — Foreign languages   151

Chapitre J — Information and communication technology   165

Annexes   189

Table of Figures   247

Acknowledgements   255

INTRODUCTION

This new edition of *Key data on education in Europe* retains its principal special feature, which is the combination of statistical data and descriptive information on the organization and operation of European education systems. It also keeps its overall structure and general presentation. Nevertheless there are many innovative aspects to this fourth edition. There are changes not only in the number of European countries covered from now on but also in the content and methodology used. The general outline of this report is presented below.

COVERAGE

Key data on education in Europe now covers 29 European countries, in other words all the countries taking part in the activities of the Eurydice network within the Socrates programme and the statistical data collections of Eurostat. Data on Albania, Bosnia-Herzegovina and the former Yugoslavian Republic of Macedonia are presented in the annex to the report.

CONTENTS

Overall, the chapters remain structured by level of education and there has been little change to the table of contents. However two new chapters have been added. Chapter I now gathers together all the information about foreign language learning that had previously been divided between the chapters on primary and secondary education. Chapter J contains a set of new indicators about information and communication technology.

Most indicators from the previous edition have been updated for the fourth edition. Some stable indicators that do not need a regular update have been dropped. New indicators have been added in each chapter. Information is now included on insecure employment among young people (A17), the way education systems are monitored (B10 and B11), the role of parents in school governing bodies (B8 and B9), the content of pre-primary level curricula (C11 – C16), the evolution of participation rates after the end of compulsory education (E18), a comparison of language learning in general and vocational education (I12), the ages at which teachers retire (G9) and the percentage of teachers who are approaching retirement (G10).

No data on the financing of education are included in the fourth edition. They are now being treated in detail in a volume that will be published in June 2000 as part of the series *Key Topics in Education*, produced by Eurydice for the European Commission. Currently being prepared, this publication will deal with the way in which the financial resources allocated to compulsory education institutions are granted and managed. Statistical indicators on the financing of tertiary education, and more particularly on public financial support for students, were published in June 1999 in the first volume of the *Key Topics* series.

It should be stressed that *Key data on education in Europe* deals exclusively with education systems as such. Thus it contains no specific indicators or descriptions on initial and continuous vocational training. To obtain detailed information on these aspects of training, the reader is invited to consult the report of the European Commission and Cedefop entitled *Key data on vocational training in the European Union,* the second edition of which is due to be published at the start of 2000.

Detailed diagrams of the structures and fields of study available in tertiary education have been removed from this edition. They have been updated, supplemented and published separately in the new *Eurydice Focus* series.

The statistical data on education gathered by Eurostat is also disseminated in other publications that are available via the Eurostat datashops network. We would particularly like to draw your attention to the annual publication *Education across Europe – Statistics and indicators.*

PRESENTATION

This publication is intended not only for policy makers but also to inform a very wide public of the numerous facets of the European education systems. The aim is to present both the diversity and the similarities that characterize their organization and way of functioning together with major trends that are apparent. To make it accessible to the greatest number of people and to facilitate consultation, it contains numerous figures in the form of histograms, maps and diagrams. The document is constructed on the basis of alternating comparative, statistical and descriptive graphs and comments bringing out the key points to emerge from the comparison. At the start of the book readers will also find a summary of all the chapters pointing out some approaches to reading them.

All the data used to create the graphics are given in the annexes. Tables containing them are structured by chapter and have the same reference number than the corresponding figure. Explanatory notes and specific explanations necessary for understanding the information are placed directly under the figures.

In the interest of combining readability and precision, a glossary of the codes and abbreviations is presented at the beginning of the book as well as the statistical and terminological tools.

Wherever possible, without damaging the quality of the presentation, information relating to the Member States of the European Union has been commented upon separately and data from those countries has been placed to the left or at the top of the histograms. Likewise, the European average calculated for a large number of indicators is always presented separately to the left of the figures and refers only to data from the European Union.

PARTNERSHIPS AND METHODOLOGY

The choice of indicators to be contained in this fourth edition was made following consultation with members of the Eurydice network and Eurostat's national partners. The contents of the fourth edition, the timetable for preparing the report and the working procedures were decided in a joint meeting of the two networks, organised in May 1998 by the European Commission.

The work was done in two main phases. Firstly the statistical part and the qualitative part were prepared separately. The statistical office of the European Communities, Eurostat, undertook the work of preparing the statistical part and prepared the commentaries about the statistical indicators. The data from the European Economic Area and Cyprus came from the joint UOE (Unesco/OECD/Eurostat) collection and the standardized Eurostat surveys. The data from the countries participating in the PHARE programme were gathered by Eurostat in the context of the "Multi-country Phare programme".

The qualitative part of the report corresponding to the descriptive indicators was the responsibility of the Eurydice network. To collect the new information, questionnaires were developed in direct collaboration with the national units of the network. They were tested and discussed amongst the network's working groups in order to ensure their feasibility and consistency. The analysis of the pre-primary programmes (figures C11 to C16) together with all the information contained in chapter J on information and communication technology are the fruit of these labours. The Eurydice European Unit drafted the analysis of the descriptive data.

Chapter H on special education was prepared with considerable input from the European Agency for Development in Special Needs Education. The national units of the Eurydice network provided all the necessary information on behalf of the pre-accession countries that do not participate in the activities of the Agency. The Agency's national partners also helped to check the whole chapter.

At the end of the first phase of this work, the network of Eurostat national partners and the Eurydice network went on to check the statistical part and the descriptive part respectively. The two parts were then merged. The last phase of checking and revising was carried out jointly by Eurydice and Eurostat. The Eurydice European Unit retained overall responsibility for the final editing of the report. It also prepared all the report's maps, diagrams and graphs.

The diversity of educational systems in Europe and the lack of homogeneity of certain data make prudence necessary when comparing and interpreting indicators. Therefore we have considered it essential to draw the attention of the reader to several specific points:

- The statistical data are structured by educational level in accordance with the Unesco International Standard Classification for Education (ISCED – 1976 edition). This does not always correspond to the structures adopted by the countries and described in the Eurydice diagrams (figures B1, C2, D1, and E1). So when necessary, a note under the diagram warns the reader of the extent to which they are comparable. This attention to detail is particularly important for the classification of ISCED 2 statistics for countries that provide compulsory education in a single structure and therefore do not have a lower secondary level of education.

- The statistical data coming from Eurostat relate to the 1996/1997 academic year while the Eurydice data present the situation in 1997/1998. For this reason, when a reform has taken place or is under way, a note indicates the subject of the changes. If the statistical data were not available for the year referred to, data for the previous or subsequent year are used. This is made clear in the notes.

*

* *

The European Commission would like to thank especially all national Eurostat partners, the units of the Eurydice network and the working partners of the European Agency for Development in Special Needs Education. We are deeply indebted to them for collecting the information and checking the texts, thereby ensuring the reliability and quality of the information.

The Commission would also like to thank the Eurydice European Unit and Eurostat teams for their close cooperation in preparing this book and for their common desire to make the fourth edition as consistent and as readable as possible.

The names of everyone who contributed, at all levels, to producing this collective work are given at the end of the book.

KEY DATA IN BRIEF

A READER'S GUIDE TO INTERPRETING THE DATA

CHAPTER A: CONTEXT

AGE DISTRIBUTION IN EUROPE IS GRADUALLY BECOMING TOP-HEAVY

The change in demographics in Europe since 1975 as revealed in Figures A1 and A2 shows clearly the significant reduction in the number of young people and more particularly of children aged less than 10. This phenomenon is at the root of a change in the distribution of students and pupils between the different levels of education. As the number of teachers is not necessarily evolving in the same direction, this change is one of the factors which, besides the decisions taken by the political policy makers regarding the teaching staff, has affected the pupil-teacher ratio at the various levels of education. For example there are fewer and fewer pupils per teacher in primary schools.

As Figures A4 and A5 show, younger generations are staying on longer at school and leaving the education system better qualified than their elders. On average, the proportion of pupils enrolled at the various levels of compulsory education is the same as that of young people who extend their training beyond the compulsory period (Figure A8).

Today, the predominance in numbers of young people aged over 20, combined with the growth of mass enrolment in tertiary education, explains the growing importance of this level of education. The measures currently being taken in certain countries to limit access to tertiary education (Figure F4) are one of the consequences of this change. And it is prompting the public authorities in some countries to reconsider the management and funding of small rural schools that take in few children at the primary level of education.

THE LEVEL OF EDUCATION STILL CONDITIONS EMPLOYMENT PROSPECTS, BUT QUALIFICATIONS ARE SOMETIMES UNDERVALUED

Generally speaking, the higher the level of education, the lower the risk of insecure employment or of unemployment (Figures A13 and A17). Nowadays, those with a tertiary level qualification form a growing proportion of the active population; this may contribute to intensifying competition among job seekers. Although there is a positive correlation between the level of qualification and access to employment, job security and the level of remuneration (Figure A18), but it is important to emphasize that more and more young graduates are accepting work for which they are overqualified or finding themselves in insecure employment. To be fair, very few of them have jobs that require no qualifications but a certain number occupy positions in the administrative and service industries, as office workers or sales people. This kind of professional experience is encountered less frequently beyond the age of 35 (Figure A16). As they get older most graduates find employment that does full justice to their qualifications.

Data about the numbers of people obtaining tertiary level qualifications (Figure F17) indicate that the social sciences provide the job market with the most graduates. On average, a third of people with tertiary level qualifications fall into this category, which includes those who have studied commerce, business administration, mass communication and documentation. So there is a fear, particularly for young graduates from this sector of finding themselves, at least temporarily, in occupations for which they are not prepared, and being most at risk of seeing their qualification undervalued on the job market.

YOUNG PEOPLE AND WOMEN FIND IT HARDER TO ENTER THE JOB MARKET

The employment market integration of young people displays certain particular characteristics. They suffer the most from unemployment (Figure A11) regardless of the overall level of unemployment in their country (Figure A10). Moreover, if they do find work before the age of 25, they are more likely to find themselves in insecure employment than older people (Figure A12). This is partly because large numbers of the active population aged between 15 and 24 do not have a tertiary level qualification (Figure A17). In this respect, the pre-accession countries differ from the European Union countries. In the former, the proportion of young people in insecure jobs is much lower, and the same applies to the total active population. This is almost certainly associated with the transitional socio-economic situation of these countries: the majority of occupational categories have traditionally been in the public sector so that employment has been relatively secure. However, privatization is increasing there, and a market-based economy is developing. Analysis of statistical trends over the next few years will give a better grasp of how the phenomenon is affecting the status of young people on the job market and their ability to access it.

Finally, women and men are not in a situation of equality as regards employment even if they possess qualifications at an equivalent level. Although more women than men obtain a tertiary level qualification (Figure F16), women, with very few exceptions, are more often unemployed (Figure A15). Only in a few countries is the employment situation for women and men more equally balanced. This applies to some Nordic countries, such as Finland and Sweden, in which the proportion of women graduating from tertiary education has been very high for many years. This may explain the success they enjoy in terms of employment.

CHAPTER B: STRUCTURES AND INSTITUTIONS

This chapter presents the education systems from different angles. Besides presenting educational structures and the numbers of pupils involved, some indicators of how management responsibilities are shared and the way the school year is scheduled are also described.

SCHOOLING EVERYWHERE IS CHARACTERIZED BY THE SAME BROAD STAGES, BUT THE ORGANIZATION AND LENGTH VARY

The first diagram (Figure B1) summarizes the main stages in the education systems. It brings out both their common characteristics and their principal differences. For a more in-depth analysis, a detailed diagram is presented for each level of education in the chapters concerned (Figures C2, D1 and E1). In short, the period of full-time compulsory education amounts today to almost the same number of years everywhere, 9 or 10 years. Three broad stages mark the path through school of all young Europeans: the pre-primary years, primary education and secondary education. However, the length of each stage varies from one country to the next. Primary education lasts four years only in the majority of the German *Länder* and Austria while in the Nordic countries, Portugal and in a good number of pre-accession countries, the nine or ten years of compulsory education are provided in a single structure without a transition. Access to secondary education there is fixed at 15 or 16 years of age. As regards the earliest stage, the diagram also indicates that the provision of pre-primary education differs from one country to another. Thus, in certain countries, school is accessible very early for young children. In others, children do not start school before primary school, and are looked after in other types of establishments described in Chapter C.

All these differences assume greater importance when one tries to compare the distribution of pupils between each level (Figure B2). In fact, the number of years covered by a given educational level is decisive in determining numbers of pupils. The longer it is, the more pupils there are at that level. When calculating the distribution of the numbers of pupils between the levels, the relative size of the figures arrived at is strongly influenced by it. Moreover, when making comparisons, it is important to take into account on one hand, widely varying proportions of children enrolled in education-oriented pre-primary institutions in different countries (Figure C3) and, on the other hand, the way participation rates diminish after the end of compulsory education (Figure E18). Nowadays, lengthening time spent in education is a global phenomenon typical of young Europeans compared with their elders (Figures A4 and A5), but the rapidity with which young people leave the education system at the end of the compulsory period varies between countries. This phenomenon cannot be explained only by the age at which compulsory training ends. In some countries, continuing in post-compulsory studies seems to have become well and truly part of the culture of young people. Far fewer of them leave the education system before having completed at least upper secondary level.

Finally, the limitations on admission to tertiary education introduced in some countries (Figure F4), should also be taken into consideration when comparing the distribution of the school population between the levels of education.

PUBLIC AUTHORITIES REMAIN RESPONSIBLE FOR BASIC EDUCATION ALTHOUGH INSTITUTIONS ARE GIVEN AUTONOMY

Several indicators testify to the considerable responsibility retained by the public authorities in matters of school education. The overwhelming majority of pupils in all countries attend a public or grant-aided private school (Figure B3). Furthermore we know[1] that while respecting freedom of education, public funding is usually made available to private institutions on the basis of operational criteria defined by the public authorities or formal requirements aimed at guaranteeing pupils an equivalent quality of education in the two sectors. The extent of the autonomy granted to schools (Figures B4 and B5) varies between countries. The areas in which it is granted also indicate that, in the majority of European countries, institutions have considerable autonomy in organizing the timetable and managing teaching. However the public authorities maintain significant control in financial matters and personnel management. In allowing institutions almost complete autonomy in most areas considered in the analysis, the Netherlands and the United Kingdom (particularly England and Wales) are the exceptions.

NEW PATTERNS OF MANAGEMENT COMBINED WITH INCREASING INSTITUTIONAL RESPONSIBILITY

The obligation on schools to draw up plans or formal proposals for activity in a good number of countries (Figure B10) has to be seen in relation to the growing autonomy given them in other respects. In the same way, the creation of management bodies at institution level enabling parents to participate and sometimes giving them decision-making powers (Figure B9) is a typical measure taken by the public authorities, following the progressive decentralization of education system management.

Finally, ways of monitoring the education system introduced in one form or another in a growing number of countries, indicate the extent to which quality control and the possibility of regulating and improving the functioning of the education system exercise the minds of political decision-makers and remain the prerogative of the public authorities. The results of national examinations for the award of certificates are the most often used to carry out the analyses. Few countries set diagnostic tests purely for monitoring purposes (Figure B11).

SCHOOL CALENDARS ARE INCREASINGLY FLEXIBLE

At a time when school partnerships and exchanges between institutions are developing at a European level in the context of Community programmes such as Socrates, it has become essential for those who run these programmes to have available some indicators on how the school year is scheduled and when the holidays fall (Figures B6 and B7) in the different countries. These data also highlight the variations that can exist even within some countries in this respect. In this way, one can distinguish between countries where the organization of school time remains fairly centralized and those in which regional and local variations are possible because authority in these matters has been decentralized. The pre-accession countries present overall the most uniform centralized pattern as regards the dates of the return to school (Figure B6). However, the way holiday periods are distributed over the year in some central and eastern European countries can vary.

---

[1] Awarding and managing the financial resources made available to institutions, *Key Topics* Volume 2, European Commission, to be published in 2000

CHAPTER C: PRE-PRIMARY EDUCATION

This chapter is concerned solely with formal institutions providing pre-primary education for young children before they start primary school. Child-minding and other private ways of catering for young children are not presented. Moreover, apart from diagram C2 that refers to many types of child care, all the other descriptions and all the statistical data concern institutions described as education oriented. These have been selected on the basis of the type of qualification required of the staff.

TRAINING REQUIREMENTS FOR THIS LEVEL ARE BECOMING MORE STRINGENT EVERYWHERE

It can be seen that, in all countries, education-oriented institutions are accessible from the age of three or four at the latest. An examination of Figure G1 makes it clear that the level of training of the adults responsible for the education of very young children is high, and is sometimes even identical to the training required for teachers within compulsory education. A comparison between existing educational structures and the level of training indicates that university education is not only a characteristic of countries that provide schools at pre-primary level. Conversely, provision of upper secondary level education for adults in charge is found both in countries where young children go to non-school centres of education and in those in which schools receive the children.

CERTAIN OPERATIONAL PARAMETERS DIFFER BETWEEN SCHOOL AND NON-SCHOOL SETTINGS

Whether or not countries opt for school or non-school pre-primary education for their very young children has nothing to do with how important they consider this level. It is the product of history and traditions. It is also attributable to different views regarding approaches to education. In any event, the choice between the two models seems to influence several operational parameters. Grouping children by age is more typical of schools (Figure C8) and the maximum number of children per adult is also often greater in schools (Figure C9). According to the official recommendations, the objectives are fairly comparable in the two types of structures. Neither do schools differ from non-school forms of provision in terms of their recommended activities. It is their approaches to teaching that distinguish them the most (Figure C16).

RISING PARTICIPATION RATES REFLECT THE IMPORTANCE ATTACHED TO THIS LEVEL

Participation rate trends alone (Figure C1) reveal how much effort has been invested everywhere in recent decades in giving the greatest possible number of very young children the opportunity to attend an education-oriented institution before entering primary school.

Of course the participation rates presented by age in Figure C3 are to be interpreted in relation to the number of places available in the different countries and thus to accessibility, the existence or not of other forms of child care for the families, and to distinct cultural perceptions of the part played by the family in educating children. Irrespective of the particular circumstances, the importance of pre-primary education is increasingly recognized. Whether or not children attend pre-primary institutions[2] can now no longer be explained simply by the necessity for working mothers to find a way of looking after their children (Figure C6).

---

[2] For detailed information on the history of pre-primary education and the results of research carried out in this area, please read the study carried out by the European Commission published in 1996 entitled *Pre-school Education in the European Union. Current thinking and provision*, Studies no. 6.

CHAPTER D: PRIMARY EDUCATION

THE LIFE OF SCHOOLCHILDREN IN EUROPE AGED BETWEEN SIX AND TEN IS SIMILAR IN MANY RESPECTS

Entry to primary school usually coincides with the start of the period of compulsory education. In all the countries surveyed, the age of children is the principal criterion for admission at this level (Figure C17) but, in most cases, all children start on the same date. In certain countries maturity and, more rarely, the results of tests are among the admission criteria. Aptitude criteria are to be found both in countries where pre-primary education is provided in a school environment, and those in which other types of provision cater for very young children.

The distribution of educational activities and subjects among the members of the teaching staff of an institution is becoming increasingly flexible and varies with the age of the pupils (Figure D3). The appearance of the compulsory teaching of foreign languages (Figure I1) and information and communication technology (Figure J11) in the primary curriculum in numerous countries is certainly one of the factors explaining this. With the growing diversity of subjects and the many skills required to teach them, teamwork or the sharing of classes by teachers has become essential. This flexibility is also no doubt partially attributable to the desire to develop interdisciplinary projects and approaches. However, the most widespread situation in the initial years of schooling is that a single teacher takes on a multiplicity of subjects. In some countries, the timetable of the youngest children is also reduced in comparison with that of the last years of primary education (Figure D6).

SCHOOL CURRICULA DIFFER IN TERMS OF THE TIME ALLOTTED TO VARIOUS SUBJECTS

The annual number of teaching hours is generally lower, at all ages, in the pre-accession countries. These countries also make precise recommendations as to the number of hours to devote to each subject in the curriculum. By contrast, in some countries of the European Union, curricula only specify the compulsory subjects, leaving the local authorities or schools at liberty to determine the time spent on each (Figures D7 and D8).

SECONDARY LEVEL IS INCREASINGLY REGARDED AS THE CONTINUATION OF BASIC STUDIES

The end of primary education is becoming less of a decisive stage in the academic career of young Europeans. Indeed, relatively few countries still award a certificate or direct pupils towards different types of courses at that age (Figure D10). In many cases, young people receive a common education during the last years of compulsory education, and their choice of study option is deferred. Today only the German speaking countries still direct pupils to different types of education at the start of secondary school.

CHAPTER E: SECONDARY EDUCATION

At the start of the chapter Diagram E1 presents the organization of secondary education in detail, showing both the range of branches and their duration. The possibilities of sandwich courses, part time courses and supplementary years are indicated, as are any compulsory changes of institution during this stage.

CHOOSING A VOCATIONAL COURSE DEPENDS ON THE RANGE OF COURSES AVAILABLE

The distribution of students between the vocational and general streams in lower secondary education (Figure E3) and upper secondary education (Figure E4) gives a numerical illustration of curricular organization in the majority of systems at these levels. Thus, the very low percentages of students in vocational courses before the age of 15 reflect the fact that few countries offer the possibility of following such courses before the end of compulsory education. By contrast, in upper secondary education as a whole, the majority of young Europeans undergo vocational training at upper secondary level. This predominance is particularly marked in the pre-accession countries and in the German speaking countries. Conversely, some countries stand out because a large majority of their students are in the general stream. This is noticeable both at national and regional levels (Figure E6).

Lastly, by choosing general courses in greater numbers than boys (Figure E5), girls outnumber them in obtaining general upper secondary education qualifications (Figure E13).

IN SOME COUNTRIES, ALL STUDENTS HAVE AN IDENTICAL COMPULSORY CURRICULUM; IN OTHERS, THEY CHOOSE THEIR SUBJECTS.

There are less striking differences between countries in compulsory minimum course workloads at secondary level (Figures E7 and E8) than at primary level. Variations are most conspicuous in the amount of teaching time devoted to compulsory subjects (Figures E10 and E11). The further students progress through secondary school, the less they follow a common core curriculum, even in the general stream. The emphasis now switches to compulsory options and, in certain countries, students assemble their own programmes of study depending on the qualifications they want to achieve.

THE AWARD OF FINAL SECONDARY SCHOOL QUALIFICATIONS IS OFTEN SUBJECT TO OUTSIDE SCRUTINY

Given the importance of an upper secondary school qualification for admission to tertiary education, this chapter contains information on procedures underlying the award of certificates to pupils. Analysis reveals that certificates are not very often awarded at the end of lower secondary education on the basis of satisfactory performance in externally set exams (Figure E14 and E15). Periodic marking and coursework done over the year are sufficient for many countries. In most cases, schools themselves set the exams at this level of education and decide whether or not to award the certificate. By contrast, at the end of upper secondary education, students often have to take exams either set by external bodies or, at least, marked or checked by an external body (Figures E16 and E17).

CHAPTER F: TERTIARY EDUCATION

MORE AND MORE YOUNG PEOPLE ARE DOING HIGHER LEVEL COURSES BUT INEQUALITIES PERSIST

There has been a constant increase in numbers of students in tertiary education over the last 20 years (Figure F2). This trend can be seen in all the EU and EFTA/EEA countries. This rise has led to a higher percentage of graduates in the under 40 age group by comparison with the generation aged 55-59 (Figure F15). However, mass student enrolment at tertiary level is not synonymous with equality of access for all young people. Disparities still exist. They can be seen between the regions (Figure F3) and in terms of the social origins of students (Figure F13). Furthermore, while women are represented as well as, or even better than, men at tertiary level (Figure F12), there are still great contrasts in the branches of study in which they obtain qualifications. Arts and social science courses remain among the most popular courses for women (Figure F18). Conversely, men predominate in engineering, architecture, mathematics and informatics studies.

STUDENTS BEAR A SMALL PROPORTION OF THE COST AND GRANTS CONSTITUTE THE MOST COMMON FORM OF FINANCIAL SUPPORT

In the EU and EFTA/EEA countries, there are two main scenarios when it comes to the individual taking on some of the cost (Figure F9). In about half the countries, the government covers all or nearly all of it. Elsewhere, the students contribute to the expense of their education. They might even have to make quite a large financial contribution. In the pre-accession countries almost all students participate in financing tertiary education via registration fees.

The forms of financial support awarded to students while they undertake their studies are under discussion in a number of countries. The main debates are described in *Key Topics in education*, published in June 1999, in which this question is given detailed consideration[3]. Here, a short description is given in Figure F10. From this, it is clear that grants represent the most common form of financial support, whether or not they are combined with loans. The pre-accession countries almost exclusively offer grants but the introduction of loans is currently being debated or planned.

---

[3] A detailed analysis of the issue of course fees and registration fees was undertaken in the first volume of the series *Key Topics in Education* devoted to financial support for students in tertiary education in Europe. Only a bare minimum of the information is included in the present volume of *Key data*. Data on the pre-accession countries have been added.

CHAPTER G: TEACHERS

LENGTH OF COURSE IS THE PRINCIPAL DIFFERENCE BETWEEN THE LEVELS OF TEACHER TRAINING

Figures G1 to G4, showing the initial training of teachers, make it clear that, with rare exceptions, it is provided at tertiary level. Some countries have even made their teacher training completely uniform for all levels. However in certain countries, secondary-level courses for the adults responsible for educating pre-primary children, are still given in parallel with those offered in tertiary education. If this is the case, the qualification obtained is generally not that of a teacher. It is also noticeable that if teachers intend teaching at the higher levels of school, they have to study for longer, and university courses are the norm.

The chapter does not include information on the content of training courses. It is however likely that the effort expended by the public authorities to raise the level of teacher training has been accompanied by revision of the courses in order to adapt them to new needs. As is clear from Chapter J on information and communication technology, many countries have integrated this field of knowledge into the curriculum for those training to teach at either primary or secondary level (Figures J21 to 23). However in a good number of cases, the courses concerned are optional for would-be teachers. Only a few EU countries make them compulsory.

PROFESSIONAL TRAINING STARTS LATER FOR SECONDARY SCHOOL TEACHERS

Professional training usually gets directly under way at the start of tertiary education for those who want to become pre-primary and primary teachers; those intending to become upper secondary level teachers start by doing a general course usually leading to a first university degree, and follow that with professional teacher training as such.

DESPITE THE REQUIREMENT FOR TRAINING, CONDITIONS GOVERNING TEACHER SALARIES ARE NOT EQUIVALENT EVERYWHERE

Seniority remains the main source of the differences in salaries within the teaching profession but, within a given country, differences in the training provided for the various levels of teaching are often reflected in the salary conditions of teachers during their careers (Figures G12 to G14). A comparison between the national situations indicates that it is difficult to establish a connection between the level of salaries with respect to GDP and the length or university status of the training. In fact, the salaries of teachers trained at university can be equivalent or even inferior to those of teachers who have trained for less time or at non-university level.

Given that the requirements for training have increased, the question of teacher salaries is being discussed in many European countries. In fact, for the most part, salaries in the teaching profession are being increased in line with the level of qualification and to make teaching more attractive, while keeping public-sector expenditure within reasonable limits.

PART TIME WORK IS NOT COMMON AND IS MORE FREQUENT FOR UPPER SECONDARY LEVEL TEACHERS

The choice of a part time career in the teaching profession is not taken up widely in the European countries. In many countries fewer than 20% of teachers work part time. However the situation varies enormously from one country to another and from one level of education to another (Figure G6). In the majority of countries, part time teaching is more common in upper secondary education. Some countries present contrasting practices by comparison to the average: up to half of all teachers may work part time, or the figure may be minimal. As the percentage of women in the profession (Figure G11) is quite high everywhere and particularly at the primary level, it is not possible to establish a link between numbers of women in teaching and part time working. On the contrary, a comparison between these two indicators tends to show that it is at the upper secondary level, which generally speaking employs the highest proportion of men, that part time working is most extensive. The explanation can be found, among other things, in the different way of dividing the subjects between teachers in the two levels. Secondary school teachers are specialists in one or more subjects and take groups of students for certain periods spread over the week. This way of arranging things opens up many more possibilities of working part time, whereas at the primary level, teachers are often responsible for the same class for the greater part of the week (Figure D3).

GROWING NUMBERS OF TEACHERS CLOSE TO RETIREMENT REFLECT THE AGEING OF THE TEACHER POPULATION

A large number of European teachers are aged over 40. This finding is particularly valid at secondary level (figures G7 and G8). In many countries the proportion is about half, and occasionally rises to over 80%. A few countries are exceptions to this trend with as many as 20% of their teachers aged under 30. Teachers' ages in themselves are not a sufficient indicator for planning long term recruitment and avoiding possible shortfalls over the next few years. It is important to take into consideration the legal age fixed for retirement (Figure G9). This is rarely identical for everyone. Criteria such as the number of years' service, and gender are often taken into account to provide for early retirement. Only the maximum retirement age is fairly comparable between countries: it is generally fixed at 65 but some countries allow staff to continue with their careers until the age of 70. Figure G10 takes account of these varying parameters and shows the proportion of teachers nearing the end of their careers. This indicator has been calculated taking account of individual situations in each country. It shows the proportion of teachers who are within ten years of the end of their career. It is obvious that, for countries for which data is available, the situation varies greatly between EU and pre-accession countries. The percentage is much higher overall for the latter; a quarter or more of the teaching population is close to retirement. The EU average is 10%, but differences between countries range from just a few percent to around 20%.

In years to come, one important issue facing educational policies will be that of tackling the replacement of a very large proportion of teachers. By recruiting young, recently trained people to the profession, educational systems will benefit from teachers who are better prepared for the new challenges confronting those systems and, in particular, the teaching of languages (Chapter I) and ICT (Chapter J).

CHAPTER H: SPECIAL EDUCATION

Over the century, education systems have evolved towards a progressively less segregated approach to providing for children with special needs. Today, the majority of European countries have several models existing side by side (Figure H1). Very few countries have maintained the "two-track" option, in which the majority of these children attend specialized institutions (Figure H2). Nevertheless some separate structures exist in almost all countries. They are fairly similar to those in ordinary education. Italy and Norway are the only countries that do not have separate institutions (Figure H4).

THE PROPORTION OF CHILDREN RECOGNIZED AS HAVING SPECIAL NEEDS VARIES ENORMOUSLY

The proportion of children in the school population, who are recognized as having special needs depends on the criteria used to identify the need(s). These criteria and evaluation procedures vary from one country to another. The percentage of children attending separate educational institutions depends on the choices as regards their school provision. As Figure H5 shows, these two proportions are not always the same. The discrepancy is an indicator of the degree to which integration is practised. Some Nordic countries stand out in having a proportion of children with recognized special needs which, at 12-16% of the school population, is noticeably higher than elsewhere. Yet few of them receive a separate form of schooling.

Conditions are generally established to ensure the children are integrated successfully. They vary from one country to another and from one need to another.

IN THE CONTEXT OF INTEGRATION, SPECIALIZED SUPPORT IS ALWAYS PROVIDED BUT THE PATTERN DIFFERS

Whether provided in separate institutions or not, the education of children with special needs requires qualified staff and specialist support. In most cases, specialist teachers provide the teaching support needed in classes receiving the children with special needs. They may or may not be officially on the staff of the school.

Depending on the country, initial training to prepare teachers for work with special needs pupils is more or less intensive (Figure H3). All teachers receive at least a minimum of training in this area. In certain countries, a specialized curriculum is provided for persons who wish to work with these children. The existence of this kind of specialist course does not seem to depend on the pattern of special needs provision in the country concerned. Indeed, it is to be found both in countries where integration is widely practised, as well as in those in which segregation remains significant.

CHAPTER I: FOREIGN LANGUAGES

FOREIGN LANGUAGES ARE COMING INTO COURSES EARLIER AND EARLIER

In the European Union, on average, half of primary school children learn a foreign language (Figure I2). The percentages observed do not only depend on whether it is compulsory to teach a language at a certain stage of school life (Figure I1). In fact, in some countries, almost all primary school children are taught a foreign language although it is not compulsory in the first years. So schools offer these courses and pupils have the option of taking them. Usually it becomes compulsory to teach a foreign language at about the age of 10, but certain countries keep the choice optional or are introducing the courses in the form of pilot projects.

The increasingly important position that foreign languages occupy in school curricula (Figure I1) and the time devoted to teaching them (Figures D8 and E10) reflect the effort put in by European policy makers convinced of the importance of everyone mastering at least one foreign language.

Reforms are under way in several countries. The objective is to make foreign language teaching available, in the near or fairly near future, to all pupils. The transition phase actually under way for this aspect of education is often justified either by the lack of teachers capable of undertaking this work, or by the difficulty of making the current education budget bear the additional expense implied by bringing the reform into general practice immediately.

THE RANGE OF LANGUAGES STUDIED IS DECREASED IN FAVOUR OF ENGLISH

Despite the desire expressed in official texts to conserve the multilingual character of Europe, English is everywhere the language studied by the greatest number of young people at primary school and general secondary school (Figures I3 and I7). In some countries this is explained in part by the choice of the decision-makers to make this language compulsory for all pupils[4].

THE PERCENTAGE OF STUDENTS LEARNING MORE THAN ONE LANGUAGE VARIES ACCORDING TO THE STREAM CHOSEN AT SECONDARY LEVEL

In certain countries, equivalent numbers of students in the vocational stream and the general stream can learn a foreign language (Figure I12). However, this is not the case everywhere and in some countries, the gap between vocational and general is widening, to the detriment of vocational training. This difference between the branches is particularly noticeable when it comes to learning a second language. Generally speaking, a lower percentage of students learn at least two foreign languages in the vocational stream.

---

[4] A study on language teaching is currently being prepared by Eurydice. It is mainly concerned with the question of teaching arrangements, curriculum content, teacher training and the reforms carried out in this area in Europe. Publication is expected in the summer of 2000.

CHAPTER J: INFORMATION AND COMMUNICATION TECHNOLOGY

This chapter examines national policies regarding teaching information and communication technology. It clearly reveals the priority given to developing this sector, certainly in line with the development of the Internet and the many instruments of communication destined to become indispensable in everyone's daily lives.

EDUCATION POLICIES ARE INCREASINGLY GEARED TO THE USE OF ICT

Information and communication technology lies at the heart of national policies. All European countries today possess official documents aiming to promote their use (Figure J1). The integration of ICT into school systems is becoming progressively more widespread. In a few cases a long-standing priority, ICT policies are increasingly being implemented. Nearly everywhere, bodies have been set up to promote or supervise the implementation of recommendations. Education systems are being directly targeted by national projects drawn up in all countries (Figure J3). The year 2000 is often a pivotal date in the implementation of these national programmes.

BUDGETS ARE RARELY MANAGED SOLELY AT CENTRAL GOVERNMENT LEVEL

National statistical data available regarding the purchase and maintenance of ICT equipment, or the ICT budget are hard to compare. No standardized database exists to this day. This chapter does not therefore contain any information on the scale of school equipment and facilities or the size of the budget allocated to ICT in the various countries. The difficulty of obtaining this sort of information is explained partly by the shared responsibilities for the purchase and maintenance of equipment. Indeed, as Figure J4 shows, in Europe it is very unusual to find financial management resting solely with the ministry in central government. Equipment budgets are most often managed either at the local level or jointly, with the responsibility shared between several layers of authority. The way budgets are allocated between equipment and human resources has also proved difficult to identify clearly in many countries. However, where the breakdown is known, equipment has taken precedence in expenditure (Figures J5 to J7).

ICT IS PRESENT IN SCHOOL CURRICULA AND OBJECTIVES PURSUED ARE FAIRLY SIMILAR

Even at primary level, numerous countries have written ICT objectives into the minimum compulsory curriculum. Elsewhere, the integration of ICT has been provided for or offered in an optional way (Figure J11). The use of ICT as a tool to be used for projects or for educational content is the approach most commonly recommended for primary schools (Figure J12). Pre-accession countries typically teach it as a separate curriculum subject. At the secondary level, ICT is more commonly taught in this way (Figure J15). The aims pursued differ little with the level of education (Figures J13, J16 and J19). The different approaches recommended are to be set in the context of teacher training. ICT specialists are most likely to be found at the secondary level (Figure J20). They teach ICT as a separate subject, whereas teachers of other subjects make use of ICT as a tool.

NOT ALL COUNTRIES HAVE INCLUDED ICT IN THE COMPULSORY CURRICULUM OF INITIAL TEACHER TRAINING

While in many countries ICT has been included as a compulsory part of curricula for pupils, this is not the case in the initial curricula for teacher training, for either primary or secondary level. An ICT course in teacher training is compulsory in fewer than half the European countries. In the remainder it is optional (Figures J21 to J23).

This appears to be inconsistent with the integration of ICT into the courses. Indeed, only teachers who have themselves been trained in the use of ICT will be in a position to supervise their pupils effectively as they become fully familiar with and gradually master its essential resources. Although all the countries have laid down a policy of in-service training for teachers taking account of these aspects, it would appear no less urgent to ensure that all future teachers acquire the necessary skills. This is an inescapable requirement if the younger generations are to master ICT.

Indeed, securing quality education in all schools presupposes that teachers are not left to provide for their own training entirely on their own initiative, in such an important priority field.

GLOSSARY

CODES AND ABBREVIATIONS

COUNTRY CODES

EU	European Union
B	Belgium
B fr	Belgium – French Community
B de	Belgium – German-speaking Community
B nl	Belgium – Flemish Community
DK	Denmark
D	Germany
EL	Greece
E	Spain
F	France
IRL	Ireland
I	Italy
L	Luxembourg
NL	Netherlands
A	Austria
P	Portugal
FIN	Finland
S	Sweden
UK	United Kingdom
E/W	England and Wales
NI	Northern Ireland
SC	Scotland
EFTA/EEA	European Free Trade Association / European Economic Area
IS	Iceland
LI	Liechtenstein
NO	Norway
Pre-accession countries	
BG	Bulgaria
CZ	Czech Republic
EE	Estonia
LV	Latvia
LT	Lithuania
HU	Hungary
PL	Poland
RO	Romania
SI	Slovenia
SK	Slovakia
CY	Cyprus

LANGUAGES CODES

DA	Danish
NL	Dutch
EN	English
FI	Finnish
FR	French
DE	German
EL	Greek
IT	Italian
PT	Portuguese
ES	Spanish
SV	Swedish

ABBREVIATIONS OF STATISTICAL TOOLS AND OTHER CLASSIFICATIONS

(:)	Not available
(*)	Estimate
Ø	Average
ESA	European system of accounts
EU	European average (tables and graphs)
F	Female/Women
FTE	Full-time equivalents
GDP	Gross domestic product
ILO	International Labour Organization
ISCED	International Standard Classification for Education
ISCO	International Standard Classification of Occupations
LFS	Labour Force Survey
M	Male/Men
NUTS	Nomenclature of territorial units for statistics
UOE	Unesco/OCDE/Eurostat

NATIONAL ABBREVIATIONS IN THEIR LANGUAGE OF ORIGIN

AEI	Anotato Ekpaideftiko Idryma	EL
BAC	Baccalauréat	F
BEP	Brevet d'études professionnelles	F
BTS	Brevet de technicien supérieur	F, L
BUP	Bachillerato Unificado y Polivalente	E
CAP	Certificat d'aptitude professionnelle	F
CAPES	Certificat d'aptitude au professorat de l'enseignement secondaire	F
CI	Contrat institutionnel	EU
COU	Curso de Orientación Universitaria	E
CPGE	Classes préparatoires aux grandes écoles	F
CS	Community school/Comprehensive school	IRL
CSPOPE	Cursos Secundários Predominantemente Orientados para o Prosseguimento de Estudos	P
CT	Cursos Tecnológicos	P
DBSO	Deeltijds beroepssecundair onderwijs	B nl
ETI	Education and Training Inspectorate	UK (NI)
EUD	Erhvervsuddannelse	DK
FHL	Fachhochschule Liechtenstein	LI
GS	Grammar school	UK (E, NI)
GCSE	General Certificate of Secondary Education	UK (E/W,NI)
HAVO	Hoger Algemeen Voortgezet Onderwijs	NL

NATIONAL ABBREVIATIONS IN THEIR LANGUAGE OF ORIGIN

HBO	Hoger Beroepsonderwijs	NL
HF	Højere Forberedelseseksamen	DK
HHX	Højere Handelseksamen	DK
HMI	Her Majesty's Inspector	UK
HTX	Højere Teknisk Eksamen	DK
IAP	Internationale Akademie für Philosophie	LI
ICT	Information and communication technology	
IEES	Institut d'études éducatives et sociales	L
ISERP	Institut supérieur d'études et de recherches pédagogiques	L
IST	Institut supérieur de technologie	L
IUFM	Institut universitaire de formation des maîtres	F
IUT	Instituts universitaires technologiques	F
LOGSE	Ley Orgánica de Ordenación General del Sistema Educativo	E
MAVO	Middelbaar Algemeen Voortgezet Onderwijs	NL
MBO	Middelbaar Beroepsonderwijs	NL
OFSTED	Office for Standards in Education	UK (E)
OHMCI	Office of Her Majesty's Chief Inspector of Schools	UK (W)
PATES	Paidagogiki techniki scholi	EL
PIC	Programme interuniversitaire de coopération	EU
PPS	Program Priprave na Šolo	SI
SCRIPT	Service de coordination de la recherche et de l'Innovation	L
STS	Sections de techniciens supérieurs	F
SV	Stredné vzdelanie (secondary education)	SK
TEE	Technika Epagelmatika Ekpaideftiria	EL
TEI	Technologiko Ekpaideftiko Idryma	EL
TES	Techniki epaggelmatiki scholi	EL
UCAS	Universities and Colleges Admissions Services	UK
ÚSV	Úplné stredné vzdelanie (secondary education)	SK
VBO	Voorbereidend Beroepsonderwijs	NL
VS	Vocational school	IRL
VWO	Voorbereidend Wetenschappelijk Onderwijs	NL
WO	Wetenschappelijk Onderwijs	NL

DEFINITIONS OF STATISTICAL TOOLS

SOURCES OF STATISTICAL DATA

THE UOE DATA COLLECTION

The UOE (Unesco/OECD/Eurostat) data collection is an instrument through which these three organizations jointly collect internationally comparable data on key aspects of education systems on an annual basis using administrative sources. Data collected cover enrolments, new entrants, graduates, educational personnel, education institutions and educational expenditure. The specific breakdowns include level of education, sex, age, type of curriculum (general, vocational), mode (full-time/part-time), type of institution (public/private), field of study and nationality. In addition, to meet the information needs of the European Commission, Eurostat collects enrolment data by region and on foreign language learning.

In 1998 the pre-accession countries participated in collecting education data for the first time; the ISCED 97 classification was used. In this volume, data collected according to the ISCED 97 classification were converted into ISCED 76 so they could be compared with data from other countries. ISCED level 4 has been assimilated into ISCED level 3.

EUROSTAT DEMOGRAPHIC DATABASE

Eurostat collects the national demographic data from responses to an annual questionnaire sent to the national statistical institutes of the Member States of the European Union and EFTA countries. The annual national population estimates are based either on the most recent census or on data extracted from the population register. Demographic data are only gathered at regional level from the Member States of the European Union.

THE COMMUNITY LABOUR FORCE SURVEY (LFS)

The LFS, which has been carried out annually since 1983, is the principal source of statistics on employment and unemployment in the European Union. This survey is directed at individuals and households. The questions mainly cover the characteristics of employment and job seeking. It also includes questions on participation in education or training during the four weeks prior to the survey and information on the level of education attained. The definitions are common for all Member States and are based in particular on the recommendations of the International Labour Organization.

NOMENCLATURE/CLASSIFICATIONS USED

INTERNATIONAL STANDARD CLASSIFICATION OF EDUCATION (ISCED 1976)

In order to facilitate comparision between countries, data on education in each country are allocated to the various level categories of the International Standard Classification of Education (ISCED). However, in making international comparisons, it is important to take account of the numerous differences in the national education and training systems.

A brief description of the ISCED levels is presented in the table below:

ISCED 0 (pre-primary education)   Education preceding primary education. In the vast majority of cases, it is not compulsory.

ISCED 1 (primary education)   Begins between the ages of four and seven, is compulsory in all cases and lasts five or six years as a rule.

ISCED 2 (lower secondary education)   Compulsory education in all EU countries. The end of this level corresponds often to the end of full-time compulsory education.

ISCED 3 (upper secondary education)   Begins around the age of 14 and 15 and refers to either general or vocational education. It may lead to the standard required for admission to tertiary education or it may be "terminal", as is sometimes the case with vocational education and training.

ISCED 5, 6, 7 (tertiary education)   Due to discrepancies in the allocation of data to the three ISCED levels comprising tertiary education, data in this report refer to the three levels combined.

The three levels are:

> **ISCED 5** Covers programmes which generally do not lead to the awarding of a university degree or equivalent, but admission to this level usually requires the successful completion of a programme at the uper secondary level.

> **ISCED 6** Covers programmes leading to a first university degree or equivalent.

> **ISCED 7** Covers programmes leading to a second, post graduate university degree.

> This classification was revised in 1997 to cover more adequetely the changing structure of education and training systems.

THE NOMENCLATURE OF TERRITORIAL UNITS FOR STATISTICS (NUTS)

This was established by Eurostat to provide a single, uniform breakdown of territorial units for the production of regional statistics for the European Union. The NUTS is a five-level hierarchical classification (three regional levels and two local levels) which in most cases subdivides Member States into a number of NUTS level 1 regions, each of which is in turn subdivided into a number of NUTS 2 regions, and so on. For Sweden, the regional breakdown only begins at NUTS level 2, Denmark and Ireland at NUTS level 3 and Luxembourg at NUTS level 4. The published data mainly cover NUTS levels 1 and 2. However, because of some recent administrative changes, the regional divisions used can differ according to the source. This is particularly the case in Sweden, Finland and in the United Kingdom.

DEFINITIONS/NOTES ON THE CALCULATIONS

Unemployment

For a comparable measure of unemployment in the EU, Eurostat applies the recommendation of the International Labour Office (ILO), according to which the unemployed comprise persons aged 15 and over who :

- are without work;
- are currently available for work, i.e. can start a job within two weeks, and
- have been actively seeking work during the past four weeks.

The unemployment rate is the percentage of the active population which is unemployed.

Participation rates

Participation rates for a given age are the ratio of the number of children of this age registered at a given level of education (or in a given type of institution) and the total population of this age.

European average

If not mentionned otherwise, the European average is calculated on the basis of the European Union Member States for which data is available.

——— FEWER AND FEWER YOUNG PEOPLE IN EUROPE ———

In 1997, the number of young people under 30 years of age stood at 142 million in the European Union. This figure has been falling constantly since 1975.

FIGURE A1: CHANGE IN THE NUMBERS OF YOUNG PEOPLE IN THE 0-9, 10-19 AND 20-29 AGE GROUPS IN THE EUROPEAN UNION, FROM 1975 TO 1997

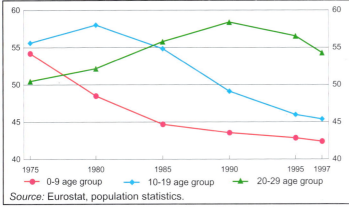

Source: Eurostat, population statistics.

The change in the different age groups illustrates the downward trend in the number of young people; the number in the 20-29 age band actually increased regularly until 1990 and declined slowly since then. In other words, this means that the birth rates have been dropping since the middle of the 1960s.

Moreover, the proportion of the youngest, continues to decrease, giving the impression that deceleration in the birth rate is continuing.

Thus, within the Member States, the 20-29 age group is generally the largest one, except in Ireland, where the 10-19 age group predominates, reflecting a later deceleration in the birth rate in this country.

FIGURE A2: PERCENTAGE OF THE POPULATION IN THE 0-9, 10-19 AND 20-29 AGE GROUPS, 1997

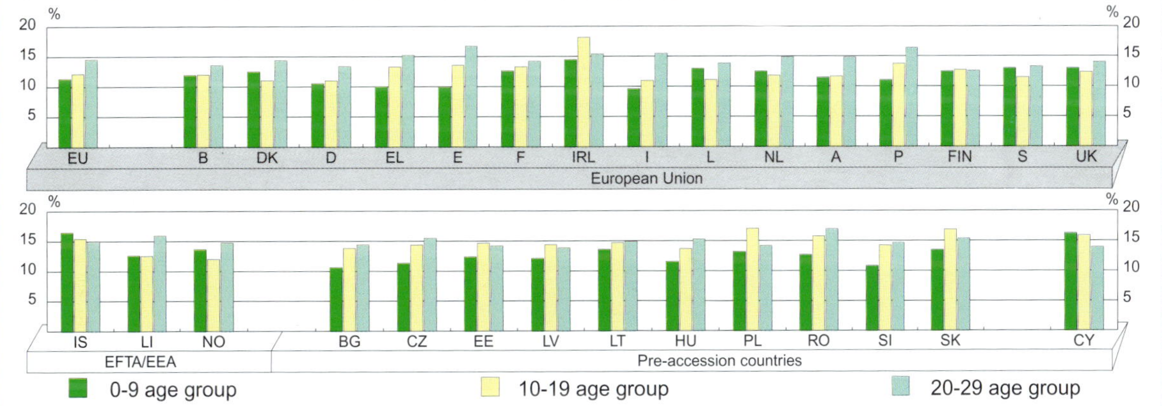

Source: Eurostat, population statistics.

As a whole, young people aged less than 30 years account for approximately 38% of the total population of the EU (against 46% in 1975). The proportion of young people is relatively homogeneous between the different Member States. The EU country with the lowest percentage is Germany (35%) and the highest percentage is recorded in Ireland (48%).

Of the EFTA/EEA countries, Iceland has a relatively high proportion of young people (47%) and presents a particular pattern as children under the age of 10 predominate because the birth rate is one of the highest in Europe and because of the significant number of young people who later leave the country to study abroad.

In all the pre-accession countries, the proportion of young people is generally larger than in the EU Member States (between 39 and 45%). However, the reduction in the number of young people can also be observed although the phenomenon is sometimes more recent (Baltic States, Poland and Slovakia), as witnessed by the lowest percentage in the under 10 age group.

SIGNIFICANT REGIONAL VARIATIONS
IN THE PROPORTION OF YOUNG PEOPLE

In the EU, the proportion of young people in relation to the total population reveals regional disparities, mainly in the southern countries.

Thus, the proportion of young people is relatively high in the south of Spain (and in the Canary Islands, not shown on the map), accounting for 45% of the total population in these regions against 40% or less in the rest of the country. Similarly, in France, a large proportion of young people is found in Nord-Pas-de-Calais, with 45% of young people against 41% on average for the whole territory. In the southern regions of Italy, the proportion of young people reaches or exceeds 42% while it is 31% or less in Lombardy, in Emilia-Romagna and in the Centro region. In the north of Portugal (and also in the Azores and in Madeira, not shown on the map), young people represent more than 45% of the population but the proportion is below 40% in Lisbon, as well as in the southern regions (Alentejo and the Algarve).

Lastly, Northern Ireland and the Pohjois-Suomi region (north of Finland) have relatively high proportions of young people compared to the rest of their respective countries.

FIGURE A3: PERCENTAGE IN THE 0-29 AGE GROUP
BY NUTS 1 AND NUTS 2 REGIONS, 1997

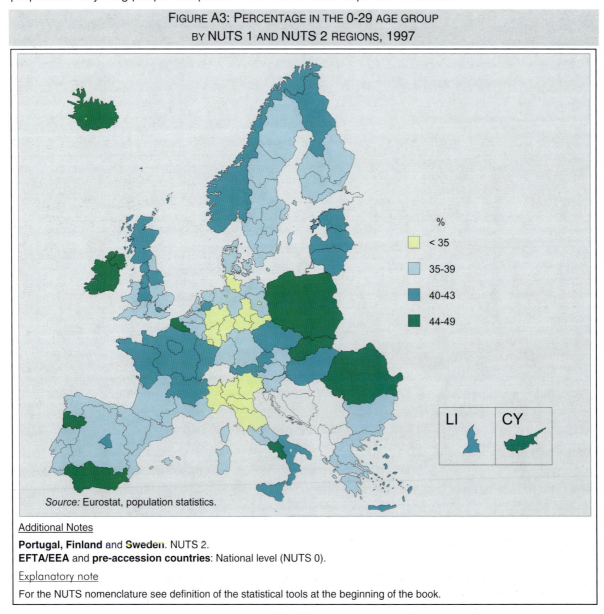

Source: Eurostat, population statistics.

Additional Notes

Portugal, Finland and **Sweden**. NUTS 2.
EFTA/EEA and **pre-accession countries**: National level (NUTS 0).

Explanatory note

For the NUTS nomenclature see definition of the statistical tools at the beginning of the book.

INCREASING NUMBERS OF WELL-QUALIFIED YOUNG PEOPLE

For several decades, increasing numbers of young people have been continuing their studies beyond upper secondary education. The percentage of the population leaving school without a qualification at this level has been progressively decreasing and as a consequence, the educational level of the population is rising. In 1997, only 31% of young people in the 20-29 age group in the EU did not have an upper secondary education qualification; the comparable figure in the 50-59 age group was 53%.

The increase in educational level is found in all Member States although it is particularly marked in Ireland and in the EU southern countries; in these countries, levels of education are relatively low. Indeed, among people aged 50-59, at least two-thirds have not achieved upper secondary education in Greece, Spain, Ireland, Italy and Portugal. Among the 20-29 age group, the same proportion exceeds 40% in three countries only (Italy, Luxembourg and Portugal). Moreover, in Germany, Denmark and also Iceland, the proportion of low-qualified persons among young people is higher than for some other categories of older people, most certainly because of a longer duration of studies.

In the EFTA/EEA countries, as well as in the pre-accession countries for which data is available, the increase in education levels is also noted.

FIGURE A4: PERCENTAGE OF PEOPLE WHO DO NOT HAVE AN UPPER SECONDARY QUALIFICATION, BY AGE GROUP, 1997

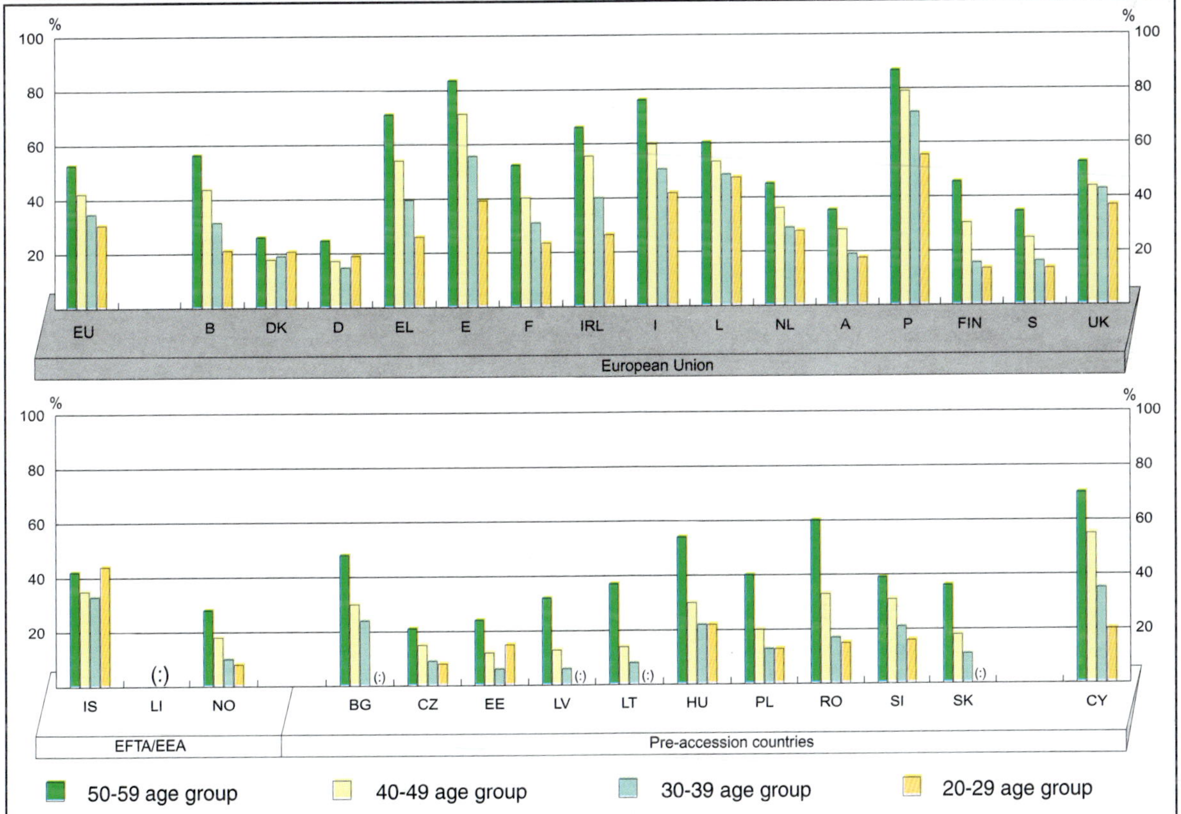

■ 50-59 age group   □ 40-49 age group   ■ 30-39 age group   □ 20-29 age group

Source: Eurostat, Labour force survey.

Additional note

United Kingdom: The GCSE and equivalent qualifications taken at the age of 16 are considered as lower secondary qualifications.
Iceland: National statistics.
Bulgaria, Latvia, Lithuania, Slovakia and **Cyprus**: National statistics.

Explanatory note

The education levels are defined here according to the International Standard Classification for Education – ISCED (see definition of the statistical tools at the beginning of the book). People who do not hold a certificate of upper secondary education come in the same category as those who have achieved ISCED 0-2.

Figure A5 also illustrates the trend towards a longer period of education. It shows the increase, between 1987 and 1997, in the percentages of young people between 15 and 24 years old who are currently in education or training.

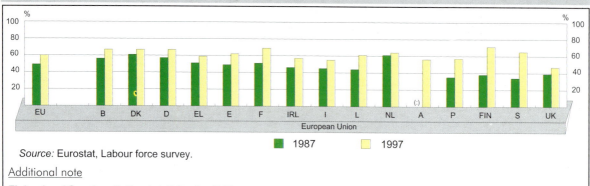

FIGURE A5: PERCENTAGE OF PEOPLE IN EDUCATION OR TRAINING AMONG YOUNG PEOPLE AGED 15 TO 24, 1987 AND 1997

Source: Eurostat, Labour force survey.

Additional note

Finland and **Sweden**: National statistics for 1987.

Explanatory note

Persons in education or training are the ones who have, during the last four weeks, attended a school (general or vocational), university or apprenticeship-type training course, whether full-time or part-time.

In 1987, fewer than 50% of young people aged 15 to 24 years old were still studying. By 1997, there were more than 60%. The increase is relatively similar throughout the Member States. The largest rises occurred in France, Luxembourg, Portugal, Finland, and Sweden.

MORE THAN 83 MILLION PUPILS AND STUDENTS IN THE EUROPEAN UNION

During the 1996/97 academic year, there were slightly more than 83 million pupils and students in the EU, representing about 22% of the total population.

In the same year, there were more than one million pupils and students in the EFTA/EEA countries, i.e. virtually a quarter of the total population.

In the pre-accession countries, the 24 million pupils and students represented slightly less than 23% of the total population in 1996/97.

FIGURE A6: PUPILS AND STUDENTS (IN THOUSANDS), 1996/97

European Union															
EU	B	DK	D	EL	E	F	IRL	I	L	NL	A	P	FIN	S	UK
83 416	2 589	1 176	16 784	1 966	9 356	14 582	1 002	10 890	70	3 510	1 641	2 274	1 192	2 159	14 224

EFTA/EEA				Pre-accession countries											
IS	LI	NO		BG	CZ	EE	LV	LT	HU	PL	RO	SI	SK		CY
82	6	1 068		1 675	2 233	341	517	772	2 205	9 662	4 688	426	1 300		162

Source: Eurostat, UOE.

Additional notes

Belgium and **Luxembourg**: Non-grant-aided schools are excluded.
Iceland: Only full-time students are included in ISCED levels 3 to 7.
Poland, Romania and **Slovenia**: Students at ISCED level 7 are excluded.

Explanatory note

Pupils in special education as well as pupils in pre-primary education controlled by the education ministries are included.

In the European Union as a whole, 57% of young people under 30 years of age are pupils or students.

As Figure A7 shows, the highest percentages are found in Belgium and France (over 60%). By contrast, in Greece, less than half of those aged under 30 are students or pupils.

In the EFTA/EEA countries with the exception of Liechtenstein, the proportion of young people who are in education is above the EU average while it is relatively lower in the pre-accession countries.

FIGURE A7: PROPORTION OF PUPILS AND STUDENTS IN THE 0-29 AGE GROUP, 1996/97

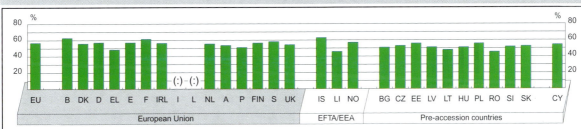

Source: Eurostat, UOE and population statistics.

Additional notes

Iceland: Only full-time students are included in ISCED levels 3 to 7.
Cyprus: National statistics.

Explanatory note

The ratio of the number of pupils and students aged between 0 and 29 years old to the total population in that age group does not take the level of education they are attending into account.

The total number of pupils and students of compulsory education age and the percentage of the population in education that they represent are indicated in Figure A8. The typical ages for the beginning and end of compulsory education explain the differences between countries to some extent. They are presented in Figure B1 which describes the organisation of the education systems.

FIGURE A8: PUPILS AND STUDENTS OF COMPULSORY SCHOOL AGE, IN THOUSANDS AND AS A PROPORTION OF THE TOTAL NUMBER OF PUPILS AND STUDENTS, 1996/97

European Union															
EU	B	DK	D	EL	E	F	IRL	I	L	NL	A	P	FIN	S	UK
45 442	1 455	508	10 833	1 046	4 646	7 716	545	4 549	(:)	2 407	840	1 069	580	956	8 260
55%	56%	43%	65%	53%	50%	53%	54%	42%	(:)	69%	51%	47%	49%	44%	58%

EFTA/EEA				Pre-accession countries										CY
IS	LI	NO		BG	CZ	EE	LV	LT	HU	PL	RO	SI	SK	
42	4	487		937	1 182	192	318	489	1 360	4 940	2 578	225	(:)	97
51%	60%	46%		56%	52%	56%	62%	63%	62%	51%	55%	53%	(:)	60%

Source: Eurostat, UOE.

Additional notes

Italy: Only ISCED levels 0 to 3 are included.
Iceland: Only full-time students are included in ISCED levels 3 to 7.
Hungary: Full-time pupils only.

Explanatory note

The number of pupils of compulsory school age is calculated by adding up the numbers of children of statutory education age, regardless of which level of education they are attending.

In the EU as a whole, 54% of all pupils and students are of compulsory education age. In Denmark, Italy, Portugal, Finland and Sweden, fewer than half are this age. This is due in part, for certain countries at least, to the inclusion of pupils in pre-primary education in the total number of pupils and students, but also to the large number of pupils remaining in education beyond the minimum school leaving age.

In some other countries, the proportion of pupils of compulsory school age exceeds 60% of all pupils and students. This is the case in Germany and the Netherlands, where this proportion is around, or exceeds, two thirds. In these two countries, the phenomenon should be seen in the light of the longer period of compulsory education.

In the EFTA/EEA countries and the pre-accession countries, the percentages of children of compulsory education age are relatively close to the EU average. The extreme percentages are recorded on the one hand in Norway (46%) and on the other hand in Latvia and Lithuania (respectively 62% and 63%).

TRENDS IN UNEMPLOYMENT RATES VARY
ACROSS COUNTRIES

During the last decade, unemployment rates across the different age groups have followed similar trends in the EU (figure A9). Unemployment rates fell during the second half of the 1980s, reaching their lowest point in 1990, then increased, to fall slightly in 1995. The recovery between 1987 and 1990 does not seem to have benefited one age group more than another. Similarly, the fall in activity after 1990 has affected all three age groups. Since 1995, levels of unemployment seem to have stabilized.

FIGURE A9: CHANGE IN THE UNEMPLOYMENT RATES BY AGE GROUP, IN THE EUROPEAN UNION, 1987-1997

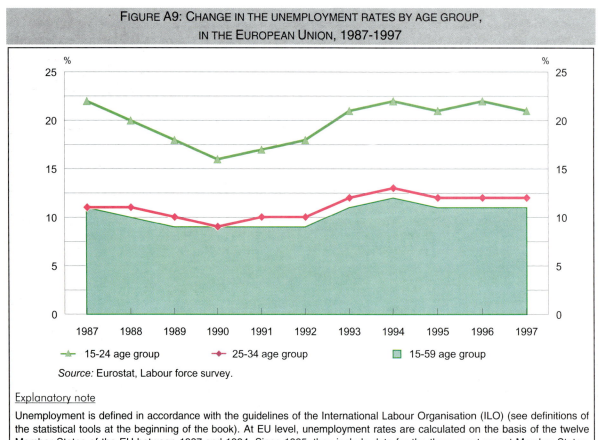

Source: Eurostat, Labour force survey.

Explanatory note

Unemployment is defined in accordance with the guidelines of the International Labour Organisation (ILO) (see definitions of the statistical tools at the beginning of the book). At EU level, unemployment rates are calculated on the basis of the twelve Member States of the EU between 1987 and 1994. Since 1995, they include data for the three most recent Member States, Austria, Finland and Sweden.

Figure A10 presents the evolution over time in unemployment rates in each of the fifteen Member States, between 1987 and 1997. It can be seen that unemployment rates differ considerably between countries.

For some countries, the trend is close to the EU average, with a fall in unemployment from 1987 to 1990/91, a subsequent increase and then a slight fall since 1994 or 1995. This is the case in Belgium, Spain, Ireland, the Netherlands, Portugal and the United Kingdom.

The evolution of unemployment rates in Germany was similar to that in the EU until 1995 but there has been a relatively recent rise in the unemployment rate.

The profile for Greece, France and Italy is also close to the EU average, even though unemployment has not fallen over the last few years.

Finland and Sweden, which had experienced relatively low unemployment rates until 1990, have witnessed a steep increase after this date.

In general, since 1987, people in the 15-24 age group have been affected more by unemployment than those in the 25-34 age group. This pattern is found everywhere in the EU except in Germany (apprentices being included in the working population), and in Denmark, where unemployment rates remain relatively close for the different age groups. In Luxembourg, the Netherlands and the United Kingdom, differences also remained moderate.

In Belgium, Greece, France, and to a lesser extent in the United Kingdom, differences between unemployment rates in the 15-24 and 25-34 age groups have tended to become more pronounced.

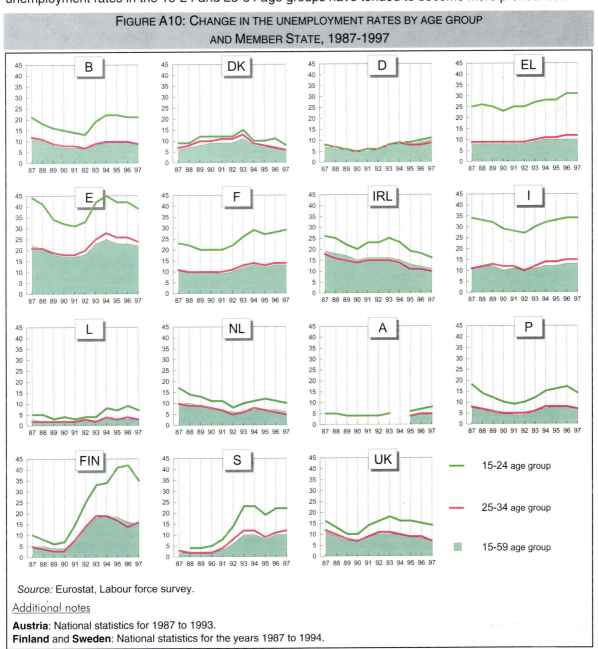

FIGURE A10: CHANGE IN THE UNEMPLOYMENT RATES BY AGE GROUP AND MEMBER STATE, 1987-1997

Source: Eurostat, Labour force survey.

Additional notes

Austria: National statistics for 1987 to 1993.
Finland and **Sweden**: National statistics for the years 1987 to 1994.

───── YOUNG PEOPLE ARE MORE AFFECTED BY UNEMPLOYMENT ─────

Young people find it difficult to enter the labour market; their integration is often delayed and progressive. Thus, in the EU, almost 25% of young people who have left education and are currently available for work are without a job. For adults aged 25 to 59 years the level is below 10%.

This observation applies to all countries, including Germany (young people in apprenticeship systems being excluded of the active population). In Denmark, the Netherlands and Austria the ratio of unemployment in the 15-24 age group to unemployment in the population of working age as a whole is the lowest of the EU. At the other end of the scale, the youth unemployment rate is proportionally very high in France, Italy and Luxembourg (approximately three times higher) and higher still in Greece (four times higher).

However, unemployment rates differ considerably between Member States, both for young people aged 15 to 24 years who have left education (from 7 to 36%) and for 25-59 year olds (from 2 to 18%). For both age categories, the highest unemployment rate is found in Spain while Denmark, Luxembourg, the Netherlands and Austria have the lowest rates.

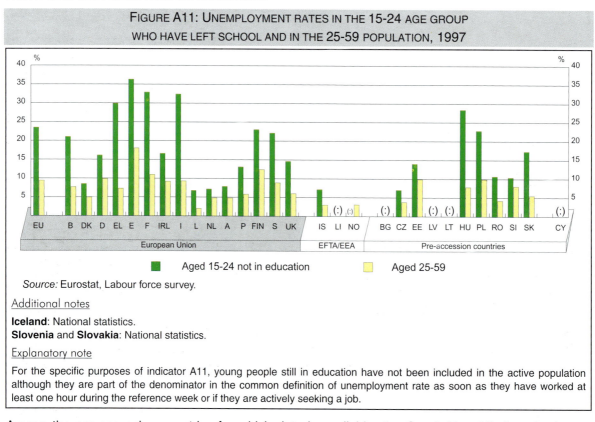

FIGURE A11: UNEMPLOYMENT RATES IN THE 15-24 AGE GROUP
WHO HAVE LEFT SCHOOL AND IN THE 25-59 POPULATION, 1997

Source: Eurostat, Labour force survey.

Additional notes

Iceland: National statistics.
Slovenia and **Slovakia**: National statistics.

Explanatory note

For the specific purposes of indicator A11, young people still in education have not been included in the active population although they are part of the denominator in the common definition of unemployment rate as soon as they have worked at least one hour during the reference week or if they are actively seeking a job.

Among the pre-accession countries for which data is available, the Czech Republic has the lowest unemployment rates for both age groups (less than 7%). In Hungary and Poland on the other hand, unemployment affects approximately one quarter of the youth labour force who have left school.

INSECURE JOBS:
——— A CHARACTERISTIC OF YOUTH EMPLOYMENT ———

Young people are more affected by unemployment than adults. Moreover, in general, their situation regarding employment is also more fragile. An insecure job is defined here as having a fixed term contract in the absence of any available permanent post, or a part-time job because no full-time job was available. In the EU, insecure job thus defined accounts for 18% of total youth employees against 7% of adult employees.

FIGURE A12: PERCENTAGE OF EMPLOYEES WITH INSECURE JOBS BY AGE GROUP, 1997

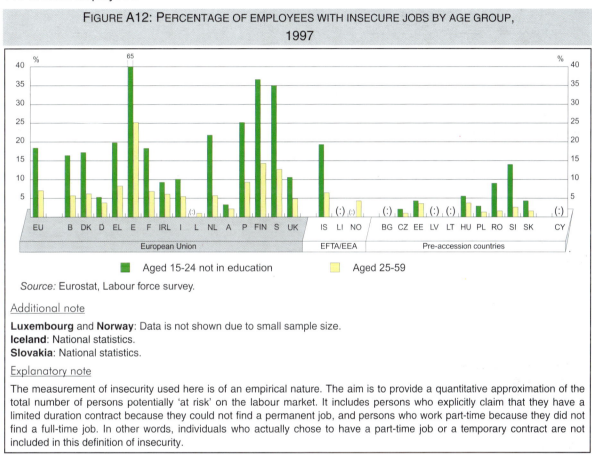

■ Aged 15-24 not in education   □ Aged 25-59

Source: Eurostat, Labour force survey.

Additional note

Luxembourg and **Norway**: Data is not shown due to small sample size.
Iceland: National statistics.
Slovakia: National statistics.

Explanatory note

The measurement of insecurity used here is of an empirical nature. The aim is to provide a quantitative approximation of the total number of persons potentially 'at risk' on the labour market. It includes persons who explicitly claim that they have a limited duration contract because they could not find a permanent job, and persons who work part-time because they did not find a full-time job. In other words, individuals who actually chose to have a part-time job or a temporary contract are not included in this definition of insecurity.

In the majority of EU Member States, the proportion of young employees with insecure jobs is at least twice that of adults. In Finland and Sweden, more than one in three young employees does not have a permanent contract or work part-time because they could not find a full-time job. In Spain, this applies to two out of three young employees.

In terms of employment insecurity, the smallest differences between young and adult employees can be observed in Germany, Ireland and Austria.

In the pre-accession countries for which data is available, insecure jobs are also more frequent among young people, although in general, the level of job insecurity seems to be lower than in the EU countries. The differences between young employees and adults are sometimes relatively small (as in Estonia and Hungary) while they are much higher in Romania and Slovenia.

CHANCES OF HAVING A JOB GENERALLY INCREASE
WITH LEVEL OF EDUCATION...

Figure A13 compares the unemployment rates and education levels of the population aged between 25 and 59. Generally speaking, the unemployment rate is lower for people with higher qualifications. In 1997, in the EU, the unemployment rate of persons with a tertiary education qualification was 6%, against 9% for persons who had completed upper secondary level and 13% for those who had at best the minimum compulsory schooling. Two Member States deviate from this pattern. In Greece and, to a lesser extent Portugal, unemployment rates of the least qualified are lower than those of people who hold an upper secondary education qualification.

Similar patterns can be observed in the pre-accession countries. Differences in the unemployment rates by level of education are particularly marked in the Czech Republic, Hungary, Poland and Slovakia. In Romania and, to a lesser extent, in Lithuania, people with upper secondary education qualification have the highest unemployment rate.

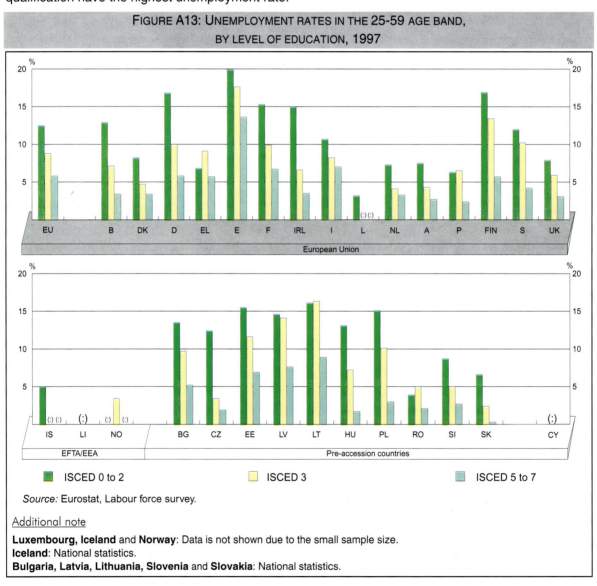

FIGURE A13: UNEMPLOYMENT RATES IN THE 25-59 AGE BAND, BY LEVEL OF EDUCATION, 1997

■ ISCED 0 to 2   □ ISCED 3   ■ ISCED 5 to 7

Source: Eurostat, Labour force survey.

Additional note

Luxembourg, Iceland and **Norway**: Data is not shown due to the small sample size.
Iceland: National statistics.
Bulgaria, Latvia, Lithuania, Slovenia and **Slovakia**: National statistics.

... BUT ALSO WITH AGE

Among those with higher education qualifications, the unemployment rate of people aged 25-34 years is higher overall than that of older graduates. In other words, while the education level is an important factor vis-à-vis unemployment, it seems that a significant number of young graduates have difficulties finding a job and are consequently faced with spells of unemployment when they finish their studies. This pattern is particularly noticeable in Greece, Spain and Italy. In Germany, Sweden and the United Kingdom, age seems to have little influence on unemployment of tertiary education graduates. In Belgium, Denmark, Greece, Finland and the United Kingdom, a slight increase in the unemployment of tertiary education graduates occurs after 45 years.

In the pre-accession countries, the youngest graduates are more likely to be unemployed than their elders, except in Estonia.

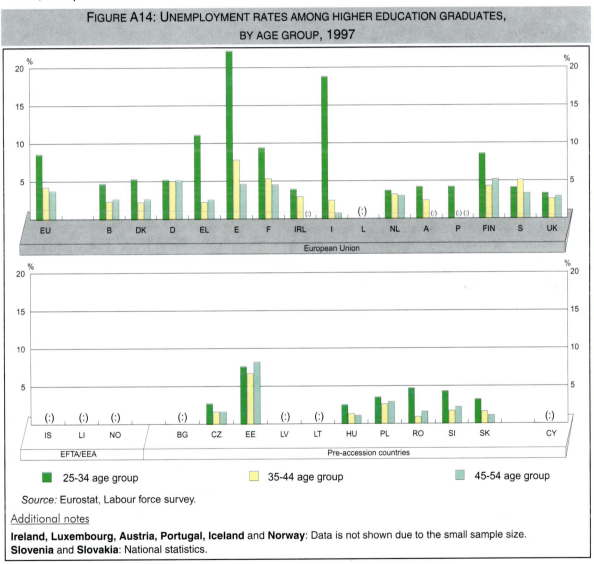

FIGURE A14: UNEMPLOYMENT RATES AMONG HIGHER EDUCATION GRADUATES, BY AGE GROUP, 1997

Legend: ■ 25-34 age group   □ 35-44 age group   ▨ 45-54 age group

Source: Eurostat, Labour force survey.

Additional notes

Ireland, Luxembourg, Austria, Portugal, Iceland and **Norway**: Data is not shown due to the small sample size.
Slovenia and **Slovakia**: National statistics.

WITH THE SAME LEVEL OF EDUCATION, MORE WOMEN THAN MEN ARE UNEMPLOYED

The increasing opportunities for women to remain in education and the growing numbers of them who obtain upper secondary and tertiary education qualifications have not completely eroded the differences between men and women vis-à-vis employment. With the same qualifications, a larger proportion of women than men is unemployed.

This situation is found in most of the EU and also in Norway, irrespective of the education level considered, although differences between the sexes are lower for tertiary education graduates. Inequalities are particularly pronounced in Greece, Spain and Italy, but also for the least qualified in Belgium, Luxembourg and the Netherlands. As far as tertiary education graduates are concerned, choices of different fields of study may partially explain disparities between the unemployment rates of men and women.

For Sweden and the United Kingdom, the unemployment rate is lower for women than men. This applies to holders of both levels of qualification under consideration.

In the pre-accession countries, women seem generally less affected than in the EU, especially the least qualified; however, among the latter, the female unemployment rate is significantly higher in the Czech Republic and Poland.

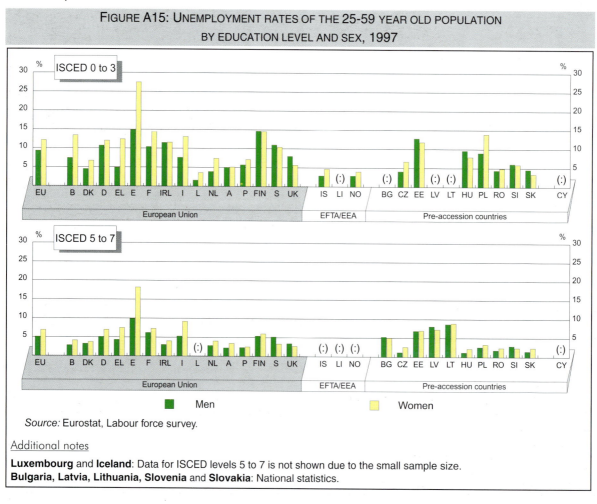

FIGURE A15: UNEMPLOYMENT RATES OF THE 25-59 YEAR OLD POPULATION BY EDUCATION LEVEL AND SEX, 1997

Source: Eurostat, Labour force survey.

Additional notes

Luxembourg and **Iceland**: Data for ISCED levels 5 to 7 is not shown due to the small sample size.
Bulgaria, Latvia, Lithuania, Slovenia and **Slovakia**: National statistics.

RECOGNITION OF SKILLS:
———— SOMETIMES A QUESTION OF TIME ————

At the beginning of a professional career, having a tertiary education qualification is rarely sufficient to guarantee a job directly related to the level of the studies undertaken. Given the difficulties of integrating young people into the labour market, a large number of tertiary education graduates have to accept an under-qualified job and to wait a few years before obtaining a more 'responsible' post.

In the EU, only 53% of young graduates are professionals or managers, compared with more than 65% of their elders. By contrast almost 40% of tertiary education graduates aged 25 to 34 are working as technicians, associate professionals, office workers or salesman. The same proportion for people aged over 35 is below 30%. This finding is true for the majority of EU Member States. Portugal reveals a different pattern – the proportion of graduates working in posts with a high degree of responsibility does not vary appreciably with age.

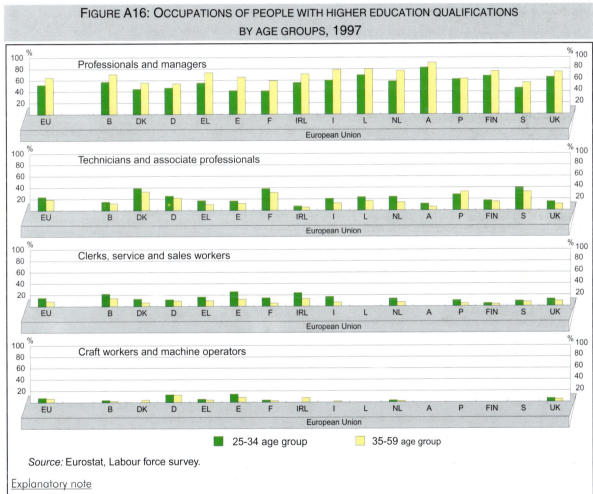

FIGURE A16: OCCUPATIONS OF PEOPLE WITH HIGHER EDUCATION QUALIFICATIONS BY AGE GROUPS, 1997

■ 25-34 age group   ☐ 35-59 age group

Source: Eurostat, Labour force survey.

Explanatory note

The International Standard Classification of Occupations (ISCO) was introduced by the International Labour Organization and is used in the Eurostat Labour Force Survey. This distinguishes ten main types of occupations which have been grouped together as follows:

1. Senior officials, managers and professionals;
2. Technicians and associate professionals;
3. Clerks, service and sales workers;
4. Craft workers, plant and machine operators, elementary occupations.

QUALIFICATIONS REDUCE INSECURITY IN EMPLOYMENT

As defined in the explanatory note below, insecure jobs account for more than 10% of total employees among poorly qualified persons in the EU (lower secondary education at best). The proportion for people who have completed upper secondary education is less than 6%.

This is true of most of the EU Member States, except for the Netherlands, where the proportion of insecure jobs among employees is the same, irrespective of the education level attained. Finland and Sweden also deviate from the EU pattern in that insecure jobs are more frequent among more highly educated persons. The countries for which qualifications seem more likely to curb the risk of job insecurity are Greece and Ireland: the proportion of insecure jobs among high qualified employees is half that of among the least qualified.

In the pre-accession countries for which information is available, the differences between the respective shares of insecure jobs according to education level attained seem to be even greater than in the EU, although the global level of job insecurity is lower here.

FIGURE A17: PERCENTAGE OF EMPLOYEES AGED 25-59 WITH INSECURE JOBS, BY EDUCATION LEVEL, 1997

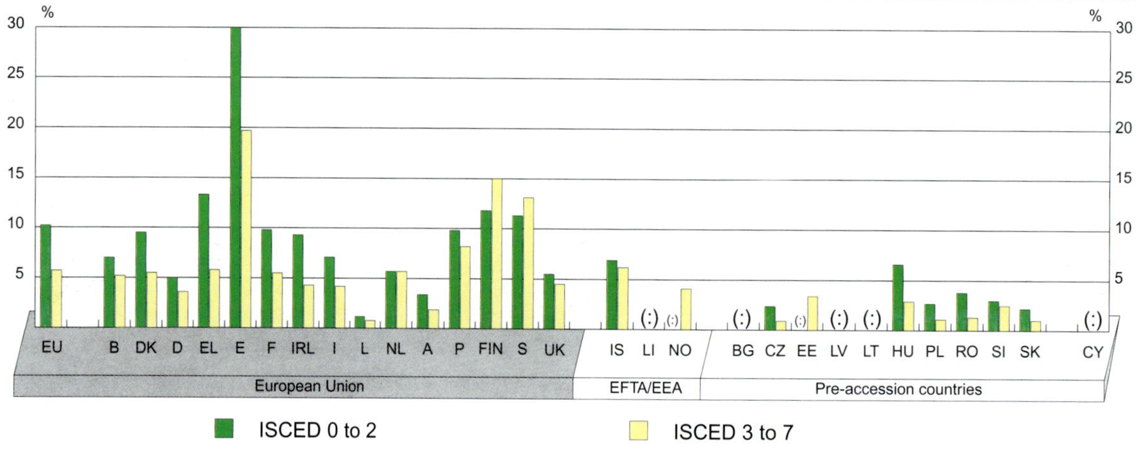

ISCED 0 to 2   ISCED 3 to 7

Source: Eurostat, Labour force survey.

Additional notes

Iceland: National statistics.
Norway: Data is not shown due to the small sample size.
Slovakia: National statistics.

Explanatory note

The measurement of insecurity used here is of an empirical nature. The aim is to provide a quantitative approximation of the total number of persons potentially 'at risk' on the labour market. It includes persons who explicitly claim that they have a limited duration contract because they could not find a permanent job, and persons who work part-time because they did not find a full-time job. In other words, individuals who actually chose to have a part-time job or a temporary contract are not covered in this definition of insecurity.

EDUCATIONAL LEVEL HAS EFFECTS ON WAGES

In 1995, employees who had a tertiary education qualification earned approximately 30 to 40% more than those having completed upper secondary education. This percentage was close to 84% in Austria and 104% in Portugal. On the other hand, the differences were much lower in Spain and Luxembourg and were particularly low in Sweden.

When comparing the overall change of earnings according to educational level, one group of countries is characterized by a progressive rise of earnings. In this group, we find Spain, Italy, Luxembourg, Sweden and the United Kingdom. In a second group composed of Greece, France, Ireland and Finland, the difference in earnings between employees with upper secondary education and those with at best lower secondary education is relatively small. The situation in Belgium and Austria falls between these two groups.

FIGURE A18: AVERAGE GROSS MONTHLY EARNINGS, BY EDUCATION LEVEL, IN EUROS, 1995

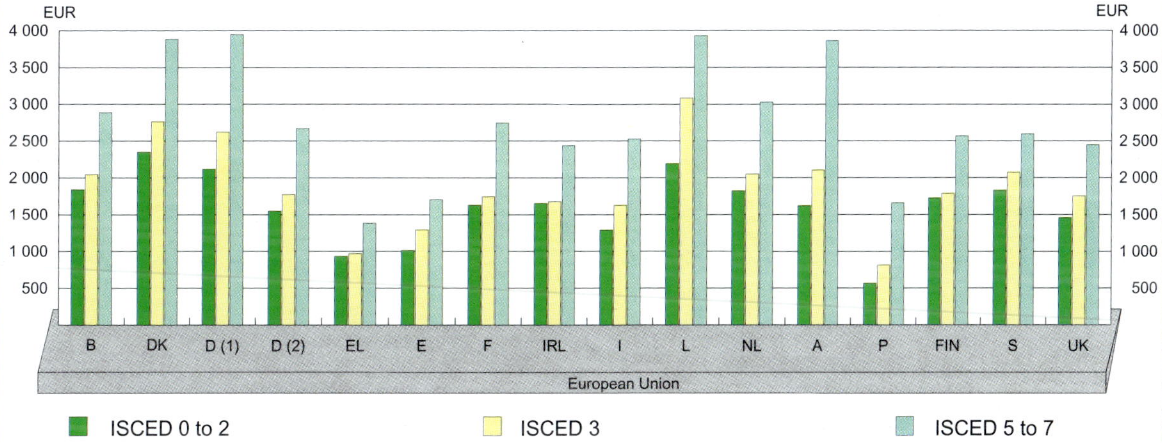

| | ISCED 0 to 2 | ISCED 3 | ISCED 5 to 7 |

Source: Eurostat, Structure of Earnings Statistics.

Additional note

Germany: (1) Federal Republic of Germany before 3/10/90; (2) new *Länder* and East Berlin.

Explanatory note

The structure of earnings statistics collected in all the Member States for the year 1995 (1994 for France) were the first to be compiled on the basis of comparable methodologies.

The figures given here are gross values and include additional payments for overtime and shift work, as well as regular bonuses. They refer only to full-time workers. Trainees' earnings are not taken into account.

STRUCTURES AND SCHOOLS

A WIDE VARIETY OF SCHOOL SYSTEMS

Figure B1 illustrates the multiplicity of approaches to structuring education in Europe. Leaving aside pre-primary institutions, which are reviewed in Chapter C, the diagrams still outline similarities and differences in structure in school and tertiary level European education. Special education organized separately is also excluded from these diagrams and can be found in Chapter H.

In half of the European Union countries, children **enter the school system** at the age of 3 or 4, but the youngest ones may have their first experience of school at age 2 in France and at 2½ in Belgium. In Denmark, Germany, Austria, Finland and Sweden, they are admitted at the age of 6.

Attendance at a **pre-primary educational institution** is optional in most member countries, parents being free to send their children if they so desire. Education is compulsory from the age of 6 in nine of the EU Member States, but begins earlier in some of them — at age 4 in Luxembourg and Northern Ireland and at age 5 in the Netherlands and Great Britain. In the Nordic Member States (Denmark, Finland and Sweden), education is not compulsory until the age of 7. The start of compulsory education generally coincides with the point of entry to primary school, except in Ireland, Luxembourg and the Netherlands. In Ireland and the Netherlands, where the school systems do not include a pre-primary level, children have access to primary school 'infant classes' and an optional year of *basisonderwijs*, respectively, from 4 years of age. In Luxembourg, attendance at the last two years of pre-primary education *(Spillschoul)* has been made compulsory.

The **pattern of education** is generally the same for all pupils until the end of lower secondary school, i.e. up to the age of 14 or 15. A common core curriculum is followed until age 16 in Denmark, Spain, Finland, Sweden and the United Kingdom. In Germany and Austria, pupils are faced with choices regarding their direction of study at the start of lower secondary education generally at the age of 10 and in Luxembourg at age 12.

In most member countries, the **end of compulsory education** coincides with the transition from lower to upper secondary education. However, in some countries, lower secondary education ends before the end of compulsory education: one year before in France and Austria, two years before in the United Kingdom (except Scotland), and can end either one or two years before in Belgium.

Full-time **compulsory education** lasts until at least age 16 in most Member States, but in Greece, Ireland, Luxembourg, Austria and Portugal it ends at 15. In Belgium and Germany, it ends at age 15 or 16. In Italy it ends at 14, but it is raised to the age of age 15 since 1999/2000. In most Member States, full-time compulsory education lasts 9 or 10 years. In Italy, it lasts 8 years, whereas in Luxembourg and the United Kingdom (England/Wales and Scotland) it lasts 11 years and in the Netherlands and Northern Ireland as long as 12 years. In the Netherlands, full-time compulsory education starts at age 5 and ends at age 16 (inclusive), but all pupils must complete at least 12 years of full-time education.

Compulsory education continues at least part-time beyond age 16 for two years in Belgium, for one year in the Netherlands and generally for three years beyond the age of 15 or 16 in Germany. In these Member States, compulsory education continues in upper secondary education or lasts until the end of upper secondary education.

The Spanish school system is currently in a transition phase, following the passing in October 1990 of the Organic Act on the General Organisation of the Education System (*LOGSE*). The process of implementing this act, initially intended to be brought in over a 10-year period, is currently going ahead at different rates in the various Communities. This reform provides for bringing together all early childhood education under the Ministry of Education.

FIGURE B1: STRUCTURES OF SCHOOLS AND TERTIARY EDUCATION INSTITUTIONS, 1997/98

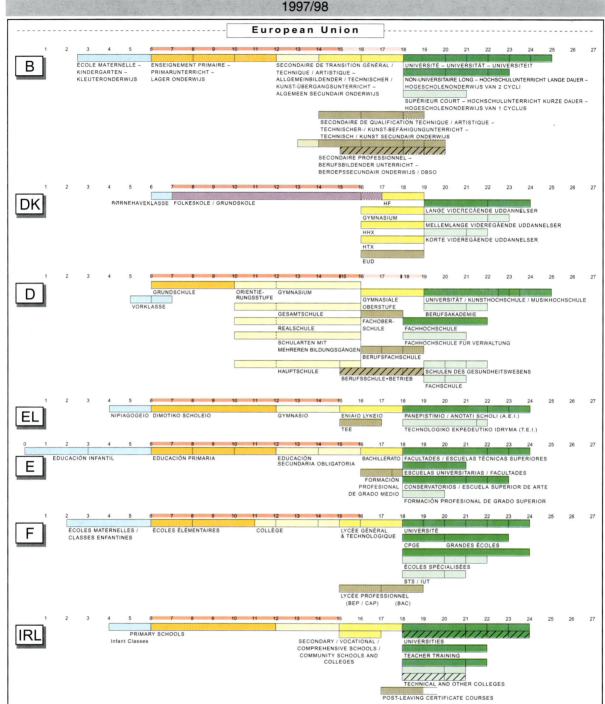

Source: Eurydice.

<u>Additional notes</u>

Belgium: Secondary education is divided into three two-year stages. The end of compulsory full-time education is set to the age of 15 for pupils who have completed the first stage or to the age of 16 for pupils who have not completed the first stage.

Germany: In two *Länder*, *Vorklassen* are provided for children aged 5 who have not yet reached compulsory school age but whose parents wish them to receive preparation for primary school. In seven *Länder*, *Vorklassen* are provided for children who have reached compulsory school age but do not have the maturity required to start school.

Spain: The graph presents the post-reform structure, even though the new system of post-compulsory secondary education has not yet been phased in.

Greece: A reform of upper secondary education was introduced during 1997/98, and the former *Lykeio* was replaced by the *Eniaio Lykeio*. Technical vocational schools (TEEs), which replace the former TESs, are planned for 1998/99.

<u>Explanatory note</u>

The ages given here represent the 'normal' ages of admission to courses and their duration. Neither early nor late starts nor extended school careers resulting from pupils having to repeat years nor breaks are taken into account in these illustrations and explanations.

FIGURE B1 (CONTINUED): STRUCTURES OF SCHOOLS AND TERTIARY EDUCATION INSTITUTIONS, 1997/98

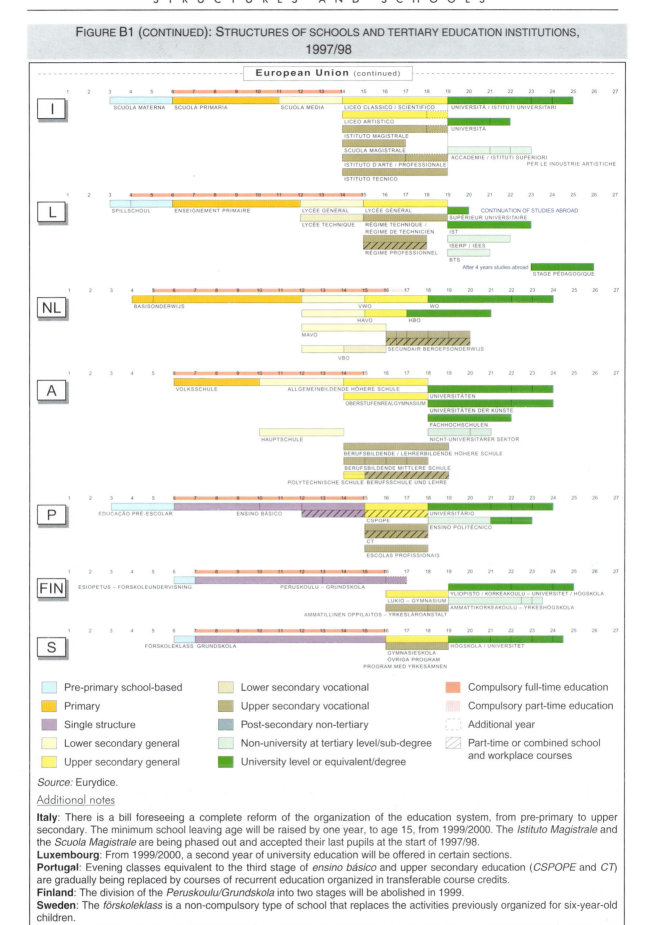

Pre-primary school-based	Lower secondary vocational
Primary	Upper secondary vocational
Single structure	Post-secondary non-tertiary
Lower secondary general	Non-university at tertiary level/sub-degree
Upper secondary general	University level or equivalent/degree

Compulsory full-time education
Compulsory part-time education
Additional year
Part-time or combined school and workplace courses

Source: Eurydice.

Additional notes

Italy: There is a bill foreseeing a complete reform of the organization of the education system, from pre-primary to upper secondary. The minimum school leaving age will be raised by one year, to age 15, from 1999/2000. The *Istituto Magistrale* and the *Scuola Magistrale* are being phased out and accepted their last pupils at the start of 1997/98.

Luxembourg: From 1999/2000, a second year of university education will be offered in certain sections.

Portugal: Evening classes equivalent to the third stage of *ensino básico* and upper secondary education (*CSPOPE* and *CT*) are gradually being replaced by courses of recurrent education organized in transferable course credits.

Finland: The division of the *Peruskoulu/Grundskola* into two stages will be abolished in 1999.

Sweden: The *förskoleklass* is a non-compulsory type of school that replaces the activities previously organized for six-year-old children.

FIGURE B1 (CONTINUED): STRUCTURES OF SCHOOLS AND TERTIARY EDUCATION INSTITUTIONS, 1997/98

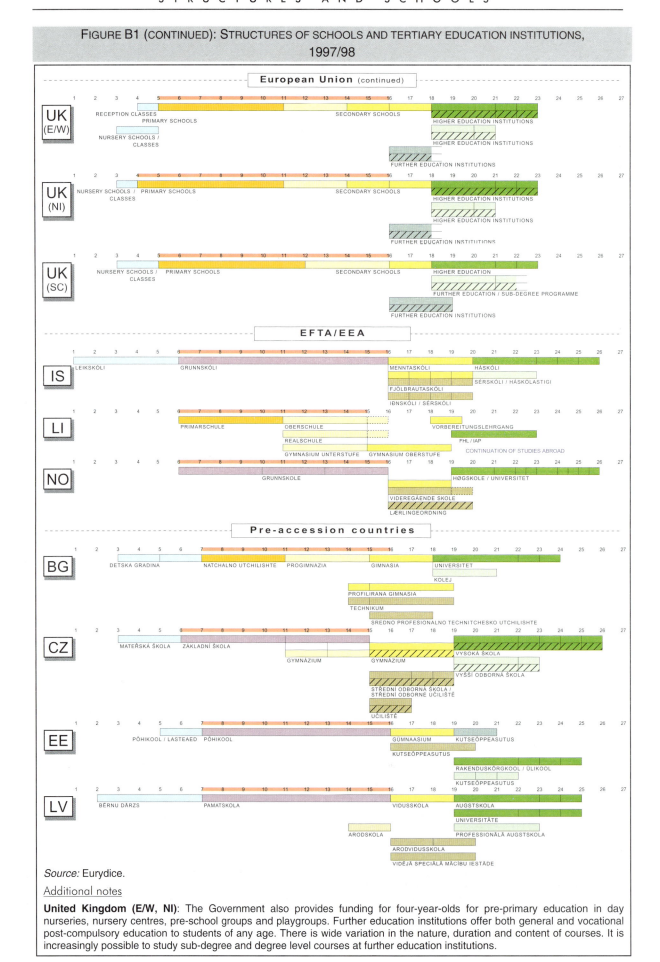

Source: Eurydice.

Additional notes

United Kingdom (E/W, NI): The Government also provides funding for four-year-olds for pre-primary education in day nurseries, nursery centres, pre-school groups and playgroups. Further education institutions offer both general and vocational post-compulsory education to students of any age. There is wide variation in the nature, duration and content of courses. It is increasingly possible to study sub-degree and degree level courses at further education institutions.

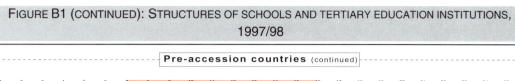

FIGURE B1 (CONTINUED): STRUCTURES OF SCHOOLS AND TERTIARY EDUCATION INSTITUTIONS, 1997/98

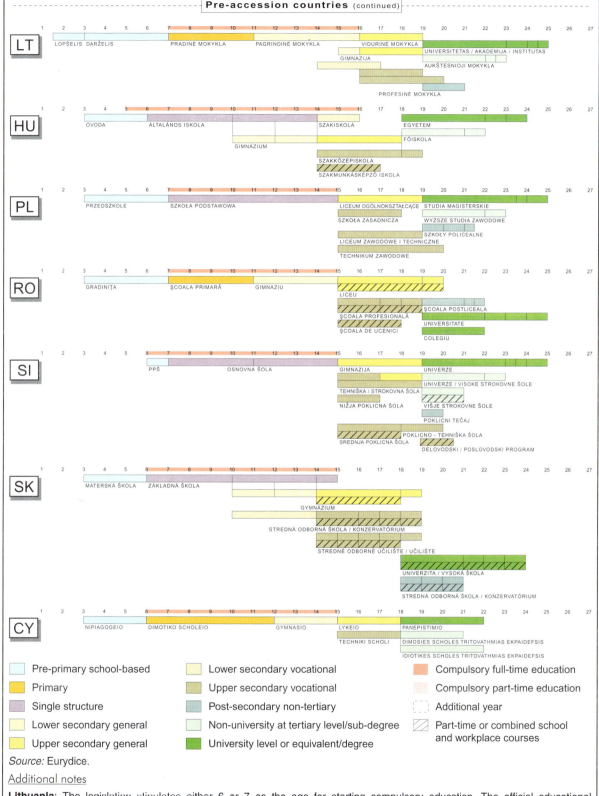

Pre-accession countries (continued)

Source: Eurydice.

Additional notes

Lithuania: The legislation stipulates either 6 or 7 as the age for starting compulsory education. The official educational guidelines recommend the age of 6. The usual practice, however, is for children to start primary school at 7 years of age.
Slovakia: From 1998/99, the duration of compulsory education will be increased from nine to ten years.

In **upper secondary education**, a vocational or technical branch is often available to students alongside the general academic branch. In Ireland, the general course is complemented by parallel courses which contain some elements of general subjects and vocational preparation. These courses lead to vocationally orientated qualifications. In Sweden, vocational and general courses have both been delivered by the same schools as modular upper secondary education. In the United Kingdom, pupils in post-compulsory education can study for qualifications in general academic subjects, in a vocational field or in a combination of the two.

Entry to **tertiary education** is usually possible from age 18, except in Luxembourg, Finland and Sweden, where it is later. The age of entry varies in Germany (at age 18 or 19) and the Netherlands, depending on the type of course chosen.

To take a first tertiary education qualification, students in a majority of the member countries have to study for a minimum of 2 years. The minimum is 3 years in Belgium, Spain, Portugal and Finland, 3½ years in Greece and 4 years in the Netherlands. This applies only to the minimum duration of study. In many Member States, students are free to complete their courses over a longer period or to opt to study part-time.

Luxembourg provides a certain number of non-university tertiary education courses. It is also possible for students to follow a one-year university-level course before continuing their studies abroad.

In Sweden, it is not possible to distinguish between courses leading to a general undergraduate degree and courses not leading to such a qualification. It depends on the duration of the course and on the depth of the studies. All courses at the universities or university colleges can be part of a general undergraduate degree but it is necessary to take a course lasting at least 3 years.

In the **EFTA/EEA countries**, young children enter the school system at the age of 6 except in Iceland, where they can enter the *leikskóli* from the age of 1 year if their parents so desire and there are places available. The start of compulsory education coincides with the start of primary education. It lasts 9 years in Liechtenstein and 10 years in Iceland and Norway.

Pupils' education is organized in a single, continuous structure up to the end of compulsory education in Iceland and Norway. In Liechtenstein, pupils make a first choice regarding their direction of study at the age of 11, at the end of their primary education. In Iceland and Norway, it is possible to choose a vocational branch from the age of 16.

Entry to tertiary education is normally possible from the age of 19 in Liechtenstein and Norway and 20 in Iceland. In Liechtenstein, only university studies are available at tertiary education level.

In most **pre-accession countries**, pre-primary schools-based institutions will admit children from the age of 3 or even earlier (in Latvia and Lithuania). In Slovenia, school attendance starts with compulsory education at the age of 6.

Compulsory education varies from country to country and may start at 5, 6 or 7 years of age, and the duration varies from eight years in Poland and Romania to 11 years in Hungary.

In Bulgaria, Lithuania, Romania and Cyprus, the primary level of education is separate from lower secondary. In the other pre-accession countries, compulsory education is provided in a single structure very similar to that found in the Nordic countries. However, in the Czech Republic, Hungary and Slovakia, pupils can proceed to separate lower secondary education at about 10 or 11 years of age. Vocational courses can be started only at upper secondary level in the majority of these countries.

Estonia, Lithuania, Poland, Romania, Slovenia and Slovakia offer non-tertiary post-secondary education. Students attending this type of institution have usually completed upper secondary education, although this is not a formal entrance requirement. The duration of the training courses offered at post-secondary level varies generally from 6 months to 2 years full-time. Some courses provide access to the job market, while others allow students to continue their studies at tertiary level.

In the pre-accession countries, tertiary education includes both university and non-university education, except in Romania and Slovakia, in which all recognized courses at tertiary education level are university courses, or included within the university category. Students can normally start tertiary education courses at the age of 18 in Hungary, Slovakia and Cyprus and at 19 in the other countries.

PROPORTIONALLY, MORE ENROLEES ——————— ARE FOUND AT PRIMARY LEVEL ———————

Figure B2 shows the distribution of those enrolled in each country's education system into the different education levels as defined in the ISCED classification. This data should be interpreted with reference to the duration of compulsory education, the relative duration of each educational level (Figure B1), the factors influencing attendance in pre-primary education (Chapter C), the age structure of the population, the tendency to stay on in education (Chapter A), etc. A comparison of participation rates has been done at pre-primary, secondary and tertiary levels; these are shown in the specific Chapters and allow a more detailed analysis.

In the EU, Denmark is the country with the highest proportion of pupils in pre-primary education (ISCED 0): slightly less than 20% of the total population of pupils/students are enrolled at this level. In Belgium, Germany, France, Italy, Luxembourg and Sweden around 15% of total enrolments are found in pre-primary education. Enrolment of children in pre-primary education does not exceed 10% of the total enrolled population in Greece, Portugal, Finland and the United Kingdom, where primary education starts at a relatively early age. In EFTA/EEA countries, percentages are particularly high (over 15%). Pre-primary enrolment in pre-accession countries ranges from 10% in Poland to 18% in Hungary. Variations between countries should be interpreted in the light of the educational provision.

Generally, primary level (ISCED 1) is the level of education with the highest enrolment. It is included in the compulsory education period and often lasts the longest. It accounts for approximately one third of all enrolees in most EU and EFTA/EEA countries. Only Germany and Austria do not follow the tendency; the smaller proportion of pupils at this level (23%) can partly be explained by the fact that primary education lasts only 4 years. Amongst the pre-accession countries, Hungary and Slovenia also show a low percentage (23%) of total enrolees in primary education. In Hungary, the situation should be seen in the light of high enrolment in pre-primary education. In Slovenia, the low proportion of primary school pupils is partly explained by only the first stage of the single structure being considered as primary level and partly by the high proportion of pupils enrolled in lower and upper secondary education.

Lower secondary education (ISCED 2) has proportionally more pupils in Germany, of the EU countries, and Latvia, Lithuania and Slovakia, of the pre-accession countries.

In Austria (EU), Hungary and in Slovenia (pre-accession countries), upper secondary (ISCED 3) students are proportionally more numerous. The greatest percentage of enrolments at ISCED 3 level is observed in the United Kingdom.

Compared with total numbers of enrolees in the educational system, the proportion of students in tertiary education (ISCED 5-7) remains low: it accounts for 15% of all pupils and students on average. However, the proportion has risen in all countries over the last 20 years (see Chapter F). Among EU and EFTA/EEA countries, the largest proportion of students enrolled in ISCED levels 5, 6 and 7 (almost 20%) is observed in Greece, Spain, Finland and Norway. Luxembourg and Liechtenstein do not have a complete system of tertiary university education. In pre-accession countries, enrolment in these levels is relatively lower (from 6 to 16%). Only Bulgaria has a higher percentage than the EU average: 16%. Romania, Slovakia and Cyprus have the lowest proportions of enrolees in tertiary education.

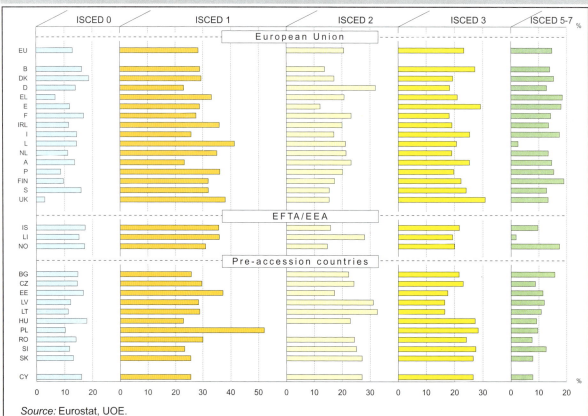

FIGURE B2: DISTRIBUTION OF PUPILS AND STUDENTS BY LEVEL OF EDUCATION, AS A PERCENTAGE, 1996/97

Source: Eurostat, UOE.

Additional notes

Germany, France, Ireland and **Luxembourg**: Percentages do not reach 100%, as a certain number of students cannot be allocated by ISCED level.
Germany: ISCED 7 is excluded.
Spain: Data on the old and the new educational system are presented jointly. As the duration of ISCED levels 2 and 3 varies from one system to another, a statistical adjustment has been made in the two levels concerned.
Luxembourg: There is no complete system of tertiary education at university; non subsidized private education is excluded.
Iceland: Only full-time students are included in ISCED levels 3 to 7.
Liechtenstein: 1995/96. There is no complete system of tertiary education at university.
Poland, Romania and **Slovenia**: ISCED 7 is excluded.
Poland: ISCED 2 is included in ISCED 1, some ISCED 5/6 education programmes are included in ISCED 3.
Slovenia: Only the first stage of the single structure is considered to be ISCED 1.

Explanatory note

The total population referred to in this indicator is the number of enrolees in the education system of the country concerned.

MOST STUDENTS ATTEND PUBLIC-SECTOR SCHOOLS

In all European countries, over 90% of primary and secondary students attend either public or subsidized private institutions. In other words, the education of most students is financed by public authorities.

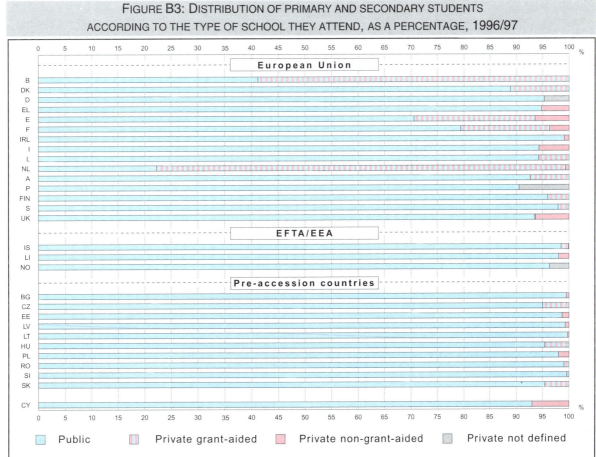

FIGURE B3: DISTRIBUTION OF PRIMARY AND SECONDARY STUDENTS ACCORDING TO THE TYPE OF SCHOOL THEY ATTEND, AS A PERCENTAGE, 1996/97

☐ Public   ☒ Private grant-aided   ☐ Private non-grant-aided   ☐ Private not defined

Source: Eurostat, UOE.

Additional notes

Luxembourg: Non subsidized private education is excluded.
Netherlands: Equal funding of public and subsidized private schools is a constitutional right.
United Kingdom: The figure does not include further education institutions that provide post-compulsory general and vocational education.
Iceland: Only full-time students from the single structure are included.
Liechtenstein: 1995/96.

Explanatory note

Students may be divided into different categories depending on whether they attend **public-sector** schools, provided and controlled directly by public authorities or **private** schools, provided and controlled by non-governmental bodies.

Private schools are further distinguished as between those that are subsidized and those that are not. Private schools are said to be **subsidized** if they receive more than 50% of their financing from public authorities. **Non subsidized** private schools receive less than 50% of their finance from the public sector.

It is not possible to distinguish between pupils attending subsidized or non-subsidized private schools in Germany, Portugal and Norway. Where data were available, the most refined form of classification possible has been used.

In all EU and EFTA/EEA countries, public-sector education is in the majority, except for Belgium and the Netherlands, where there are proportionally more pupils in the subsidized private sector. In Belgium, Denmark, Luxembourg, Austria, Finland and Sweden, school attendance of primary and secondary pupils is financed, entirely or largely, by public authorities. In pre-accession countries, even more students are enrolled in public-sector schools: more than 93% of pupils attend a public-sector school. School attendance of primary and secondary students are financed, wholly or largely, by public authorities in the Czech Republic, Hungary, Romania, Slovenia and Slovakia.

In EU and EFTA/EEA countries, non-subsidized private education accounts for less than 6.5% of enrolees. It concerns more than 5% of pupils in Greece, Spain, Italy and the United Kingdom. The situation is similar in pre-accession countries. Around 5% of Czech, Hungarian and Slovakian students attend subsidized private sector schools. In five countries (Bulgaria, Estonia, Latvia, Lithuania and Poland), only 0.2 to 2% of the pupils are enrolled in this type of schools. Cyprus is the only country where the proportion of pupils in private sector schools reaches 7%.

PUBLIC-SECTOR SCHOOLS: FROM CONSIDERABLE AUTONOMY TO VERY LIMITED DECISION-MAKING POWERS

Four broad areas of school organization are examined in this section: the demarcation of school time, the management of teaching staff, the use of financial resources and finally pedagogical matters or teaching as such. Information has been gathered on the freedom that schools enjoy in relation to a number of parameters in these four areas. In view of the variety of management situations, depending on whether the school comes under a private body or not, only public-sector schools at primary and lower secondary level are included in the analysis.

Three main modes of decision making have been defined:
— the school has full powers and autonomy;
— the school takes decisions in consultation with the competent authority and/or within the limits set by the latter, and its autonomy is limited; or
— the school is not involved in the decision-making process and has no autonomy.

Figures B4 and B5 show the autonomy of the public-sector schools for each country at two levels of compulsory education, i.e. primary and lower secondary level. Each cell refers to one of the parameters under examination. The autonomy of a school can be more or less restricted depending on the field and parameter concerned.

Within the same country, whether it be a Member State of the EU, an EFTA/EEA or a pre-accession country, there are usually few differences in the scope of the decision-making power granted to public-sector schools between the two levels of education, especially in countries where these two levels of education are provided within a single-structure system or are administered at the same level of power. However, in France the parameters for which schools do or do not have decision-making power differ sharply depending on the level of education considered. In Luxembourg and Austria, lower secondary schools have more autonomy than primary schools, where decisions are more frequently taken in consultation with the competent authorities.

Explanatory note (Figures B4 and B5)

The school is considered as a whole, represented either by its headteacher or by a management body. The sharing of responsibility for decisions on internal matters is not taken into consideration.
The term 'public-sector school' is taken to mean schools provided and controlled directly by public or government authorities. Schools controlled by private or non-governmental authorities are excluded, even when they are financed entirely from public funds.
The competent authority at the level above the school can, depending on the situation, be a public authority at local, regional or central level.
Only the financial resources provided by public authorities are taken into account.
For secondary education, insofar as all teachers are subject teachers, the parameter 'allocation of posts' relates to fixing the number of teaching posts for teachers of compulsory subjects and options.

FIGURE B4: AUTONOMY OF PUBLIC-SECTOR PRIMARY SCHOOLS, 1997/98

Source: Eurydice.

Additional notes

Denmark: For major building work, the responsibility lies with the municipality, but, for renovation and minor building projects, schools have some autonomy.

Ireland: While primary schools enjoy autonomy in the number of hours per subject, recommendations are made by the Department of Education and Science as to the appropriate distribution of school time.

Italy: A large number of schools are enjoying greater autonomy in organization, teaching methods, development and research. In the year 2000, this autonomy will be granted to all schools.

Luxembourg: In primary schools, there are no headteacher posts. The function is fulfilled on behalf of the State by the primary education inspector who is responsible for several schools and on behalf of the municipality by the commune.

Austria: Where schools use their right to curricular autonomy, they have limited autonomy as regards the number of hours per week. The school is entitled to comment on applicants for the post of a headteacher.

Portugal: 1st stage of *ensino básico* only.

Finland: The organising authority, usually a municipality, has decision-making power in most areas, and it is up to this authority to delegate decision-making to the schools. There are therefore differences between municipalities.

Norway: It is up to the municipality to decide to what extent the municipal autonomy is delegated to the individual school.

Hungary: The appointment of the headteacher is the responsibility of the competent authority, but it requires the approval of the teaching staff.

FIGURE B5: AUTONOMY OF PUBLIC-SECTOR LOWER SECONDARY SCHOOLS, 1997/98

🔴 Autonomy for decisions   🟡 Limited autonomy   🟤 No autonomy   ⚪ Data not available

Source: Eurydice.

Additional notes

Denmark: For major buildings work, the responsibility lies with the municipality, but, for renovation and minor building projects, schools have some autonomy.

Italy: A large number of schools are enjoying greater autonomy in organization, teaching methods, development and research. In the year 2000, this autonomy will be granted to all schools.

Austria: The school is entitled to comment on applicants for the post of a headteacher.

Portugal: 2nd and 3rd stages of *ensino básico*.

Finland: The organising authority, usually a municipality, has decision-making power in most areas, and it is up to this authority to delegate decision-making to the schools. There are therefore differences between municipalities.

Norway: It is up to the municipality to decide to what extent the municipal autonomy is delegated to the individual school.

Hungary: The appointment of headteacher is the responsibility of the competent authority, but it requires the approval of the teaching staff.

Overall, among the countries of the EU, schools have the greatest degree of autonomy in the Flemish Community of Belgium (at primary level) and in the Netherlands and the United Kingdom (England/Wales and Northern Ireland), at both levels of education. For most of the areas of decision-making under consideration here, they have total autonomy. For a few parameters, decisions are taken in consultation with the competent authority or within the limits that it has laid down. Only a very small number of decisions are taken solely by the competent authority at a higher level than the institution.

On the other hand, the schools with the most limited autonomy in decision-making are to be found in Germany and Luxembourg. Only timetabling subjects over the week is left entirely in the hands of the school, at both levels of education in Germany and at lower secondary level in Luxembourg.

In the Flemish Community of Belgium (at lower secondary level), Ireland, Finland and Liechtenstein, most of the decisions are taken at school level but with the agreement with a supervisory competent authority or within the limits the authority has laid down.

In the pre-accession countries, most decisions are taken by or in consultation with the authorities. In Cyprus, the only area left to schools' discretion is the distribution of subjects over the school week. In Romania, schools are also allowed to choose their teaching methods. Estonia is the pre-accession country in which schools enjoy the greatest autonomy, except for the management of school time.

SCHOOLS HAVE GREATER AUTONOMY TO ARRANGE THEIR TIMETABLES THAN TO DETERMINE ——— THE AMOUNT OF TIME ALLOCATED TO TEACHING ———

As regards decisions linked to the **management of school time**, schools are seldom free to decide how much time they will devote to teaching. Thus, the number of days and hours of teaching time per year is often set by the competent authorities. Sweden is an exception: here these issues are subject to a decision taken in consultation with the competent authority; schools even enjoy complete autonomy to set the annual number of hours of teaching. In Germany, the Netherlands and Austria, while schools have limited freedom to decide on the number of days per year, they play no part in setting the overall volume of annual teaching time.

In some countries of the EU, the curriculum lays down the compulsory subjects but leaves the school free to allocate the teaching time among these subjects. This is the case, at primary level, in the Flemish Community of Belgium, Ireland, the Netherlands and Portugal and, for the two levels of education being considered, in the United Kingdom.

Almost everywhere in the EU and EFTA/EEA countries, schools have greater autonomy when it comes to timetabling periods in schools over the week or over the day. More especially, the responsibility for allocating time for subjects in the timetable is left to schools in all countries with the exception of Ireland and Luxembourg (primary level), the Flemish Community of Belgium (lower secondary level) and Liechtenstein (both levels).

The same trend can be observed in the pre-accession countries, where decisions on teaching time (number of days per year and number of hours per year and per week) are usually taken by the competent authorities, whereas the organisation of the school day is left to the school itself.

SCHOOLS HAVE LITTLE AUTONOMY WHEN IT COMES TO ADMINISTERING LARGE BUDGETS

As regards the **use of financial resources**, in EU countries, schools have no autonomy in Germany, France (primary), Luxembourg (primary) and Portugal (in the first stage of *ensino básico*). In the member countries in which schools have a certain degree of freedom in the use of their financial resources, the larger the expenditure involved, the more the decisions are taken by the competent authorities. Schools therefore have more responsibility for their running costs than for deciding capital expenditure, in particular for buildings. Schools in the Flemish Community of Belgium, Greece, Spain, Ireland, Austria, the United Kingdom (England/Wales and Northern Ireland) Liechtenstein and Norway can take some or all decisions in relation to capital expenditure on buildings in consultation with the competent authority.

Among the pre-accession countries, in Hungary and Romania, schools have no decision-making power in the use of financial resources. In Bulgaria (with the exception of capital investment in buildings), in Lithuania and Poland, these decisions are the subject of consultation between the school and the competent authorities. In the Czech Republic, Latvia and Slovakia, schools have total control over their operating budget. Schools in Estonia manage their operating budgets and equipment expenditure.

MANAGEMENT OF TEACHING STAFF SELDOM IN THE HANDS OF SCHOOLS

Within both the EU and EFTA/EEA countries, whether at primary or lower secondary level, as far as the **management of teaching staff** is concerned, the most common model is one in which schools have little or no autonomy. In only a few countries (Ireland, Finland, Sweden, the United Kingdom [Scotland only], Liechtenstein and Norway) are most decisions on staffing matters taken by the school in consultation with the competent authorities. The Flemish Community of Belgium (primary), the Netherlands and the United Kingdom (England and Wales) are exceptions in that schools there enjoy full powers in relation to the selection and management of staff. In Finland, Sweden and Norway, teachers are employed by the municipalities. Frequently, the task of recruiting teachers there, and thus the determination of the number of teaching posts in the different subjects, is the responsibility of the headteacher, even though this function falls within the competence of the municipalities.

Similarly, the appointment of headteachers is generally subject to a decision taken at a level above that of the school, except in the Flemish Community of Belgium (primary), the Netherlands and the United Kingdom (England and Wales). In Portugal they are elected by the *conselho de escola* or by the staff of the school. In Spain, they are appointed following agreement between the schools and the competent authorities. In Ireland, the selection of the headteacher is a matter for the school (all primary and most post-primary schools) or a local education authority (schools under vocational education committees), but the rules concerning the eligibility of candidates and the selection process are determined by the central authority.

Finally, the power to fix the total number of teaching posts often goes hand in hand with the allocation of posts to class teachers or to specialist subject teachers at primary school level and with the fixing of the number of teachers required for the compulsory subjects or for optional subjects at lower secondary level.

In most pre-accession countries, schools enjoy total autonomy as regards the recruitment of teaching staff. The decision on the appointment of the headteacher takes place at a higher level of authority, except in Slovenia. In Poland, headteachers are appointed following agreement between schools and the competent authorities. Teaching posts are allocated at school level or in consultation with the competent authorities, except in Cyprus, where schools have the least autonomy in the area of the administration of teaching staff.

SCHOOLS ENJOY TOTAL DECISION-MAKING POWER IN PEDAGOGICAL MATTERS

We thus find fairly generally that schools at both primary and lower secondary level usually have considerable autonomy as regards the **choice of textbooks and teaching methods**. Among the countries of the EU and of the EFTA/EEA, in Germany, Spain (education is a matter for the Autonomous Communities), Luxembourg (at lower secondary level), Iceland and Liechtenstein the autonomy of schools is limited in the choice of school textbooks. Teachers at both primary and lower secondary level must choose their textbooks from a list or on the basis of criteria set by the competent authorities. Moreover, in some of these countries, teaching methods are laid down on the basis of recommendations and suggestions made by the competent authorities.

In most pre-accession countries, the teaching methods are decided by the school. In contrast, textbooks are chosen in consultation with the competent authorities, except in Estonia, where the school can decide which textbooks to use outside the list approved by the Minister of Education. In Cyprus, these two areas are totally administered by the competent authorities.

STAGGERING THE RETURN TO SCHOOL

Within the framework of the European programmes (in particular Socrates), partnerships between schools and exchanges of teachers and pupils have meant that it is increasingly necessary to take into account the timing of the school year in each country when it comes to organising activities.

In a number of countries of the EU and of the EFTA/EEA and in all the pre-accession countries, school resumes in the autumn on the same day for all pupils at a given level of education. In contrast, the start and the end of the summer holidays varies from *Land* to *Land* in Germany, from region to region in Spain, Italy, the Netherlands, Austria and Portugal, and according to the local education authorities in Finland, Sweden, the United Kingdom and Norway. In some of these countries, the return to school can be spread over one or even several weeks.

The return to school is spread over a period of about eight weeks from the start of August (in Denmark, in Germany and in some municipalities in Sweden) to the second fortnight in September (in Spain at secondary level, in certain regions of Italy, in Luxembourg and in Portugal). The largest spread of the return to school is to be found in Germany because of a system operated in the country whereby the date of the start and end of the summer holidays differs from *Land* to *Land*. These dates vary according to a system whereby they are rotated every year. All pupils in Denmark and certain pupils in Sweden return to school before 15 August. It is in the south of Europe that, mainly due to climatic conditions, school resumes latest after the summer break.

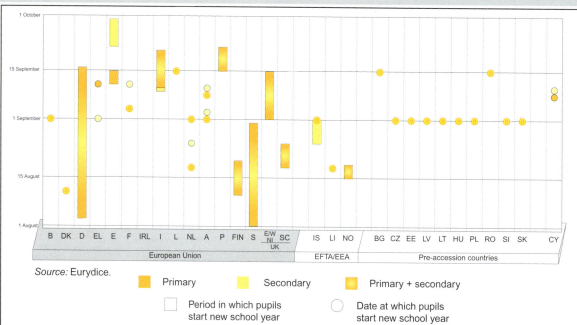

FIGURE B6: RANGE OF DATES OF THE RETURN TO SCHOOL, PRIMARY AND SECONDARY EDUCATION, 1997/98

Source: Eurydice.

Primary — Secondary — Primary + secondary

Period in which pupils start new school year — Date at which pupils start new school year

Additional notes

Germany: In accordance with the school legislation of the *Länder*, school year begins for all pupils in theory on 1 August and ends on 31 July. The actual beginning of the school year depends on the end of the summer holidays, which have been restricted to the period between mid-June and mid-September.

France: The school year starts on 11 September at upper secondary level.

Ireland: Schools must remain closed during July and August, but the date of return to school in September is set by the school. In general the return occurs as close to 1 September as possible.

Iceland: The school year starts between 25 August and 1 September at upper secondary level.

Explanatory note

When the date or the period during which the school year starts only concerns primary schools, it is indicated in orange. When it only concerns secondary schools, it is indicated in yellow. When both levels of education are concerned, this is indicated by a mixture of orange and yellow.

SCHOOL HOLIDAYS

The timing of the school year is generally similar at primary and secondary level. However, there are differences in certain countries. In Greece and, among the pre-accession countries, in Bulgaria and Lithuania, the school year for secondary pupils is spread over a longer period than for primary school pupils, while the reverse is the case in Spain, Ireland and the Netherlands.

The length of the summer holidays differs from country to country and sometimes within the same country from one level of education to another. The countries where the pupils have the shortest summer holidays (around 6 weeks) are Germany, the Netherlands (primary schools), the United Kingdom (England/Wales and Scotland) and Liechtenstein. At the opposite end of the spectrum, the holidays last 13 weeks in Ireland (at secondary level), in Iceland and in a number of pre-accession countries (in Bulgaria, at lower secondary level, in Latvia and Romania). Bulgarian primary school children have the longest holidays in summer (15 to 16 weeks).

During the year, in all countries pupils are given a break at Christmas generally lasting at least ten days. In most countries pupils have a break of similar duration at Easter; in the Czech Republic and Slovenia, pupils only get one or two days.

There are few breaks between Easter and the summer holidays. In most countries, there are in fact no days off school. When the pupils are given a break, it can last several days (Belgium, Austria and Scotland), a week (Luxembourg, the Netherlands and the United Kingdom – England/Wales, Northern Ireland) or even two weeks (Germany).

In certain countries (Greece, Italy and Iceland for the EU and EFTA/EEA countries, and in Hungary, Romania and Cyprus for the pre-accession countries), apart from the summer holidays and the Christmas and Easter breaks, pupils have no time off school except for weekends, legal holidays and national or local holidays.

In several countries, school breaks are organized differently from region to region (Germany, the Netherlands and Austria) or according to the municipality in which the school is located (Finland, Sweden and the United Kingdom). Similarly, among the pre-accession countries, in the Czech Republic, Latvia, Poland, Slovenia and Slovakia, regional or local variations exist and affect the timing of the winter breaks.

Explanatory note

In Figure B7, the comparison is based on days or in some cases weeks of school attendance or holidays. For a comparison based on the annual number of hours of teaching time per annum, we refer the reader to the chapters on 'Primary Education' and 'Secondary Education'.
For each country, the first line indicates the arrangement of school holidays at primary level and the second line the arrangement of school holidays at secondary level.
In certain countries, all the pupils at a given educational level have the same number of days off school. The period of the year when these breaks are given sometimes depends on the region, the municipality or the school. This is indicated by the variations.
The school, municipality or education authority can sometimes grant additional breaks beyond the basic minimum that applies for all pupils. These additional days off are granted within certain limits that are shown on the graph by the maximum number of days.

FIGURE B7: DISTRIBUTION OF SCHOOL HOLIDAYS OVER THE SCHOOL YEAR, PRIMARY AND SECONDARY EDUCATION, 1997/98

| | Fixed or minimum number of days |
| | Maximum number of days |

Variations

Country — Primary / Secondary

Source: Eurydice.

Additional notes

Denmark: Only the number of school days and the date of the beginning of the summer holidays are fixed. The ministry issues guidelines to the distribution of holidays. Otherwise it is up to the municipal authorities to decide how to distribute the holidays.

Netherlands: The dates and duration of the summer holidays and the maximum number of days off are decided by the ministry. The graph presents these recommendations. Schools are free to follow these recommendations, which they generally do, albeit with regional variations.

Sweden: In certain municipalities, there is a week's holiday in November.

THE ROLE OF PARENTS IN CONSULTATIVE COUNCILS AND DECISIONS TAKEN BY THE COUNCIL

Participatory bodies which include the parents exist in all countries. However, they are not found at all levels of administration within the education system.

Some of these bodies are made up exclusively of parents. In some countries of the EU and of the EFTA/EEA (the French-speaking Community of Belgium, at the *Länder* level in Germany, Ireland, Austria, Portugal, Finland, Sweden and Norway), these councils or parents' associations are found at national level. They generally act in a consultative capacity with the ministry and as an information platform for their members.

This analysis does not take into account the councils made up exclusively of parents nor the councils organized at regional and local level which include parents. It therefore focuses on bodies in which the parents participate which are set up by the ministries nationally or within the school.

FIGURE B8: ROLE OF NATIONAL-LEVEL BODIES WHICH INCLUDE REPRESENTATIVES OF PARENTS. COMPULSORY EDUCATION, 1997/98

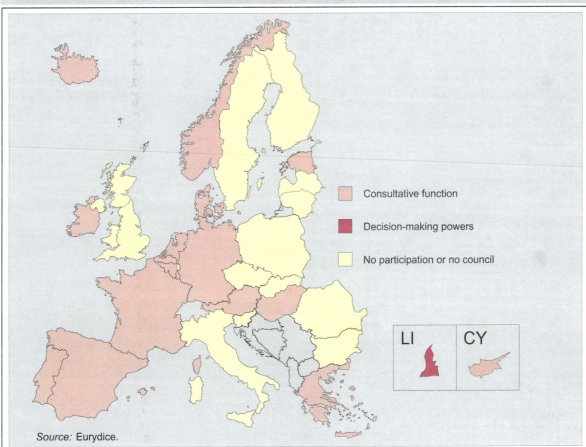

Consultative function

Decision-making powers

No participation or no council

Source: Eurydice.

Additional notes

Germany: The *Länder* enjoy legal status and have State authority. School legislation and administration of the education system are the responsibility of the *Länder*.
Luxembourg: The powers of the *Commission d'instruction* are confined to primary education.
Liechtenstein: The powers of the National Education Council are confined to secondary education.
Poland: A national education council which includes parents is enshrined in the law of 1991. This council has not yet been set up, but it should act in a consultative capacity on education policy, the budget, the curriculum and legislation.

Explanatory note

Parents' associations are not taken into account in this map.

In most countries within the EU and the EFTA/EEA, **at national or central level (in relation to the education system)** there is at least one participatory body which includes parents as well as representatives of the other stakeholders of the education system. These bodies act in a consultative capacity on most educational issues.

In Liechtenstein, within the National Education Council (for secondary education), the parents are involved in decisions concerning the distribution and allocation of pupils in the event of a disagreement between parents and teachers. In certain countries, a consultative body exists but the parents are not represented. For example, in Italy, a consultative council is organized at central level but does not include any parents. Finally, in the German-speaking Community of Belgium, Finland, Sweden and the United Kingdom, there are no consultative councils at this level.

In most of the pre-accession countries, at national level there are no consultative councils that include parents. However, in Hungary, the national parents' association is represented on a council that carries out preparatory work for decision-making in the field of public education policy. Parents are also represented at national level in Estonia and Cyprus (in the education council). In these two countries, these councils are consulted on education-related issues.

In almost all countries, there are consultative councils that include parents **at school level**. However, in a few countries only bodies made up exclusively of parents exist at school level. This is the case, among the countries of the EU and the EFTA/EEA, in the German-speaking Community of Belgium, Iceland and Liechtenstein, and, among the pre-accession countries, in Cyprus.

Figure B9 shows the nature and scope of the councils in which parents are involved at school level in a number of broad-based areas within the education system. These areas are: clarification of school rules, drafting of the school's development plans, setting the teaching syllabus and objectives, control of expenditure and allocation of the budget assigned to the school.

In general, the decision-making powers of these councils are exercised more often in the drafting of internal rules than in the other fields analysed in this document. In most countries, these councils are consulted when the school development plan is drawn up. As regards decisions relating to the budget, the situation varies considerably from country to country.

In a number of countries, these councils enjoy considerable decision-making powers. For example, in the United Kingdom (England/Wales and Northern Ireland), parents' representatives are included on the council (the school governing body or board of governors) which has decision-making powers in all the areas taken into account. In Romania, this is also the case for most of the fields analysed. Conversely, in Greece, of these different fields, only decisions relating to the budget are taken by the council involving the parents.

In other countries, these councils act in a consultative capacity for all decisions relating to the school (the Flemish Community of Belgium, the Netherlands, Lithuania) or virtually all decisions (French-speaking Community of Belgium, Norway and Estonia). In Austria, depending on the subject, these councils either have consultative capacity or decision-making power.

Finally, in Finland and Sweden, the powers of the council in which parents are involved vary according to the municipality or the school.

FIGURE B9: POWERS OF SCHOOL-LEVEL BODIES WHICH INCLUDE PARENT REPRESENTATIVES, IN 5 AREAS. COMPULSORY EDUCATION, 1997/98

	B fr	B de	B nl	DK	D	EL	E	F	IRL	I	L	NL	A	P	FIN	S	UK (E/W, NI)	UK (SC)
School rules	●	(–)	●	●	●	○	●	●	●	●	●	●	●	●	●	●	●	●
Drafting of the school development plan	●	(–)	●	○	●	●	○	○	●	●	●	●	●	●	●	●	●	●
Setting of the teaching syllabus and objectives	●	(–)	●	●	○	○	○	○	○	●	○	●	●	●	●	●	●	○
Control of expenditure	○	(–)	●	●	●	●	●	●	○	●	●	●	●	●	●	●	●	●
Allocation of the budget granted to the school	●	(–)	●	●	○	●	●	●	●	●	●	●	●	●	●	●	●	○

	IS	LI	NO	BG	CZ	EE	LV	LT	HU	PL	RO	SI	SK	CY
School rules	(–)	(–)	●	●	○	●	●	●	●	●	●	○	○	(–)
Drafting of the school development plan	(–)	(–)	●	●	●	●	●	●	●	●	●	○	●	(–)
Setting of the teaching syllabus and objectives	(–)	(–)	○	○	●	●	○	●	●	●	●	○	○	(–)
Control of expenditure	(–)	(–)	●	●	●	○	○	○	●	●	●	○	●	(–)
Allocation of the budget granted to the school	(–)	(–)	●	○	●	●	○	○	●	●	●	○	●	(–)

● Consultative function   ● Decision-making power   ○ No power

Source: Eurydice.

(-): Only bodies made up exclusively of parents exist at school level.

<u>Additional notes</u>

Belgium (B de): Since the basic decree of August 1998 and the decree on pre-primary and primary education of April 1999, each school must set up a consultative council. Among other things, this council must decide on the school plan and oversee self assessment in the school. It must seek the advice of parents in these matters.

Belgium (B nl): The school councils exercise their consultative function under the supervision of the central education council of the Community. Under a decree that will come into force in 1999, these councils are to be wound up and replaced by a structure that will permit greater decentralisation of the administration of secondary schools.

Germany: The scope of the regulations and the framework for the participation of parents differ from *Land* to *Land*. However, in all *Länder*, parents can participate either at the level of the class attended by their child or at the level of the school.

Spain: The council that includes parents has decision-making powers in the area of management and monitoring of expenses up to 2 million pesetas. If the expenses exceed this amount, the council acts in a consultative capacity.

Netherlands: The participating council is entitled to ratify the decisions taken by the *bevoegd gezag* (authorities) in the field of internal rules, the school development plan and the setting of the curriculum and the educational aims. The *bevoegd gezag* consults the participating council concerning the decisions to be taken, inter alia, as regards the budget.

Finland: The powers of the councils vary between municipalities and even between schools within the same municipality. The new school legislation, effective since 1/1/1999, does not contain any provisions on the administrative or consultative bodies of municipal schools.

Sweden: Most councils have an advisory function, but on an experimental basis some councils have decision-making powers. The powers of the councils vary between municipalities and even between schools within the same municipality.

United Kingdom (E/W, NI): School-level bodies may delegate some decisions to the headteachers.

Iceland: In 1997/98, there were only bodies made up exclusively of parents at school level. This council comments on the school plan and monitors its implementation.

Norway: In the schools that have a management council, the parents are consulted on decisions relating to the management of expenses.

Slovenia: The school council takes some decisions concerning the allocation of the budget: whether or not to give the headteacher a bonus, adopt the annual finance plan etc.

ALL COUNTRIES HAVE SET UP
—— SOME FORM OF MONITORING OF THE EDUCATION SYSTEM ——

Any monitoring of an education system assumes there is, at some administrative level (central or institutional), a clear definition of the standards and objectives which it must seek to achieve and that regulatory mechanisms which allow the system to be properly adjusted have been put in place.

For the education system to be monitored and for adjustment to be possible, it must first and foremost be evaluated. The education system can be assessed either at the level of the school or at the level of the overall education system. External evaluation of schools may also be carried out by an inspectorate. Various reference criteria can be applied according to the levels at which the evaluation is organized and according to the individual countries: school plans (or action plans), school self-evaluation, external examinations, the construction of indicators based on results, the definition of skills bases or final objectives, national attainment testing, international evaluations and the involvement of experts or an authority (for example, the setting up of a council to follow up the implementation of a reform).

Initiatives in this direction have been taken in most countries in one form or another. In some countries, specific bodies have been put in place to carry out this task. However, only a few countries have made monitoring compulsory. In other countries, monitoring exists in the form of *ad hoc* initiatives and plans or is currently in the planning stage.

Given the variety of models, two main forms are considered here, the first at school level and the second at the central level. Only procedures that have been made compulsory are analysed. At the level of the school, the most common form that has been made compulsory is the school plan or school action plan. However, with the education system, the most common form of monitoring is to set external examinations with publication of overall results, which enables the state of health of the system to be analysed with a view to improving results.

SCHOOL PLANS:
——— COMPULSORY IN MORE THAN HALF THE COUNTRIES ———

Generally speaking, a school plan or school development plan is finalized by the school's teaching staff or board of management before being approved by the authorities and then possibly being submitted to inspection. Often, this plan, drawn up at the start of the school year, describes the school's educational principles and teaching strategies, providing an overview of the educational and developmental objectives pursued by the school, the choice of subjects, the organisation of the school and the methods adopted for assessing and grading pupil progress. Rather than being an assessment of current activities, it is a statement of future prospects.

Thus, of the EFTA/EEA and EU countries, in the French Community of Belgium, each institution of basic education (pre-primary, primary) and secondary school is required to draw up a school plan. The *Conseil de participation*, which is organized within the school, is responsible for periodically reviewing how the plan is being implemented. In the Flemish Community, only primary schools are required to draw up a plan that mainly describes their approach to teaching, their operating and organisational principles and their methods of assessment. In Spain, in pre-primary, primary and secondary schools, the *Consejo Escolar* and the school management committee evaluate the extent to which the *proyecto curricular* (plan by which the institution delivers the core curriculum) has been implemented at the end of each year. In France, at the end of each school year, the school council (primary education) or the administrative council (secondary education) undertakes an evaluation of the functioning of the school on the basis of the school plan.

FIGURE B10: MONITORING THE EDUCATION SYSTEMS AT THE PRIMARY AND/OR SECONDARY LEVEL.
COMPULSORY PREPARATION OF A SCHOOL PLAN, 1997/98

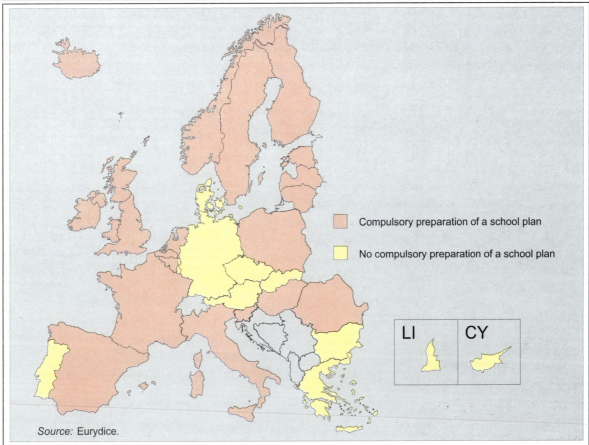

Compulsory preparation of a school plan

No compulsory preparation of a school plan

Source: Eurydice.

Additional notes

Belgium (B de): Based on the Decree of August 1998, all the primary and secondary schools are required to prepare a school plan and submit it for evaluation by the school council (the *Pädagogische Rat*).
Denmark: Since 1997, the municipalities have been obliged to issue declarations indicating the targets and framework set for individual public services, including the quality level offered by its school system.
Germany: In October 1997, the *Kultusministerkonferenz* concluded an agreement containing measures designed to safeguard the quality of teaching in lower secondary education, such as the development of evaluation instruments and studies, within and between the *Länder*, of pupils' skills and performance (for example, internal and external evaluation, greater autonomy for each school, school plans).
Greece: In addition to the assessment of activities drawn up at the end of each school year, a Ministerial Decree (1998) has made it obligatory to prepare an action plan. This was already common practice in recent years.
Italy: From 1999/2000 a new type of school plan has been introduced as an experiment, the *Piano dell'offerta formativa*.
Netherlands: Since 1998/99, the school plan is to be revised every four years.
Portugal: Since the law on school autonomy, administration and management (1998), schools are required to prepare a development plan, the *projecto educativo*.
Czech Republic: Schools do not prepare action plans, but are required to return an annual report of their activities and to make it public.
Cyprus: Schools have to draft an assessment of activities at the end of each year but do not have to prepare an action plan.

In Ireland, since the enactment of the Education Act (1998), the board of management of each recognized primary and post-primary school is required to draw up a school plan. In Italy, since 1995, primary and secondary schools must draw up a *Progetto Educativo d'istituto* (school educational plan) every year. This plan is drawn up by a group of teachers and the headteacher and submitted to the general meeting of the school's teachers for approval. In the Netherlands, all primary and secondary schools must prepare a school plan (*schoolwerkplan*) at least every two years. In Finland, the education provider has to approve the local curriculum and draw up an annual action plan based on the curriculum. In Sweden, since 1980 for compulsory education and 1994 for upper secondary level, each municipality has been required to draw up an activity plan for the schools under its responsibility. On this basis, the teachers and the headteacher of each school, with the cooperation of the parents and pupils, draw up an annual plan of work and activities that is reviewed on a regular basis. In the United Kingdom (England/Wales and Northern Ireland), schools are expected to prepare school development plans and to set targets for pupil performance. The school-level bodies may be required to draw up an action plan highlighting areas of concern mentioned in an inspection report and detailing measures to be taken. In Iceland, each school in compulsory education and at upper secondary level must produce a guide to the operation of the school, *Skólanámskrá* that defines its objectives, teaching methods and plans. In Norway, all schools are required to produce a work and development plan based on the national curriculum. They must also undertake a self evaluation and prepare an annual report to the local or regional authorities.

In seven pre-accession countries schools are now required to draft action plans. In Estonia, each school has to draw up a development plan. This plan is approved by the teachers' council (*Õppenõukogu*) and discussed with the school board (*Hoolekogu*). In Latvia, each school is required to prepare two school plans, one covering the coming school year, the second covering the period of the coming 3 to 5 years (development plan). In Lithuania, each school has to draw up an action plan. In Hungary, schools are evaluated on the basis of the plan that they have drawn up. This plan sets out the aims and objectives of the school as well as details of its organisation in infrastructure, academic and pedagogical terms. In Poland, annual school plans are targeted at the organisational and teaching priorities defined by the school. In Romania, at primary and secondary level, each school is required to draw up a school plan to ensure quality education. This plan is prepared by the teaching staff and approved by inspectors from the county. In Slovenia, headteachers and the school staff of primary and secondary schools must devise an annual plan covering organisation and teaching aspects.

RESULTS OF EXTERNAL CERTIFICATED EXAMINATIONS OFTEN BEING USED —— AS A PERFORMANCE INDICATOR OF THE EDUCATION SYSTEM ——

The purpose of a global evaluation of the education system is to account to the nation for the performance of its schools and to improve their performance. In this context, several countries have opted for compulsory **external tests** at certain stages in the pupil's school career. Two groups of countries may be distinguished according to the purpose for which these tests are designed and their timing.

In two countries only, does this external evaluation have a strictly diagnostic objective and it takes place at the start of the school year. In the French Community of Belgium, it assesses the pupils' skills and is scheduled at the start of the 3rd year of primary school, the 5th year of primary school and the 1st year of secondary school, (in reading and mathematics). The results of these tests are compared with the skills that should have been mastered at these ages, and teaching guidelines are drawn up and distributed to the teachers. In France, pupil attainment is assessed by national tests set at the start of the 3rd year of primary and the 1st year of secondary school (in reading, writing and mathematics) and also at the start of the 1st year of upper secondary school (in the mother tongue, mathematics and the first modern language). In the United Kingdom (England/Wales, Northern Ireland), as an overall evaluation of the education system, the Government publishes the national average results in National Curriculum end-of-key-stage assessments. These results are used to measure progress towards nationally defined targets.

Moreover, in France and the United Kingdom (England/Wales and Northern Ireland), the overall results of national public examinations such as the *baccalauréat* and GCSEs are also published nationally by the awarding bodies.

FIGURE B11: MONITORING THE EDUCATION SYSTEMS AT THE PRIMARY AND/OR SECONDARY LEVEL.
PUBLICATION OF THE OVERALL RESULTS OF EXTERNAL TESTS, 1997/98

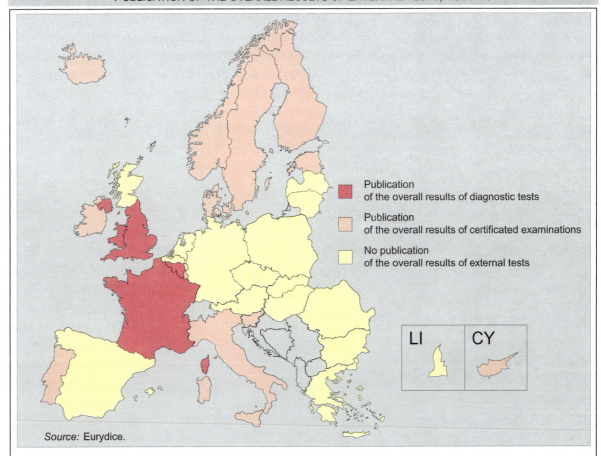

Publication
of the overall results of diagnostic tests

Publication
of the overall results of certificated examinations

No publication
of the overall results of external tests

Source: Eurydice.

Additional notes

Belgium (B fr): During 1998/99, external tests on pupils skills were set in the 3rd year secondary.
Germany: In October 1997, the *Kultusministerkonferenz* concluded an agreement containing measures designed to safeguard the quality of teaching in lower secondary education, such as the development of evaluation instruments and studies, within and between the *Länder*, of pupils' skills and performance (for example, internal and external evaluation, greater autonomy for each school, school plans).
France: The overall results of the baccalaureate are also published.
Portugal: In 1999/2000 standardized tests are to be administered nationally in the 4th year of *ensino básico* (mother tongue and mathematics). Then they will be set for the 6th year (2000/2001) and the 9th year (2001/2002).
United Kingdom (E/W, NI): The overall results of national public examinations, such as GCSEs, are also published nationally by the awarding bodies.
Bulgaria: A national centre has recently been set up to investigate the performance of the education system.
Lithuania: An analysis of the results of internal tests is carried out regularly, and was done during 1997/98. As an experiment, externally set tests have been administered in one of the 10 regions (counties).

In order to enable the general public to become acquainted with the state of the system, other countries have opted to publish the overall results of external certificating examinations that take place either at the end of compulsory education, or at the end of upper secondary education. These results are analysed to shed light on the overall state of the educational system at a given moment, and are sometimes used to compare and rank schools. When the results of tests only serve to evaluate the institutions and are published exclusively by schools or by the local authorities, they are not considered here. In Denmark, Italy and Portugal, the results of the final examinations in upper secondary school are published each year at national level. In Ireland, the National Council for Curriculum and Assessment publishes a global review of pupils' results in the national examinations that are undertaken at the end of the lower secondary level and at the end of the upper secondary level. In Luxembourg, the *Service de Coordination de la Recherche et de l'Innovation* (SCRIPT) regularly evaluates how the education system is evolving. This service publishes data on the assessment of overall pupil performance.

In Finland, the National Board of Education is responsible for evaluating the performance of the education system and must publish the significant results of the external tests that it sets and is responsible for administering. Pupils' skills in their mother tongue and mathematics at the end of compulsory education are assessed regularly, other subjects are evaluated in turn. In Sweden, the schools use compulsory national tests in Swedish, English and mathematics at the end of compulsory education. The results are used for assessment at school and national level but not as an individual examination. In Iceland, the results of the national tests at the end of compulsory education are published each year at national level. In Norway, national tests in three subjects are organized for pupils at the end of compulsory education. The pupils must sit at least one of the subjects, and the overall results are published only with the national and regional averages. Each school receives its own results individually to enable it to see how it ranks in relation to the national average.

As regards the overall external evaluation of their systems, of the pre-accession countries, only Estonia, Slovenia and Cyprus have made the national publication of results compulsory. Other countries have no external evaluation or are currently implementing specific initiatives and experimental projects. In Slovenia, since 1992, external tests have been organized for pupils at the end of basic education (8th year), the overall results of which are published in a report submitted to the national council of education experts. Since 1995, the results of the external examinations leading to the *matura* certificate at the end of upper secondary education have also been published, with the national average, but with no possibility of comparison between schools. Schools are informed of their individual results and can therefore see how they stand in relation to the national average. In Cyprus, the overall results of external examinations held at the end of secondary school are published. Comparisons are drawn up on developments from year to year in order to improve the curriculum and teaching methods.

PRE - PRIMARY EDUCATION

PARTICIPATION OF 4-YEAR-OLDS IN PRE-PRIMARY EDUCATION KEEPS ON RISING

In 1997, participation rates of 4-year-old children in education-oriented pre-primary institutions exceed 50% in all European Union and EFTA/EEA countries, except in Finland and Liechtenstein, where they are around one third of the 4-year-old population. The highest participation rates (over 90%) are found in Belgium, Spain, France, Italy, Luxembourg and the Netherlands. In pre-accession countries, percentages range from 28% in Poland to 96% in Hungary.

Figure C1 illustrates how enrolment has evolved from 1960 to 1997 in the EU. Generally, more and more 4-year-old children are attending an education-oriented pre-primary institution except in Ireland, where enrolment remained stable. This increase should be connected to the recognition of the importance of pre-primary education to young children's development and socialisation. Among the highest participation rates, those of France, Luxembourg and the Netherlands have risen significantly in the 1960s and 1970s. In Spain, the rise can be observed in the 1970s and 1980s. In Belgium, enrolment was already high in 1960. Among the countries the enrolment of which was lowest in 1980, the percentages observed in Portugal, Finland and Sweden have at least doubled in the last two decades.

FIGURE C1: PARTICIPATION RATES OF 4-YEAR-OLDS IN EDUCATION-ORIENTED PRE-PRIMARY INSTITUTIONS, AS A PERCENTAGE, FROM 1960 TO 1997

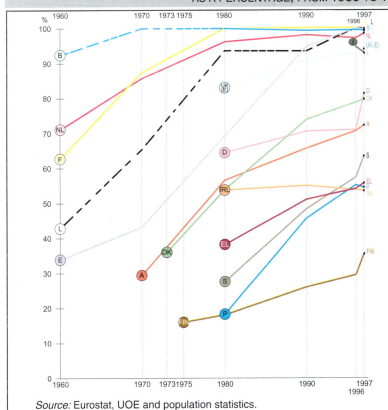

Additional notes

NB: The 1997 data available for **EFTA/EEA countries** and **pre-accession countries** are set out in the annex.

Belgium: The data prior to 1980 are shown as a dotted line because they are available only for all children enrolled in nursery schools (*écoles maternelles/kleuteronderwijs*) regardless of their age.
Greece: Only children between 3½ and 4½ years old in public-sector nursery schools are included.
Ireland: Pupils attending certain private schools are not included.
Luxembourg: The data are shown as a dotted line as the percentages include enrolment of both 4- and 5-year-olds.
United Kingdom (E): The data are shown as a dotted line as they cover children in nursery schools, nursery and infant classes in primary schools, special schools and independent schools.

Source: Eurostat, UOE and population statistics.

Explanatory note

Education-oriented pre-primary institutions provide education-oriented care for young children. They can either be schools or non-school settings, which generally come under authorities or ministries other than those responsible for education. They obligatorily recruit staff with specialized qualifications in education. Day nurseries, playgroups and day care centres, where the staff are not required to hold a qualification in education, are not included.

A WIDE RANGE OF PROVISION
IN PRE-PRIMARY EDUCATION

There is a wide range of facilities which children in Europe may attend before entering primary school. Further details of them, with their names in the original languages, are presented in Figure C2.

FIGURE C2: ORGANIZATION OF PRE-PRIMARY INSTITUTIONS, PUBLIC AND PRIVATE SECTORS, 1997/98

Age/years	0	1	2	3	4	5	6	7

European Union

- **B** — CRÈCHES / KINDERDAGVERBLIJF / KRIPPEN | ENSEIGNEMENT MATERNEL / KLEUTERONDERWIJS / KINDERGARTEN
- **DK** — VUGGESTUER | ALDERSINTEGREREDE INSTITUTIONER | BØRNEHAVER | BØRNEHAVEKLASSE
- **D** — KRIPPEN | KINDERGARTEN | VORKLASSEN (2 *Länder* only)
- **EL** — IDIOTIKI VREFONIPIAKI STATHMI | KRATIKI STATHMI | NIPIAKA TMIMATA | IDIOTIKI PAIDIKI STATHMI, KRATIKI PAIDIKI STATHMI | NIPIAGOGEIA / OLOIMERA NIPIAGOGEIA
- **E** — GUARDERÍAS and other institutions | ESCUELAS DE EDUCACIÓN INFANTIL / CENTROS DE EDUCACIÓN INFANTIL
- **F** — CRÈCHES | ÉCOLES MATERNELLES / CLASSES ENFANTINES
- **IRL** — DAY CARE / DAY NURSERIES | PLAYGROUPS | PLAYGROUPS FOR TRAVELLER CHILDREN | PRIMARY SCHOOLS (Infant Classes)
- **I** — ASILO NIDO | SCUOLA MATERNA
- **L** — FOYERS DE JOUR | Classes enfantines SPILLSCHOUL
- **NL** — PEUTERSPEELZALEN | BASISONDERWIJS | KINDERDAGVERBLIJVEN / HALVEDAGOPVANG
- **A** — KRIPPEN | KINDERGARTEN
- **P** — CRÈCHES | JARDINS DE INFÂNCIA | JARDINS DE INFÂNCIA
- **FIN** — PÄIVÄKOTI / DAGHEM | PERUSKOULU / GRUNDSKOLA
- **S** — FÖRSKOLA | FÖRSKOLEKLASS
- **UK (E/W)** — DAY NURSERIES / NURSERY CENTRES | PRE-SCHOOL GROUPS / PLAYGROUPS | NURSERY SCHOOLS / CLASSES | RECEPTION CLASSES
- **UK (NI)** — DAY NURSERIES / NURSERY CENTRES | PRE-SCHOOL GROUPS / PLAYGROUPS | NURSERY SCHOOLS / CLASSES
- **UK (SC)** — DAY NURSERIES | PLAYGROUPS | DAY NURSERIES / PLAYGROUPS | NURSERY SCHOOLS / CLASSES

▢ Nurseries/Day care/Playgroups   ▢ Non-school education-oriented settings   ▢ Schools

Source: Eurydice.

Additional notes

Germany: In two *Länder*, *Vorklassen* are provided for children aged 5 who have not yet reached compulsory school age but whose parents wish them to receive preparation for primary school. In seven *Länder*, *Vorklassen* are provided for children who have reached compulsory school age but do not have the maturity required to start school.

Spain: The *centros de Educación Infantil* are private institutions recognized as schools. The education law (*LOGSE*) provides for the *escuelas de Educación Infantil* to admit children from the age of 3 months and to provide the first stage of education (for children from 3 months to 3 years of age), the second stage (for those aged 3-6) or both.

Ireland: The Early Start Pilot Pre-school Project is located in some primary schools in selected disadvantaged areas. It provides an intervention programme for the most needy children from these areas who are between the ages of 3 and 4 and who are most at risk of educational failure.

Luxembourg: Since 1998, the national Ministry of Education has offered early education to children from the age of 3. The aim is to develop the pupils' social integration and language capacities. This pilot project will be brought into general use in 2004/2005.

Netherlands: *Basisonderwijs* is compulsory from 5 years of age, but children are admitted from the age of 4.

Sweden: The *förskoleklass* is a non-compulsory type of school that, since 1 January 1998, has replaced the activities that were previously provided for six-year-old children.

United Kingdom (E/W, NI): In April 1997, the Government introduced a scheme to fund a full year of at least part-time pre-primary education for all 4-year-olds (3- and 4-year-olds in Northern Ireland) in day nurseries, nursery centres, pre-school groups, playgroups and private schools. These institutions (like public nursery schools and classes) are expected to work towards the official goals for learning for children by the time they enter compulsory education; they are now also inspected by the Office for Standards in Education.

United Kingdom (SC): The Government funds some day nurseries and playgroups for children aged 3 to 5; they are therefore subject to the same regulations as nursery schools/classes.

In facilities belonging to the school system as such, staff members responsible for children's education always have specialized qualifications in education. On the other hand, in the non-school settings (day nurseries, playgroups or day care centres) which generally or partly come under authorities or ministries other than those responsible for education, staff members are not required to hold a qualification in education. However, the *Kindergärten* in Germany and Austria and the non-school *jardins de infância* in Portugal must employ staff with a qualification in education. (Assistants may be employed in addition.) In the United Kingdom (England, Wales and Northern Ireland), although staff are not obliged to have teacher qualifications in non-school institutions, those receiving funding from the education authorities are strongly advised to involve a qualified teacher in planning. In Denmark, Finland and Sweden, all settings catering for young children employ staff qualified in education.

Attendance at a pre-primary institution is voluntary in all Member States of the EU with the exception of Luxembourg, where the *Spillschoul* is compulsory from the age of 4. In Northern Ireland, compulsory primary education starts at age 4.

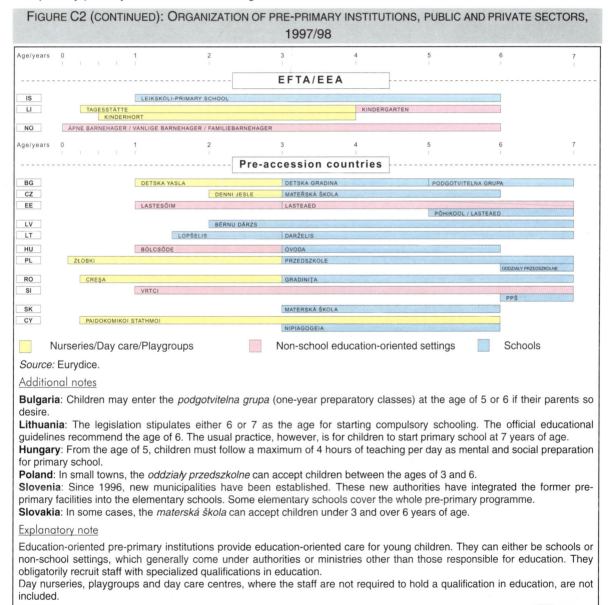

FIGURE C2 (CONTINUED): ORGANIZATION OF PRE-PRIMARY INSTITUTIONS, PUBLIC AND PRIVATE SECTORS, 1997/98

Nurseries/Day care/Playgroups   Non-school education-oriented settings   Schools

Source: Eurydice.

Additional notes

Bulgaria: Children may enter the *podgotvitelna grupa* (one-year preparatory classes) at the age of 5 or 6 if their parents so desire.
Lithuania: The legislation stipulates either 6 or 7 as the age for starting compulsory schooling. The official educational guidelines recommend the age of 6. The usual practice, however, is for children to start primary school at 7 years of age.
Hungary: From the age of 5, children must follow a maximum of 4 hours of teaching per day as mental and social preparation for primary school.
Poland: In small towns, the *oddziały przedszkolne* can accept children between the ages of 3 and 6.
Slovenia: Since 1996, new municipalities have been established. These new authorities have integrated the former pre-primary facilities into the elementary schools. Some elementary schools cover the whole pre-primary programme.
Slovakia: In some cases, the *materská škola* can accept children under 3 and over 6 years of age.

Explanatory note

Education-oriented pre-primary institutions provide education-oriented care for young children. They can either be schools or non-school settings, which generally come under authorities or ministries other than those responsible for education. They obligatorily recruit staff with specialized qualifications in education.
Day nurseries, playgroups and day care centres, where the staff are not required to hold a qualification in education, are not included.

In three Member States of the EU, schools are the only form of provision for children from the age of two-and-half (Belgium) or 3 years (France and Italy). A wide range of educational provision is available in the other member countries and children go to school later. There are pre-primary classes for 6-year-olds in Denmark, Finland and Sweden. In most of the German *Länder,* school provision starts with compulsory primary education. In Denmark and in Sweden, parents may opt to enrol their children in the *folkeskole* and the *grundskola* respectively from age 6.

A similar diversity is also found in the EFTA/EEA countries and in the pre-accession countries. Many of these, however, share a common characteristic in that there is only one type of institution for children of a given age. This may be a playgroup, a non-school education-oriented setting or a school.

In all these countries, attendance at a setting is also voluntary, depending on the wishes of the parents and the availability of the provision. It is therefore optional in all countries, except in Hungary where attendance of the last year of the *óvoda* is compulsory for 5-year-olds, and in Slovenia where it is compulsory from 6 years of age.

In Iceland, the main provision for pre-primary children is in the *leikskóli*. In Liechtenstein and Norway, there is no school provision for children before they start primary school at the age of 6. The non-school education-oriented settings in these two countries are, however, required to recruit staff with qualifications in education.

In several pre-accession countries, children under 3 are catered for in crèches and day nurseries. In Estonia, Hungary and Slovenia, there are non-school education-oriented settings for these children. In most pre-accession countries, children can attend a pre-primary school from the age of 3. In Latvia and Lithuania, they can attend a pre-primary school-based institution from the age of 2 and 1½ years respectively. In Estonia, children can attend school from the age of 5.

PRE-PRIMARY ATTENDANCE INCREASES
—————— WITH THE AGE OF CHILDREN ——————

Figure C3 sets out, by country, participation rates of children aged 3-7 in education-oriented pre-primary and primary levels and when transition from the one level to the other occurs.

In half of the EU and EFTA/EEA countries, mass attendance at education-oriented institutions is observed from 3 years of age (Belgium, France, Italy and Iceland) or from 4 years (Denmark, Germany, Spain, Luxembourg, and the Netherlands). The United Kingdom also has mass attendance from 4, but the majority of pupils are in primary schools. In the other countries, pre-primary attendance increases together with the age of children. In Ireland, Austria and Liechtenstein, the overwhelming majority of 5-years-olds attend pre-primary education. In Sweden and Norway, participation in pre-primary education is only predominant from 6.

One year before the beginning of compulsory education, pre-primary participation rates exceed 80% in all the countries with early enrolment in pre-primary education as well as in Austria, Sweden, Iceland and Liechtenstein. In Greece, Portugal and Finland, however, the rates do not exceed 70%.

Among pre-accession countries, more than half of 3-year-olds attend an education-oriented pre-primary institution in Bulgaria (55%), Estonia (67%) and Hungary, where enrolment is particularly high (88%). It is lower in Lithuania and Poland, where respectively 40% and 38% of children aged 5 are enrolled in pre-primary education.

In the EU and EFTA/EEA, transition to primary school occurs at 6 for almost all children in Belgium, Greece, Spain, France, Italy, Luxembourg, the Netherlands, Portugal and Iceland and at 7 in the other countries. In the United Kingdom, by the age of 5, all pupils are in primary schools.

In pre-accession countries, entry into primary school occurs at 7 for most children, except in Hungary, where it occurs at 6.

FIGURE C3: PARTICIPATION RATES IN EDUCATION-ORIENTED PRE-PRIMARY INSTITUTIONS AND PRIMARY INSTITUTIONS, BY AGE, AS A PERCENTAGE, 1996/97

Source: Eurostat, UOE and population statistics.

Additional notes

Greece: Only children attending the *nipiagogeia* (public-sector nursery schools) are included.
France: 1997/98.
Ireland: Pupils attending certain private schools are not included.
Luxembourg: Early entry into pre-primary education (for 3-year-olds) has been provided since the 1998/99 school year. In ISCED 0, children aged 4 are included with 5-year-olds.
Netherlands: 4-year-olds attend the non-compulsory year of *basisonderwijs*. Compulsory primary education starts at age 5, but for the purposes of international statistics, 5-year-olds are included under ISCED 0.
United Kingdom: The data are presented for the United Kingdom as a whole; disparities between the component parts are therefore concealed. ISCED 1 data include reception classes and 4-year-olds in Northern Ireland (compulsory education starts at age 4). The data cover pupils in nursery schools and nursery and infant classes in primary schools.
Liechtenstein: 1995/96.
Norway: As of 1997/98, compulsory schooling starts at 6.
Slovenia: Data for children aged 3 and 4 at ISCED 0 are included with those aged 5 and set out in the annex.

Explanatory note

Education-oriented pre-primary institutions provide education-oriented care for young children. They can either be schools or non-school settings, which generally come under authorities or ministries other than those responsible for education. They obligatorily recruit staff with specialized qualifications in education. Day nurseries, playgroups and day care centres, where the staff are not required to hold a qualification in education, are not included.

MOST PROVISION IS IN SCHOOLS RATHER THAN IN OTHER TYPES OF INSTITUTION

Children enrolled in education-oriented pre-primary provision attend schools in almost all EU and EFTA/EEA countries. All pre-primary pupils go to school in Belgium, Greece, Spain, France, Ireland, Italy, Luxembourg, the Netherlands and Iceland. In most countries, this is the only type of pre-primary institution for children of that age (see Figure C2). In other countries, data are not available on other facilities; they account for a low percentage however. In Denmark, Germany, Austria, Finland and Sweden, the vast majority of children attend non-school education-oriented settings. In Norway, this is the case for all pupils.

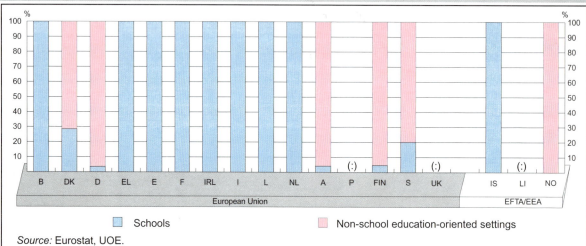

FIGURE C4: DISTRIBUTION OF CHILDREN ATTENDING EDUCATION-ORIENTED PRE-PRIMARY PROVISION ACCORDING TO THE TYPE OF INSTITUTION THEY ATTEND, AS A PERCENTAGE, 1996/97

Schools

Non-school education-oriented settings

Source: Eurostat, UOE.

Explanatory note

Education-oriented pre-primary institutions provide education-oriented care for young children. They can either be schools or non-school settings, which generally come under authorities or ministries other than those responsible for education. They obligatorily recruit staff with specialized qualifications in education. Day nurseries, playgroups and day care centres, where the staff are not required to hold a qualification in education, are not included.

The category 'schools' includes pre-primary classes in primary school and pre-primary schools in separate educational settings.

The category 'non-school education-oriented settings' includes pre-primary children groups in settings outside the school system and managed by other pre-primary service providers.

REGIONAL VARIATIONS IN ATTENDANCE OF 3-YEAR-OLDS ——— AT EDUCATION-ORIENTED PRE-PRIMARY INSTITUTIONS ———

Referring back to Figure C3, enrolment of 4-year-olds in education-oriented pre-primary education is fairly high in most countries. Examination of the map showing the regional variations at that age would show not only an increase in the rate in most countries but also small variations between the regions.

However in most EU countries, attendance by 3-year-olds at education-oriented pre-primary institutions varies from one region to another. The smallest regional variations are observed in France, where percentages reach the maximum, which suggests the early schooling tradition is well established throughout the country. Considerable regional variations are found in the United Kingdom, where regional rates range from 20% to 84%.

FIGURE C5: PARTICIPATION RATES OF 3-YEAR-OLDS IN EDUCATION-ORIENTED PRE-PRIMARY INSTITUTIONS, BY NUTS 1 AND NUTS 2 REGIONS, AS A PERCENTAGE, 1996/97

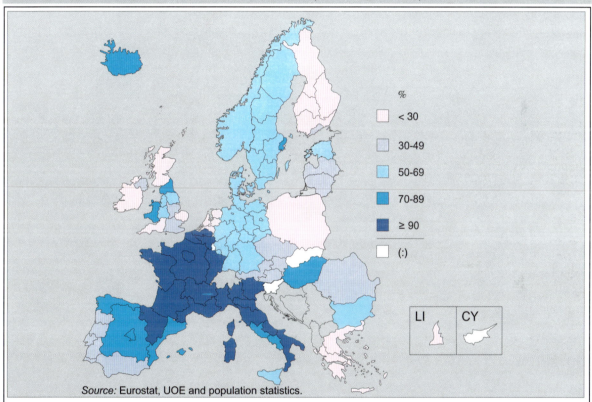

%
- ☐ < 30
- ☐ 30-49
- ☐ 50-69
- ☐ 70-89
- ☐ ≥ 90
- ☐ (:)

LI   CY

Source: Eurostat, UOE and population statistics.

Additional notes

Germany, Greece, Austria and **Portugal**: Only data from the national level (NUTS 0) are presented.
France: 1997/98.
Ireland: Pupils attending certain private schools are not included.
United Kingdom: The data cover children in nursery schools and nursery and infant classes in primary schools. 1995/96 population data are used for NUTS regions Scotland and Northern Ireland as well as parts of NUTS South East and South West.
Liechtenstein: 1995/96.
Hungary: Only full-time pupils are included.

Explanatory note

For most Member States, the nomenclature used here is that of NUTS 1. NUTS 2 is however used for Finland and Sweden. For the EFTA/EEA countries and the pre-accession countries, only national data are provided.

For the definition of the NUTS classification, please refer to the definition of statistical tools at the beginning of the book.

Education-oriented pre-primary institutions provide education-oriented care for young children. They can either be schools or non-school settings, which generally come under authorities or ministries other than those responsible for education. They obligatorily recruit staff with specialized qualifications in education. Day nurseries, playgroups and day care centres, where the staff are not required to hold a qualification in education, are not included.

NO DIRECT CONNECTION BETWEEN ATTENDANCE OF EDUCATION-ORIENTED PRE-PRIMARY INSTITUTIONS BY 3-YEAR-OLD CHILDREN AND ——————— THE EMPLOYMENT STATUS OF MOTHERS ———————

Figure C6 shows that the uptake of pre-primary provision is not directly related to the child-care needs of mothers who go out to work. The phenomenon is more complex and enrolment in pre-primary education certainly depends partly on the provision. Whereas percentages of mothers with a 3-year-old child and a paid job range from 37 to 74%, participation rates of 3-year-olds vary to a larger extent (from 3 to 100%).

In the three countries in which there is full coverage of pre-primary provision (Belgium, France and Italy), the percentage of 3-year-olds attending education-oriented pre-primary institutions is very much higher than the percentage of mothers with a 3-year-old child and a paid job. The situation is similar in Germany, Spain and Iceland, but to a lesser degree. In Greece, Ireland, Austria, Portugal, Finland, Sweden and the United Kingdom, on the contrary, the percentage of mothers who have a 3-year-old child and who work outside the home is greater than that of 3-year-olds attending education-oriented pre-primary institutions. In these countries, in addition to education-oriented institutions, a network of child care centres and playgroups or family day care for 3-year-olds is found (see Figure C2).

FIGURE C6: ENROLMENT OF 3-YEAR-OLDS IN EDUCATION-ORIENTED PRE-PRIMARY INSTITUTIONS, AS A PERCENTAGE, IN COMPARISON TO PERCENTAGE OF MOTHERS WITH A 3-YEAR-OLD CHILD AND IN EMPLOYMENT, 1996/97

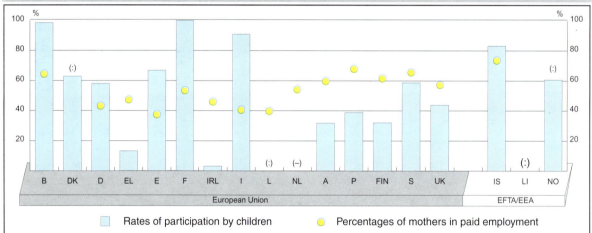

☐ Rates of participation by children   ● Percentages of mothers in paid employment

Source: Eurostat, UOE, Labour force survey and population statistics.

Additional notes

France: 1997/98.
Ireland: Pupils attending certain private schools are not included.
Luxembourg: Early entry into pre-primary education (for 3-year-olds) has been provided since 1998/99.
Sweden and **Iceland**: National estimates are used in percentages of mothers with a job.
United Kingdom: The data cover children in nursery schools and nursery classes in primary schools.

Explanatory note

The data on mothers with a 3-year-old child and in employment are drawn from the 1997 Eurostat Labour Force Survey. Data on 3-year-old enrolment in education-oriented pre-primary institutions are drawn from the UOE questionnaires.

Education-oriented pre-primary institutions provide education-oriented care for young children. They can either be schools or non-school settings, which generally come under authorities or ministries other than those responsible for education. They obligatorily recruit staff with specialized qualifications in education. Day nurseries, playgroups and day care centres, where the staff are not required to hold a qualification in education, are not included.

THE AVERAGE DURATION OF ATTENDANCE IN PRE-PRIMARY EDUCATION —— IS OFTEN SHORTER THAN THE DURATION OF PROVISION ——

In most European countries, the average duration of attendance at an education-oriented pre-primary institution is shorter than the theoretical duration of official provision. The average duration can be influenced by various factors: the minimum age of admission to educational provision, the starting age of compulsory primary education and the participation rates of children in pre-primary institutions. Thus, a short average period of attendance can be found for different reasons – either because the official provision extends to only a few years or because attendance at such schools or other settings is not widespread.

Theoretical and average duration values coincide in Belgium, Germany, Spain, Ireland, Italy, the Netherlands, Liechtenstein and Hungary.

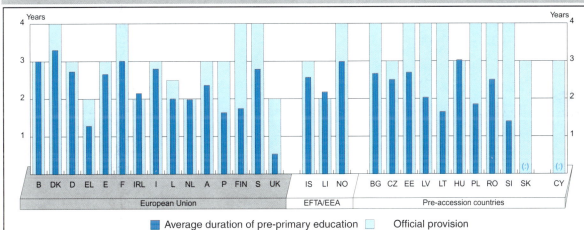

FIGURE C7: AVERAGE DURATION OF ATTENDANCE BY CHILDREN AGED 3-7 AT AN EDUCATION-ORIENTED PRE-PRIMARY INSTITUTION IN COMPARISON TO DURATION OF OFFICIAL PROVISION, IN YEARS, 1996/97

Legend:
- Average duration of pre-primary education
- Official provision

Source: Eurostat, UOE and Eurydice.

Additional notes

France: 1997/98.
Greece: Only children enrolled in the public-sector nursery schools (*nipiagogeia*) are included. An educational structure is only in place for children aged 4 and over.
Ireland: Children aged 6 and 7 who are of compulsory school age but who are in the infant classes are included. There is no genuine theoretical duration of attendance at an education-oriented pre-primary institution: revised policy is being formulated for the pre-primary level.
Luxembourg: Early entry into pre-primary education (for 3-year-olds) has been provided since school year 1998/99.
Netherlands: 4- and 5-year-olds from the *basisonderwijs* are classified in ISCED 0.
United Kingdom: The data cover children in nursery schools and nursery classes in primary schools.
Liechtenstein: 1995/96.
Norway: From school year 1997/98 onwards, the single structure starts at age 6, and no longer at age 7.

Explanatory note

The average duration of children's attendance at an education-oriented institution is obtained by adding together the attendance rates for the different age groups from the age of 3 to 7 years. In Belgium, for example, the pre-primary rate for children aged 3 years is 98.6%, 99.5% at 4 years and 98.0% at 5 years, 4.3% at 6 and 0.1% of 7-year-olds, the duration of pre-primary education would equal (0.986 + 0.995 + 0.980 + 0.043+ 0.001) x 1 year = 3.00 years.
The official duration of provision corresponds to the number of years – starting at the age of 3 years – during which the pre-primary institution can take children prior to their entry into primary school.

Education-oriented pre-primary institutions provide education-oriented care for young children. They can either be schools or non-school settings, which generally come under authorities or ministries other than those responsible for education. They obligatorily recruit staff with specialized qualifications in education. Day nurseries, playgroups and day care centres, where the staff are not required to hold a qualification in education, are not included.

The countries with the **shortest theoretical duration (2 years)** are Greece, Ireland, the Netherlands, the United Kingdom and Liechtenstein. Among these countries, the gap between theoretical and average duration is large in Greece and even more in the United Kingdom. The short average duration of pre-primary in the United Kingdom can be explained by a lower starting age for primary education.

In the majority of EU and EFTA/EEA countries, where it is possible to attend pre-primary education for **3 years**, the average duration of attendance varies from 2.5 to 3 years. The situation is different in Portugal and Austria, where a shorter duration is found (1.6 and 2.4 years respectively). The observation is also true for two pre-accession countries (the Czech Republic and Hungary).

In four EU Member States (Denmark, France, Finland and Sweden), Norway and in most pre-accession countries, it is possible to attend pre-primary education for **4 years**. Among those countries, a gap of over two years between theoretical duration and average duration of attendance is observed in Finland, Latvia, Lithuania and Poland.

GROUPING OF CHILDREN:
AGE GROUPS OR 'FAMILY GROUPS'

In education-oriented institutions (whether or not they are school based) that cater for children before they enter the compulsory primary school, the groups of children are formed according to one of two main models.

— The first anticipates the pattern of organization in classes that is used in primary schools, the children being grouped according to age. This pattern is called the 'school model'.

— The second is closer to the pattern of the family, children of different ages being placed in the same group. This is the 'family model'.

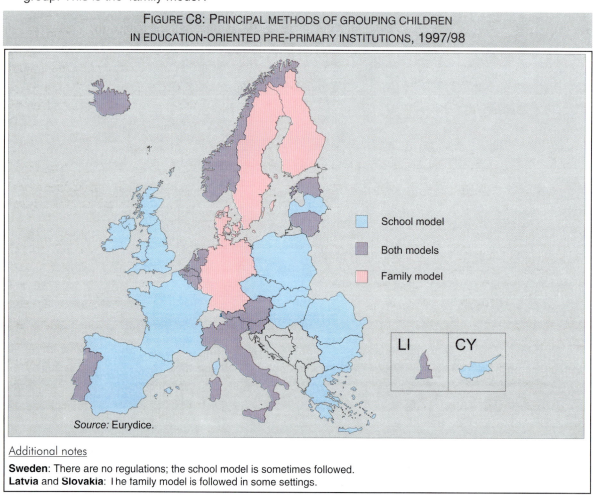

FIGURE C8: PRINCIPAL METHODS OF GROUPING CHILDREN
IN EDUCATION-ORIENTED PRE-PRIMARY INSTITUTIONS, 1997/98

School model

Both models

Family model

LI   CY

Source: Eurydice.

Additional notes

Sweden: There are no regulations; the school model is sometimes followed.
Latvia and **Slovakia**: The family model is followed in some settings.

Within the EU, in schools in Greece, Spain, France, Ireland and the United Kingdom, the tendency is to make up classes of children of the same age, according to the school model. This situation is also found in the pre-primary classes, which take children at the age of 6 in Denmark and Finland.

On the other hand, in the non-school education-oriented settings for children under 6 years of age in Denmark, Germany, Finland and Sweden, children of different ages are grouped together, rather on the family model. In Luxembourg, in the *Spillschoul*, the family model is also the most common. In Luxembourg, Finland and Sweden, there is a tendency to group together children of the same family.

In the other EU countries, institutions may adopt either model. This is the case in the schools in Belgium, Italy and the Netherlands, in the *Kindergärten* in Austria and in the *jardins de infância* in Portugal.

In the EFTA/EEA countries, institutions catering for children before they start primary school organize groups on both the school and the family models, although in Liechtenstein the *Kindergarten* usually places children aged 4 and 5 together.

In the pre-accession countries, the most common model is the school model, while in Estonia, Lithuania and Slovenia, the two models coexist and schools can choose one or other organization.

NUMBER OF CHILDREN PER ADULT: OFTEN SUBJECT ———— TO REGULATIONS BUT WITH DIFFERENT NORMS ————

Most of the EU Member States and all the EFTA/EEA and pre-accession countries have regulations prescribing the maximum and/or minimum number of children in a class or group of children in education-oriented institutions, whether these are schools or not. Figure C9 shows the maximum number of children for which each adult is responsible, and not the size of the groups. In the countries in which two adults work together routinely, the maximum number of children in the group is divided by two.

These norms in relation to class sizes vary widely from one country to another and even within the same one, depending on the age of the children. The numbers shown here are therefore those prescribed for 4-year-olds. The comparison shows that the norms are relatively high in a number of EU countries, in particular those in which the children are in schools. The norms of the *Kindergärten* in Austria are similar.

EU countries that have no regulations on class or group sizes operate in a variety of ways. In some of them, the number of teachers in an institution is fixed on the basis of the total number of pupils enrolled. This is the case in Belgium and the Netherlands (in *basisonderwijs*). The basis used for the calculation is, however, very different from one country to another. In France, the *Inspecteur d'Académie* determines annually the average number of pupils per class in his area and can also set the maximum number of pupils in a class according to criteria unique to that *Académie*. In the United Kingdom (England, Wales and Northern Ireland), an indication is given as to recommended minimum number of adults to be provided for a group of children, depending on their age.

In Norway, there are no regulations on the size of groups but there are on the number of children per teacher.

In most of the pre-accession countries, the permitted numbers are high (between 20 and 26 children per adult). The norms appear more favourable in Bulgaria (under 10 children per adult), in Lithuania and Slovenia (15 and 12 children per adult respectively).

FIGURE C9: PRESCRIBED OR RECOMMENDED MAXIMUM NUMBERS OF 4-YEAR-OLD CHILDREN PER ADULT IN SCHOOLS AND OTHER EDUCATION-ORIENTED PRE-PRIMARY INSTITUTIONS, 1997/98

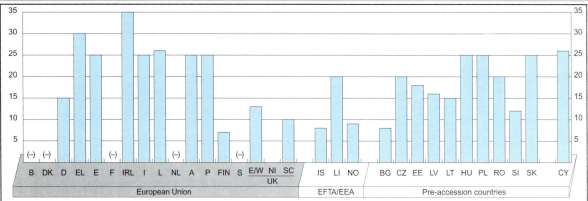

Source: Eurydice.

(–): No regulations regarding maximum and/or minimum group size, or number of adults per group.

Additional notes

Germany: A group should have between 15 and 30 children with at least one person with a qualification in education and usually an assistant.

France: The average number of pupils per class can be 25 in nursery schools in educational priority areas.

Ireland: The recommendations presented concern only the number of children in the infant classes of primary schools. From September 1999, the maximum number per class is 30. The maximum number of children per class in the Early Start Pilot Pre-school Project is 15, and the classes are taken by a primary teacher and a qualified child care worker.

Finland: The law prescribes, for full-time education-oriented pre-primary institutions, the number of qualified staff in relation to the number of children: one adult for every 4 children under 3 years of age and one adult for every 7 children over 3 years of age.

United Kingdom (E/W): Government guidance recommends a minimum of two adults per group of 26 pupils in schools (20 if the teacher also has administrative duties) and in non-school provision where staff include a qualified teacher and a qualified nursery assistant.

United Kingdom (NI): Compulsory primary education begins at age 4. A maximum of 25 pupils is recommended on the basis of the size of the classroom.

United Kingdom (SC): Legislation requires a minimum staff/child ratio of 1:10 in local authority nursery schools and classes.

Czech Republic: Decisions on class sizes are taken by headteachers after consultation with the school's organising body and the local authority responsible.

Estonia: The maximum number for groups of children of the same age is 18, and this figure is reduced to 16 for groups of children of different ages.

Latvia: Depending on the financial situation of the authorities and the actual demand, the number of children per group can be 20.

Hungary: The maximum number can be reduced subject to consultation with the competent authority.

Slovenia: Two adults per group of 24 children are required to be present during the time reserved for educational activities (4 hours a day). Outside these hours, only one adult is in charge of the group.

Cyprus: For children under 3½ years of age, the maximum number is 20 children per adult; for children over 4½, the maximum is 30.

FEE-PAYING IS MORE FREQUENT IN THE PRIVATE SECTOR THAN IN THE PUBLIC SECTOR

In most of the countries of the EU and of the EFTA/EEA, admission to public-sector pre-primary schools and other settings is free of charge. On the other hand, in the private sector, parents often have to make a financial contribution. In several countries (Denmark, Austria, Finland, Sweden, Iceland and Norway), a fee must be paid for admission to non-school settings in both sectors and this applies to all or nearly all children. In Belgium and the Netherlands, all children are guaranteed free admission to schools, even in the private grant-aided sector.

In certain pre-accession countries access to the public sector is often free of charge, but in the Czech Republic, Estonia, Hungary and Poland, some public pre-primary institutions may be fee-paying. In Slovenia and Cyprus the pre-primary institutions are always fee-paying. In Bulgaria and Lithuania, all settings are free of charge.

FIGURE C10: FEE-PAYING/FREE ADMISSION TO EDUCATION-ORIENTED PRE-PRIMARY INSTITUTIONS AND PERCENTAGE OF FEE-PAYING CHILDREN, 1997/98

	FREE OF CHARGE		FEE-PAYING		PERCENTAGE OF FEE-PAYING CHILDREN
	PUBLIC	PRIVATE	PUBLIC	PRIVATE	
European Union					
B	*Enseignement maternel, kleuteronderwijs, Kindergarten*	*Enseignement maternel, kleuteronderwijs, Kindergarten*			0%
DK	*Børnehaveklasse*		*Aldersintegrerede institutioner, Børnehaver*	*Aldersintegrerede institutioner, Børnehaver, Børnehaveklasse*	(:)
D	*Vorklassen, Schulkindergärten*		*Kindergärten* (with some exceptions)	*Kindergärten* (with some exceptions), *Vorklassen, Schulkindergärten*	(:)
EL	*Nipiagogeia*			*Idiotika nipiagogeia*	3.5%
E	*Escuelas de Educación Infantil*	*Centros de Educación Infantil*	*Escuelas de Educación Infantil* (some)	*Centros de Educación Infantil*	22.7%
F	*Écoles maternelles Classes enfantines*			*Écoles maternelles Classes enfantines*	12.5%
IRL	Playgroups for Traveller children Primary schools (Early Start included)			Private schools	2%
I	*Scuola materna*			*Scuola materna*	(:)
L	*Classes enfantines, Spillschoul* (*éducation précoce* included)				0%
NL	*Basisonderwijs*	*Basisonderwijs*			0%
A			*Kindergärten* (with some exceptions)	*Kindergärten*	(:)
P	*Jardins de infância (ME)*	*Colégios*	*Jardins de infância (MSSS)*	*Jardins de infância*	(:)
FIN	*Peruskoulu/Grundskola*	*Peruskoulu/Grundskola*	*Päiväkoti/Daghem*	*Päiväkoti/Daghem*	± 94%
S	*Förskoleklass*	*Förskoleklass*	*Förskola*	*Förskola*	(:)
UK (E/W)	Day nurseries, Nursery centres Nursery schools/classes Reception classes	Pre-school groups/ playgroups, Day nurseries, Nursery centres Nursery schools/classes/ Reception classes		Pre-school groups/ playgroups, Day nurseries, Nursery centres Nursery schools/classes (independent schools)	(:)
UK (NI)	Day nurseries, Nursery centres Nursery schools/classes	Pre-school groups/ playgroups, Day nurseries, Nursery centres Nursery schools/classes		Pre-school groups/ playgroups, Day nurseries, Nursery centres Nursery schools/ classes (independent schools)	(:)
UK (SC)	Nursery schools/classes		Pre-school centres	Pre-school centres	(:)
EFTA/EEA					
IS			*Leikskóli*	*Leikskóli*	100%
LI	*Kindergärten*	*Sonderschulkindergärten*	*Kinderhort*	*Tagesstätte, Waldorf-Kindergärten*	2%
NO			*Åpne barnehager, Vanlige barnehager, Familiebarnehager*	*Åpne barnehager, Vanlige barnehager, Familiebarnehager*	100% (*)
Pre-accession countries					
BG	*Poludnevna detska gradina*	*Detska gradina*			0%
CZ	*Mateřská škola*		*Mateřská škola*	*Mateřská škola*	(:)
EE	*Põhikool*		*Koolieelne lasteasutus*	*Koolieelne lasteasutus*	(:)
LV	*Bērnu dārzs*			*Privātais bērnu dārzs*	1.3%
LT	*Lopšelis/Lopšelis-darželis/Darželis-mokykla*	*Lopšelis-darželis/Darželis-mokykla*			0%
HU	*Óvoda, Bölcsöde*	*Óvoda, Bölcsöde*	*Óvoda, Bölcsöde*	*Óvoda, Bölcsöde*	(:)
PL	*Przedszkole*		*Przedszkole*	*Przedszkole*	(:)
RO	*Gradiniţa*			*Gradiniţa*	0.7%
SI			*Vrtci*	*Vrtci*	96%
SK	*Materská škola*			*Materská škola*	(:)
CY			*Nipiagogeia*	*Nipiagogeia*	± 100%

Source: Eurydice.

Additional notes

Ireland: Children enrolled in certain private schools are not included in the percentage calculation.
United Kingdom (E/W, NI): Fees are payable in private and voluntary settings for children who are too young to qualify for the current Government-funded scheme and for all children in settings not participating in the scheme.
Estonia and **Slovenia**: The enrolment fee that parents are required to pay varies according to the municipality and is based on the parents' income. For some children, all or part of the enrolment fee is paid by the municipality.

Explanatory note

'Fee-paying' means that parents are required to pay an enrolment fee for access to educational activities; it does not refer to fees they may pay for meals or certain optional, specific or additional activities (such as day care).

PRE-PRIMARY CURRICULA

In all the countries, pre-primary institutions use written guides, manuals, recommendations, etc. that do not have the status of official programmes. These materials have been prepared by the authorities that regulate the pre-primary institution, sometimes in collaboration with the teachers involved. In this case, they reflect the approaches and teaching concepts practised in these settings. Documents about education can also be produced by specialized publishers. These can sometimes be very influential over everyday practices in pre-primary education because they may be used by many people. These reference documents vary from one region to another, one municipality to another, even from one institution to another. Thus their heterogeneity precludes comparison. Therefore the following indicators (Figures C11 to C16) only cover the contents of guidelines published in one or more official documents prepared by a Ministry or a central body. In Germany, the Children and Youth Welfare Act (*Kinder- und Jugendhilfegesetz*) of the Federal Government is binding on all settings of the pre-primary sector, while legislation for a certain *Land* is binding on all settings in the pre-primary sector in that *Land*. In certain countries, these official documents relate only to pre-primary education or to at least two education levels. The official document relates to primary schools in Ireland where the first two years of primary education, between the ages of 4 and 6 years, are regarded as pre-primary. In the Netherlands, the official document deals with *basisonderwijs* (primary level), which covers the education of children from 4 to 12 years of age.

FIGURE C11: LEVELS OF EDUCATION COVERED BY THE OFFICIAL DOCUMENT SETTING OUT GUIDELINES FOR EDUCATION-ORIENTED PRE-PRIMARY PROVISION, 1997/98

THE OFFICIAL DOCUMENT COVERS	
ONLY THE EDUCATION-ORIENTED PRE-PRIMARY LEVEL	THE EDUCATION-ORIENTED PRE-PRIMARY LEVEL AND ONE OR MORE OTHER LEVEL(S) OF EDUCATION
B de, D, EL, E, I, L, A, P, FIN, S (*Förskola*), **UK**	**B fr, B nl, DK, F, IRL, S** (*Förskoleklass*)
IS, LI, NO　　　**BG, EE, LV, LT, HU, PL, SI, SK**	**LI**　　　**CZ, RO, CY**
Source: Eurydice.	

In the majority of the European countries, when pre-primary education takes place within a school, the guidelines generally cover the following four components: objectives, subjects/activities, teaching approach and assessment.

When they cover non-school education-oriented settings, the official documents outline at least the aims to be pursued, sometimes in a very general way (Germany and Austria). They also specify the arrangements for pupil assessment in Austria and Sweden. In Finland, the United Kingdom, Liechtenstein and Norway, the documents cover the four components.

In Estonia and Slovenia where pre-primary education is provided both in non-school education-oriented settings and schools, the official texts give guidelines on the same components for the two types of institution.

The degree of freedom given to the different institutions as regards the application of the recommendations issued in the official documents varies from country to country and according to the aspect in question. So with regard to objectives, all countries limit autonomy. In some of the countries, the institutions have no freedom as regards objectives. As regards the three other aspects (subjects/activities to be organized, recommended methods and assessment), the institutions enjoy greater freedom. In some countries autonomy is almost total: in general, this is the case in countries whose official documents do not deal with one or other of the key aspects.

FIGURE C12: CONTENTS OF THE OFFICIAL GUIDELINES, IN SCHOOLS AND OTHER EDUCATION-ORIENTED PRE-PRIMARY INSTITUTIONS, 1997/98

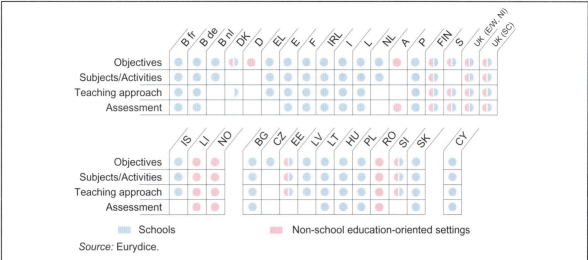

Source: Eurydice.

Additional notes

Denmark: The general aims are defined in the Social Services Act for the *Aldersintegrerede Institutioner* and the *Børnehaver* and in the Act on the *Folkeskole* for the *Børnehaveklasse*.

Germany: The general aims are defined in the Children and Youth Welfare Act *(Kinder- und Jugendhilfegesetz)* and in legislation of the individual *Länder*.

Finland: The curriculum covers pre-primary education for children aged 6 provided in *Päiväkoti/Daghem* and *Peruskoulu/ Grundskola*.

United Kingdom: Non school education-oriented settings dealt with by this diagram include day nurseries, nursery centres, pre-school groups and playgroups in receipt of nursery education grant.

United Kingdom (E/W, NI): Teaching methods are left to the discretion of the individual institution. However, common features of good practice are suggested in the guidelines.

Explanatory note

The category 'teaching approach' includes not only the approach to teaching, but also recommendations on the activities provided and the attitude to be adopted.

——————— ALL COUNTRIES DEFINE OBJECTIVES ———————

In all countries, official documents state **objectives, in very general and/or more precise terms**. The terms used for general objectives are fairly similar in all countries: development, autonomy, responsibility, well-being, self-confidence, citizenship, preparation for school life and future education, etc.

Among their aims the majority of countries also stress the importance of **cooperation with the family.** Here too, the same terms are often used: communication, information, understanding, cooperation, dialogue, support, mutual assistance, participation, involvement of the parents in the project, the educational process, continuity, coherence, etc.

In addition to these very general objectives, in almost all countries more precise details are given on the aims to be pursued in more specific areas. In this analysis, they are grouped under six headings: socio-affective development, adaptation to school life, physical development, the development of intellectual skills, the development of creativity and relations with the environment.

The skills the children should theoretically have mastered by the end of pre-primary education or before starting compulsory education are also defined by several countries of the EU (the French Community of Belgium, France, Ireland, Italy, the Netherlands, Austria, the United Kingdom (England, Wales and Northern Ireland)), in the three EFTA/EEA countries, and in several pre-accession countries (Bulgaria, Lithuania, Hungary, Romania, Slovakia and Cyprus). In the United Kingdom, these skills are assessed in the evaluation carried out at the start of primary school (baseline assessment) during the first seven weeks in England and Wales and during the first year of compulsory education in Northern Ireland.

PRE - PRIMARY EDUCATION

FIGURE C13: GENERAL AND SPECIFIC OBJECTIVES STIPULATED IN THE OFFICIAL GUIDELINES, EDUCATION-ORIENTED PRE-PRIMARY INSTITUTIONS, 1997/98

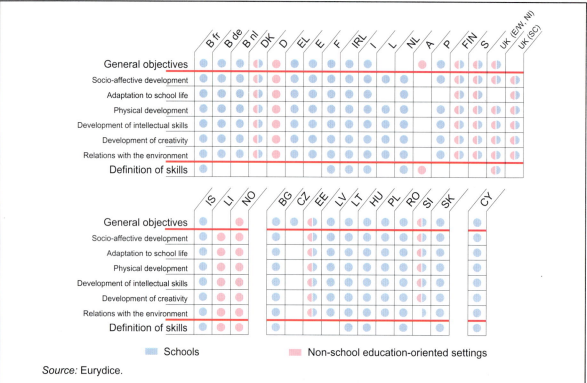

Schools   Non-school education-oriented settings

Source: Eurydice.

<u>Additional notes</u>

Denmark: The aims are included in the Act of Social Services for the *Aldersintegrerede Institutioner* and the *Børnehaver* and in the Act on the *Folkeskole* for the *Børnehaveklasse*.
Germany: The aims are included in the Children and Youth Welfare Act *(Kinder-und Jugendhilfegesetz)* and legislation of the individual *Länder*.
United-Kingdom: Non school education-oriented settings dealt with by this diagram include day nurseries, nursery centres, pre-school groups and playgroups in receipt of nursery education grant.
United-Kingdom (E/W, NI): Recommendations about adaptation to school life are implicit within the guidelines on personal and social development.

——— MOST COUNTRIES SPECIFY FIVE BROAD SPHERES OF ACTIVITY ———

Where the official guidelines specify the subjects and the educational content to be taught, they generally define at least five general areas in which pre-primary education must foster the acquisition of knowledge: written and oral language, mathematics, introduction to art, introduction to science and physical education. These broad categories are the ones most often presented in detail with examples of activities. The official documents of the Flemish Community of Belgium, Spain and Finland cover these five areas, but do not illustrate them with examples of activities. In Hungary, mathematics is not specified in the official document.

Elements of folklore are also mentioned in the guidelines of Finland and Latvia. Other subjects are information and communication technology in Finland, foreign language teaching in Bulgaria and elements of health education in Cyprus.

In only a few countries do the official guidelines not provide any information on the subjects to be taught: Denmark, Germany, Austria, Sweden for the countries of the EU, and the Czech Republic for pre-accession countries.

58

FIGURE C14: THE FIVE AREAS OF ACTIVITY SELECTED ARE SPECIFIED IN THE OFFICIAL GUIDELINES,
SCHOOLS AND OTHER EDUCATION-ORIENTED PRE-PRIMARY INSTITUTIONS, 1997/98

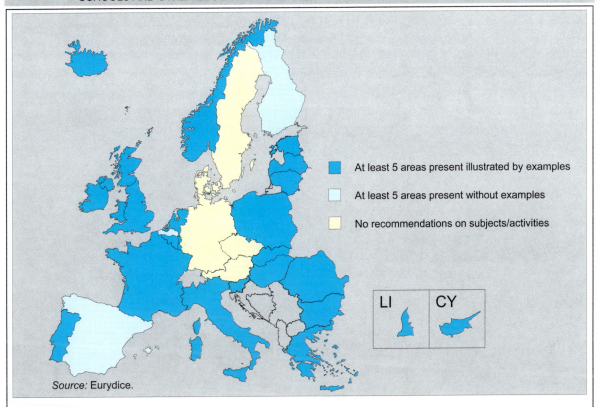

■ At least 5 areas present illustrated by examples

■ At least 5 areas present without examples

□ No recommendations on subjects/activities

Source: Eurydice.

Additional notes

Denmark: There are no official guidelines. Only the aims are included in the Act of Social Services for the *Aldersintegrerede Institutioner* and the *Børnehaver* and in the Act on the *Folkeskole* for the *Børnehaveklasse*.
Germany: There are no official guidelines. Only the aims are included in the Children and Youth Welfare *Act (Kinder- und Jugendhilfegesetz)* and legislation of the individual *Länder*.
Hungary: The official guidelines do not specify mathematics.

Explanatory note

Figure C14 specifically covers the presence of five areas of activity/subjects in the official guidelines and/or the legislation. These areas are written and oral language, mathematics, introduction to art, introduction to science and physical education. The absence of recommendations in the official guidelines does not mean that pre-primary educational settings do not teach these subjects or do not provide any activities.

THE MOST COMMON EVALUATION METHOD:
CONTINUOUS ASSESSMENT

The official guidelines or legislation of almost all countries specifically mention evaluation and underline the importance of continually monitoring the child's progress, particularly mentioning observation. Exceptions are the Flemish Community of Belgium, Denmark, Germany, the Netherlands, Iceland, the Czech Republic, Latvia, Hungary and Slovenia.

FIGURE C15: RECOMMENDATIONS FOR PUPIL EVALUATION IN THE OFFICIAL GUIDELINES, SCHOLS AND OTHER EDUCATION-ORIENTED PRE-PRIMARY INSTITUTIONS, 1997/98

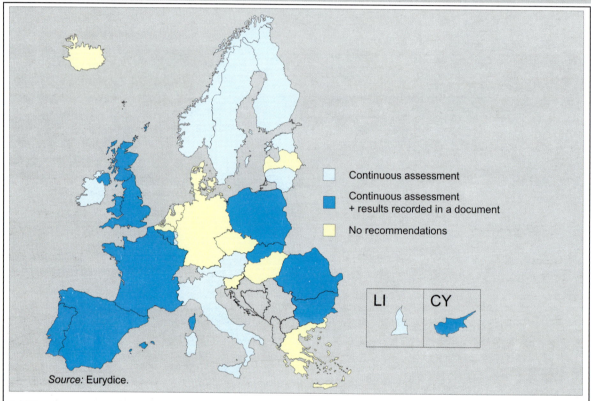

Source: Eurydice.

Additional notes

Denmark: There are no official guidelines. Only the aims are included in the Act of Social Services for the Aldersintegrerede Institutioner and the *Børnehaver* and in the Act on the *Folkeskole* for the *Børnehaveklasse*.
Germany: There are no official guidelines. Only the aims are included in the Children and Youth Welfare Act *(Kinder- und Jugendhilfegesetz)* and legislation of the individual *Länder*. The importance of continuous assessment by observation is laid down in the individual pedagogical concept of each institution.
Netherlands: There are no official recommendations, but primary schools have the obligation to describe their procedure of assessment in their school plan.
Iceland: A new curriculum guide for pre-schools (published in 1999) recommends that schools continually assess the children's progress and that the results be recorded in a document.
Bulgaria and **Romania**: An assessment at the end of pre-primary education is mentioned in the guidelines.
Hungary: The official guidelines do not specify assessment procedures because the education act determines them.

Explanatory note

Figure C15 only reflects written recommendations for the assessment of pupils in official guidelines and/or legislation. The absence of recommendations in the official guidelines does not mean that pre-primary settings are not assessing pupils' progress.

In some countries the official guidelines are more precise and stipulate that the results of this assessment process must be recorded (either in an individual document or one kept by the teacher). These countries are the French Community of Belgium, Spain, France, Portugal, the United Kingdom, Bulgaria, Poland, Romania, Slovakia and Cyprus. In Cyprus, teachers are to assess the children when they start a new activity.

In Ireland, suggestions are made as to the use of diagnostic and standardized tests.

THE MOST FREQUENTLY RECOMMENDED APPROACH: ADAPT TO THE NEEDS OF THE CHILD

In most countries, recommendations on the approach to teaching are mapped out in both the official guidelines and at school level. However the official guidelines of some EU and EFTA/EEA countries do not make recommendations on the methods or approach to be adopted: the Flemish Community of Belgium, Germany, the Netherlands and Austria.

Where the documents go into recommendations on the teaching approach to be adopted, some appear more often than others. The need to adapt practices to the needs of the child (taking account each child's rhythm and individual differences) and the importance of educational teamwork (to ensure continuity within pre-primary education and with primary education) are always mentioned.

Most official documents, with the exception of those in France, Sweden and the United Kingdom (England, Wales and Northern Ireland), also give recommendations on the way to go about different activities such as play-related learning, activities in small groups, etc. The United Kingdom documents give examples of good practice, but not methods in the strict sense ('recognition of the value of providing first hand experience, of giving clear explanations, of appropriate adult interventions', etc. and 'principle of appropriateness').

The documents also specify the importance to be given to different fields or activities, except in France, Finland and the United Kingdom. In the French Community of Belgium and the United Kingdom (Scotland), the documents advise against partitioning the various fields, suggesting an interdisciplinary approach be adopted.

A timetable is suggested in three countries of the EU and the EFTA/EEA: the French Community of Belgium, Greece and Liechtenstein. In the German-speaking Community of Belgium, it is suggested that a balance should be struck between the different activities.

No official document specifies the textbooks to be used in pre-primary education. In Liechtenstein, recommendations are issued on the documents to be used by the teachers, primarily in the field of music.

All guidelines from pre-accession countries contain recommendations regarding methods, with the exception of the Czech Republic. In five of the countries, all the aspects mentioned in this analysis are recommended for all types of pre-primary institution. Other countries only cover some of the recommendations. In Hungary the only recommendation made for methods deals with the importance to be attached to different areas or activities.

FIGURE C16: TEACHING APPROACHES RECOMMENDED BY THE OFFICIAL GUIDELINES, EDUCATION-ORIENTED PRE-PRIMARY INSTITUTIONS, 1997/98

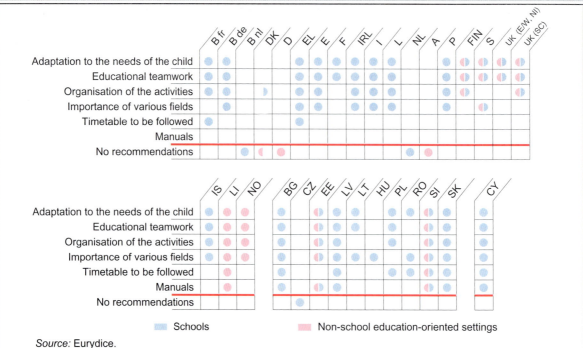

Schools   Non-school education-oriented settings

Source: Eurydice.

Additional notes

Denmark: There are no official guidelines. Only the aims are included in the Act of Social Services for the *Aldersintegrerede Institutioner* and the *Børnehaver* and in the Act on the *Folkeskole* for the *Børnehaveklasse*.

Germany: There are no official guidelines. Only the aims are included in the Children and Youth Welfare Act (*Kinder- und Jugendhilfegesetz*) and legislation of the individual *Länder*. Methods are laid down in the individual pedagogical concept of each institution.

United Kingdom: Non school education-oriented settings dealt with by this diagram include day nurseries, nursery centres, pre-school groups, playgroups in receipt of nursery education grant.

Explanatory note

Figure C16 only covers approaches to teaching written in official guidelines and/or legislation. The absence of recommendations in the official guidelines does not mean that pre-primary settings are not adopting the approaches mentioned.

By organisation of activities is meant working in small groups, learning through play, etc.

AGE IS THE PRINCIPLE CRITERION FOR ACCESS TO COMPULSORY PRIMARY EDUCATION

Two criteria can be applied to decide on the admission of children to compulsory primary education: age and maturity. **Age** is the more widespread of these criteria, since it is applied in all countries, but the age limits that determine admission vary from one country to another. These are maximum age limits. In practice, in most countries, it is possible to start primary school before reaching compulsory school age. In some countries, the child's maturity is an additional criterion taken into account for admission to compulsory primary school.

FIGURE C17: AGE LIMITS FOR THE ADMISSION OF CHILDREN TO COMPULSORY PRIMARY EDUCATION, 1997/98		
ADMISSION TO COMPULSORY PRIMARY EDUCATION		
COINCIDES WITH THE START OF THE SCHOOL YEAR		DURING THE SCHOOL YEAR
THE CHILD MUST HAVE REACHED THE AGE OF THE START OF COMPULSORY EDUCATION		
DURING THE CALENDAR YEAR	BY A SPECIFIC DATE	
B fr, B de, B nl, DK, EL, E, F, I, FIN, S; **IS, NO**; **BG, LV, LT, PL, RO**	**D** (according to the *Land*, between 30/6 and 30/9), **L** (15/9), **A** (31/8), **P** (31/8), **UK (NI)** (1/7), **UK (SC)** (between 1/3 and 1/8); **LI** (between 1/5 and 31/8); **CZ** (1/9), **EE** (1/10), **HU** (31/5), **SI** and **SK** (start of the school year); **CY** (1/9)	**IRL, NL, UK (E/W)**

Source: Eurydice.

Additional note

Germany: The *Länder* can in certain circumstances allow children to start compulsory education during the school year (rather than at the beginning). This degree of flexibility allows the school to take account of the child's maturity.

In almost all countries, compulsory education starts at the same time as the school year. In more than half of these countries, the age for starting school must be reached during the calendar year in which the child starts school. In some countries, the required age must have been reached before a date which, generally, precedes or corresponds to, the start of the school year. In the United Kingdom (Scotland), children born between September and February have the option of starting school either in the August preceding their 5th birthday or of deferring to the next August.

In three EU countries, children may start school during the school year (rather than at the beginning). In Ireland, children do not have to attend school until the start of the term following their 6th birthday. In the Netherlands, compulsory education starts on the first day of the month which follows the child's 5th birthday. In the United Kingdom (England and Wales), children reach compulsory school age on one of three designated dates following their 5th birthday: 31 August, 31 December and 31 March. However, they are not normally required to begin school before the start of the next school term.

The child's **maturity** is an additional criterion taken into account for admission to compulsory primary school in the German-speaking Community of Belgium, Denmark, Germany, Austria, Finland, Liechtenstein, for the countries of the EU and the EFTA/EEA, and in almost all pre-accession countries, with the exception of Estonia and Poland. In Denmark, Finland, Slovenia and Slovakia, the child's maturity is taken into account only when the child wants to start school before the statutory school age. Various procedures are used in different countries to assess the child's maturity: a medical examination, a psychological examination, an aptitude test, the opinion of the educational team and/or the future teacher, the opinion of the headteacher, the opinion of the parents, etc.

PRIMARY EDUCATION

A SEPARATE LEVEL OF EDUCATION OR PART OF ———— A SINGLE CONTINUOUS STRUCTURE ————

In eleven Member States, primary education is a separate level of education. In most of these countries, it lasts six years. The shortest duration (four years) is found in the majority of the *Länder* in Germany and in Austria. In four European Union countries (Denmark, Portugal, Finland and Sweden), compulsory education is organized in a single, continuous structure with no distinction being made between the primary and lower secondary stages. The information presented in this chapter refers to the first six years of the single structure in these countries.

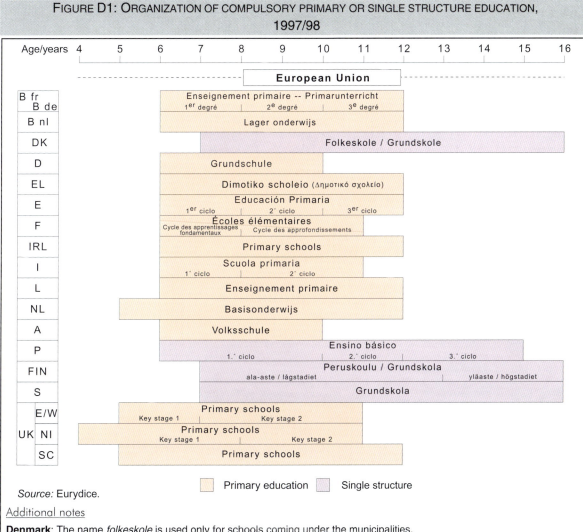

FIGURE D1: ORGANIZATION OF COMPULSORY PRIMARY OR SINGLE STRUCTURE EDUCATION, 1997/98

Source: Eurydice.

Legend: Primary education / Single structure

Additional notes

Denmark: The name *folkeskole* is used only for schools coming under the municipalities.
Germany: The *Grundschule* lasts 4 years in 14 *Länder*. It lasts 6 years in Berlin and Brandenburg.
Ireland: Primary education is offered from the age of 4 and most pupils start it at that age. Compulsory education starts at age 6.
Netherlands: *Basisonderwijs* lasts 8 years. Compulsory education starts at age 5. Most children start *basisonderwijs* at age 4. Children who start at age 5 spend 7 years in *basisonderwijs*.
Finland: The division of the *Peruskoulu/Grundskola* into two stages was abolished in 1999.
United Kingdom (E): In some regions of England, the education system is divided into three levels: first schools, middle schools and high schools. Pupils move from first school to middle school at age 8 or 9 and from middle school to secondary school at age 12 or 13.

Explanatory note

The diagram D1 shows the age of pupils from the start of compulsory primary education to the end of primary education or the single structure. In most countries, children can, under certain circumstances and if their parents so desire, start school before they reach compulsory school age.

Primary education is divided into three stages in French and German-speaking Communities of Belgium and Spain and into two in France, Italy and the United Kingdom (except Scotland). The single structures in Portugal and Finland are divided into three and two stages respectively.

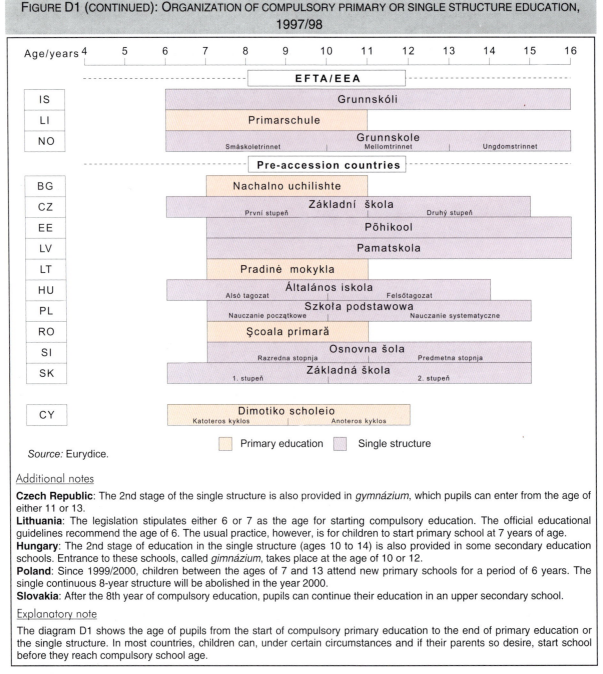

FIGURE D1 (CONTINUED): ORGANIZATION OF COMPULSORY PRIMARY OR SINGLE STRUCTURE EDUCATION, 1997/98

Source: Eurydice.

Primary education | Single structure

Additional notes

Czech Republic: The 2nd stage of the single structure is also provided in *gymnázium*, which pupils can enter from the age of either 11 or 13.

Lithuania: The legislation stipulates either 6 or 7 as the age for starting compulsory education. The official educational guidelines recommend the age of 6. The usual practice, however, is for children to start primary school at 7 years of age.

Hungary: The 2nd stage of education in the single structure (ages 10 to 14) is also provided in some secondary education schools. Entrance to these schools, called *gimnázium*, takes place at the age of 10 or 12.

Poland: Since 1999/2000, children between the ages of 7 and 13 attend new primary schools for a period of 6 years. The single continuous 8-year structure will be abolished in the year 2000.

Slovakia: After the 8th year of compulsory education, pupils can continue their education in an upper secondary school.

Explanatory note

The diagram D1 shows the age of pupils from the start of compulsory primary education to the end of primary education or the single structure. In most countries, children can, under certain circumstances and if their parents so desire, start school before they reach compulsory school age.

Among the EFTA/EEA countries, in Liechtenstein primary education consists of a separate level lasting five years. In Norway and Iceland, compulsory education is organized, as in the other Nordic countries, in a single structure, lasting ten years. Iceland has one continuous stage running from age 6 to age 16. In Norway, the system is divided into three stages, the first two corresponding to the first seven years.

Among the pre-accession countries, Bulgaria, Lithuania, Romania and Cyprus organize primary education separately from secondary education. Primary school lasts four years in the first three of these countries. In Cyprus, it lasts six years and is divided into two stages (*kyklos*). In the other pre-accession countries, compulsory education consists of a single structure which is divided into two stages, except in Estonia and Latvia.

CLASS SIZE NORMS:
A MAXIMUM OF 25 TO 35 PUPILS

Most EU and EFTA/EEA countries have regulations stipulating the maximum and/or minimum number of pupils in a class or group. The norms for maximum class sizes vary considerably from one country to another.

Where norms are defined, the maximum never exceeds 35. However, in Greece, Spain, Ireland, Iceland and Norway, lower norms can be set for particular situations such as the start of primary education and the inclusion of several age groups or for schools serving areas that are socially or economically disadvantaged. In some countries, a minimum number of pupils is also required to establish a class. This figure is lowest in Austria (10) while in Portugal the minimum is 20. In Greece, the minimum number of pupils can be less than 15 according to the type of school (one- or two-teacher schools).

In the countries with no regulations on class size, individual local authorities or schools have the power to decide how classes are made up. They generally do this taking into account educational guidelines and classroom sizes. In France, however, the *Inspecteur d'Académie* (a central government official) can set both the average number of pupils per class for his area and also the maximum number according to the specific criteria of that *département*. In the Netherlands, measures were taken during 1997/98 to improve the quality of teaching. Through the deployment of additional staff, these measures were designed to reduce class sizes in the first four years of *basisonderwijs*.

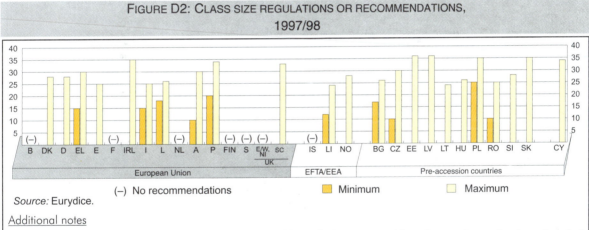

FIGURE D2: CLASS SIZE REGULATIONS OR RECOMMENDATIONS, 1997/98

Source: Eurydice.

(–) No recommendations   ▢ Minimum   ▢ Maximum

Additional notes

Germany: The minimum and maximum cannot be indicated but only the average of the reference figures for class size of all *Länder*.
Ireland: Since 1999/2000, maximum class size in primary schools is 30 pupils.
Portugal: The minimum and maximum numbers are 26 and 34 for 40 m² classrooms, and 20 and 26 for classrooms between 35 and 40 m².
United Kingdom (E/W, NI): The local education authorities are preparing and implementing plans to satisfy a forthcoming requirement to limit class sizes for 5-7 year olds to a maximum of 30.
United Kingdom (SC): Since 1999/2000, primary school teachers may have the help of a classroom assistant.
Iceland: In accordance with the law of 1995 on compulsory education, there are no longer any recommendations on class size. The municipalities decide on the organization of classes.
Czech Republic: In exceptional cases, there can be more than 30 pupils in a class.
Hungary: Regulations prescribe an average number of pupils per class (21) as well as a maximum.
Poland: Since 1999/2000, with respect to the reformed primary schools, there are no longer any recommendations on class size.

In all the pre-accession countries, the maximum number of pupils per class is laid down in regulations and varies from 36 in Estonia and Latvia to 24 in Lithuania. The maximum number can be lower in classes with disadvantaged pupils (Slovenia) or in composite classes with pupils of different ages (Slovenia, Cyprus) or at the start of primary education (Slovakia and Cyprus). In some countries, minimum class sizes are also laid down. In the Czech Republic and Romania, the statutory minimum is 10 pupils while in Poland it is 25.

ONE TEACHER PER CLASS, BUT
———— OFTEN REPLACED FOR SOME SPECIALIZED SUBJECTS ————

In most EU and EFTA/EEA countries, at the start of primary education or in the first years of the single structure, one teacher is usually responsible for the class. These teachers teach most of the subjects and are sometimes replaced by other teachers for certain specialized activities, such as physical education and sport, music and religious education. In Denmark, however, each subject is taught by a different teacher but there is team-teaching at some levels and there is interdisciplinary teaching for some subjects. In Italy, two or three teachers routinely share the teaching of all subjects. They take the class in turns and also have a spell of some hours in the day where they work together. In Germany, Ireland, Finland and the United Kingdom (England, Wales and Northern Ireland), one teacher is usually responsible for the class for the whole week and usually has sole responsibility for all subjects. Finally, in France, the Netherlands, Portugal, Sweden and Norway, several patterns of dividing up the teaching among the teachers are found at the same time.

In the pre-accession countries, at the start of primary education or in the first years of the single structure, pupils usually have a number of teachers, one of whom is responsible for the class while the others teach subjects such as sport and music, but in Estonia, Lithuania, Poland and Slovenia one teacher has sole responsibility for all subjects.

Given the extent of variation in the way teaching is divided among the teachers, the situations described above and in Figure D3 refer exclusively to children of about 7 years of age. These variations are related in particular to the pupils' progress through the school. Thus in the German-speaking Community of Belgium and Sweden, differences in organization are found between the start and the end of primary education. In Germany and Finland, pupils are gradually introduced to subject teachers from the third year so as to prepare them for the transition to the secondary school or the last years of the single structure where they will have only subject teachers. In Portugal, in the 2nd stage of *ensino básico*, different teachers are each responsible for a group of subjects. In the United Kingdom (England, Wales and Northern Ireland), primary school teachers may have the help of a classroom assistant.

FIGURE D3: MAIN MODELS FOR DIVIDING TEACHING AND SUBJECTS AMONG THE TEACHERS (AROUND AGE 7), 1997/98

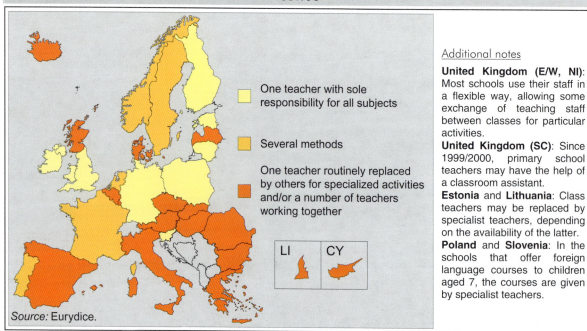

Source: Eurydice.

FROM 377 TO 950 HOURS A YEAR OF
TEACHING FOR 7-YEAR-OLDS

In most countries, pupils attend school five days a week (six days in Luxembourg and in some regions of Italy). In Germany, Austria and Portugal (in the 2nd stage of *ensino básico*), teaching can be spread over five or six days a week. The number of hours spent in class in any day also varies according to the country, the day of the week and the age of the pupils. Given the wide variations in the organization of time in schools, an indicator showing the total annual hours of teaching has been calculated to permit comparison. Variations – sometimes considerable – may be observed in the annual number of taught hours across the different countries.

Figure D4 shows the annual course load of pupils around the age of 7. At this age, pupils are at very different points in their education depending on the education system that they are in. While Danish, Finnish and Swedish children are in their 1st year of compulsory education, others (in the Netherlands and the United Kingdom (England, Wales and Scotland)) are starting their 3rd year, or even their 4th year for those in Luxembourg and the United Kingdom (Northern Ireland).

There are less marked differences in the school experience of children in the EFTA/EEA countries and in the pre-accession countries, where at age 7 they are all in the 1st or 2nd year of compulsory education.

In half the EU and EFTA/EEA countries, children aged 7 are taught for over 800 hours a year. In some countries (Greece, Finland, Northern Ireland and Norway) the number of teaching hours is under 600. Overall in the pre-accession countries, the number of teaching hours for children aged 7 is lower than in the countries of the EU. The maximum number is 719 hours, and usually the figure is around 500 hours.

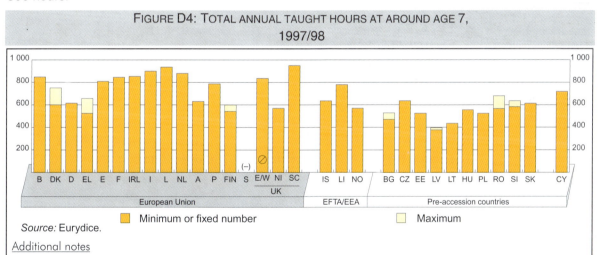

FIGURE D4: TOTAL ANNUAL TAUGHT HOURS AT AROUND AGE 7, 1997/98

Source: Eurydice.

Legend: ■ Minimum or fixed number   □ Maximum

Additional notes

Italy: The calculation takes into account a deduction of 30 minutes a day for breaks, although the duration of such breaks is not officially set, but left to the teacher's discretion. The official annual load comes to 1 000 hours, including breaks.

Finland: The calculation is based on periods of 45 minutes each. The law also authorizes 50-minute periods.

Sweden: The new timetable introduced in 1995/96 represents 6 665 hours of teaching. The local authorities/schools are free to divide up these hours over the 9 years of the *grundskola*, whilst ensuring that the children attain certain targets at the end of the 5th and 9th years.

United Kingdom (E/W): The annual number of taught hours is an average based on information collected in 1996. The figures exclude time spent on registration and the daily act of worship.

United Kingdom (NI): The figures are based on the minimum number of recommended hours, but the actual taught hours may be greater.

Bulgaria: If the three additional non-compulsory hours per week (often spent on foreign languages, sport or art subjects) are taken into account, the annual load varies from a minimum of 533 hours to a maximum of 600 hours.

Explanatory note

The taught time presented in this graph does not represent the teacher's work-load but that of the pupil. Annual taught time is calculated by taking the average daily load multiplied by the number of school days in the year. Breaks of all types (recreation or other) and time spent on optional extra courses are excluded from the calculation. The tables showing the method of calculation appear in the appendix.

MORE HOURS OF TEACHING
AT AROUND AGE 10

Figure D5 shows the annual course load of pupils around the age of 10. At that age, depending on the education system, children are fairly close to the end of primary school. In Germany, France, Italy, Austria and the United Kingdom (England, Wales and Northern Ireland) children are in their final or penultimate year of primary school.

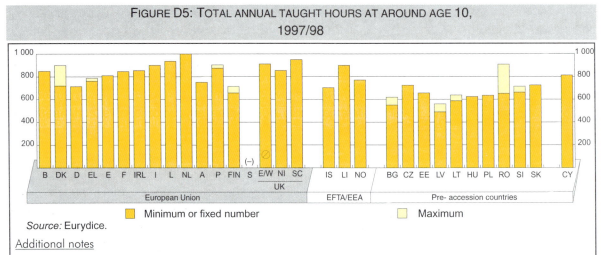

FIGURE D5: TOTAL ANNUAL TAUGHT HOURS AT AROUND AGE 10, 1997/98

■ Minimum or fixed number   □ Maximum

Source: Eurydice.

Additional notes

Germany and **Austria**: The data refer to the age of 9 (4th and final year of primary school).
Italy: The calculation takes into account a deduction of 30 minutes a day for breaks, although the duration of such breaks is not officially set, but left to the teacher's discretion. The official annual load amounts to 1 000 hours, including breaks.
Finland: The calculation is based on periods of 45 minutes each. The law also authorizes 50-minute periods.
Sweden: The new timetable introduced in 1995/96 represents 6 665 hours of teaching. The local authorities/schools are free to divide up these hours over the 9 years of the *grundskola*, whilst ensuring that the children attain certain targets at the end of the 5th and 9th years.
United Kingdom (E/W): The annual number of taught hours is an average. The figures exclude time spent on registration and the daily act of worship.
United Kingdom (NI): The figures are based on the minimum number of recommended hours, but the actual taught hours may be greater.
Bulgaria: If the four additional non-compulsory hours (often spent on foreign languages, sport or art subjects) are taken into account, the annual load varies from a minimum of 638 hours to a maximum of 718 hours.

Comparison of the annual load of pupils aged 7 and 10 shows that more than half of the countries of the EU and of the EFTA/EEA have adopted a slightly reduced timetable for younger children at the start of their primary education. This reduction can range from 50 to over 100 hours and is particularly marked in Northern Ireland and Liechtenstein.

In all the pre-accession countries, the same pattern appears, with the annual taught time of pupils being less at the start of primary education than at around 10 years of age.

FIGURE D6: MINIMUM ANNUAL HOURS OF TAUGHT TIME AT AROUND AGE 7 AND AGE 10, 1997/98

	European Union											
	B	**DK**	**D**	**EL**	**E**	**F**	**IRL**	**I**	**L**	**NL**	**A**	**P**
About age 7	849	600	615	525	810	846	854	900	936	880	630	788
About age 10	849	720	713	761	810	846	854	900	936	1 000	750	875

	European Union (continued)							EFTA/EEA		
	FIN	**S**	**UK (E/W)**	**UK (NI)**	**UK (SC)**			**IS**	**LI**	**NO**
About age 7	542	(–)	836	570	950			635	780	570
About age 10	656	(–)	912	855	950			703	900	770

	Pre-accession countries											
	BG	**CZ**	**EE**	**LV**	**LT**	**HU**	**PL**	**RO**	**SI**	**SK**		**CY**
About age 7	470	637	525	377	436	555	524	567	583	614		719
About age 10	550	724	656	490	587	624	635	652	662	725		812

Source: Eurydice.

COMPULSORY SUBJECTS:
———— A COMMON BASIS BUT DIFFERENCES IN EMPHASIS ————

In some Member States, the curricula and official directives specify the subjects that must be taught, while giving teachers or schools freedom to determine how much time to allocate to different subjects or when to introduce a specific subject. This is the case in the Flemish Community of Belgium, the Netherlands, Portugal (1st stage of *ensino básico*), Sweden and the United Kingdom. For these countries compulsory subjects are indicated by a bullet in figures D7 and D8. The curricula in the other countries of the European Union and in all the EFTA/EEA and pre-accession countries prescribe the timetabling of the various subjects, so it is possible to compare the relative amount of time devoted to each of these subjects. In Denmark, the municipalities are free to choose whether or not to follow the ministry guidelines concerning the weekly distribution of lessons on the individual subjects.

Whether or not the curricula specify any time allocation between subjects, the compulsory subjects are generally the same in all countries. The only differences observed relate to foreign language teaching, the inclusion of courses in information and communication technology or the requirement to provide religious or ethical instruction.

In primary education in the countries of the EU, at about 7 years of age, major disparities are observed in the time allocated to the teaching of the mother tongue. Thus, whereas nearly half of the teaching hours are devoted to this in Denmark, only 4% of time is spent on it in Luxembourg. This very small percentage is explained by the fact that teaching is mainly in French and German (national languages) while Letzeburgesch, the mother tongue, is essentially a vernacular language.

The teaching time allocated to certain subjects (science, sport, art subjects and even mother tongue and mathematics in Italy) is relatively low in certain countries, where, due to the fact that part of the timetable is flexible, schools are given freedom to increase the time devoted to these subjects depending on the specific needs of the pupils.

In the pre-accession countries, for children of around 7 years of age, the mother tongue has a major place in the curriculum, along with mathematics and art. These three subjects account for at least 64% of the timetable and as much as 80% in the Czech Republic, Poland, Romania and Slovakia.

At around age 10, the relative amount of mother tongue teaching drops in almost all countries of the EU and of the EFTA/EEA. Only in France and Ireland does it still occupy more than one third of the timetable. In Ireland, this large percentage is due to both Irish and English being learned.

At this age, compulsory foreign language learning tends to be a general phenomenon in most countries. Whereas at the start of primary school, art education often took up more of the timetable than scientific subjects, at the age of 10 this trend is reversed.

In the pre-accession countries, the trend of the allocation of teaching time is similar to the pattern observed in the countries of the EU.

FIGURE D7: RECOMMENDED ALLOCATION OF ANNUAL HOURS OF TEACHING OF COMPULSORY SUBJECTS AT AROUND AGE 7, 1997/98

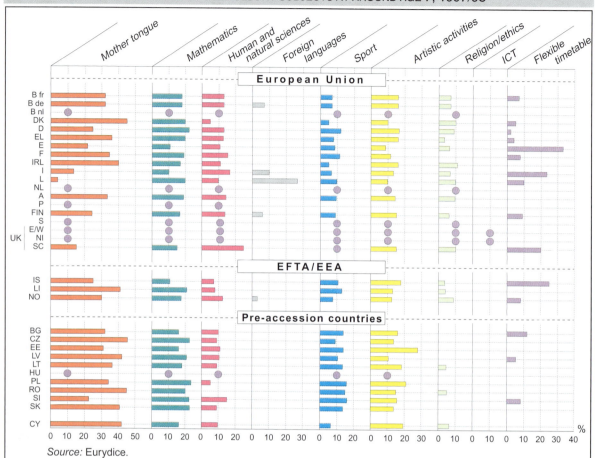

Source: Eurydice.

Additional notes – Figures D7 and D8

Denmark: These graphs follow the Ministry's guidelines for the distribution of subjects.

Germany: The calculation of the annual hours of teaching in each subject is based on the half-day school (*Halbtagsschule*) with a five-day school week for 7-year-olds in the 2nd year of primary school and for 9-year-olds in the 4th year of primary school. In some *Länder*, 9-year-olds can learn a foreign language as a separate subject. In the other *Länder*, foreign language teaching is integrated into other subjects. Other subjects are included under the heading 'flexible timetable'.

Spain: In the autonomous communities with two official languages (the community's language and Spanish), the flexible portion of the timetable is 45%, which provides a means of increasing the number of hours allocated to the second official language.

France: The 130 hours of 'discovery of the world and civic education' (Figure D7) and of 'history, geography, civic education, science and technology' (Figure D8) are included under the heading 'human and natural sciences'. The 195 hours (Figure D7) and the 178 hours (Figure D8) of art, physical education and sport have been distributed between these two subjects. The 65 hours of supervized homework are included under the heading 'flexible timetable'. 32 hours (at age 7) or 47 hours (at age 10) of modern language teaching can be taken from the mother tongue timetable.

Ireland: 'Mother tongue' refers to English (18%) and Irish (22%). Since 1999/2000, the distribution of time between Irish and English reflects the status of these languages as first or second languages in the schools.

Austria: Foreign languages and ICT are taught according to an integrated approach along with other subjects where this is advised. ICT will soon be incorporated in the primary school curriculum.

Portugal: In Figure D8, technology is included in the art activities. The number of hours of sport depends on the availability of human resources and school infrastructure. Religious and moral education is optional; the pupils can instead choose 'Personal and social development'.

Finland: Within the limits of the national core curriculum, schools can decide when a subject should be introduced and how to distribute the subjects over the 6 years of the 1st stage of *peruskoulu*. The figures show a theoretical average based on the minima given for the whole 1st stage and assuming that the subjects are spread equally throughout the 6 years.

Sweden: Schools are free to decide when to introduce a subject and how to distribute the teaching hours over the 9 years of the *grundskola*, provided the pupils reach certain targets at the end of the 5th and 9th years.

United Kingdom (E): In September 1998, a daily literacy hour was introduced. This will be followed from September 1999 by a daily numeracy session of between 45 and 60 minutes. Each will account for approximately 20% of total taught time (based on figures collected in 1996 of 836 hours for 7 year olds and of 912 hours for 10 year olds).

FIGURE D8: RECOMMENDED ALLOCATION OF ANNUAL HOURS
OF TEACHING OF COMPULSORY SUBJECTS AT AROUND AGE 10, 1997/98

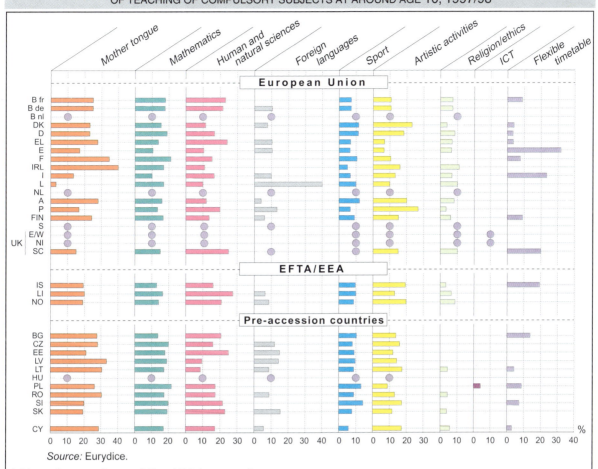

Source: Eurydice.

Additional notes – Figures D7 and D8 (continued)

United Kingdom (SC): The curriculum in Scottish primary schools is determined by the Scottish Executive. Five broad curriculum areas are specified with time allocations, which are not compulsory but are contained in national guidelines to schools. The percentage allocated to artistic activities should also include physical exercise. In Figure D8, ICT is included in environmental studies.

Norway: In Figure D7, 'free activities' have been included under the heading 'flexible timetable'.

Czech Republic: The number of hours devoted to natural science, history, art, music and practical activities is decided by the head of the school in cooperation with the teachers (Figure D8).

Estonia: The hours of teaching are allocated by subject for pupils who speak Estonian. Those whose mother tongue is not Estonian follow a timetable that has more hours of Estonian as a foreign language.

Latvia: In Figure D7, one of the 19 weekly periods shown as flexible is allocated as chosen by the class.

Lithuania: In Figure D8, depending on the choice of the school or on the specific needs of a class, one of the 23 weekly periods, indicated in the flexible timetable, is allocated either to mother tongue, a foreign language, mathematics or physical education.

Hungary: Within certain limits, schools are free to decide how to allocate time to the different subjects. For example, at age 7, the time devoted to the mother tongue must account for between 32% and 40% of the total teaching time.

Poland: ICT is taught in schools, equipment permitting (Figure D8).

Slovenia: Compulsory options and other disciplines have been included under the heading 'flexible timetable'.

Cyprus: Home economics, design and technology have been included under the heading 'artistic activities'.

Explanatory note

Figures D7 and D8 show the relationship between the annual time to be allocated to the various compulsory subjects and the total minimum number of hours of teaching in the year. The figures expressed as hours of teaching and as a proportion of taught time are set out in the annex. Bullets indicate compulsory subjects in those countries where the curricula specifies which subjects must be taught, but where schools or teachers are free to decide how much time to allocate to each subject.

In the interest of clarity, some subjects have been grouped together. This is the case, for example, with human and natural sciences which include subjects such as 'school life and culture', environmental studies, history, geography, social and political instruction, and craft activities.

The category 'flexible timetable' indicates either that the time to be allocated to the various compulsory subjects has not been fixed, or that as a supplement to the time allocated to the various compulsory subjects, the curriculum provides for a certain number of teaching hours that the pupils or the school can devote to subjects of their choice.

PROGRESSION TO THE NEXT YEAR: EITHER AUTOMATIC OR SUBJECT TO REPEATING THE YEAR

The management of pupils' learning difficulties varies from one country to another. In several countries of the EU and of the EFTA/EEA, pupils who have not acquired an adequate mastery of the curriculum at the end of the year or do not have the required maturity are made to repeat the year. This decision is taken by the teacher or by the teaching team. However, in certain countries where pupils can repeat a year, the percentage of those who actually repeat is very low: 0.6% in Italy and 0.5% in Finland.

FIGURE D9: PROGRESSION TO THE NEXT YEAR DURING PRIMARY EDUCATION, 1997/98

☐ Automatic progression

☐ Repeat for exceptional reasons

☐ Possible to repeat a year at the end of a stage

☐ Possible to repeat each year

LI   CY

Source: Eurydice.

Additional notes

Belgium (B fr, B de): Repeating a year is possible, but this is only allowed once or twice throughout the 6 years of primary school.
Denmark: Repeating a year is possible, if special reasons indicate that the child will benefit from such measures.
Germany and **Austria**: Pupils move automatically from the 1st to the 2nd year of the primary school. Subsequently, pupils can be made to repeat a year based on their results.
Spain: Pupils can only repeat a year at the end of a stage once during primary education.
Portugal: Repeating is exceptional in the 1st stage. At the end of the 2nd stage, pupils can be made to repeat the year if they are considerably behind in three subjects including Portuguese and mathematics.
Bulgaria: It is possible to repeat a year, except in the 1st year of primary school where summer courses are organized for those in difficulty.
Estonia: The decision to make a pupil repeat the 1st or 2nd year is taken only for exceptional reasons (e.g. for medical reasons).
Hungary: Pupils automatically move up from the 1st to 2nd year. After that, pupils may have to repeat a year if they do not achieve the required attainment level.

Repeating is only required for exceptional reasons in Greece, Ireland, Portugal and Liechtenstein. These exceptional reasons vary from country to country and consist of either a very long period of absence during the school year or a recommendation by a person (or a team) outside the school (a psychologist, a doctor, a social worker, etc.). The decision is usually taken with the agreement of the head of the school and the pupil's parents.

The decision to keep a child in one stage of education can be taken only at the end of each stage in Spain and France.

Denmark, Sweden, the United Kingdom, Iceland and Norway have opted for automatic progression from year to year throughout compulsory education and they provide other educational support measures for pupils in difficulty.

The practice of making pupils with difficulties repeat a year is a feature of most of the pre-accession countries. In Cyprus pupils only exceptionally repeat a year, and the decision depends on the recommendation of the teacher, the inspector concerned, a psychologist and the pupil's parents. This decision can only be taken once during the child's primary school career (with the agreement of the parents).

CONDITIONS OF ADMISSION TO LOWER SECONDARY EDUCATION

The organization of compulsory education varies from country to country. In certain countries, pupils complete all or virtually all their compulsory education within a single structure. In other countries, there are two successive levels, primary education and secondary education. In most of these countries, at the start of secondary education there is a common core that offers all pupils a common basic course. In a number of countries, pupils are given the choice of several streams or types of school at the start of secondary level.

FIGURE D10: CONDITIONS OF ADMISSION TO LOWER SECONDARY EDUCATION, PUBLIC AND PRIVATE GRANT-AIDED SECTORS, 1997/98

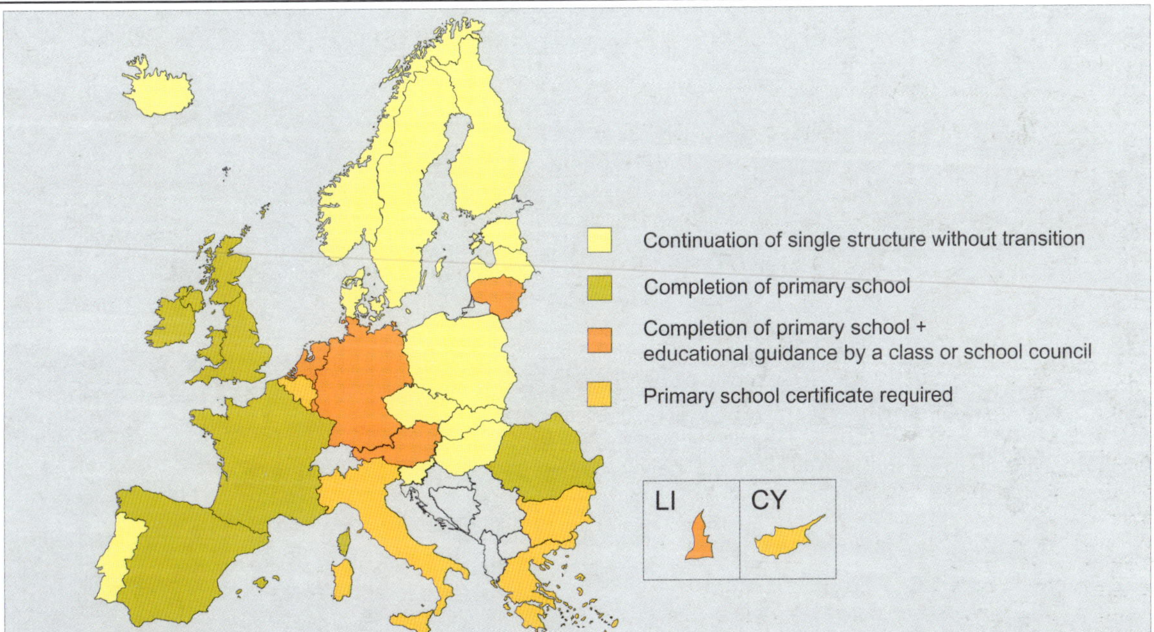

Continuation of single structure without transition

Completion of primary school

Completion of primary school + educational guidance by a class or school council

Primary school certificate required

Source: Eurydice.

Additional notes

Belgium (B fr, B de): Pupils who have not obtained the primary school leaving certificate or who are at least 12 years old are admitted to lower secondary level in a reception class.
United Kingdom (E, NI): Admission to grammar schools in England and Northern Ireland depends on the results of an examination.
Poland: From 1999, the completion of the 6-year primary school is required for admission to *gimnazjum*.

In certain countries, pupils' results also have a bearing on the arrangements for the transition between primary and secondary education. There are four main groups of countries.

In the first group of countries where compulsory education forms one single structure, admission to the final years of the educational stage is automatic without any transition. Thus, among the countries of the EU and of the EFTA/EEA, in Denmark, Portugal, Finland, Sweden, Iceland and Norway, and among the pre-accession countries, in the Czech Republic, Estonia, Latvia, Hungary, Poland, Slovenia and Slovakia, pupils progress to the next year if they have fulfilled the requirements of the previous year. However, it should be noted that in the Czech Republic, Hungary and Slovakia, when pupils choose to complete their compulsory education in a secondary school rather than within the single-structure system, they must take an examination set by the school.

In the second group of countries, to gain admission to lower secondary education, the pupil must have completed the last year of primary school. This is the case, among the countries of the EU, in Spain and Ireland, and in the pre-accession countries, in Romania. In France and the United Kingdom, children are normally admitted to secondary level when they reach the appropriate age, although admission to *grammar schools* in England and Northern Ireland also depends on the results of an examination.

In the third group of countries, the transition between the two levels of education depends on the decision of a class council or school council. In all these countries, with the exception of Lithuania, lower secondary education is divided into different types of courses. Pupils who have completed primary school are therefore streamed towards different types of schools depending on their results. In Germany, the recommendation of the primary school forms the basis for deciding on the pupil's future school career or for guidance. In all cases, the recommendation involves in-depth consultation with the parents. Depending on the different *Länder*, the final decision is taken by the parents, by the future school or by the school supervisory authority. In Luxembourg, a guidance recommendation is issued at the end of the sixth year primary school. If the parents decide not to accept the recommendation, the pupil must take a national entrance examination to be admitted to general secondary education. In the Netherlands, the primary school leaving report depends partly on the assessment of the pupil which, in most cases, involves tests organized at central level during the final year of *basisonderwijs*. In Austria, to be accepted for the *allgemeinbildende höhere Schule*, the pupil must have successfully completed the fourth year of primary school and must have obtained the grade 'Excellent' or 'Good' in German and mathematics. Pupils who are not automatically admitted to the *allgemeinbildende höhere Schule* can always take an entrance examination set by the school.

Finally, in a number of countries where primary education is separate from secondary education, the decision to move pupils up to the next level depends on whether or not they have a primary school leaving certificate. The certificate is awarded on the basis of work during the school year (Greece, Bulgaria and Cyprus) or following an examination organized by the school (Italy). In Belgium, the certificate is awarded to pupils who have successfully completed the final year (based on the work of the year and perhaps examinations). The authorities in the grant-aided private and public sectors also hold an external examination which the schools and the pupils are free to take. In these five countries, the certificate is issued by the individual school, and there is no external control.

SECONDARY EDUCATION

EDUCATIONAL PATHWAYS IN DIFFERENT COUNTRIES: —— FROM A COMMON CURRICULUM TO SPECIALIZED BRANCHES ——

Most of the countries of the European Union and of the EFTA/EEA have 'integrated' structures in lower secondary education, with all pupils following a common curriculum of general education. Only a few countries have different types of courses at the lower secondary level. In upper secondary education, a variety of courses is provided in all countries. Leaving aside name differences, we can distinguish two major categories: general education leading to the possibility of entry to tertiary education, and vocational, providing qualifications both in preparation for working life and for pursuing further studies.

In Denmark, Portugal, Finland, Sweden, Iceland and Norway, there is no separate lower secondary education, compulsory education being organized in one single, continuous structure over nine or ten years.

In Greece, France and Italy, the two levels of secondary education are provided in different schools. The first level is referred to as 'integrated', meaning that all pupils receive exactly the same curriculum of general education. In France, however, it is possible to choose a technical type of course in the last two years of the lower secondary *collège*. At upper secondary level, in these countries, a range of types of course is available to pupils, who choose their school according to the kind of course they wish to take.

Belgium, Spain, Ireland and the United Kingdom (Scotland) all aim to give all pupils a common educational foundation in the first years of secondary education. This common course continues until the end of compulsory education, except in Belgium and the United Kingdom (Scotland) where it lasts for two years and is followed by a choice of course options. Moreover, in Belgium, Spain and Ireland, pupils can complete their full secondary education in the same school, although a change of school may be necessary at the end of lower secondary education or of compulsory education for pupils wishing to enter vocational education. In the United Kingdom (England, Wales and Northern Ireland), there is no separate phase of lower secondary education; compulsory secondary education is organized in a single continuous structure over five years.

In Germany, the Netherlands and Austria, at lower secondary level, all pupils receive general education but at different academic levels depending on the type of school. There are, however, 'harmonized' foundation curricula in the first years preparatory to decisions being taken regarding pupils' directions of study. In Germany and the Netherlands, these do not lead to equivalent qualifications. Some types of school provide only lower secondary education while others cover both lower and upper secondary education. Luxembourg has two distinct types of education - general and technical - from the start of secondary education.

In Liechtenstein, pupils are selected for separate branches of education at the end of primary education. At upper secondary level, only general education is provided within Liechtenstein. Vocational courses alternate between school and workplace – students participate in practical in-company training in Liechtenstein and attend theory courses in a neighbouring country.

The Czech Republic, Hungary and Slovakia are among the pre-accession countries where two types of structure coexist for the compulsory stage of secondary education. Pupils can either continue their education under the single structure until the age of 14 or 15, or opt to transfer to a secondary school at age 10 or 11. In the latter case, they can complete all their secondary education in the same school.

In Estonia, Latvia, Poland, Slovenia, as in the Nordic countries, the final stage of the single structure coincides with lower secondary level.

In Bulgaria, Lithuania, Romania and Cyprus, all pupils enter lower secondary education at the end of their primary education and follow a common curriculum of general education. Students in Bulgaria do not have to change schools after lower secondary school unless they decide to follow vocational training. On the other hand, in Lithuania, Romania and Cyprus, the two levels of secondary education are usually organized in different schools.

All the pre-accession countries offer a wide range of different upper secondary provision and provide both general and vocational education.

Figure E1 shows the organization of the secondary education structures by country. Different branches of education, their duration and their position in this level of education are indicated.

FIGURE E1: ORGANIZATION OF SECONDARY EDUCATION STRUCTURES, 1997/98

Source: Eurydice.

Additional notes

Belgium: Except in exceptional circumstances, pupils who have not obtained the primary school leaving certificate *(CEB)* are taught in a reception class referred to as 1st B.

Germany: The first 2 years of lower secondary education can be provided in separate organizational units independent of the standard school types. Compulsory education normally comprises 9 years of full-time education (10 years in 4 *Länder*). Once students have completed their full-time compulsory education, those who do not continue in full-time general upper secondary or vocational education must attend part-time education, normally for 3 years, in accordance with the duration of training for recognized occupations for which formal training is required *(anerkannter Ausbildungsberuf)*. *Gesamtschulen* exist which only offer years 5 to 10 and therefore a transfer to the *Gymnasium* is necessary if students want to enter the *Gymnasiale Oberstufe*, and *Gesamtschulen* which offer years 5 to 13 with the *Gymnasiale Oberstufe*.

Explanatory note

According to the ISCED classification, the first two years of secondary education in Belgium coincide with ISCED level 2 (lower secondary education). According to this same classification, the final three years of *folkeskole* (in Denmark), of *ensino básico* (in Portugal), of *peruskoulu/grundskola* (in Finland) and of *grundskola* (in Sweden) are included in the same level as lower secondary education (ISCED 2).

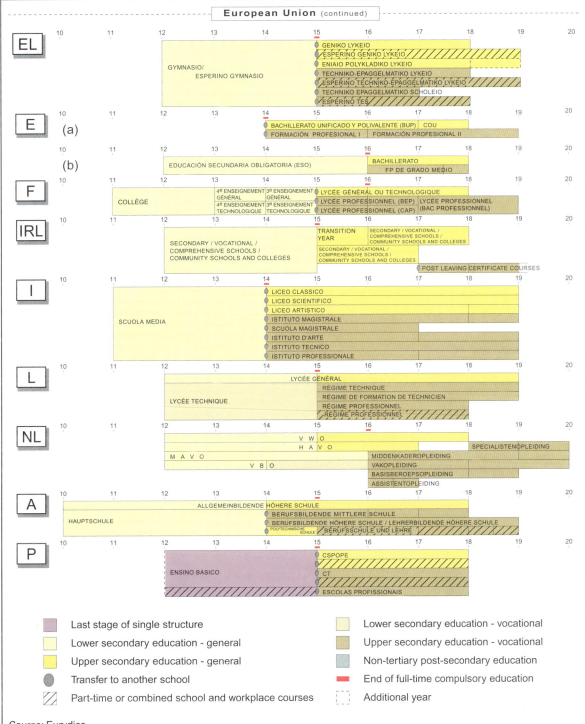

FIGURE E1 (CONTINUED): ORGANIZATION OF SECONDARY EDUCATION STRUCTURES, 1997/98

Legend:
- Last stage of single structure
- Lower secondary education - general
- Upper secondary education - general
- Transfer to another school
- Part-time or combined school and workplace courses
- Lower secondary education - vocational
- Upper secondary education - vocational
- Non-tertiary post-secondary education
- End of full-time compulsory education
- Additional year

Source: Eurydice.

Additional notes

Spain: The pre-reform structure is shown because the post-reform structure (*LOGSE*) in upper secondary education is not yet complete. In certain cases, students must change school if they choose an option that is not offered by their school.

Italy: Pending the complete reorganization of the education system, the minimum school leaving age will be raised by one year, to age 15, from 1999/2000. The *Istituto Magistrale* and the *Scuola Magistrale* are being phased out and accepted their last students at the start of 1997/98.

Netherlands: Since 1 August 1997, the various courses of vocational education have been organized on a modular basis. They can therefore be followed either full-time or part-time. This system replaces the former *MBO* and apprenticeships.

Portugal: Evening classes equivalent to the 3rd level of *ensino básico* and upper secondary education (*CSPOPE* and *CT*) are gradually being replaced by recurrent courses according to a system of transferable course credit units.

FIGURE E1 (CONTINUED): ORGANIZATION OF SECONDARY EDUCATION STRUCTURES, 1997/98

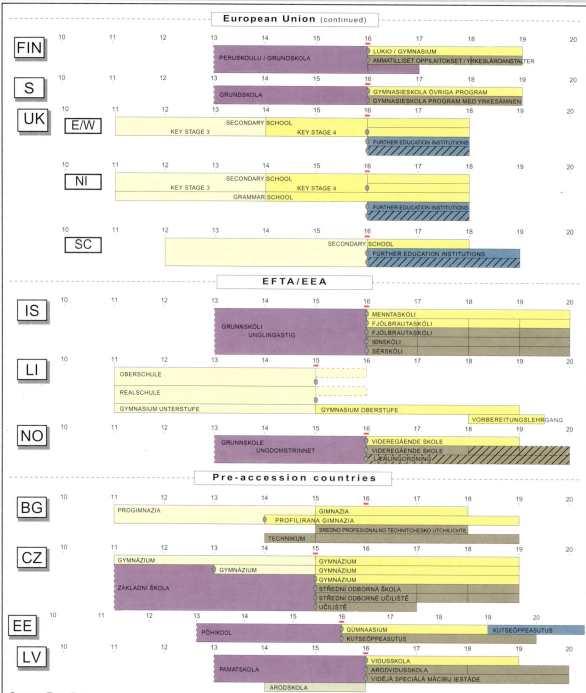

Source: Eurydice.

Additional notes

United Kingdom (E/W, NI): In some areas, the education system is divided into three levels: first schools, middle schools and high schools. In these areas, pupils move from first school to middle school at age 8 or 9 and from middle school to secondary school at age 12 or 13. Some areas of England also have grammar schools. Further education institutions offer both general and vocational post-compulsory education to students of any age. There is wide variation in the nature, duration and content of courses.

Bulgaria: According to the latest amendments to the National Education Act (1998), the duration of total school attendance will be increased by one year (making it twelve years). There will be no change in the duration of compulsory education.

Explanatory note

According to the ISCED classification, the first three years of secondary education in the United Kingdom (E/W, NI), the final three years of the single-structure system in Iceland and Norway (in the countries of the EFTA/EEA) and in Estonia are included in the level of lower secondary education (ISCED 2). In the other pre-accession countries, in the Czech Republic, Hungary and Slovenia, the last four years of the single structure correspond to ISCED level 2 and in Latvia, Poland and Slovakia the last five years.

FIGURE E1 (CONTINUED): ORGANIZATION OF SECONDARY EDUCATION STRUCTURES, 1997/98

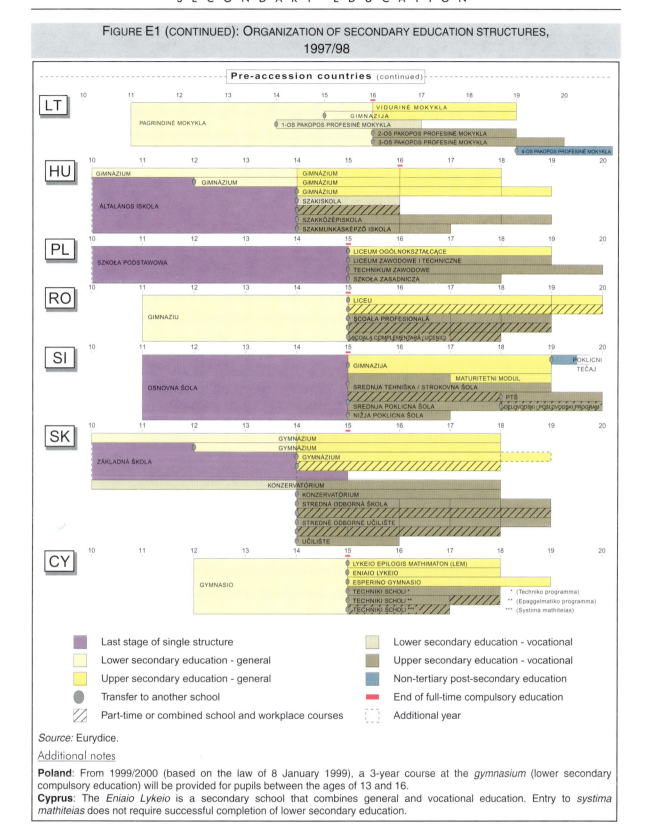

Pre-accession countries (continued)

Source: Eurydice.

Additional notes

Poland: From 1999/2000 (based on the law of 8 January 1999), a 3-year course at the *gymnasium* (lower secondary compulsory education) will be provided for pupils between the ages of 13 and 16.

Cyprus: The *Eniaio Lykeio* is a secondary school that combines general and vocational education. Entry to *systima mathiteias* does not require successful completion of lower secondary education.

THE ORGANIZATION OF THE FINAL YEARS OF FULL-TIME COMPULSORY ——— EDUCATION VARIES FROM COUNTRY TO COUNTRY ———

Three different models of organization can be distinguished for the end of compulsory full-time education, depending on whether the countries have a single structure, separate types of education or compulsory integrated secondary education.

FIGURE E2: PUPILS' AGE OF THE END OF COMPULSORY FULL-TIME EDUCATION AND THE ORGANIZATION OF LOWER SECONDARY EDUCATION, 1997/98

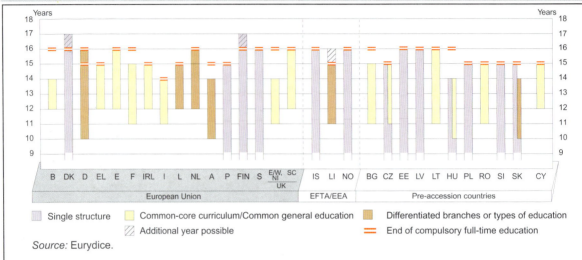

Source: Eurydice.

<u>Additional notes</u>

Belgium: Secondary education is divided into three two-year stages. The end of compulsory full-time education is set to the age of 15 for pupils who have completed the first stage or to the age of 16 for pupils who have not completed the first stage.
Germany: The duration of full-time compulsory education is defined as nine years in 12 *Länder* and ten years in 4 *Länder*. It therefore finishes at the age of 15 or 16.
Italy: Pending the complete reorganization of the education system, the minimum school leaving age will be raised by one year, to age 15, from 1999/2000.
Netherlands: Depending on the school the pupil attends, lower secondary education ends at the age of 15 (*VWO, HAVO*) or 16 (*MAVO, VBO*).
United Kingdom (E/W, NI): There is no separate phase of lower secondary education. Compulsory secondary education is organized in a single continuous structure over five years.
Czech Republic, Hungary and **Slovakia**: In parallel with the single-structure system that ends at the age of 14 or 15 depending on the country, pupils can be admitted to lower secondary school at the age of 10 or 11.
Lithuania: Pupils wishing to gain a vocational qualification can go to a vocational school from the age of 14.
Hungary: The common core curriculum lasts until the age of 16.

<u>Explanatory note</u>

According to the ISCED classification, the first two years of secondary education in Belgium and the first three years of secondary education in the United Kingdom (E/W, NI) coincide with ISCED level 2 (lower secondary education).
According to this same classification, the final three years of *folkeskole* (in Denmark), of *ensino básico* (in Portugal), of *peruskoulu/grundskola* (in Finland) and of *grundskola* (in Sweden) are included in the same level as lower secondary education (ISCED 2). This also applies for the final three years of the single-structure system in Iceland and Norway (in the countries of the EFTA/EEA) and in Estonia. In the other pre-accession countries, in the Czech Republic, Hungary and Slovenia, the last four years of the single structure correspond to ISCED level 2 and in Latvia, Poland and Slovakia the last five years.

In the single-structure countries (Denmark, Portugal, Finland, Sweden, Iceland and Norway for the countries of the EU and of the EFTA/EEA, and Estonia, Latvia, Poland and Slovenia for the pre-accession countries), the end of single-structure education generally coincides with the end of compulsory education. In Estonia, however, compulsory education continues until the students have completed basic education or they have reached the age of 17.

In Germany, Luxembourg, the Netherlands, Austria and Liechtenstein, pupils are streamed into different branches or schools before the end of full-time compulsory education. This is also the case in Slovakia, where pupils who do not complete their compulsory education within the single-structure system have a choice between general and vocational courses. In Germany, even though pupils attend different schools, they follow harmonized curricula for the first two years in order to delay the decision as to which course option to take. In the Netherlands, usually during the first three years, pupils follow a common core curriculum whose level varies depending on the type of school. Attainment targets have been defined for all pupils.

There is a final group of countries where during the first years of secondary school all pupils learn the same general set of subjects (referred to as the 'common core'). In some of these countries, the end of lower secondary education or of the single structure coincides with the end of full-time compulsory education. In some countries (Belgium, France, Austria, the United Kingdom – England, Wales and Northern Ireland, Bulgaria and Hungary), the end of full-time compulsory education does not correspond to the end of lower secondary education; the final years of compulsory education belong to upper secondary level. In Belgium, France and Bulgaria pupils choose between general and vocational education one or two years before the end of full-time compulsory education. In the Czech Republic and in Hungary, for the final years of compulsory education, pupils can stay in the single structure or attend a general lower secondary education institution.

AT UPPER SECONDARY LEVEL, MORE STUDENTS ―― IN THE VOCATIONAL STREAM THAN IN GENERAL EDUCATION ――

The vocational stream is only open to **lower secondary** pupils in some EU and EFTA/EEA countries (see Figure E1). The highest percentages of pupils enrolled in this stream are observed in the Benelux countries: 27% in Belgium, 67% in Luxembourg and 18% in the Netherlands. In France, a small proportion of pupils in lower secondary education (6%) attend vocational courses. The vocational stream is also present at this level, though in marginal proportions in some countries. In pre-accession countries, percentages of pupils enrolled in the vocational stream do not exceed 3%.

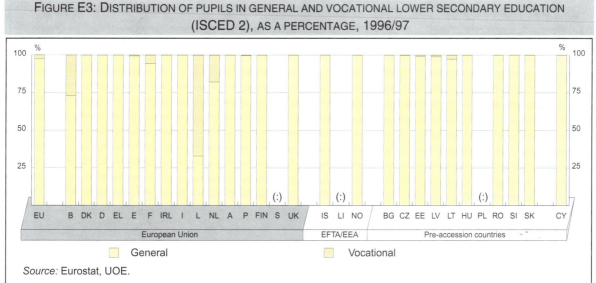

FIGURE E3: DISTRIBUTION OF PUPILS IN GENERAL AND VOCATIONAL LOWER SECONDARY EDUCATION (ISCED 2), AS A PERCENTAGE, 1996/97

Source: Eurostat, UOE.

Additional notes

Belgium: Pupils in (transitional) secondary technical and art education are included with pupils in vocational education. The high percentage of pupils in lower secondary vocational education is explained by pupils in social advancement education, which is not shown in Figure E1.
France: Pupils in technological education are included with pupils in vocational education.
Luxembourg: Pupils in technical secondary education are considered as pupils in the vocational stream.
United Kingdom: For international statistical purposes, all pupils in secondary schools are classified as following general programmes.
Bulgaria: A small number of pupils enrolled in vocational programmes at ISCED 2 are included in ISCED 3.
Poland: ISCED 2 pupils are included in ISCED 1.
Slovakia: Data are given in full-time equivalents, special education is excluded.

In the EU on average, more students are enrolled in the vocational stream than in general education at **upper secondary level**. This pattern is found in most EU and EFTA/EEA countries but is particularly pronounced in Germany, Austria and Liechtenstein, where more than three quarters of students are in the vocational stream. In Ireland and Portugal, conversely, more than three quarters are found in general education and, in Greece, Spain and Iceland, more than two thirds of students and in are found in that stream.

Vocational education predominates in pre-accession countries, especially in the Czech Republic, Slovenia and Slovakia, where more than three quarters of students follow vocational courses. Four countries have a different pattern: Estonia, Latvia, Lithuania, where around 60% of upper secondary students are enrolled in general education, and Cyprus, where the percentage is 84%.

FIGURE E4: DISTRIBUTION OF STUDENTS IN GENERAL AND VOCATIONAL UPPER SECONDARY EDUCATION (ISCED 3), AS A PERCENTAGE, 1996/97

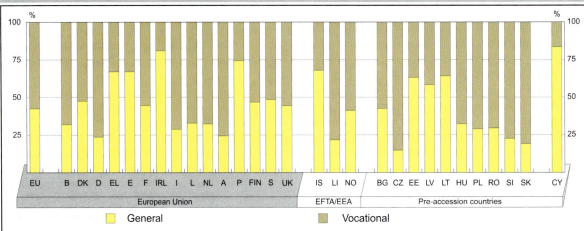

Source: Eurostat, UOE.

Additional notes

Belgium: Students in (transitional) secondary technical and art education are included with students in vocational education. The high percentage of students in upper secondary vocational education is explained by students in social advancement education, which is not shown in Figure E1.
France: Students in technological education are included with students in vocational education.
Luxembourg: Students in technical secondary education are considered as students in the vocational stream.
Sweden: Adult education (mature students) is included. Some students (in adult and special education) cannot be split into general and vocational education.
United Kingdom: For international statistical purposes, all students in secondary schools are classified as following general programmes. All students on further education courses, some of which are academic, are classified as following vocational programmes. The majority of these students are also over theoretical school age.
Iceland: Only full-time students are included.
Liechtenstein: Only the *Gymnasium (Oberstufe)* are regarded as providing general education. Vocational courses alternate between school and workplace – pupils participate in practical in-company training in Liechtenstein and attend theory courses in a neighbouring country. 1995/96.
Bulgaria: A small number of students enrolled in vocational programmes at ISCED 2 are included in ISCED 3.
Hungary: Students in pre-vocational education are included in vocational.
Slovakia: Data are given in full-time equivalents, special education is excluded.

Explanatory note

Students in vocational training spending 90% of their time or more within the company are not included in the UOE data collection.

Three groups of countries with a similar profile can be distinguished.

The first group comprises the Benelux countries, Germany, Italy, Austria and Liechtenstein (for EU and EFTA/EEA countries), and the Czech Republic, Hungary, Poland, Romania, Slovenia and Slovakia (among pre-accession countries). In these countries, the vocational stream is largely in the majority.

Greece, Spain, Ireland, Portugal and Iceland (for EU and EFTA/EEA countries), Estonia, Latvia, Lithuania and Cyprus (among pre-accession countries) constitute a second group of countries. In these countries, more students are enrolled in general education than vocational courses.

The third group is made of the Nordic countries (except Iceland) and France. It is characterized by almost equal numbers in both streams.

MORE FEMALES THAN MALES FOLLOW THE GENERAL STREAM IN UPPER SECONDARY EDUCATION

The male/female distribution between the general and vocational streams in upper secondary education illustrated in Figure E5 confirms the main observations concerning the overall distribution between the two (Figure E4). Moreover, it allows a finer analysis and shows that in all European countries, apart from Ireland and the United Kingdom, more females than males are enrolled in the general stream.

Within the EU and the EFTA/EEA, the difference between gender attendance in upper secondary education is minimal in four countries: 5% in Belgium and Austria and 2% in Spain and Ireland. The largest differences between percentages of males and females are found in Greece, Sweden, Iceland and Norway (14 to 22%).

In pre-accession countries, differences in the percentages of males and females enrolled in the different streams are appreciably larger than in the EU. The largest differences can be found in Bulgaria (28%), Romania and Cyprus (21%). In the Czech Republic however, percentages are comparable for males and females.

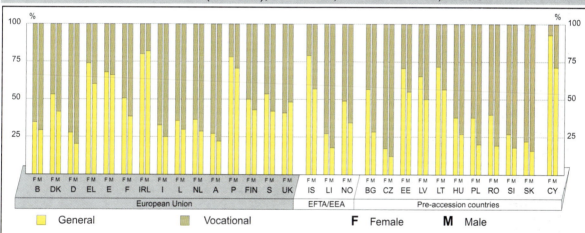

FIGURE E5: DISTRIBUTION OF STUDENTS BETWEEN GENERAL AND VOCATIONAL STREAMS AT UPPER SECONDARY LEVEL (ISCED 3), BY GENDER, AS A PERCENTAGE, 1996/97

General   Vocational   **F** Female   **M** Male

Source: Eurostat, UOE.

Additional notes

Belgium: Students in (transitional) secondary technical and art education are included with students in vocational education. The high percentage of students in upper secondary vocational education is explained by students in social advancement education, which is not shown in Figure E1.
France: Students in technological education are included with students in vocational education.
Luxembourg: Students in technical secondary education are considered as students in the vocational stream.
Sweden: Some students (in adult and special education) cannot be split into general and vocational education.
United Kingdom: For international statistical purposes, all students in secondary schools are classified as following general programmes. All students on further education courses, some of which are academic, are classified as following vocational programmes. The majority of these students are also over theoretical school age.
Iceland: Only full-time students are included.
Liechtenstein: 1995/96. Only the *Gymnasium (Oberstufe)* are regarded as providing general education. Vocational courses alternate between school and workplace – students participate in practical in-company training in Liechtenstein and attend theory courses in a neighbouring country.
Bulgaria: A small number of pupils enrolled in vocational programmes at ISCED 2 are included in ISCED 3.
Hungary: Students in pre-vocational education are included in vocational.
Slovakia: Data are given in full-time equivalents, special education is excluded.

ENROLMENT IN GENERAL EDUCATION IS COMPARABLE AT REGIONAL AND NATIONAL LEVELS

The regional distribution of upper secondary students into general and vocational education is quite similar to the national distribution. Some regions or capitals do not follow the national pattern. This is the case of Berlin in Germany, Madeira in Portugal and Scotland in the United Kingdom, where the percentage of students enrolled in general education is higher than the national rate. Conversely, *Ahvenanmaa* in Finland has a smaller proportion of students in general education at the upper secondary level.

The EU regions with the highest proportions of students enrolled in general upper secondary education are the Portuguese regions (from 70 to 85% of enrolees). On the other hand, in three German *Länder* (Baden-Württemberg, Bavaria and Mecklemburg-Western Pomerania), the general stream has fewer enrolees (fewer than 20% of students at that level).

FIGURE E6: PERCENTAGE OF UPPER SECONDARY STUDENTS (ISCED 3) IN GENERAL EDUCATION BY NUTS 1 AND NUTS 2 REGIONS, 1996/97

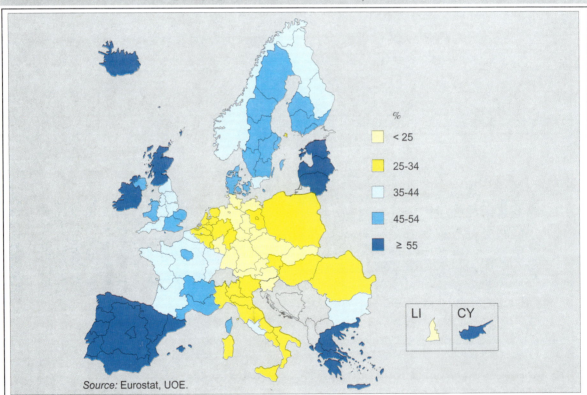

%
< 25
25-34
35-44
45-54
≥ 55

Source: Eurostat, UOE.

Additional notes

Belgium: Students in (transitional) secondary technical and art education are included with students in vocational education.
Greece: Only data from the national level (NUTS 0) are presented.
Sweden: Adult education and distance learning are excluded.
United Kingdom: For international statistical purposes, all students in secondary schools are classified as following general programmes. All students on further education courses, some of which are academic, are classified as following vocational programmes. The majority of these students are also over theoretical school age.
Iceland: Only full-time students only are included.

Explanatory note

For most of the Member States, the nomenclature used here is that of NUTS 1, which is the largest of the regional units. NUTS 2 is, however, used for Portugal, Finland and Sweden. For the EFTA/EEA and the pre-accession countries, only national data are presented.

For the definition of the NUTS classification, please refer to the definition of statistical tools at the beginning of the book.

PUPILS RECEIVE DIFFERENT AMOUNTS OF TEACHING ACCORDING TO ——— COUNTRY, COURSE AND YEAR OF STUDY ———

There are wide variations between countries in the organization of school time, as illustrated in Figures E7 and E8 for lower and general upper secondary education respectively. In most countries of the EU and of the EFTA/EEA, at lower secondary level, the annual number of teaching hours varies between a compulsory minimum which applies to all pupils, and a maximum. Variations result from pupils having subject options (Belgium, France, Italy) or the number of lesson periods increasing as pupils progress through school (Denmark, Germany, Austria) or both (Spain). In the countries with no set maximum, variations exist between schools. In most of these countries, particularly Finland, Sweden and the United Kingdom, schools enjoy a considerable measure of freedom in setting the timetable. For Finland, the figure illustrates a notional average and for England and Wales it gives an average derived from an annual census of schools. In Iceland, the municipalities are free to add extra hours to the minimum. Luxembourg and the Netherlands are the only countries where all lower secondary general pupils follow the same number of lesson periods per year.

At this level of education, Ireland, the Netherlands, the United Kingdom (Scotland) and Liechtenstein have the highest annual minimum load – over 1 000 hours. In Italy, some pupils have classes for more than 1 200 hours per year. This maximum is calculated taking into account the hours of optional language lessons. Pupils in Denmark, Germany and Iceland, on the other hand, receive an annual minimum of about 800 hours of teaching.

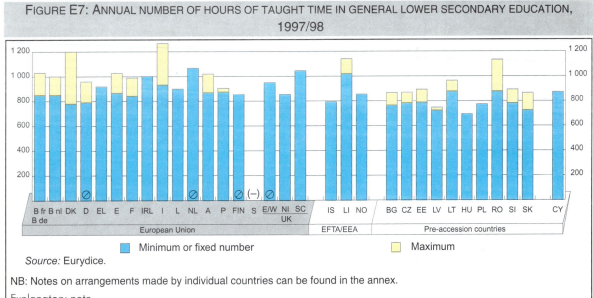

FIGURE E7: ANNUAL NUMBER OF HOURS OF TAUGHT TIME IN GENERAL LOWER SECONDARY EDUCATION, 1997/98

Minimum or fixed number ◼   Maximum ☐

Source: Eurydice.

NB: Notes on arrangements made by individual countries can be found in the annex.

<u>Explanatory note</u>

The last three years of the *folkeskole* (in Denmark), *ensino básico* (in Portugal), *peruskoulu/grundskola* (in Finland), and of *grundskola* (in Sweden) are classified as lower secondary education. This also applies to the final three years of the single-structure system in Iceland and Norway (in the countries of the EFTA/EEA), and in Estonia. In the other pre-accession countries, in the Czech Republic, Hungary and Slovenia, the last four years of the single structure correspond to ISCED level 2 and in Latvia, Poland and Slovakia the last five years.
The annual teaching load is calculated by taking the average daily load multiplied by the number of days of teaching in the year. Tables giving the detailed method of calculation appear in the annex.

In most pre-accession countries, the annual number of taught hours for pupils at lower secondary level varies between a minimum and a maximum figure. In Lithuania, this variability is due to the possibility of schools adding a number of taught hours to the minimum required for all. In Estonia, the annual number of taught hours increases over the years.

The fewest hours are found in Hungary and Slovakia, where they are about 700 hours a year.

SECONDARY EDUCATION

As illustrated in Figure E9, in Greece, Italy, Portugal and Iceland the minimum annual number of hours of teaching is less in general upper secondary education than in lower secondary. In Belgium, Ireland, Luxembourg, the United Kingdom, Liechtenstein and Norway, the number of taught hours is the same in general upper secondary education as it is in lower secondary education. However, in the United Kingdom (England, Wales and Northern Ireland), that is only the case for the compulsory phase of upper secondary education. The number of taught hours is higher in Denmark, Germany, Spain, France and Austria. In all countries, the annual teaching load differs from one pupil to another, even in countries for which the graph shows no set maximum. In these countries, schools have considerable freedom in distributing the number of lesson hours over the years. The graph therefore shows an average. In upper secondary education, differences can mainly be explained by the numerous options available to students (languages, mathematics, sciences, literature, etc.) in the different branches.

In the pre-accession countries, students' annual lesson load is greater at upper secondary level than at lower secondary, except in Romania and Cyprus. As in the countries of the EU and of the EFTA/EEA, the annual number of taught hours varies according to the section and option chosen by the student.

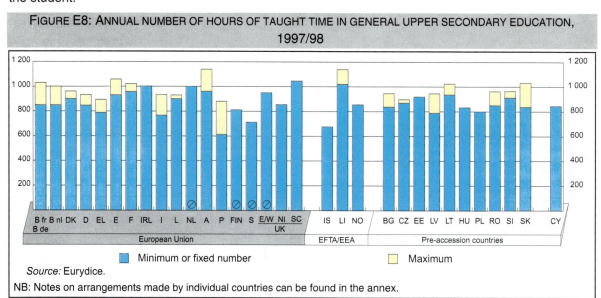

FIGURE E8: ANNUAL NUMBER OF HOURS OF TAUGHT TIME IN GENERAL UPPER SECONDARY EDUCATION, 1997/98

Source: Eurydice.

NB: Notes on arrangements made by individual countries can be found in the annex.

FIGURE E9: MINIMUM ANNUAL HOURS OF TAUGHT TIME IN SECONDARY EDUCATION, 1997/98

| | European Union | | | | | | | | | | | |
	B	DK	D	EL	E	F	IRL	I	L	NL	A	P
Lower secondary - general	849	780	790	919	866	842	1 002	933	900	1 067	870	875
Upper secondary - general	849	900	846	788	930	957	1 002	767	900	1 000	960	613

| | European Union (continued) | | | | | | EFTA/EEA | | |
	FIN	S	UK (E/W)	UK (NI)	UK (SC)			IS	LI	NO
Lower secondary - general	855	(–)	950	855	1 045			793	1 020	855
Upper secondary - general	812	712	950	855	1 045			677	1 020	855

| | Pre-accession countries | | | | | | | | | | | |
	BG	CZ	EE	LV	LT	HU	PL	RO	SI	SK		CY
Lower secondary - general	765	782	788	723	878	694	773	878	783	725		872
Upper secondary - general	837	869	919	788	936	833	800	850	912	837		845

Source: Eurydice.

88

AT AROUND AGE 13, THE SAME COMPULSORY SUBJECTS, BUT DIFFERENT TIMETABLE LOADS

Where the curricula indicate the time allocation among the different compulsory subjects, it is possible to compare the relative amount of time allocated to the different subjects. Figures E10 and E11 show the proportions of the annual timetable allocated to each of the compulsory subjects, at around ages 13 and 16. In some countries, schools are completely free to determine the amount of time they allocate to the various subjects in the timetable; for these countries, the compulsory subjects are indicated on the chart by a bullet in figures E10 and E11.

FIGURE E10: PERCENTAGES OF MINIMUM ANNUAL TIMETABLE ALLOCATED TO COMPULSORY SUBJECTS AROUND AGE 13 IN GENERAL LOWER SECONDARY EDUCATION, 1997/98

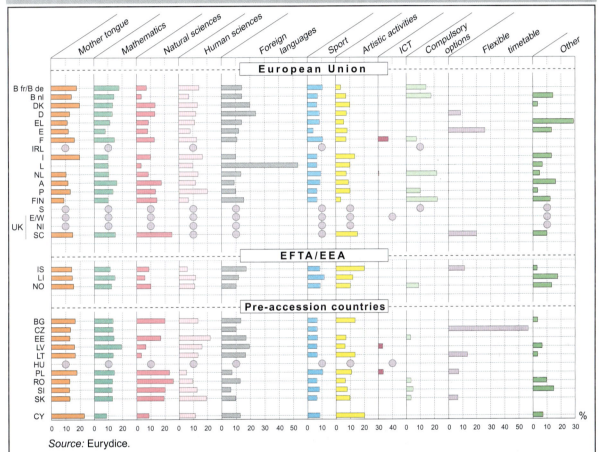

Source: Eurydice.

NB: Notes on individual countries' arrangements can be found in the annex.

Explanatory note

The proportion of time allocated to each subject is calculated on the basis of the ratio between the minimum number of class hours of teaching to be allocated to each compulsory subject and the total minimum number of class hours at ages 13 and 16. These are set out in the annex.

Subjects have been grouped together as follows: human sciences includes history and geography; natural sciences takes in biology, physics and chemistry; the 'other' category includes religious education and the classics (Latin and Greek).

ICT is indicated in this figure if it is a separate subject, provided outside the compulsory options and the flexible timetable. For more information on the presence of ICT in the curricula, see chapter J.

The category 'flexible timetable' indicates either that the time allowed for various compulsory subjects is not fixed, or that, in addition to the time to be allocated to various compulsory subjects, the curriculum allows for a certain number of teaching hours that can be used to study subjects chosen by the pupils or the school.

The 'compulsory options' category indicates where pupils must choose one or more subjects from a specific group within the compulsory curriculum.

At about age 13, in general education, all pupils follow the same compulsory subjects. However, the proportion of time allocated to each of these subjects varies from one country to another. At this level of education, the mother tongue, mathematics and a foreign language are relatively the most important subjects in most countries.

Thus, the time devoted to mother tongue teaching accounts for one fifth of teaching time in Denmark and Italy. In the Netherlands and Finland, the compulsory minimum amount of time allocated to this subject represents 10% of the total timetable. In Luxembourg, at this age, Letzeburgesch is no longer included in the curriculum. This is explained by the fact that this language is essentially oral. Pupils in Luxembourg have the greatest number of hours of foreign language courses, which include both German and French in addition to English, which are also used in the teaching of other subjects. The French Community of Belgium has the greatest proportion of the compulsory teaching hours allocated to the teaching of mathematics (18%).

In some countries, 13-year-old pupils have to choose between a number of compulsory options. The proportion of the timetable set aside for such subjects is fairly high in the Netherlands and Finland (22%). The amount of time allocated to 'other' subjects is considerable in Greece (29%). This is largely accounted for by the compulsory teaching of ancient Greek. In most other countries, this category mainly comprises the teaching of religion.

In Iceland, Liechtenstein and Norway, a sizeable amount of time is allocated to artistic activities, and there are no compulsory options at this level of education.

All the pre-accession countries devote between one quarter and one third of the timetable to mother tongue and mathematics at this level of education. Poland and Romania attach considerable importance to science (around one quarter of the timetable). In Estonia and Lithuania, the time allocated to the teaching of foreign languages accounts for 17% of the timetable at the age of 13. In Latvia, Hungary and Poland, the compulsory subjects include a course on information and communication technology. In the Czech Republic, more than 50% of the curriculum is organized in a flexible timetable.

AT AROUND AGE 16, DIFFERENT COMPULSORY SUBJECTS —— IN THE SCIENCE SECTION OF UPPER SECONDARY EDUCATION ——

In the majority of countries, at upper secondary level, students are able to choose between a variety of courses, whose curricula specify a core of compulsory subjects to be studied. In Ireland and the United Kingdom (England, Wales, Northern Ireland), at the upper secondary level (after the end of compulsory education), students can choose an individual combination of subjects from the range offered by their institution but there are no compulsory subjects. In view of the diversity of the options and courses at the upper secondary level, the science section of general education has been selected so as to make comparison possible.

At about the age of 16, considerable differences are found in timetables in the science section of general education. At this point in their school careers, students do not necessarily all have the same compulsory subjects. In this section of general upper secondary education, the teaching of the mother tongue, mathematics and foreign languages usually retain a fairly important relative position in the majority of countries. However, where the curriculum regulates the time allowed to the different subjects, the proportion of time devoted to science has increased considerably compared with that at age 13. The time devoted to science sometimes exceeds the minimum compulsory time spent teaching mathematics. In countries where art and sport activities are still included in the compulsory curriculum, they are allocated less time than in lower secondary, except in Denmark where it is the same. More time is often allocated to foreign languages at this age. The flexible timetable is a feature of Germany, Ireland, Finland, Sweden and the United Kingdom. In Germany, subjects are taught in basic and advanced courses (*Grundkurse* and *Leistungskurse*) according to students' aptitudes and attainments. The curriculum includes compulsory subjects (2/3) plus compulsory options (1/3). The proportion of time allocated to compulsory options is particularly high in the Netherlands, where it accounts for over 70% of the timetable.

Among the pre-accession countries, at the age of 16 artistic activities are still compulsory in the Czech Republic, Estonia, Latvia, Lithuania and Hungary. Almost everywhere, less time is allocated to the teaching of mathematics and mother tongue than at the age of 13. Courses in ICT are compulsory in Lithuania, Hungary and Poland.

FIGURE E11: PERCENTAGES OF MINIMUM ANNUAL TIMETABLE ALLOCATED TO COMPULSORY SUBJECTS AROUND AGE 16 IN THE SCIENCE SECTION OF GENERAL UPPER SECONDARY EDUCATION, 1997/98

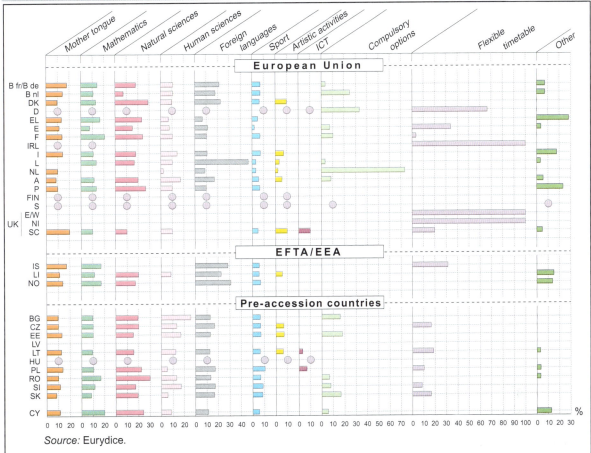

Source: Eurydice.

NB: Notes on individual countries' arrangements can be found in the annex.

Explanatory note

The proportion of time allocated to each subject is calculated on the basis of the ratio between the minimum number of class hours of teaching to be allocated to each compulsory subject and the total minimum number of class hours at ages 13 and 16. These are set out in the annex.

Subjects have been grouped together as follows: human sciences includes history and geography; natural sciences takes in biology, physics and chemistry; the 'other' category includes religious education and the classics (Latin and Greek).

ICT is indicated in this figure if it is a separate subject, provided outside the compulsory options and the flexible timetable. For more information on the presence of ICT in the curricula, see chapter J.

The category 'flexible timetable' indicates either that the time allowed for various compulsory subjects is not fixed, or that, in addition to the time to be allocated to various compulsory subjects, the curriculum allows some or all taught hours to be used to study subjects chosen by the student or the school.

The 'compulsory options' category indicates where students must choose one or more subjects from a specific group within the compulsory curriculum.

ALMOST THREE QUARTERS OF YOUNG PEOPLE HAVE SUCCESSFULLY ──── COMPLETED THE UPPER SECONDARY LEVEL OF EDUCATION ────

In the EU as a whole, on average, 71% of 22-year-olds have successfully completed at least upper secondary education. Finland and Sweden exceed 90%. Conversely, Portugal has the lowest percentage (52%).

Percentages should be interpreted taking into account the proportion of students studying abroad.

FIGURE E12: PERCENTAGE OF THOSE AGED 22 WHO HAVE SUCCESSFULLY COMPLETED AT LEAST UPPER SECONDARY EDUCATION (ISCED 3), 1997

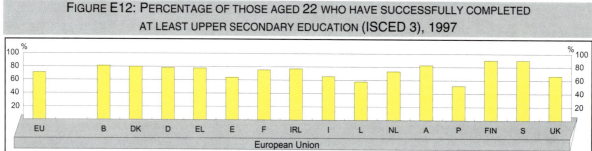

Source: Eurostat, Labour force survey.

Additional notes

Luxembourg: Most young people taking tertiary education courses are abroad. All of them have completed at least the upper secondary education level. The percentage is therefore under-estimated.
United Kingdom: The GCSE and equivalent qualifications taken at the end of compulsory schooling at the age of 16 are considered as lower secondary qualifications.

Explanatory note

In the Eurostat Labour Force Survey, all vocational training in schools (including sandwich courses) has been allocated to ISCED 3. This may explain a relative over-estimate of the number of students having completed ISCED 3 in Denmark, France and especially in the Netherlands.

The conditions of successful completion vary and can be determined by various criteria: the award of a certificate, a number of hours of attendance, passing exams, etc.

MORE GIRLS QUALIFY FROM ──────── GENERAL UPPER SECONDARY EDUCATION ────────

In the EU as a whole, slightly over 4 million students obtained a general upper secondary education qualification in 1996 or 1997. In all EU and EFTA/EEA countries for which data are available, more girls than boys obtain a general upper secondary education qualification: the average ratio in the EU is 129 females completing upper secondary education per 100 males.

The phenomenon is more marked in Denmark, France, Finland, Sweden and Iceland than in other countries, with around three females per two males. Conversely, in Ireland, the ratios are closest to 100 indicating little difference between girls and boys.

In pre-accession countries, the proportion of females completing upper secondary education is even higher than in the EU. In the Czech Republic, Estonia, Lithuania, Hungary, Slovenia and Slovakia, around three girls per two boys obtained general upper secondary education qualifications. In Bulgaria and Romania, the number of successful female students is as high as twice that of male students.

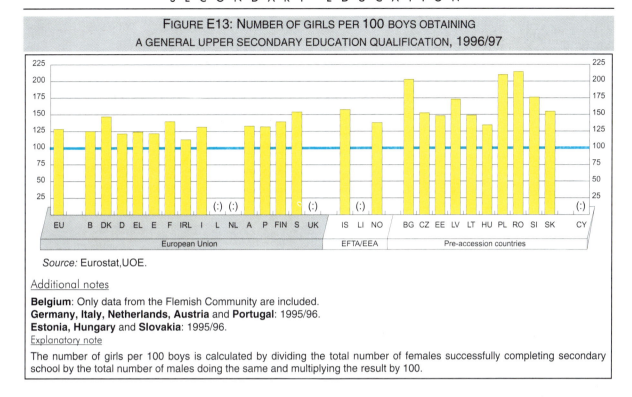

FIGURE E13: NUMBER OF GIRLS PER 100 BOYS OBTAINING
A GENERAL UPPER SECONDARY EDUCATION QUALIFICATION, 1996/97

Source: Eurostat,UOE.

Additional notes

Belgium: Only data from the Flemish Community are included.
Germany, Italy, Netherlands, Austria and **Portugal**: 1995/96.
Estonia, Hungary and **Slovakia**: 1995/96.

Explanatory note

The number of girls per 100 boys is calculated by dividing the total number of females successfully completing secondary school by the total number of males doing the same and multiplying the result by 100.

CERTIFICATION AT THE END OF EITHER GENERAL LOWER SECONDARY EDUCATION OR COMPULSORY FULL-TIME EDUCATION

In most countries of the EU and the EFTA/EEA, a certificate is awarded to pupils who complete compulsory full-time education. In France and Austria, this certificate is awarded at the end of general lower secondary education. In the Netherlands, pupils in *MAVO* and *VBO* schools receive a certificate at this stage of their school career, but not the pupils in *VWO* and *HAVO* schools. In the Flemish Community of Belgium, pupils do not receive a certificate at the end of lower secondary education.

In the majority of countries, this certificate is awarded to pupils at least partly on the basis of results obtained in a final examination. However, in the French and German-speaking Communities of Belgium, the majority of the German *Länder*, Greece, Spain, Luxembourg, Austria, Finland and Sweden, this certificate is awarded only on the basis of the pupil's marks and the work over the year.

When a final examination is set, it includes at least one written part. Sometimes the tests, written and/or oral, are compiled by a team from outside the school but are usually administered by the school. It is only in Portugal and Liechtenstein that this examination is written within the school and under its entire responsibility. In Italy, the chairman of the examination board, who is not a member of the school, gives his opinion on the tests set by the teachers and supervizes the correction and marking. In the Netherlands, the final examination consists of two tests: an internal test (*schoolexamen*), which is oral and/or written and set and marked by the teacher, and an external test (*centraal examen*), which is written and set by an external body and corrected by the teachers according to the standards established by the external body. Finally, in Iceland pupils take internal and external examinations at the end of the single structure.

In most cases, teachers decide the grade that will appear on the certificate if the certificate is awarded on the basis of grades obtained and on work completed over the year or by taking into account the results of an internally set examination. In several countries, the mark given by the teachers is either weighted by an external grade (for example, the results obtained in the external examination) or decided on the basis of criteria established by an external authority. In Ireland and the United Kingdom (England, Wales, Northern Ireland), the final grade is given by examiners from outside the school.

In the pre-accession countries, except in the Czech Republic and in Slovakia, pupils also receive a certificate at this stage in their school career. In Bulgaria, Hungary, Poland and Slovenia, this certificate is issued on the basis of the pupil's grades and work over the year. In contrast, in Estonia, Latvia, Lithuania, Romania and Cyprus, the results obtained in a final examination are at least partially taken into account in the decision whether or not to issue the certificate.

FIGURE E14: CERTIFICATION AT THE END OF GENERAL LOWER SECONDARY EDUCATION OR COMPULSORY FULL-TIME EDUCATION, 1997/98

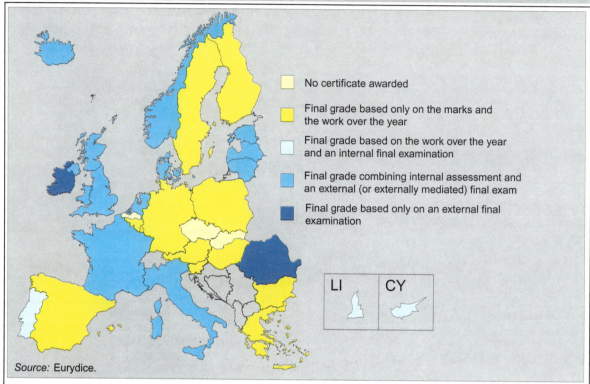

Source: Eurydice.

Additional notes

Belgium (B nl): At the end of the second stage of secondary education, a certificate is awarded on the basis of written and oral tests (set by the school) and the work over the year.

Denmark: The certificate always contains marks for the work over the year. Pupils who sit for the optional final examinations receive a certificate which also contains marks for these examinations.

Germany: In most *Länder*, certificates are awarded at the end of *Hauptschule* and *Realschule* on the basis of the pupils' marks and their work over the year. In a number of *Länder*, pupils must take a final examination (written and oral) to receive the certificate at the end of *Realschule*. Depending on the *Land*, the *Schulaufsichtsbehörde* (school supervisory authority) either set the topics for the written examination centrally or merely give approval if they are set by individual schools.

Netherlands: Certificates are issued in *MAVO* and *VBO* schools, but not in *VWO* and *HAVO* schools, at this level of education.

Sweden: The final mark is awarded on the basis of the pupil's work during the final years of *grundskola*, even if there are national tests for mother tongue, English or mathematics. These tests are organized as part of the scheme to monitor the education system.

United Kingdom (E/W, NI): The pupils take external qualifications on a single subject basis, at the end of compulsory education. The final grade is awarded on the basis of external final examinations and may also take into account externally controlled assessment of specific work during the course.

Slovenia: A non-compulsory external assessment in mother tongue and mathematics is offered at the end of *osnovna šola*. The results obtained do not affect the mark that appears on the certificate at the end of compulsory education, but they are one of the selection criteria for admission to upper secondary schools (where the number of places is limited).

Explanatory note

In the category 'Final grade combining internal assessment and an external (or externally mediated) final exam', the internal assessment can mean a final internal test or an evaluation of the marks obtained or the coursework done during the year.

When there is a final examination, it is either set by an external body (Latvia, Lithuania) or by the school (Cyprus). In Estonia, there are two examinations, one set by the school and one set externally. In Romania, after it is set within the school, the regional education authorities must approve the examination.

In most pre-accession countries, the teachers decide on the final grade that appears on the certificate awarded at the end of lower secondary level. However, in Latvia and Lithuania, teachers mark pupils' scripts according to the marking scheme defined by a national body. In Romania, external examiners award the final grade.

FIGURE E15: CERTIFICATION AT THE END OF GENERAL LOWER SECONDARY EDUCATION OR COMPULSORY FULL-TIME EDUCATION, 1997/98	
THE CERTIFICATE IS AWARDED ON THE BASIS OF	
a final examination	**D** (in certain *Länder* for the *Realschule*), **IRL, NL, P, LI, RO**
the grades and work over the year	**B fr, B de, D** (most *Länder*), **EL, E, L, A, FIN, S, BG, HU, PL, SI**
a final examination and the grades and work over the year	**DK** (optional final examination), **F, I, UK, IS, NO, EE, LV, LT, CY**
WHEN THERE IS AN EXAMINATION, IT IS	
Written	**F, IRL, NL** (*centraal examen*), **P, UK (E/W, NI), EE, LV, CY**
Written and oral	**DK, D** (in certain *Länder* for the *Realschule*), **I, NL** (*schoolexamen*), **UK (SC), IS, LI, NO, LT, RO**
WHEN THERE IS A WRITTEN EXAMINATION, IT IS SET	
by the school (internally)	**NL** (*schoolexamen*), **P, IS, LI, EE, CY**
by the school but under the mediation of an external authority	**D** (in certain *Länder* for the *Realschule*), **I, RO**
by an external body	**DK, D** (in certain *Länder* for the *Realschule*), **F, IRL, NL** (*centraal examen*), **UK, IS, NO, EE, LV, LT**
WHEN THERE IS AN ORAL EXAMINATION, IT IS SET	
by the school (internally)	**DK, D** (in certain *Länder* for the *Realschule*), **NL** (*schoolexamen*), **IS, LI**
by the school but under the mediation of an external authority	**I, UK (SC), NO, RO**
by an external body	**UK (E/W, NI), LT**
THE FINAL GRADE IS AWARDED BY	
only the pupil's teachers	**B, D** (most *Länder*), **EL, E, L, A, P, FIN, S, LI, BG, HU, PL, SI, CY**
the teachers, but weighted by an external grade	**DK, D** (in certain *Länder* for the *Realschule*), **F** (work of 2 years and examination), **I, IS, NO, EE**
the teachers, on the basis of criteria defined by an external body	**NL, LV, LT**
external examiners	**IRL, UK, RO**

Source: Eurydice.

Additional notes

Belgium (B nl): At the end of the second stage of secondary education, a certificate is awarded on the basis of written and oral tests (set by the school) and the work done over the year.
Netherlands: The final grade is the average of the results obtained by the pupil in the two examinations (internal and external).
United Kingdom (E/W, NI): A range of assessment methods may contribute to the final grades, including the assessment of specific work during the course, but written examinations predominate.
Liechtenstein: The final examination is compulsory for the *Realschule* and optional for the *Oberschule*.
Estonia: From 1999, written examinations will be set by an external body.
Poland: From 1999/2000 (based on the law of 8 January 1999), a 3-year course at the *gymnasium* will be provided for pupils between the ages of 13 and 16. Pupils will be assessed through external examinations at the end of these three years.

CERTIFICATION AT THE END
—————— OF GENERAL UPPER SECONDARY EDUCATION ——————

In all countries, a certificate is awarded to students who complete general upper secondary education and have met the set requirements. This certificate is normally a minimum admission requirement for tertiary education.

In the vast majority of the countries of the EU and of the EFTA/EEA, this certificate is awarded on the basis of the results obtained by the student in a final examination. However, in Belgium, Spain and Sweden, the certificate is awarded on the basis of continuous assessment during the final year or years of general secondary education. In a number of countries (Denmark, Germany, Greece, Italy, United Kingdom, Iceland, Liechtenstein and Norway), the certificate is awarded on the basis of the results of the final examination and the work over the final year or years. In Finland, students receive two certificates, one based on the work throughout the upper secondary school, the other on the grades obtained in the matriculation examination.

In the majority of the countries of the EU and of the EFTA/EEA, when a final examination is set, it is in two parts (written and oral). At this level of education, the written examination is very often compiled by a body external to the school, although it is still sometimes administered by the institution. However, in Greece and Iceland, the final written examination is set by a teacher or a team of teachers within the school. In Austria, the chairman of the examination committee selects the examination questions from those proposed by school's teachers. In Portugal, the students take two written examinations, one internal and one external.

In the majority of countries where the final examination is in two parts (written and oral), these two parts are organized in the same manner, either within the school or by an external body. In the Netherlands, the final examination consists of two tests: an internal test (*schoolexamen*), which is oral and/or written and set and marked by the teacher, and an external test (*centraal examen*), which is written, set by an external body and corrected by the teachers according to the standards established by the external body.

In several countries, the teachers in the school decide on the grade to be given to the student and on whether the certificate can be awarded. In some countries, the final grade is awarded by a jury or by examiners from outside the school. In Italy and Luxembourg, external examiners award the final grade taking into account the results obtained by the student in the external examination and the work over the year. Finally, in Denmark, Germany, Finland and Norway, the certificate gives the grades obtained by the student in the final examination (for the subjects assessed) and the results of the work of the final year or years (for the other subjects). In the Netherlands and Portugal, the final grade is the average of the results in the two examinations (internal and external). In the United Kingdom, the final grade may take account of internally marked coursework and grades achieved for examinations set externally.

In all the pre-accession countries, the awarding of the certificate at the end of general upper secondary level depends - at least partly - on the results obtained in a final examination. In Bulgaria, Estonia, Latvia, Lithuania and Cyprus, the marks and the work over the year are also taken into account. In Hungary and Poland, a general secondary school leaving certificate can be awarded without a final examination based on the student's results over the year, but this does not allow the student access to tertiary education.

The final examination includes a written part and an oral part in all the pre-accession countries with the exception of Bulgaria and Cyprus, where it is mainly written. In these countries, with the exception of the Czech Republic and Slovakia, the written examination is set by an external body. In Bulgaria, Latvia, Hungary and Poland, external authorities set the written part. Each school is responsible for the oral part (under the supervision of an external examiner in Latvia and Hungary).

The teachers award the grade that appears on the certificate in the Czech Republic, Poland and Slovakia. In contrast, in Romania and Slovenia external examiners give the grade. In Estonia, internal tests are graded by the teachers while external tests are marked by the external examiners. In Latvia, external examiners award a mark for the subjects assessed by centralized exams and for the other subjects the teachers correct the papers on the basis of criteria established by an external body. In the other countries, the student's teachers award the final grade taking into account the results of the external examination and the work over the year.

FIGURE E16: CERTIFICATION AT THE END OF GENERAL UPPER SECONDARY EDUCATION, 1997/98

Final grade based only on the marks and the work over the year

Final grade based on the work over the year and an internal final examination

Final grade combining internal assessment and an external (or externally mediated) final exam

Final grade based only on an external final examination

LI   CY

Source: Eurydice.

Additional notes

Denmark: The data relate to the certificate obtained at the end of the *Gymnasium*. The certificate also contains marks for the work over the year. No certificate is issued if the leaving examination has not been passed.
Germany: In 7 *Länder*, the *Schulaufsichtsbehörde* (school supervisory authority) set the topics for the written examination.
Italy: The examination at the end of upper secondary level will be reformed from 1998/99. Half of the jury will be external examiners and half will be teachers from the school.
Finland: All students receive a leaving certificate; the final grades of this certificate are awarded, by the school, on the basis of the grades and work throughout the whole upper secondary school. The students who have passed the matriculation examination receive a certificate of matriculation. These two certificates are not exclusive alternatives; both have a recognized status and either of the certificates can be taken into account when applying for future studies.
Sweden: The final grades are based on the work over the three years of upper secondary education. There are national tests which are used for monitoring at school and national level. It is voluntary for the schools to use these tests, but as from 2000/2001, the national tests will be made compulsory.
United Kingdom (E/W, NI): The students take external qualifications on a single subject basis. The final grade is awarded on the basis of external final examinations and may also take into account externally controlled assessment of specific work during the course.
Hungary: The situation presented concerns the *Gimnáziumi Érettségi Bizonyítvány* certificate.
Poland: Written examinations for the *matura* certificate are set by the regional education authorities, but the teachers are responsible for the assessment and awarding of marks.

Explanatory note

In the category 'Final grade combining internal assessment and an external (or externally mediated) final exam', the internal assessment can mean a final internal test or an evaluation of the marks obtained or the coursework done during the year.

FIGURE E17: CERTIFICATION AT THE END OF GENERAL UPPER SECONDARY EDUCATION, 1997/98

THE CERTIFICATE IS AWARDED ON THE BASIS OF	
a final examination	**F, IRL, L, NL, A, P, FIN** (*Matriculation Examination*), **CZ, HU** (*Gimnáziumi Érettségi Bizonyítvány*), **PL** (*Świadectwo maturalne*), **RO, SI, SK**
the grades and work over the year	**B** (assessment of two final years), **E** (continuous assessment), **FIN** (*leaving certificate*), **S, HU** (*Gimnáziumi Bizonyítvány*), **PL** (*Świadectwo ukónczenia liceum ogólnokształcącego*)
a final examination and the grades and work over the year	**DK, D, EL, I, UK, IS, LI, NO, BG, EE, LV, LT, CY**
WHEN THERE IS AN EXAMINATION, IT IS	
Written	**EL, IRL, NL** (*centraal examen*), **P, FIN** (*Matriculation Examination*), **UK (E/W, NI), BG, CY**
Written and oral	**DK, D, F, I, L, NL** (*schoolexamen*), **A, UK (SC), IS, LI, NO, CZ, EE, LV, LT, HU** (*Gimnáziumi Érettségi Bizonyítvány*), **PL, RO, SI, SK**
WHEN THERE IS A WRITTEN EXAMINATION, IT IS SET	
by the school (internally)	**EL, NL** (*schoolexamen*), **P, IS, CZ, EE, SK**
by the school but under the mediation of an external authority	**D** (in some *Länder*), **A, LI**
by an external body	**DK, D** (in some *Länder*), **F, IRL, I, L, NL** (*centraal examen*), **P, FIN** (*Matriculation Examination*), **UK, NO, BG, EE, LV, LT, HU** (*Gimnáziumi Érettségi Bizonyítvány*), **PL, RO, SI, CY**
WHEN THERE IS AN ORAL EXAMINATION, IT IS SET	
by the school (internally)	**DK, NL** (*schoolexamen*), **IS, CZ, EE, PL, SK**
by the school but under the mediation of an external authority	**D, A, UK (SC), LI, NO, LV, HU** (*Gimnáziumi Érettségi Bizonyítvány*)
by an external body	**F, I, L, UK (E/W, NI), EE, LT, RO, SI**
THE FINAL GRADE IS AWARDED BY	
only the student's teachers	**B, EL, E, FIN** (*leaving certificate*), **S, IS, CZ, HU** (*Gimnáziumi Bizonyítvány*), **PL, SK**
the teachers, but weighted by an external grade	**DK** (oral), **D** (results in *Abitur*), **A, P** (average), **FIN** (*Matriculation Examination*), **LI, NO** (marks obtained in course work + in the examination), **BG** (marks in 3 final years + in the examination), **EE, HU** (*Gimnáziumi Érettségi Bizonyítvány*), **CY** (marks of the year + final examination)
the teachers, on the basis of criteria defined by an external body	**NL, LV, LT**
external examiners	**DK** (written), **F** (jury), **IRL, I** (jury), **L, UK, LV** (for centralized examinations), **RO, SI**

Source: Eurydice.

<u>Additional notes</u>

Italy: In 1998/99, a new final upper secondary education examination came into force. It includes three written tests and one oral test. The first two written tests are set by an external body; the third written test and the oral test are set by the school. The final grade is awarded by the student's teachers and an external examination board.
Netherlands: The final grade is the average of the results obtained by the student in the two examinations (internal and external).
Austria: The final grades are awarded by the matriculation examination committee including the chairman (external authority).
Finland: The external examination is first marked by the teacher and then assessed by the National Matriculation Examination Board.
United Kingdom (E/W, NI): A range of assessment methods may contribute to the final grades, including the assessment of specific work during the course, but written examinations predominate.
Iceland: In a few schools there are also external examiners.

PARTICIPATION RATES DECLINE GRADUALLY
AT THE END OF COMPULSORY EDUCATION

Figure E18 shows the evolution of participation rates in education – overall and by gender – observed at four different points in time: one year before the end of compulsory education, at the end of compulsory education and one year and two years years after the end of that period.

Compulsory education generally comes to an end with completion of the lower secondary level or during the upper secondary level. Compulsory education limits vary from one country to another (see Figure B1) and should be kept in mind when analysing this indicator.

In the EU and the EFTA/EEA as a whole, participation rates decline gradually at the end of compulsory education: enrolment decreases by around 10% each year. The extent of the decrease varies however from one country to another. Participation rates decline particularly slowly in France, Ireland, Italy, Austria, Sweden and Norway; in those countries, they still exceed 80% at the end of the second year after the end of compulsory education. On the contrary, the fall is sharper in Germany, Portugal and the United Kingdom and rates go below 50% during the third year. In a third group of countries (Greece, Luxembourg and Finland), participation rates go up one year after the end of compulsory schooling, before decreasing again. The sharpest decrease is observed during the first year in Belgium, the Netherlands, Austria, Portugal, the United Kingdom, Iceland and Liechtenstein. The decrease is sharper during the second year in Germany and during the third year in the other countries.

In all pre-accession countries, the reduction accelerates over time and is thus the sharpest during the third year. The phenomenon is most obvious in Hungary; two years after the end of compulsory education, only 40% of girls and boys are still in education. Participation rates diminish very slowly in Poland and Slovenia. The percentages of the three Baltic countries decrease gradually but sharply.

In most EU and EFTA/EEA countries, girls stay in education slightly longer than boys. Two years after the end of compulsory schooling, female participation rates are up to 10% higher than males'. This is the case for Belgium, Spain, Ireland and Luxembourg. In contrast, in the Netherlands, Austria and Portugal, male participation rates decrease less quickly than females'. In Denmark, France, Sweden and Norway, rates change in a similar way for both genders.

In all pre-accession countries (for which data are available), girls stay in education longer than boys. The largest gender differences for remaining in education are observed in Latvia (13%) and Lithuania (11%) and the smallest in Hungary (less than 1%) and Poland (2%).

FIGURE E18: PARTICIPATION RATES, OVERALL AND BROKEN DOWN BY SEX, AT THE END OF COMPULSORY EDUCATION, AS A PERCENTAGE, 1996/97

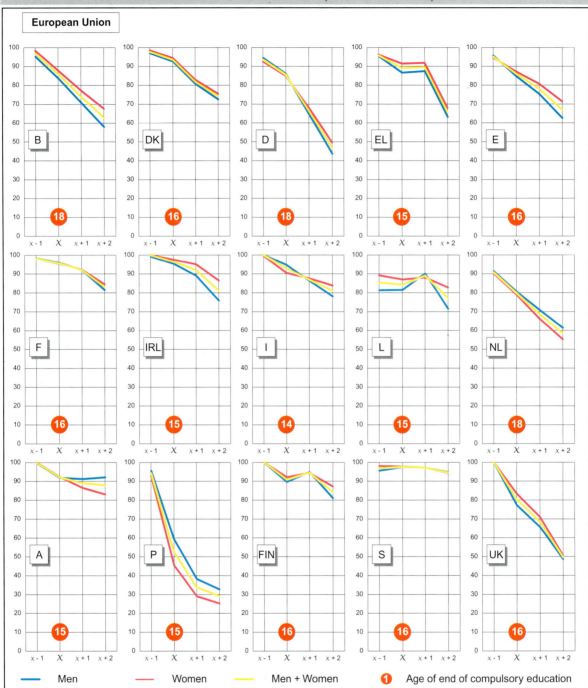

European Union

── Men	── Women	── Men + Women

① Age of end of compulsory education

Source: Eurostat, UOE and population statistics.

Additional notes

Luxembourg: Data do not include students enrolled in non subsidized private education, international schools nor residents studying abroad.
Liechtenstein: 1995/96.

Explanatory note

In the countries where compulsory schooling is continued by part-time education, the part-time limit is used in calculations. x corresponds to the age marking the end of the compulsory education period.

FIGURE E18 (CONTINUED): PARTICIPATION RATES, OVERALL AND BROKEN DOWN BY SEX, AT THE END OF COMPULSORY EDUCATION, AS A PERCENTAGE, 1996/97

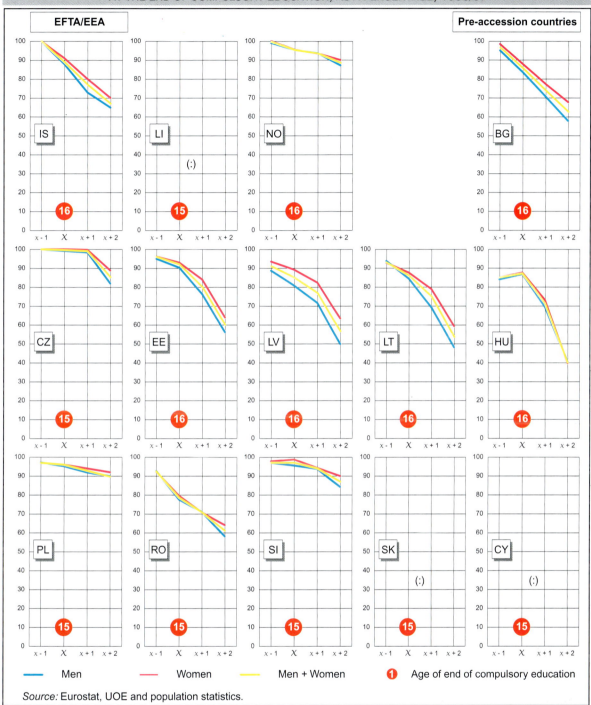

EFTA/EEA

Pre-accession countries

— Men   — Women   — Men + Women   ● Age of end of compulsory education

Source: Eurostat, UOE and population statistics.

T E R T I A R Y   E D U C A T I O N

ALMOST 15 MILLION STUDENTS IN EUROPE

More than 12 million students are enrolled in tertiary education in the European Union, which is 15% of all pupils and students enrolled in the educational system.

Among EU and EFTA/EEA countries, the proportion of students studying in tertiary education as a percentage of all those in education is relatively high in Greece, Spain (18%), Finland (19%) and Norway (17%). The low percentages found in Luxembourg, Liechtenstein and to a smaller extent in Iceland can be explained by the number of students studying abroad.

The proportions of students in tertiary education in pre-accession countries are lower than those in the EU. They are below 10% in the Czech Republic, Hungary, Romania, Slovakia. The low percentage in Cyprus is due to a large number of students studying abroad. Bulgaria is the only country with a value comparable to the European average (16%).

The rate of uptake of tertiary education has been calculated in relation to the total number of pupils and students. So it is important to view these percentages in the context of the educational structure (variable length of compulsory education and tertiary education, for example), the number of places available in tertiary education institutions and demographic variations.

FIGURE F1: PROPORTION OF STUDENTS IN TERTIARY EDUCATION (ISCED 5, 6, 7), IN THOUSANDS AND AS A PERCENTAGE OF ALL PUPILS AND STUDENTS, 1996/97

European Union															
EU	B	DK	D	EL	E	F	IRL	I	L	NL	A	P	FIN	S	UK
12 266	361	180	2 132	363	1 684	2 063	135	1 893	2	469	241	351	226	275	1 891
15%	14%	15%	13%	18%	18%	14%	13%	17%	3%	13%	15%	15%	19%	13%	13%

EFTA/EEA				Pre-accession countries											
IS	LI	NO		BG	CZ	EE	LV	LT	HU	PL	RO	SI	SK		CY
8	0	185		263	196	39	62	84	203	927	354	53	102		10
10%	2%	17%		16%	9%	11%	12%	11%	9%	10%	8%	13%	8%		6%

Source: Eurostat, UOE.

Additional notes

Germany: ISCED 7 is excluded.
Luxembourg: The majority of students study abroad.
Iceland: Very few ISCED 7 programmes are provided in the country. Only full-time students are included. 1655 students received a student loan to study in foreign universities.
Liechtenstein: 1995/96; the majority of students study abroad.
Poland: Only ISCED 6 students are included.
Romania and **Slovenia**: ISCED 7 is excluded.
Cyprus: A large number of students study abroad.

Explanatory note

Tertiary education is treated globally in this chapter: the different types of education (both full-time and part-time, university and non-university) and the different ISCED levels (ISCED 5, 6 and 7) are considered as a whole.

The total population in education referred to in this indicator is the total number of pupils and students enrolled in the country's educational system.

INCREASING STUDENT NUMBERS
DURING THE LAST TWENTY YEARS

Figure F2 illustrates, for EU and EFTA/EEA countries, the evolution in the number of students enrolled in tertiary education since 1975. It is shown by an index of the growth of student numbers based on the reference year 1975/76. The data should be interpreted with caution: the stabilisation or decrease in figures might only reflect a population diminution.

In the EU, on average, the number of students in tertiary education has more than doubled over the last twenty years. In Portugal, 4 times as many students were enrolled in 1997 than in 1975; it is the country with the greatest growth. The increase is also very clear in Greece, Spain and Ireland (number of students has tripled). The slowest growth is observed in Germany and the Netherlands (1.6 times). The values were already high in 1975/76, however. In Iceland, the number of enrolees in tertiary education has increased by a factor of 2.5 in two decades and in Norway by 2.5 in one decade.

Over the last reference year (1996/97), while the increase continued in most countries, numbers tended to stabilize in Belgium, Germany and Austria and to decrease in France and the Netherlands.

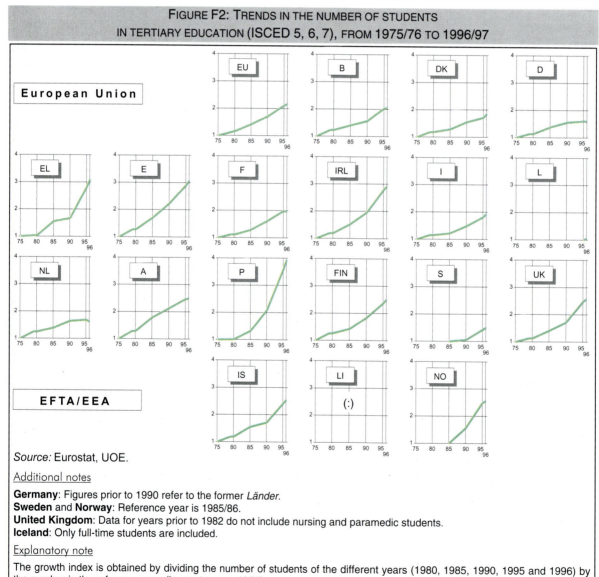

FIGURE F2: TRENDS IN THE NUMBER OF STUDENTS IN TERTIARY EDUCATION (ISCED 5, 6, 7), FROM 1975/76 TO 1996/97

Source: Eurostat, UOE.

Additional notes

Germany: Figures prior to 1990 refer to the former *Länder*.
Sweden and **Norway**: Reference year is 1985/86.
United Kingdom: Data for years prior to 1982 do not include nursing and paramedic students.
Iceland: Only full-time students are included.

Explanatory note

The growth index is obtained by dividing the number of students of the different years (1980, 1985, 1990, 1995 and 1996) by the number in the reference year (in most cases, 1975).

—— UNEVEN DISTRIBUTION OF STUDENTS ACROSS THE REGIONS ——

Analysis of the map shows large regional disparities in the percentage of enrolees at tertiary level.

The highest percentages of students in tertiary education (between 21 and 27%) are found in Belgium in the Bruxelles-Brussel region, in Germany in the *Land* of Hamburg, in Spain in the region of Madrid, in Italy in the regions of Emilia-Romagna, Centro and Lazio, in Eastern Austria and Finland in the Uusimaa region. These are regions with large cities, probably well endowed with tertiary education institutions and facilities.

Relatively high proportions of students are also found in the northern European regions and around the Mediterranean basin.

FIGURE F3: TERTIARY EDUCATION STUDENTS (ISCED 5, 6, 7) AS A PERCENTAGE OF ALL PUPILS AND STUDENTS, BY NUTS 1 AND NUTS 2 REGIONS, 1996/97

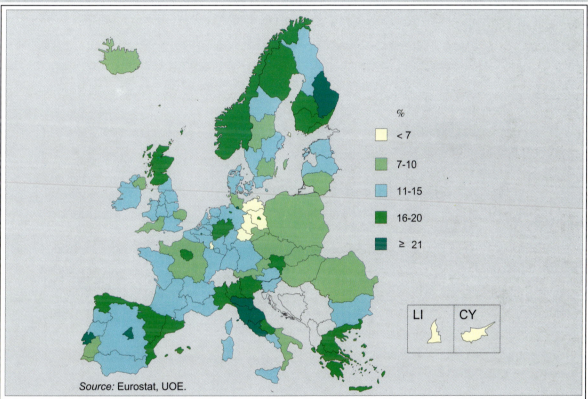

%
- < 7
- 7-10
- 11-15
- 16-20
- ≥ 21

Source: Eurostat, UOE.

Additional notes

Greece and **Netherlands**: Only data from the national level (NUTS 0) are presented.
Portugal: 1995/96.

Explanatory note

For most Member States, the nomenclature used here is that of NUTS 1, which is the largest of the regional units. NUTS 2 is however used for Portugal, Finland and Sweden. For the EFTA/EEA countries and the pre-accession countries, only national data are presented.

For the definition of the NUTS classification, please refer to the definition of statistical tools at the beginning of the book.

The total population in education referred to in this indicator is the total number of pupils and students enrolled in the country's educational system.

LIMITING THE NUMBER OF PLACES ON ADMISSION: FROM FREE ACCESS TO CENTRALIZED SELECTION

In all EU, EFTA/EEA and pre-accession countries, the minimum requirement for gaining access to tertiary education is generally an upper secondary certificate or equivalent. In most countries, other admission procedures may be added to this, such as passing an entrance examination or competition, submitting a personal record of achievement or attending an interview. Such procedures are usually used to limit the number of admissions, either because the number of candidates exceeds the capacity of the institution or because of a national *numerus clausus* system.

Selection procedures and limits on the numbers of places available contribute significantly to the regulation of the size of the student population. The political will to increase the population in tertiary education is matched by the need for financial management of this increased population. The reasons for controlling the number of places available can of course also be related to labour market conditions, when too many – or too few – young people are graduating in particular subjects relative to the jobs available.

Selection procedures vary across Europe and according to the course chosen; they are presented in detail in a table in the annex.

Figure F4 presents the three main models:

- A *numerus clausus* is set at national level. In such cases, the government limits the number of places available and exercises direct control over the selection procedure. The *numerus clausus* may be laid down in relation to courses in certain subjects or all courses.

- The institutions themselves decide on selection procedures to limit the number of places available. Institutions are free to decide to apply these procedures, either based on their capacity or on criteria defined at central level. Limitation can be applied for certain courses or for all courses. Moreover, regardless of the number of places available, institutions can decide to select students on the basis of ability. This happens particularly in certain art, technical or medical courses.

- Finally, the certificate awarded on satisfactory completion of upper secondary education or an equivalent qualification may be the only requirement for admission to some or all courses. In such cases, admission is free and institutions accept all applicants.

In some EU and EFTA/EEA countries, places are limited in all courses. Limitation and selection are decided directly at national level in Greece.

The selection procedure is applied by institutions, according to the number of places available and/or to national criteria, in Denmark, Spain, Ireland, Portugal, Finland, Sweden, the United Kingdom and Norway. In the four latter countries, this selection procedure also takes account of national standards limiting the total number of enrolments accepted or the number of graduates. In the United Kingdom and Norway, universities and other tertiary education institutions, as autonomous institutions, determine their own admissions policies. However, planning is undertaken centrally for overall student numbers. Applicants may make up choices of institution and course (six in the United Kingdom, 15 in Norway) on a single application form. In the United Kingdom this is sent to each of the institutions concerned via the Universities and Colleges Admissions Service (UCAS). UCAS processes applications on behalf of all United Kingdom universities and most colleges of tertiary education. Each institution makes its own decision on offers of places. In the United Kingdom, firm offers of places are normally made in August following the publication of examination results; applicants who have failed to secure a place, or who have applied late, can reapply for those courses which still have vacancies. In Ireland, there is a similar system of admissions. The institution determines the number of places and the admission requirements, and application for almost all full-time undergraduate courses is made through a Central Applications Office. In Spain, the national university entrance examination is in principle not compulsory for certain university courses. However, since the capacity of the institutions is often lower than the demand for places, they give priority to those students who have passed the entrance examination.

FIGURE F4: LIMITS ON THE NUMBER OF PLACES AVAILABLE IN MOST BRANCHES OF PRIVATE, GRANT-AIDED AND PUBLIC TERTIARY EDUCATION, 1997/98

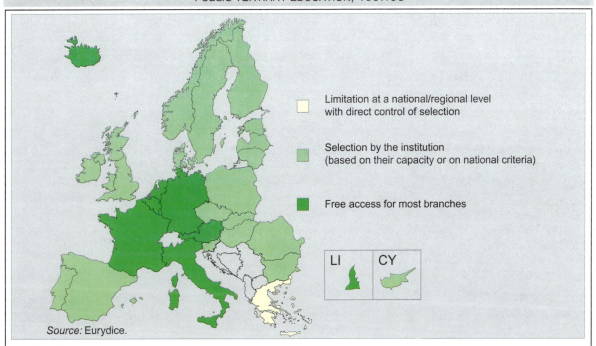

Limitation at a national/regional level with direct control of selection

Selection by the institution (based on their capacity or on national criteria)

Free access for most branches

LI   CY

Source: Eurydice.

Additional notes

Belgium (B fr): A *numerus clausus* system is being introduced for medicine.
Belgium (B nl): Access to some courses requires passing an entrance examination organized by the government (courses in medicine and dentistry) or by the universities (engineering).
Denmark: There is a *numerus clausus* for a few courses, e. g. medicine and education.
German, Italy, Austria and **Iceland**: Students generally have free access to universities, but some non-university institutions apply selection procedures.
Portugal: The 1997 law that reformed the education system introduced the possibility of institutions setting aptitude tests in addition to the national examination set at the end of secondary education, but these tests will not be applied until 2000/2001.
Lithuania: Based on a government decision, from 1998 the selection procedure organized by each institution must be approved by the Ministry of Education and Science.
Poland: The number of places is limited at central level by the Ministry of Health and Social Welfare for access to the medical faculty.
Cyprus: The system of access to tertiary education is currently under review. At the present time, to be eligible for the university entrance examination students must pass the examination taken at the end of upper secondary education. Under the terms of the reform, these two exams are expected to be replaced by one.

Finally, in other countries there are no entrance requirements for most courses, and in particular for general university courses. In Belgium, where there is a very strong tradition of free access, any attempt to introduce an entrance examination meets with resistance. It is only for courses in applied science and for certain courses in medicine, dentistry and architecture (university courses) in the Flemish Community of Belgium that institutions require students to take an entrance examination. In Austria, universities (except *Universitäten der Künste*) are legally obliged to admit all students who register, although the *Fachhochschulen* and some academies are more selective. In the majority of countries where the principle of free access is largely applied, admission to certain courses of study is regulated. Depending on the course or the level of study, the conditions for admission are set either by the institutions based on their capacity (Germany, the Netherlands and Iceland) or by the government by means of a *numerus clausus* system (France, Italy and the Netherlands).

In Italy, the universities decide which faculties will offer either open or limited access. In tertiary non-university education, access to courses is systematically based on admission procedures defined by the institutions themselves. In Luxembourg, only access to pre-primary and primary teacher training is limited on the basis of a decision taken at national level. In the Netherlands, all branches of tertiary education have open access in principle. However, the number of admissions can be limited at national level when the number of people with a qualification exceeds the labour market needs. Such a decision can also be taken by the institution when the number of applicants exceeds the places available. For some courses, the minister can impose a requirement that candidates must have studied one or two specific subjects during secondary education.

In the pre-accession countries, the number of places available is limited for all courses. In Cyprus, university entrance examinations are organized by the Ministry of Education and Culture. Institutions decide on the number of places available for the different faculties. There is no limit to the number of students allowed to take the entrance examinations for a particular faculty. In the Czech Republic, Hungary, Poland and Slovakia, for all courses the institutions decide on the number of places available and the selection procedures. In Estonia and Romania, each institution decides on the number of places available and the selection procedures, but the government sets the number of places for which it provides funding. In Bulgaria, Latvia and Lithuania, each institution organizes the selection of students taking account of the national standards limiting the number of enrolments. In Slovenia, the number of places available is decided by the institutions but approved by the Government. The admission procedures are organized by the institutions.

ERASMUS: STUDENT MOBILITY ATTRACTS INCREASING NUMBERS OF APPLICANTS

Support for student mobility, contributing to the creation of a European dimension in education, is one of the major strengths of the Socrates programme, which Erasmus has been part of since 1995. New managerial arrangements were made with the advent of the Socrates programme so that all Inter-university Cooperation Programmes (ICPs) have been, from 1995 onwards, carried out by the tertiary educational institutions through an 'Institutional Contract' (IC) established with the European Commission. Following these new arrangements, Erasmus has progressively extended to include more and more universities (more than 1 600 institutions took part in 1998/99) and geographical areas (new non-Member States have joined the initial group of 18 EU/EEA countries, and others are asking to be included). The programme now makes it possible for tertiary level students to study for between three months and one year in one of the 30 participating countries (the 15 countries of the EU, Iceland, Liechtenstein, Norway, most central and eastern European countries and Cyprus). This period abroad is part of the student's study programme at his/her home university. The grant contributes to cover the extra cost of staying and studying abroad.

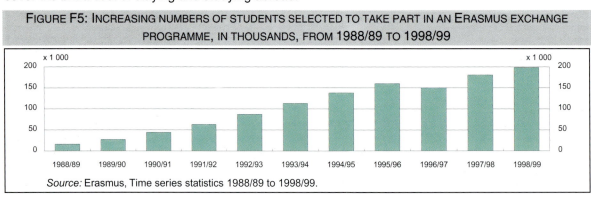

FIGURE F5: INCREASING NUMBERS OF STUDENTS SELECTED TO TAKE PART IN AN ERASMUS EXCHANGE PROGRAMME, IN THOUSANDS, FROM 1988/89 TO 1998/99

Source: Erasmus, Time series statistics 1988/89 to 1998/99.

As the Figure F5 shows, the demand for student mobility is growing constantly (by 8 to 10% a year). The critical threshold of 100 000 was passed by the middle of the decade 1989 – 1999. From 27 000 available places in 1989/90, numbers have swelled to 181 000 available places in 1998/99.

FIGURE F6: THE GROWTH IN THE BUDGETS ALLOTTED TO ERASMUS STUDENTS, IN MILLIONS OF ECU, FROM 1988/89 TO 1998/99

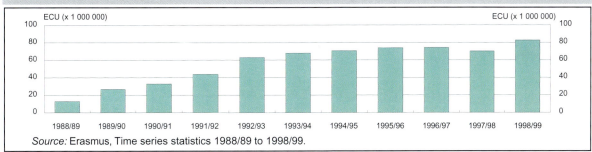

Source: Erasmus, Time series statistics 1988/89 to 1998/99.

Erasmus takes 40% of the total budget of the Socrates programme (all Erasmus activities). The proportion of the Erasmus budget devoted to student mobility is approximately 60%, even though demand eased in 1997/98: 74 000 MECU in 1995/96, 74 300 MECU in 1996/97, 70 000 MECU in 1997/98, 82 700 MECU in 1998/99. However the increase in the Erasmus budget devoted to student mobility does not match the soaring demand, therefore the level of the grant is lower and lower. Moreover the cost of staying and studying abroad is very heavy for students coming from countries where public support for mobility is weak or even non existent, as well as for their families as the survey on the socio-economic background of Erasmus students shows. This survey has been realized by the European Commission in 1998/99 in cooperation with the Socrates/Erasmus National Agencies.

FIGURE F7: PERCENTAGE OF TERTIARY LEVEL STUDENTS SELECTED TO GO ABROAD AND BE RECEIVED WITHIN THE ERASMUS PROGRAMME, 1997/98

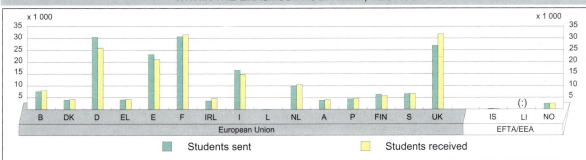

	European Union										
	B	**DK**	**D**	**EL**	**E**	**F**	**IRL**	**I**	**L**	**NL**	**A**
Sent	7.59	3.96	30.54	4.08	23.16	30.68	3.57	16.56	0.04	10	3.78
Received	8.07	4.26	25.96	4.33	21.23	31.54	4.61	14.72	0.03	10.53	4.03

	European Union (continued)					**EFTA/EEA**		
	P	**FIN**	**S**	**UK**		**IS**	**LI**	**NO**
Sent	4.48	6.34	6.57	26.91		0.25	(:)	2.47
Received	4.70	5.72	6.64	31.79		0.29	(:)	2.53

Source: Erasmus, Times series statistics 1988/89 to 1998/99.

Explanatory note

Between 1990 and 1994, some of the students moving under the Inter-university Cooperation Programmes (ICP) were financed under Action II of the Lingua programme. This action implemented in 1990 aimed to promote foreign language learning at tertiary education level and involved, in particular, future teachers of modern languages. The application and management arrangements in relation to these scholarships were identical to those introduced for Erasmus students. Since 1995, all inter-university Cooperation Programmes were carried out at the tertiary educational institutions through an inter-institutional contract (IC) established with the European Commission. Following these new managerial arrangements, no difference was made from then on between Lingua and Erasmus students.
All the statistics provided in this note are for the numbers of students included in the ICPs approved by the Commission and therefore eligible for an Erasmus travel scholarship.

As the Figure F7 shows, the most active countries remain the four most populous countries of the EU (Germany, Spain, France and the United Kingdom) for obvious quantitative reasons. The language remains a prominent criterion for choosing the destination country: so places in England and Ireland are always most sought after, closely followed by Spain. While Sweden and Finland have made a breakthrough in recent years, this is partly due to the fact that a large number of the courses given there are in English.

——— FEW YOUNG PEOPLE STUDY OUTSIDE THEIR OWN COUNTRY ———

In the EU, on average, a large majority of students pursue tertiary education in their own country: only 2% of young people in the EU study in another Member State or EFTA/EEA country. This number is, however, increasing.

Within the EU, mobility of students in tertiary education is more widespread in Luxembourg (80%), Iceland (17%) and, to a smaller extent, in Greece and Ireland, where it accounts for more than 10% of students. Luxembourg deserves to be mentioned: there is only limited tertiary education provision, which obliges students to study abroad, and therefore, students abroad outnumber students enrolled in Luxembourg.

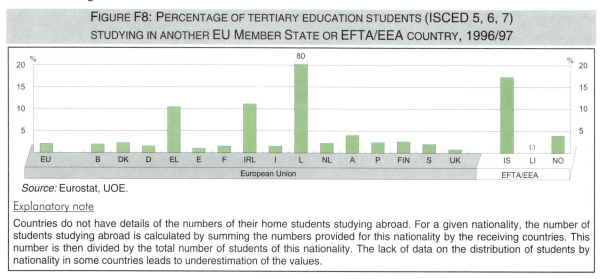

FIGURE F8: PERCENTAGE OF TERTIARY EDUCATION STUDENTS (ISCED 5, 6, 7) STUDYING IN ANOTHER EU MEMBER STATE OR EFTA/EEA COUNTRY, 1996/97

Source: Eurostat, UOE.

Explanatory note

Countries do not have details of the numbers of their home students studying abroad. For a given nationality, the number of students studying abroad is calculated by summing the numbers provided for this nationality by the receiving countries. This number is then divided by the total number of students of this nationality. The lack of data on the distribution of students by nationality in some countries leads to underestimation of the values.

——— REGISTRATION AND TUITION FEES ———

In some countries, tertiary education institutions are run and funded entirely by the public authorities. In other countries, public-sector tertiary education institutions receive a state grant but at the same time receive registration or tuition fees. The expression 'registration fees' is normally used for the payment associated with the enrolment of students and/or the certification of each student, whereas 'tuition fees' refers to contributions to the cost of their education borne by tertiary education institutions.

In virtually half the countries of the EU and of the EFTA/EEA, students do not make any contribution towards the cost of their tertiary education, to which access can therefore be regarded as free of charge. This is the case in Denmark, Greece, Luxembourg, Austria, Finland and Sweden and in Norway. It is also the case in Germany, apart from two *Länder* (Baden-Württemberg and Berlin) where regulations for raising registration fees have been introduced.

In several of these countries (Germany, Austria, Finland, Sweden and Norway), the students have to pay contributions either to a student organization or to organizations that offer support to students, mostly in the form of subsidized services (accommodation, meals, cultural services, etc.).

In the other countries, the students pay registration or tuition fees to the tertiary education institution. This is the case in Belgium, Spain, France, Ireland, Italy, the Netherlands, Portugal, the United Kingdom and Iceland. The amounts can vary from one country to another and, within the same country, from one education sector or course to another.

In all these countries, there are exemptions or other types of assistance for the payment of registration or tuition fees. The assistance can be targeted at particular groups of students (usually students from underprivileged economic backgrounds) or can apply to most students.

In some countries, in addition to registration and tuition fees, students pay an additional contribution to an organization other than the tertiary education institution: a payment to cover medical care in France, a tax paid to the regional bodies which administer all the forms of student support in Italy, and a membership fee to the student organization in Iceland.

FIGURE F9: REGISTRATION AND TUITION FEES AND OTHER PAYMENTS MADE BY STUDENTS ON FULL-TIME UNDERGRADUATE COURSES, PUBLIC SECTOR, 1997/98

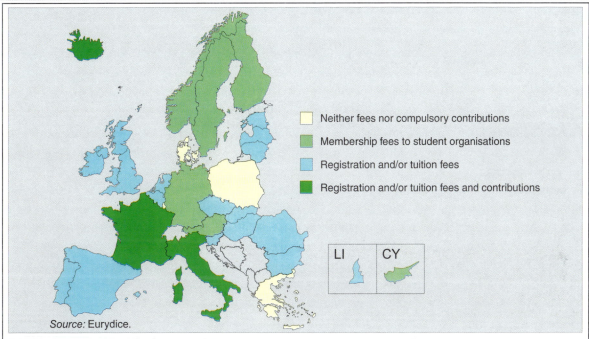

Source: Eurydice.

Additional notes

Germany: In two *Länder* (Baden-Württemberg and Berlin), regulations aimed at raising registration fees have been introduced.
Ireland: Tuition fees for EU nationals on full-time undergraduate courses were abolished in 1996. However a small student service charge is levied to cover examination, student services and other costs.
Netherlands: Statutory tuition fees are covered by the grants/loans received by students who are eligible for student finance under the Student Finance Act (most students).
Finland: Union membership fees are only compulsory in the universities and are optional for students studying in the *Ammattikorkeakoulu* institutions.
United Kingdom: Tertiary education institutions charge tuition fees. However, until 1997/98, these fees were directly paid for most students by the relevant authorities. From 1998/99, most full-time students starting tertiary education courses are required to make a means-tested contribution towards the cost of tuition fees (the maximum amount for 1999/2000 is £1,025).
Bulgaria: From 1999/2000, in addition to registration fees, all students will pay tuition fees.
Latvia: Almost 50% of the students have to pay tuition fees.
Poland: Access to tertiary education day courses is totally free. The only charge made is for entrance examinations. Public tertiary education institutions charge tuition fees for full-time evening courses.
Cyprus: The situation presented on the map applies to the university.

Explanatory note

Figure F9 shows all the compulsory payments (registration fees or tuition fees paid to the tertiary education institutions and/or contributions paid to other bodies) by students who follow full-time undergraduate courses in public-sector institutions. These fees also include any certification fees.

In most pre-accession countries, students pay registration fees to the tertiary education institution. In Bulgaria, Estonia, Latvia, Lithuania, Hungary and Romania, some students have to pay tuition fees and thus contribute towards the funding of their studies. In most cases, these measures are for students who have not obtained a state-subsidized place. In Hungary, tuition fees cannot exceed 20% of the subsidy received by each institution per student. In addition to registration and tuition fees, in Lithuania students pay a contribution to bodies that offer them services (accommodation, meals, etc.). Poland is the only pre-accession country where access to tertiary education day courses is totally free of charge (with the exception of re-enrolment for a course for which the student has not obtained satisfactory results). In Cyprus, the situation varies from institution to institution. Students pay registration fees and/or contributions in certain tertiary education institutions. In other institutions, access is free of charge.

GRANTS AND LOANS

Grants (non-refundable) and loans (to be refunded after the course) are the main forms of financial support offered to students by the public authorities.

During 1997/98, in most countries of the EU and the EFTA/EEA, the same financial support system was applied to students enrolled in all the different types of institutions that offer tertiary level university or non-university education courses. Greece is an exception.

The financial support for students in the countries of the EU and of the EFTA/EEA may be regarded as a continuum ranging from exclusively grant-based systems to exclusively loan-based systems such as the scheme implemented in Iceland. Grants are the most widespread form of support, but many countries also offer loans that are guaranteed and/or subsidized by the State.

In most countries in which loans are obtainable, they are an integral part of support and, together with grants, constitute a combined system. The two components are usually awarded on the same terms, and only students entitled to a measure of support in the form of a grant are entitled to a supplementary loan. In most combined systems, students are generally free to decide whether they will accept the supplementary loan entitlement. An exception to this is found in Germany where students who are eligible for financial assistance are obliged to receive a grant and an interest-free loan in equal proportions, which are regarded as constituting an all-inclusive support package. In some countries, however, the systems of grants and loans are separate and operate independently of each other. The conditions governing their award can therefore be different. Students who are not entitled to a grant may be eligible for a loan. This was the case in the United Kingdom where loans were introduced in the early 1990s. From September 1999, loans will be the only form of support available for the majority of new students. This is also the case in the French Community of Belgium, France and Italy, where only a very small proportion of students have loans (fewer than 1%).

In the Flemish Community of Belgium, Greece, Spain, Ireland, Austria and Portugal, only grants are available. It is important to note that in several countries where the system offers only or mainly grants, the introduction of a system of loans is an issue that is being or has been debated. Thus, in Greece, loans for university students introduced in 1991 were abolished in 1995. In Spain, an experimental loan scheme was devised in 1996 together with guidelines for its introduction but the system has not yet been adopted. Finally, Portugal has introduced a state-subsidized loan system for students that has not been implemented.

FIGURE F10: COMPONENTS OF GRANT AND/OR LOAN SUPPORT TO STUDENTS ON UNDERGRADUATE COURSES, 1997/98

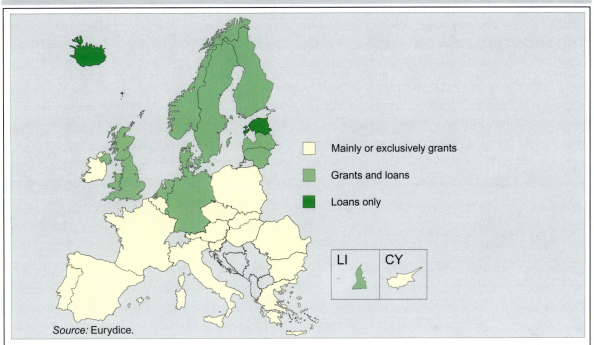

Source: Eurydice.

Additional notes

Portugal: A system of loans has been introduced by legislation but it has not been implemented.
United Kingdom: New arrangements will be in place from September 1999, when maintenance grants will be replaced by loans.
Lithuania: The conditions for the awarding of grants vary according to the institution.
Cyprus: Financial support is granted mainly to students who study at recognized institutions abroad.

Explanatory note

Figure F10 only deals with financial support in the form of grants and/or loans. These financial schemes contribute towards student maintenance, at least in part. Support in kind (provision of goods or services) are excluded. Grant linked to academic results or to specific educational needs have not been included here.

In most pre-accession countries, only grants are awarded to students. However, in Bulgaria and Hungary, the introduction of a loan scheme is under discussion. In Poland and Romania, it has been possible to obtain state-subsidized loans, since 1998/99 and 1999/2000 respectively. In Slovenia, there are plans to reintroduce a combined system of grants and loans that was in operation 25 years ago. In Slovakia, a loans system was introduced in 1997, but fewer than 1% of students are eligible, because there are very strict award criteria.

In Estonia, only loans are available. In Latvia and Lithuania, a system of loans is organized separately and independently from the system of grants. In Cyprus, grants are the main form of financial support. Only a very small percentage of Cypriot students in tertiary education have obtained a loan.

A VERY WIDE AGE RANGE IN TERTIARY EDUCATION

In EU and EFTA/EEA countries, the age range varies greatly from one country to another. Entry to tertiary education occurs later in northern countries.

Peaks in participation rates appear at different ages and the shapes of curves also vary. At one extreme – in Belgium, Greece and Ireland – high participation rates are concentrated between 18-19 years and 23-24 years and peaks occur at 18-19 years of age, reflecting high enrolment in tertiary education and a relatively short duration of study. At the other extreme – in Denmark, Germany and Austria – the width of the curve is larger and participation rates are lower but stable over a longer period, which suggests longer study for a certain number of students or entry into tertiary education at varying ages.

Among pre-accession countries, curves can be classed as of two types: high rates concentrated in lower ages in Bulgaria, Estonia, Latvia, Lithuania, and Slovenia; a more gentle and extended profile in the Czech Republic and Romania on the other hand.

Overall, male and female participation rates in tertiary education follow a similar pattern. They are usually higher for women than for men, especially in Belgium, Spain, France, Finland and Norway. With increasing age male rates catch up or even exceed those of females in some countries. This tendency is particularly marked in Germany, the Netherlands and Austria. In most countries, peak rates can be observed at the same ages for both genders, or there might be a difference of just one year. In Germany and Austria, it is greater (from 2 to 4 years). This can be explained partly by the compulsory military or alternative service for men.

The male/female participation difference is more marked in pre-accession countries, and this is the case up to the age of 23. Female participation rates are clearly higher in Bulgaria, Lithuania and Slovenia. In Bulgaria and Poland, peaks can be observed earlier for females.

FIGURE F11: PARTICIPATION RATES IN TERTIARY EDUCATION (ISCED 5, 6, 7), BY AGE AND BY GENDER, AS A PERCENTAGE, 1996/97

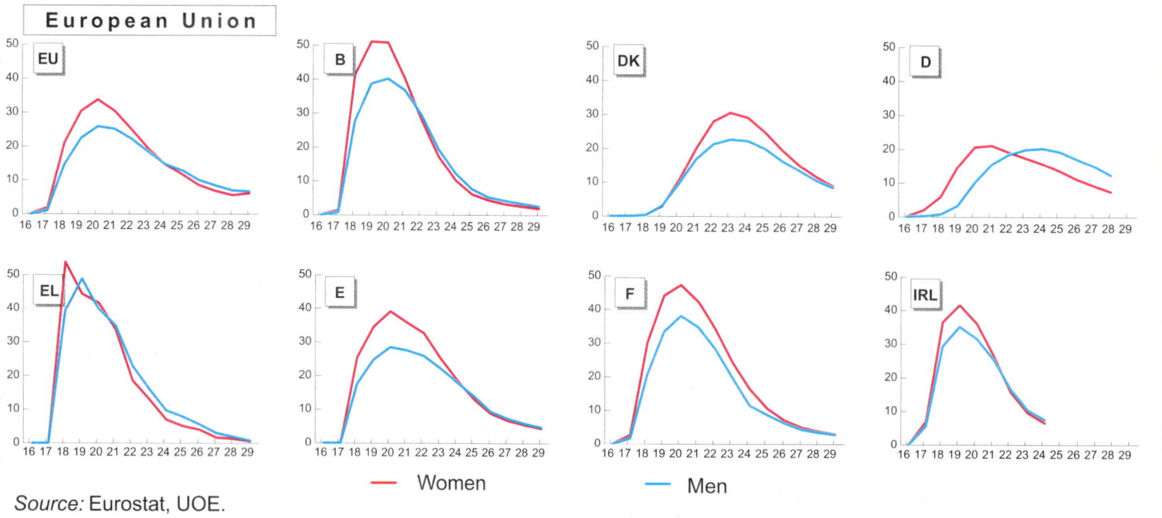

Source: Eurostat, UOE.

Additional notes

Germany: The '29-year-olds' category includes people aged 29 and over.
Ireland: The '25-year-olds' category includes people aged 25 and over.

Explanatory note

Participation rates are calculated separately for men and women.

FIGURE F11 (CONTINUED): PARTICIPATION RATES IN TERTIARY EDUCATION (ISCED 5, 6, 7),
BY AGE AND BY GENDER, AS A PERCENTAGE, 1996/97

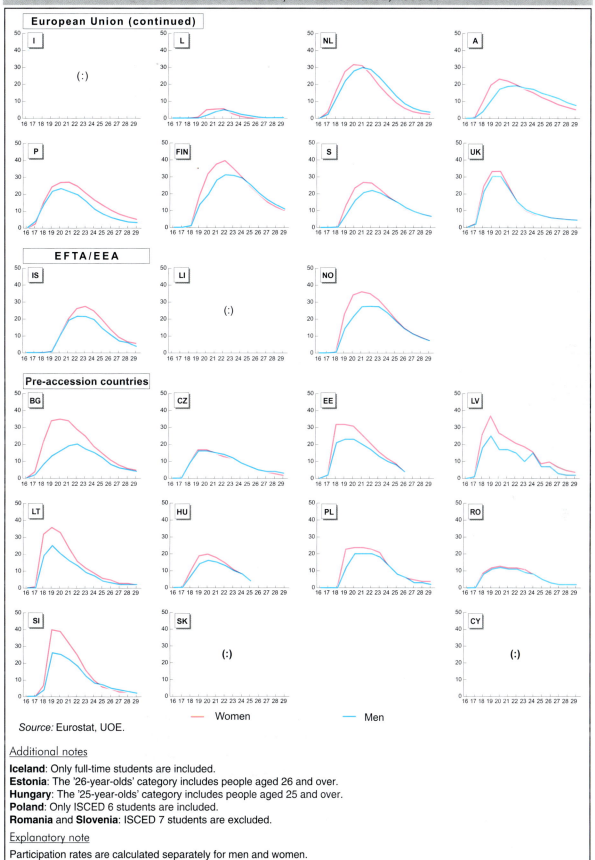

Source: Eurostat, UOE.

Additional notes

Iceland: Only full-time students are included.
Estonia: The '26-year-olds' category includes people aged 26 and over.
Hungary: The '25-year-olds' category includes people aged 25 and over.
Poland: Only ISCED 6 students are included.
Romania and **Slovenia**: ISCED 7 students are excluded.

Explanatory note

Participation rates are calculated separately for men and women.

PROPORTION OF WOMEN STUDENTS
—— IN TERTIARY EDUCATION CONSTANTLY INCREASING ——

Together with the overall increase in student numbers since 1975, there has also been a marked increase in the proportion of female enrolment in tertiary education.

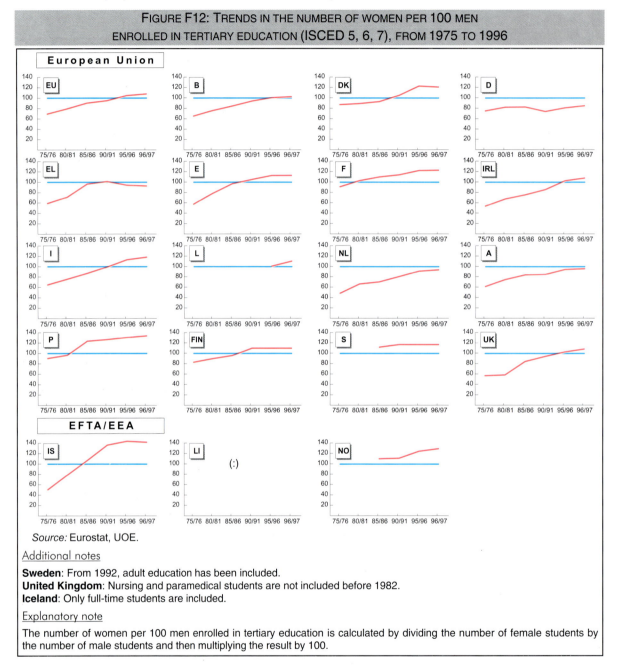

FIGURE F12: TRENDS IN THE NUMBER OF WOMEN PER 100 MEN
ENROLLED IN TERTIARY EDUCATION (ISCED 5, 6, 7), FROM 1975 TO 1996

Source: Eurostat, UOE.

Additional notes

Sweden: From 1992, adult education has been included.
United Kingdom: Nursing and paramedical students are not included before 1982.
Iceland: Only full-time students are included.

Explanatory note

The number of women per 100 men enrolled in tertiary education is calculated by dividing the number of female students by the number of male students and then multiplying the result by 100.

Twenty years ago, women were in the minority in tertiary education in all EU and EFTA/EEA countries. Over time, the proportion of women has increased and they are now in the majority in most countries. Since 1980 there have been more women than men in tertiary education in France and Portugal. It has also been the case in Sweden, Iceland and Norway since 1985. Women students outnumbered men a few years later in Denmark, Spain, Italy, Finland and more recently in Ireland, Luxembourg and the United Kingdom. Although all countries show an increase in the proportion of women students, women remain a minority in Germany, the Netherlands, Austria, and also in Greece where the difference between male and female rates has been minimal since 1985.

PARTICIPATION IN TERTIARY EDUCATION INCREASES TOGETHER WITH PARENTS' EDUCATIONAL LEVEL

Figure F13 compares the rates of participation in tertiary education in young people aged 19 to 24 living with their parents, according to the head of household's educational level.

In the EU as a whole, the tertiary education participation rates increase as the parents' educational level increases. A similar pattern emerges whichever country is considered: proportionally greater numbers of young people from families in which the head of household has a tertiary education qualification participate in tertiary education and proportionately fewer participate from families in which the head of household has completed only primary or lower secondary education. The difference is more marked in Greece and Austria.

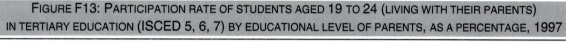

FIGURE F13: PARTICIPATION RATE OF STUDENTS AGED 19 TO 24 (LIVING WITH THEIR PARENTS) IN TERTIARY EDUCATION (ISCED 5, 6, 7) BY EDUCATIONAL LEVEL OF PARENTS, AS A PERCENTAGE, 1997

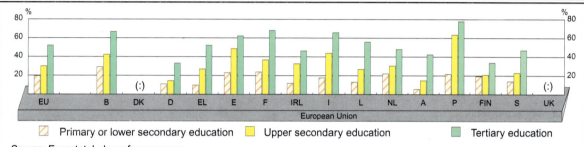

Primary or lower secondary education   Upper secondary education   Tertiary education

Source: Eurostat, Labour force survey.

Explanatory note

The Labour Force Survey (LFS) enables the connection between parents and children to be analysed to the extent that they live in the same household. Students living away from their family and being heads of households themselves are thus not taken into account.

Since a large proportion of United Kingdom students live away from their family, data on educational level of parents could not be collected from the LFS.

TODAY ONE YOUNG PERSON IN FIVE HOLDS A TERTIARY EDUCATION QUALIFICATION

In the EU, 22% of young adults between 30 and 34 years of age hold a tertiary education qualification. However, this percentage conceals major disparities between countries. In Belgium and Sweden, over 29% of those in this age band have a qualification at this level while in Italy, Austria and Portugal, the proportions with such qualifications are under 15%.

FIGURE F14: PROPORTION OF YOUNG PEOPLE AGED BETWEEN 30 AND 34 WITH TERTIARY EDUCATION QUALIFICATIONS (ISCED 5, 6, 7), AS A PERCENTAGE, 1997

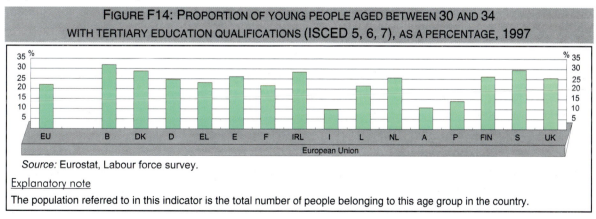

Source: Eurostat, Labour force survey.

Explanatory note

The population referred to in this indicator is the total number of people belonging to this age group in the country.

GRADUATION RATES RISE FROM
GENERATION TO GENERATION

Among the younger generation, the number of people holding a qualification from tertiary education is higher than in older generations. Whereas 21% of EU citizens aged between 35 and 39 have a tertiary education qualification, the proportion for those aged 55-59 years is only 14%.

This trend is apparent throughout the EU and is particularly strong in Greece, Spain and Italy: there are twice as many graduates among the 35-39 age group than among those aged 55-59. In other countries, the age-based differences are less marked since the percentage of people with tertiary education qualifications in the 55-59 age group is relatively high (around 20% in Denmark, Germany and Sweden). In Italy, Austria and Portugal, the proportions of those with qualifications are relatively small across all the age groups considered.

FIGURE F15: PROPORTION OF PEOPLE AGED BETWEEN 35 AND 59 WITH TERTIARY EDUCATION QUALIFICATIONS (ISCED 5, 6, 7), BY AGE GROUP, 1997

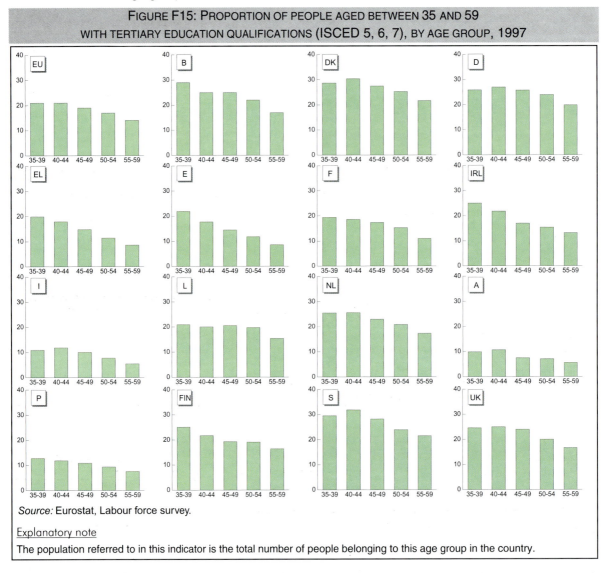

Source: Eurostat, Labour force survey.

Explanatory note

The population referred to in this indicator is the total number of people belonging to this age group in the country.

MORE WOMEN THAN MEN ──── GRADUATE FROM TERTIARY EDUCATION ────

In the EU on average, more women than men graduated from tertiary education in 1997. This is true in all EU countries, except Germany. Portugal has the highest ratio of women to men with tertiary education qualifications (7 women per 4 men). Conversely, in Germany, around 4 women graduate from tertiary education for every 5 men. In Greece, Ireland, the Netherlands and Austria, values are almost equal for both genders.

In pre-accession countries, the predominance of women graduates is clearer still. In only three countries (the Czech Republic, Romania and Slovakia) are values comparable to those observed in the EU.

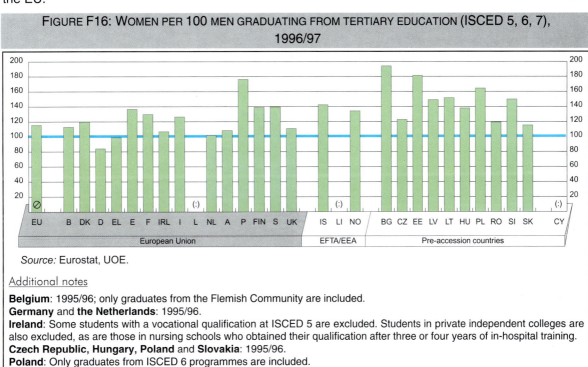

FIGURE F16: WOMEN PER 100 MEN GRADUATING FROM TERTIARY EDUCATION (ISCED 5, 6, 7), 1996/97

Source: Eurostat, UOE.

Additional notes

Belgium: 1995/96; only graduates from the Flemish Community are included.
Germany and **the Netherlands**: 1995/96.
Ireland: Some students with a vocational qualification at ISCED 5 are excluded. Students in private independent colleges are also excluded, as are those in nursing schools who obtained their qualification after three or four years of in-hospital training.
Czech Republic, Hungary, Poland and **Slovakia**: 1995/96.
Poland: Only graduates from ISCED 6 programmes are included.
Romania: Only graduates from the first degree of ISCED 6 are included.

Explanatory notes

The number of female graduates per 100 males is calculated by dividing the total number of female graduates by the total number of male graduates and multiplying the result by 100.

MORE THAN A QUARTER OF THOSE WITH TERTIARY EDUCATION ──── QUALIFICATIONS HAVE STUDIED SOCIAL SCIENCES ────

Analysis of the numbers of graduates per field of study has to take into account enrolment in that field, which is in turn limited by any restrictions on admission (entrance examination, *numerus clausus* etc.).

In the EU, on average, almost 30% of those obtaining a tertiary education qualification did 'social science' courses, which include commercial and business administration, mass communication and documentation. Engineers and architects account for 16% of the graduates. The lowest percentage (3%) is observed in 'mathematics and computer science'.

The 'social sciences' produce the greatest proportion of tertiary education graduates in almost all Member States and EFTA/EEA countries; in France and the Netherlands, nearly 40% of the graduates come from this field. Germany, Finland, Sweden and Iceland do not follow the same pattern. In those countries, the fields with the highest numbers of graduates are respectively 'engineering and architecture' (22%), 'medical sciences' (28%), 'education science and teacher training' (22% in Sweden and 24% in Iceland).

In most pre-accession countries, the 'social science' category predominates as well. Three countries are exceptions: Hungary and Poland, where 'education science and teacher training' accounts for 38% and 28% and Slovakia where 30% of graduates are engineers or architects.

FIGURE F17: DISTRIBUTION OF GRADUATES AMONG THE DIFFERENT FIELDS OF STUDY (ISCED 5, 6, 7), AS A PERCENTAGE, 1996/97

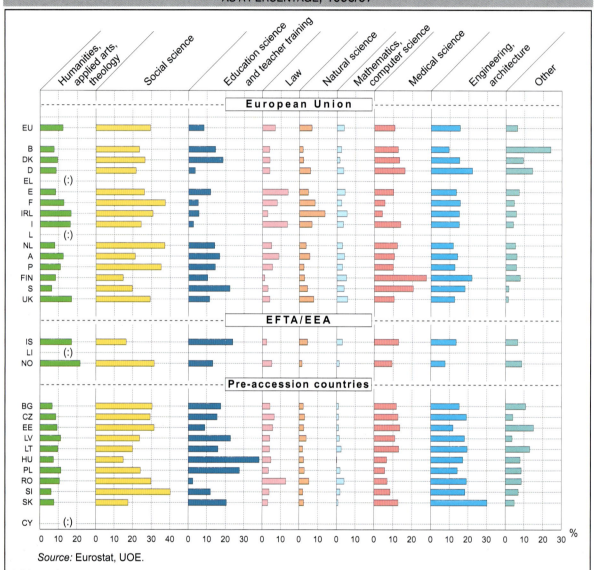

Source: Eurostat, UOE.

Additional notes

Belgium: 1995/96; only graduates from the Flemish Community are included.
Germany, Italy and **Netherlands**: 1995/96.
Ireland: The total number of those with tertiary education qualifications is included here, including those with two qualifications (about 4 000). Some students with a vocational qualification at ISCED level 5 are excluded. Students in private independent colleges are also excluded, as are those in nursing schools who obtained their qualification after three or four years of in-hospital training.
Luxembourg: Data refer only to the tertiary education institutions in Luxembourg.
Czech Republic, Hungary, Poland and **Slovakia**: 1995/96.
Poland: Only graduates from ISCED 6 programmes are included.
Romania: Only graduates from the first stage of the ISCED 6 are included.

Explanatory note

Using the ISCED definitions of fields of study, Eurostat classifies subjects into nine groups in the following terms: humanities, applied arts and theology; social science (including commercial and business administration, mass communication and documentation); education sciences; law; natural science; mathematics and computer science; medical science; engineering and architecture (including trade, craft and industrial programmes); other and unspecified (including agriculture, home economics and the service trades).

THE MOST EQUAL DISTRIBUTION BETWEEN GENDERS IS OBSERVED IN THE 'NATURAL SCIENCES' FIELD

In the EU, on average, the distribution of qualifications between males and females is contrasted in numerous disciplines. Most qualifications in 'education science and teacher training', 'humanities, applied arts and theology' as well as 'medical sciences' are given to females (respectively 73, 71 and 65%). Conversely, 80% of graduates from 'engineering and architecture' are males. 'Mathematics and computer science' graduates are also mainly males (66%). The same patterns can be observed in Iceland and Norway. The most equal distribution between genders is observed in the 'natural sciences' field.

Pre-accession countries' general trends are similar to those in the EU. 'Engineering and architecture' studies seem a little more attractive to women: over a quarter of these degrees are gained by women. In Bulgaria and Romania and to a lesser degree Estonia, more women than men obtain a degree in 'mathematics and computer science'.

FIGURE F18: PROPORTION OF FEMALES WITH TERTIARY EDUCATION QUALIFICATIONS (ISCED 5, 6, 7), BY FIELD OF STUDY, AS A PERCENTAGE, 1996/97

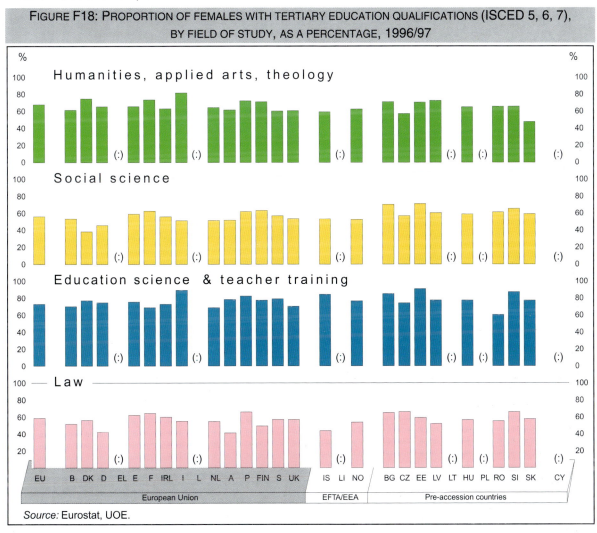

Source: Eurostat, UOE.

FIGURE F18 (CONTINUED): PROPORTION OF FEMALES WITH TERTIARY EDUCATION QUALIFICATIONS (ISCED 5, 6, 7), BY FIELD OF STUDY, AS A PERCENTAGE, 1996/97

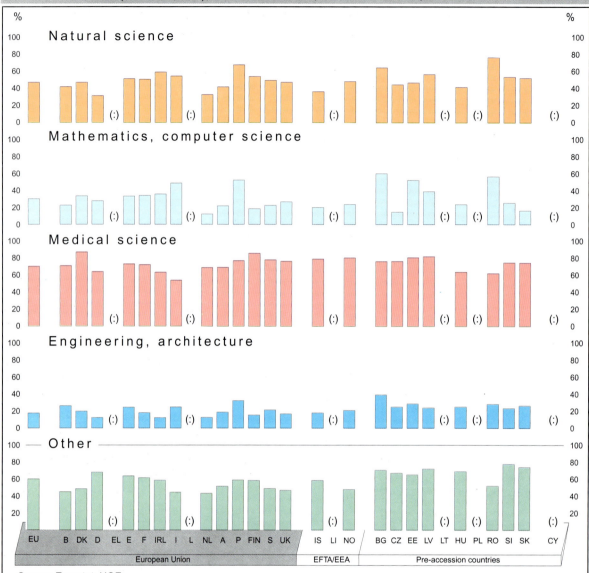

Source: Eurostat, UOE.

Additional notes

Belgium: 1995/96; only graduates from the Flemish Community are included.
Germany, Italy and **Netherlands**: 1995/96.
Ireland: The total number of those with tertiary education qualifications is included here, including those with two qualifications (about 4 000). Some students with a vocational qualification at ISCED level 5 are excluded. Students in private independent colleges are also excluded, as are those in nursing schools who obtained their qualification after three or four years of in-hospital training.
Czech Republic, Hungary, Poland and **Slovakia**: 1995/96.
Poland: Only graduates from ISCED 6 programmes are included.
Romania: Only graduates from the first stage of the ISCED 6 are included.

Explanatory note

Using the ISCED definitions of fields of study, Eurostat classifies subjects into nine groups in the following terms: humanities, applied arts and theology; social science (including commercial and business administration and mass communication and documentation); education sciences; law; natural science; mathematics and computer science; medical science; engineering and architecture (including trade, craft and industrial programmes); other and unspecified (including agriculture; home economics and the service trades).

G

TEACHERS

INCREASING TREND TOWARDS UNIVERSITY-LEVEL EDUCATION AND TRAINING

In the European Union and EFTA/EEA countries today, training for teachers working in primary and secondary schools is provided at tertiary education level, either in universities or in non-university tertiary education institutions. University level training is becoming the norm at higher levels of education. In Italy, however, the reform passed in 1990 providing for the university training of primary teachers has not yet been implemented (1997/98) and teachers are still being trained in the *istituti magistrali* at upper secondary level.

In the pre-accession countries, the initial training of primary and secondary school teachers is also mainly organized within tertiary education, with the possibility of university-level training. In Romania, it is still possible to teach at primary school level with only an upper secondary education. In Hungary, upper secondary teachers are the only ones to be trained at university level.

TWO MAIN MODELS OF PROFESSIONAL TRAINING

The professional and practical training of teachers is provided either at the same time as their general course (**the concurrent model**) or following the general course, for instance at post-graduate level (**the consecutive model**). The entrance requirement for admission to teacher education and training following the concurrent model is the school-leaving certificate awarded at the end of upper secondary education, and also, in some cases, a certificate of aptitude for tertiary education. Under the consecutive model, students who have already obtained a first tertiary education qualification (university or non-university) in a particular discipline train for the teaching profession by taking a post-graduate university or non-university course.

In most EU and EFTA/EEA countries, the concurrent model is adopted for training primary level teachers. Conversely, the consecutive model characterizes the training of secondary level teachers. In the pre-accession countries, the concurrent model is the most common whatever the level of education. However, in Bulgaria the consecutive model is the only possible option for teachers (from pre-primary to upper secondary).

In some countries, teacher training ends with a period of **practical training in a school** which forms an integral part of the course and has to be successfully completed before the qualification is awarded. This is a long period during which the future teachers are responsible for a class but maintain regular contacts with the training institution, to which they are still answerable. They are often paid during this time.

Thus, within the EU, in Germany, after a first stage of concurrent training provided by a tertiary education institution, future primary and secondary school teachers complete a programme of practical training in the form of preparatory service called *Vorbereitungsdienst*. During this period they are remunerated and usually have the status of temporary civil servants. In Denmark, pedagogical training for upper secondary teachers is open only to university graduates who have been recruited to work in a school. The training course lasts six months and consists of seminars on educational theory. This training is assessed by way of written tests and supervised practice. In France, during the second year in *Instituts universitaires de formation des maîtres* (IUFM), those who have been successful in open competition follow a theoretical course that alternates with a practical phase lasting several weeks; in it they have the status of paid student teachers. In Luxembourg, admission to practical training for secondary school teachers is dependent on success in a national open entrance competition. Student teachers are paid during this professional training placement.

The duration and level of courses are presented by level of education in Figures G1 to G4. The phases of general and professional training are also illustrated.

In the countries of the EU and the EFTA/EEA, **pre-primary teacher training** takes place within tertiary education except in Germany, where it is provided at upper secondary level for the adults responsible for children in *Kindergärten*. In Italy pre-primary teachers were still being trained in *scuole magistrali* in 1997/98. In Austria, teachers are trained at either upper secondary or tertiary education level.

In France and the United Kingdom, training for pre-primary teachers is the same as for primary teachers. In Ireland and the Netherlands, there is no distinct pre-primary level.

In the pre-accession countries, the training of teachers who are responsible for children at pre-primary level is provided mainly within tertiary education, whether or not this is at a university. In Bulgaria, Lithuania and Poland, several training models coexist. In the Czech Republic, Romania and Slovakia, upper secondary level training is still provided in parallel with tertiary level (university) training.

FIGURE G1: DURATION AND LEVEL OF THE INITIAL EDUCATION AND TRAINING OF PRE-PRIMARY TEACHERS, 1997/98

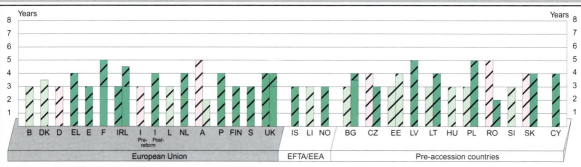

Source: Eurydice.

Additional notes

Germany: The figure refers to state-recognized youth or child-care workers (*Erzieher*), who have neither the training nor the status of teachers. In addition to a lower secondary school certificate, entrance to training in a *Fachschule für Sozialpädagogik* requires an appropriate vocational qualification in advance (a minimum of two years' training) or two years of practical experience.
Ireland: No distinction is made between pre-primary education and primary education, children of 4 to 6 years being integrated in the primary schools in the infant classes. The graph therefore presents the initial training of primary teachers.
Italy: According to the law passed in 1990, since 1998/99 the initial training of pre-primary and primary school teachers should be at university level. The duration of the course has been set at 4 years.
Netherlands: Children aged 4 to 6 years are integrated in primary schools. The figure shows the training of primary teachers. It requires 168 units (which is equivalent to 4 years' study).
Portugal: The pre-primary teaching qualification is university level and can be awarded by *Escolas Superiores de Educação* or universities.
United Kingdom: There are several routes to qualified teacher status, including part-time training. The most common model is the concurrent model. In England, from September 1999, newly qualified teachers will be required to complete an induction year.
Iceland: Since 1 January 1998, the training of pre-primary teachers has been at university level.
Bulgaria: University level courses can last 4 or 5 years.
Lithuania: The institutions providing non-university courses are in a state of transition. It will take between 5 to 10 years to recognise institutions at this level.
Poland: There are 3 possible training routes. The 2 most common models are shown here. The third one is a three-year university level course resulting in award of a *licencjat*.
Romania: University level training can last two or three years. As of 1999/2000, only university level training will be provided.
Slovenia: The training course can last three or four years.

General education (1st phase of the consecutive model)		General and professional training (2nd phase of the consecutive/concurrent model)	
■	University level education	▨	University level education
▢	Non-university tertiary education	▨	Non-university tertiary education
		▨	Non-tertiary education
▨	Practical training in a school		

In most EU and EFTA/EEA countries, the **initial training of primary school teachers** is provided at tertiary education level (university). In Belgium, Denmark, Luxembourg, Austria and Liechtenstein, it is provided at non-university tertiary education level. In Italy, in 1997/98 primary school teachers were still trained at upper secondary level.

In most of the pre-accession countries, future primary school teachers are trained at university level. In Hungary, only non-university level training is offered. In Bulgaria, Lithuania and Poland, university and non-university level training courses are provided in parallel. In Romania, there are two possible models of training, a university level course and an upper secondary course.

In almost all countries, teachers at pre-primary and primary level are trained according to the **concurrent model**. In France, however, they are all trained according to the consecutive model. In Ireland and the United Kingdom, the two models coexist, but the concurrent model is more common. Among the pre-accession countries, in Bulgaria university level training is organized according to the consecutive model.

FIGURE G2: DURATION AND LEVEL OF THE INITIAL EDUCATION AND TRAINING OF PRIMARY TEACHERS, 1997/98

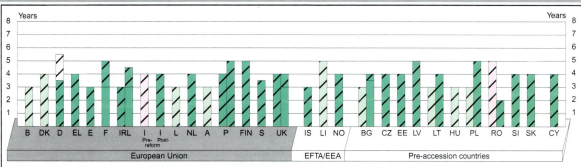

Source: Eurydice.

Additional notes

Germany: At least 7 semesters (three-and-a half years) of university-level training at a university (*Universität*) or equivalent institution of tertiary education depending on the *Land*.

Italy: According to the law passed in 1990, since 1998/99 the initial training of pre-primary and primary school teachers should be at university level. The duration of the course has been set at 4 years.

Netherlands: Initial training requires 168 units (which is equivalent to 4 years' study).

Portugal: The first model shown corresponds to teacher training for the first stage of *ensino básico*. The second model is one of the training possibilities for teachers for the second level of *ensino básico*. Since 1997, primary school teacher training has been at university level and can be given by *Escolas Superiores de Educação* or universities.

Finland: These data refers mainly to class teachers in the first 6 years of *peruskoulu/grundskola*.

Sweden: This data refer to teachers in the first 7 years of *grundskola*.

United Kingdom: There are several routes of training. The concurrent model is more common for primary school teachers. In Scotland, a 4-year university degree followed by one year of professional training is also possible In England, from September 1999, newly qualified teachers will be required to complete an induction year.

Bulgaria: University level courses can last 4 or 5 years.

Czech Republic: Training can last from 4 to 6 years, but it usually lasts 4 years.

Lithuania The institutions providing non-university courses are in a state of transition. It will take between 5 to 10 years to recognise institutions at this level.

Hungary: The model shown here refers only to teachers for the first 4 years of the single structure.

Poland: There are 3 possible training routes. The 2 most common models are shown here. The third one is a three-year university level course resulting in award of a *licencjat*.

Romania: University level teacher training can last 2 or 3 years. As of 1999/2000, only university level training will be provided.

Slovenia: The training course can last four or five years.

Slovakia: The course duration is fixed at 4 years for the first stage of *základná škola* and 5 years for the second stage.

In all countries, future **lower secondary teachers** gain access to the profession after a training course at tertiary education level. In most countries, this course is university level. However, among the Member States of the EU, in Belgium, Denmark and Austria (for teachers in the *Hauptschulen*), and, among the pre-accession countries, in Hungary, teachers follow a non-university tertiary education level training course. In Liechtenstein, both levels are possible.

When the training course is provided at non-university level, it always follows the **concurrent model**. In contrast, when it is at university level the **consecutive model** is most common in EU countries. In the majority of pre-accession countries, the concurrent model is used at university level. In Ireland, Finland, Sweden, the United Kingdom, Iceland, Norway, Lithuania and Slovenia, both models coexist at university level.

FIGURE G3: DURATION AND LEVEL OF INITIAL EDUCATION AND TRAINING OF TEACHERS
FOR LOWER SECONDARY SCHOOLS (GENERAL EDUCATION), 1997/98

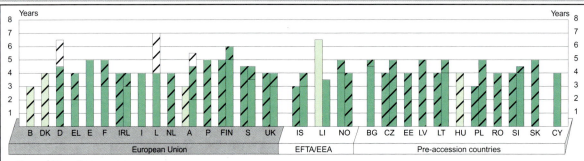

Source: Eurydice.

Additional notes

Germany: 7 to 9 semesters (between three-and-a-half and four-and-a-half years) of university-level training at a university (*Universität*), or equivalent institution of tertiary education, college of art (*Kunsthochschule*) or college of music (*Musikhochschule*), depending on the *Land*.

Greece: Courses last from 4 to 6 years depending on the university faculty. In faculties of education, professional and practical training takes the concurrent form. Future teachers who have studied in other faculties must obtain an education qualification from the teacher training school (*PATES*).

Spain: After obtaining a university qualification (4, 5 or 6-year courses), it is necessary to take a teacher training course of a minimum of 300 hours.

France: Students who have been successful in the open competition for the *Certificat d'aptitude au professorat de l'enseignement secondaire* (*CAPES*) are admitted to the year of professional training in the *IUFM*. As *professeurs certifiés* they may teach in lower and upper secondary schools *(collèges* and *lycées,* respectively). *Professeurs agrégés* (see Figure G4) may also teach at this level, but there are very few of them; their training is not included here.

Ireland: The consecutive model is more common for secondary school teachers.

Italy: The university qualification obtained after a minimum of 4 years is not a qualification for teaching at secondary level. Currently, to obtain this qualification, the candidate must sit the examination called *abilitazione* on teaching norms, theories and methods. However, preparation for this examination is left to the candidate's own initiative. The 1990 reform envisages that, from 1999/2000, a professional qualification can be obtained after a 2-year post-graduate course leading to an examination.

Netherlands: Candidates obtaining grade 2 may teach general subjects in lower secondary schools and vocational upper secondary schools only. Initial training requires 168 units (which is equivalent to 4 years' study).

Portugal: This diagram illustrates the training of teachers for the third stage of *ensino básico*. Some institutions offer training following the consecutive model over 5 or 6 years.

Finland: The information relates mainly to subject teachers in the last 3 years of *peruskoulu/grundskola*. Training lasts 5 or 6 years.

Sweden: The information relates to teachers in the last 6 years of *grundskola*. Depending on the subject chosen, training ranges from three-and-a-half to four-and-a-half years (the latter being more common), whether it is done according to the concurrent model or according to the consecutive model.

United Kingdom: There are several routes to qualified teacher status. The consecutive model is more common for secondary school teachers. In Scotland, the most common model is a general 4-year university course followed by one year of professional training. In England, from September 1999, newly qualified teachers will be required to complete an induction year.

Bulgaria and **Romania**: Training can last 4 or 5 years.

Czech Republic: Training can last from 4 to 6 years, but it usually lasts 4 years.

Lithuania: There are three training routes. The two most common models are shown here. A three-year training course can be followed in a teacher training college.

Poland: Foreign language teachers can also be trained for 3 years in a non-university course.

Slovenia: The training course can last four or five years.

University-level training is provided everywhere for **upper secondary education teachers**. Non-university training is only offered in a few countries. At this level, teacher training lasts a minimum of four years. Teacher training is longest in Luxembourg (seven years).

In most countries of the EU and EFTA/EEA, the **consecutive model** is the standard for teacher training at this level. In contrast, all teachers at this level in Germany and some of the teachers in Ireland, Portugal, Finland, Sweden and the United Kingdom are trained according to the concurrent model.

The **concurrent model** predominates in the pre-accession countries. In Bulgaria and Hungary, all upper secondary teachers are trained according to the consecutive model. In Estonia, Lithuania and Slovenia, training is available via both models.

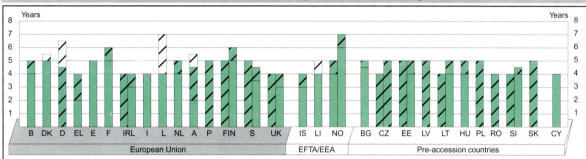

FIGURE G4: DURATION AND LEVEL OF INITIAL EDUCATION AND TRAINING OF TEACHERS FOR UPPER SECONDARY SCHOOLS (GENERAL EDUCATION), 1997/98

Source: Eurydice.

Additional notes

Belgium: Training usually lasts 4 years. Post-graduate teacher training may be undertaken either parallel to the university course (along with the degree, in one or 2 years) or following the university course (in one year, or 2 years part-time). Lower secondary level teachers (see Figure G3) can teach in the first two years of general upper secondary school and in vocational upper secondary institutions.

Germany: At least 9 semesters (four-and-a-half years) of university-level training at a university (*Universität*), or equivalent tertiary education institution, college of art (*Kunsthochschule*) or college of music (*Musikhochschule*), depending on the *Land*.

Greece: Courses last from 4 to 6 years depending on the university faculty. In faculties of education, professional and practical training takes the concurrent form. Future teachers who have studied in other faculties must obtain an education qualification from the teacher training school (*PATES*).

Spain: After obtaining a university qualification (4-, 5- or 6-year courses), it is necessary to take a teacher training course of a minimum of 300 hours.

France: Two types of teachers can work at this level: *professeurs certifiés* who have obtained the *CAPES* (see Figure G3) and *professeurs agrégés*. After 5 years of university level training and obtaining the *agrégation*, they are admitted to the year of professional training in the *IUFM*.

Ireland: The consecutive model is more common for secondary teachers.

Italy: The university qualification obtained after a minimum of 4 years is not a qualification for teaching at secondary level. Currently, to obtain this qualification, the candidate must sit the examination called *abilitazione* on teaching norms, theories and methods. However, preparation for this examination is left to the candidate's own initiative. The 1990 reform envisages that, from 1999/2000, a professional qualification can be obtained after a 2-year post-graduate course leading to an examination.

Netherlands: Teachers who have grade 2 can obtain grade 1 by following a course parallel to the university course, requiring 68 units (equivalent to one and a half years of study), or a post-graduate university course, requiring 42 units (equivalent to one year of study).

Portugal: Some institutions offer training following the consecutive model over 5 or 6 years.

Finland: Training lasts 5 or 6 years.

Sweden: Depending on the subjects chosen, training ranges from four to five years.

United Kingdom: There are several routes to qualified teacher status. The consecutive model is more common for secondary school teachers. In Scotland, the most common model is a general 4-year university course followed by one year of professional training. In England and Wales, from September 1999, newly qualified teachers will be required to complete an induction year.

Norway: Training can last between four and a half and seven years depending on the subject chosen.

Czech Republic: Training can last from 4 to 6 years, but it usually lasts 4 years.

Latvia: A two-year supplementary training course is optional.

Poland: Foreign language teachers can also be trained for 3 years in a non-university course.

Romania and **Slovenia**: Training can last 4 or 5 years.

General education (1st phase of the consecutive model)		General and professional training (2nd phase of the consecutive/concurrent model)	
▣	University level education	▨	University level education
▢	Non-university tertiary education	▨	Non-university tertiary education
		▱	Non-tertiary education
▱	Practical training in a school			

6 MILLION TEACHERS IN EUROPE

Figure G5 shows the number of full-time and part-time teachers in primary, lower and upper secondary levels (in absolute values and full-time equivalents) as well as their ratio to the total active population during the 1996/97 school year.

In view of the variety of situations around Europe, caution is necessary when comparing percentages between countries. Analysis of this sort should take into account factors such as the duration of compulsory education and the number of young people in the educational systems as well as the magnitude of the ratio of the active population to the total population.

At present, the EU has nearly 4.5 million teachers in the primary and secondary levels taken together; the European total is almost 6 million.

The teaching profession employs 3% of the total active population in the EU. Percentages vary however from one member country to another: from 2% in Germany to 5% in Belgium. In EFTA/EEA countries, primary and secondary teachers account for a rather larger proportion of the active population (over 3%). The rates in pre-accession countries are close to those of the EU: from 2% in Romania to 4% in Hungary.

FIGURE G5: TEACHERS AS A PERCENTAGE OF THE TOTAL ACTIVE POPULATION. PRIMARY AND SECONDARY LEVELS (ISCED 1, 2 AND 3), PUBLIC AND PRIVATE SECTORS COMBINED, 1996/97

	Teachers/ total active population	FTE/ total active population	Total active population/ total population		Teachers/ total active population	FTE/ total active population	Total active population/ total population
European Union				**EFTA/EEA**			
EU (*)	2.7	(:)	45.0	IS	3.4	3.3	53.6
				LI	(:)	(:)	(:)
B	5.1	4.5	41.4	NO	3.8	(:)	51.9
DK (*)	3.0	2.6	53.6				
D	2.0	1.7	47.8	**Pre-accession countries**			
EL	2.8	1.5	40.6	BG	(:)	(:)	(:)
E	2.8	2.6	40.9	CZ	2.7	2.3	49.7
F	2.7	2.6	43.4	EE	2.8	2.6	47.7
IRL	2.8	2.7	41.9	LV	(:)	(:)	(:)
I	3.2	(:)	39.8	LT	(:)	(:)	(:)
L	2.9	(:)	41.5	HU	3.8	3.6	38.7
NL	(:)	2.0	48.9	PL	2.7	(:)	44.0
A	2.9	2.8	47.2	RO	2.1	1.2	52.5
P	3.0	(:)	48.7	SI	2.5	2.2	48.2
FIN	2.6	2.6	48.6	SK	2.9	2.7	45.4
S	3.1	2.4	49.4				
UK	2.6	2.1	48.6	CY	3.3	3.2	46.8

Source: Eurostat, UOE and Labour force survey.

Additional notes

Belgium: ISCED 0 teachers are included as well.
Ireland and **Austria**: Non-teaching heads are included.
Luxembourg: 1997/98; only teachers from the public sector are included.
Netherlands: Only data in full-time equivalents are included.
Portugal: 1995/96.
Finland: ISCED 5 teachers and some ISCED 6 teachers from vocational and technical programmes are also included in ISCED 3.
Iceland: In ISCED 3, only teachers from the public sector are included.
Liechtenstein: 1995/96.
Lithuania: Only full-time teachers are included.
Slovakia: Non-teaching heads are included.

Explanatory note

Only teachers in post are taken into account (allowing for exceptions): staff allocated to duties other than teaching (inspectors, non-teaching heads, teachers on secondment, etc.) and teachers-to-be doing teaching practice in schools are excluded.

PART-TIME TEACHING IS NOT A VERY COMMON PRACTICE

In the EU, on average, one in five teachers works part-time at primary and secondary levels taken together. The proportion of teachers working part-time varies considerably from one country to another. The highest percentages of part-time teachers are found in Germany, the Netherlands and Sweden, with respectively 39%, 53 % and 48% part-time staff. On the other hand, fewer than 10% of teachers work part-time in Spain, Luxembourg, Austria or Finland. In Italy, the percentage of part-time teachers is negligible.

The extent of part-time work also differs depending on the level of education. In the EU, the highest percentage of part-time teachers is found at upper secondary level and the next highest is found at lower secondary level. The reverse is observed in Germany, where the percentage of part-time teachers is highest in primary education.

In the EFTA/EEA countries, the proportion of teachers working part-time amounts overall to more than one quarter of the teaching population. The proportion is larger in the single structure (corresponding to primary and lower secondary levels) than in upper secondary education.

In pre-accession countries, as in EU countries, part-time work is more frequent in upper secondary education than in lower secondary or primary education; only Latvia is the exception. It is also the country with the largest proportion of part-time teachers.

FIGURE G6: PERCENTAGE OF TEACHERS WORKING PART-TIME, PRIMARY (ISCED 1) AND SECONDARY (ISCED 2 AND 3) LEVELS, 1996/97

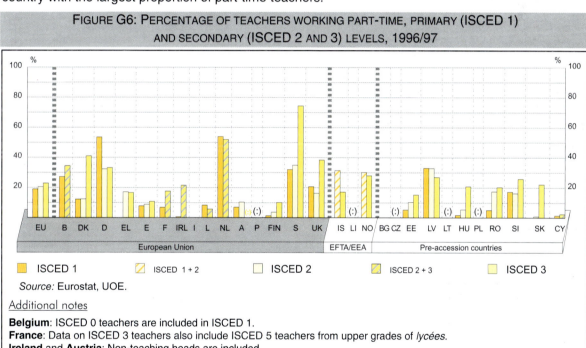

ISCED 1   ISCED 1 + 2   ISCED 2   ISCED 2 + 3   ISCED 3

Source: Eurostat, UOE.

Additional notes

Belgium: ISCED 0 teachers are included in ISCED 1.
France: Data on ISCED 3 teachers also include ISCED 5 teachers from upper grades of *lycées*.
Ireland and **Austria**: Non-teaching heads are included.
Luxembourg: 1997/98; only teachers from the public sector are included.
Netherlands: Part-time teachers are defined as any teachers whose workload is lower than the full-time workload; all heads (whether with teaching duties or not) are excluded; ISCED 0 teachers are included in ISCED 1.
Finland: ISCED 5 teachers and some ISCED 6 teachers from vocational and technical programmes are also included in ISCED 3.
Slovakia: Non-teaching heads are included.

Explanatory notes

Those whose workload is lower than 75% of the full-time workload are considered part-time. All degrees of part-time work are taken into account.

Only teachers in post are taken into account (allowing for exceptions): staff allocated to duties other than teaching (inspectors, non-teaching heads, teachers on secondment, etc.) and teachers-to-be doing teaching practice in schools are excluded.

———— NEARLY HALF OF TEACHERS ARE OVER 40 YEARS OLD ————

The analysis of the distribution of teachers by age shows that in most European countries, the proportion of teachers aged 40 and over is more than half of the teaching staff. The high proportion of older teachers can be observed in both primary and secondary levels.

FIGURE G7: DISTRIBUTION OF TEACHERS BY AGE BAND, AS A PERCENTAGE.
PRIMARY EDUCATION (ISCED 1), PUBLIC AND PRIVATE SECTORS COMBINED, 1996/97

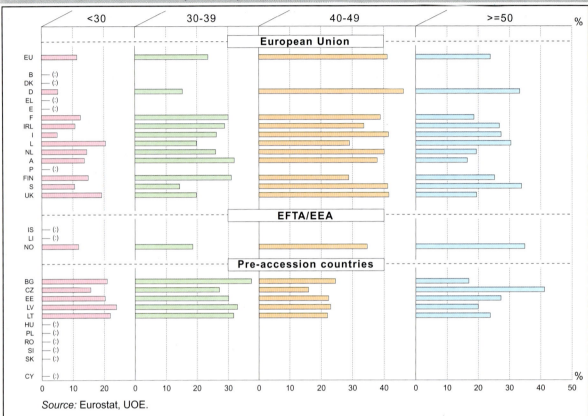

Source: Eurostat, UOE.

Additional notes

Germany, Ireland, Italy and **Norway**: Teachers whose age is unknown are not included.
France: ISCED 0 teachers are included as well.
Ireland and **Austria**: Non-teaching heads are included.
Luxembourg: 1997/98; only teachers from the public sector are included.
Netherlands: 1997/98; all heads (whether with teaching duties or not) are excluded.
Norway: Data on ISCED 1 teachers include ISCED 2 teachers from the public sector.
Slovakia: Non-teaching heads are included.

Explanatory note

Only teachers in post are taken into account (allowing for exceptions): staff allocated to duties other than teaching (inspectors, non-teaching heads, teachers on secondment, etc.) and teachers-to-be doing teaching practice in schools are excluded.

Taking the EU and EFTA/EEA countries, at **primary level**, Germany and Sweden have a relatively elderly teaching staff (80% and 75% teachers respectively are aged 40 or over). On the contrary, Finland and Austria have a relatively young teaching staff (46% teachers are under 40). Luxembourg has the greatest proportion of primary teachers who are under 30 years old (21%). In Germany and Italy, conversely, the percentage of young teachers is very small (5%).

In the pre-accession countries for which data are available, primary teachers are younger than in the EU. In Bulgaria, Estonia, Latvia and Lithuania, more than half the primary teachers are under 40 and more than one teacher in five is under 30. In the Czech Republic, primary teachers are somewhat older: 57% are over 40.

In all countries except Ireland and the United Kingdom, the teaching staff is older in **secondary education** than in primary.

Of the EU and EFTA/EEA countries, at secondary level, teachers in Germany, Italy and Sweden are relatively elderly (81, 79 and 80% of teachers respectively are aged 40 or over) while teachers are relatively youthful in Austria (44% of teachers below 40). Ireland and the United Kingdom have the greatest proportion of secondary teachers under 30 years old (respectively 15 and 16%). In contrast, Italy shows the smallest percentage of young teachers with only 0.5% of teachers under 30.

In the pre-accession countries for which data are available, young secondary teachers are more numerous than in the EU: at least 13% are under 30. Although the proportion of teachers aged 40 or over is in the majority, the percentages are lower than those observed in the EU.

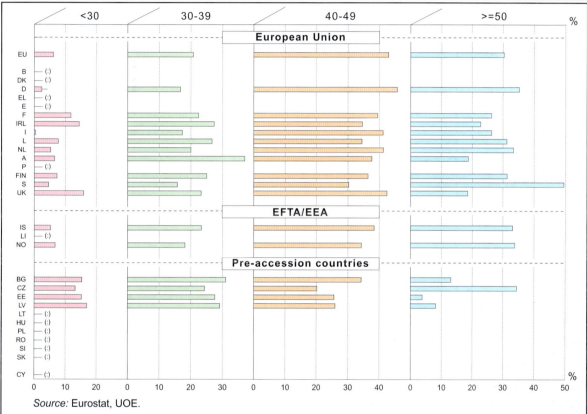

FIGURE G8: DISTRIBUTION OF TEACHERS BY AGE BAND, AS A PERCENTAGE. SECONDARY EDUCATION (ISCED 2 AND 3), PUBLIC AND PRIVATE SECTORS COMBINED, 1996/97

Source: Eurostat, UOE.

Additional notes

Germany, Ireland, Italy and **Norway**: Teachers whose age is unknown are not included.
Ireland and **Austria**: Non-teaching heads are included.
Luxembourg: 1997/98; only teachers from the public sector are included.
Netherlands: 1997/98; all heads (whether with teaching duties or not) are excluded.
Finland: ISCED 5 teachers and some ISCED 6 teachers from vocational and technical programmes are also included in ISCED 3.
Iceland and **Norway**: Only teachers from ISCED 3 and the public sector are included.
Slovakia: Non-teaching heads are included.

Explanatory note

Only teachers in post are taken into account (allowing for exceptions): staff allocated to duties other than teaching (inspectors, non-teaching heads, teachers on secondment, etc.) and teachers-to-be doing teaching practice in schools are excluded.

RETIREMENT

In almost all countries, a minimum and a maximum age for retirement are set. Differences between the countries are explained by taking into account criteria such as the number of years' service or gender.

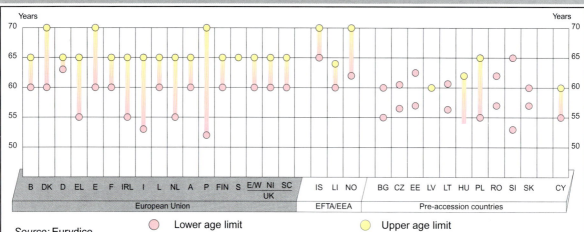

FIGURE G9: AGE OF RETIREMENT, PRIMARY AND SECONDARY EDUCATION, 1997/98

Source: Eurydice.

○ Lower age limit   ○ Upper age limit

Additional notes

Greece: Teachers who have not completed 35 years of service can work until the age of 67.

Spain: The maximum retirement age is usually 65, but a regulation passed on 31 December 1996 allows teachers to work until the age of 70.

France: The *instituteurs* who come under the 1972 legislation are allowed to retire at the age of 55. All female civil servants who have children may take advantage of certain arrangements under certain conditions.

Ireland: Primary and secondary school teachers can retire at 55 if they have completed 35 years of service. They can also retire at 55 if they have completed 34 years of service and have followed 3 years of initial training, or if they have completed 33 years of service and 4 years of initial training.

Italy: Teachers can postpone retirement until the age of 67/70 by personal request and subject to certain conditions.

Netherlands: A flexible retirement plan introduced on 1 April 1997 allows employees to retire or to reduce their working hours if they wish between 55 and 65 years of age.

Portugal: a) The maximum retirement age is 65 for primary school teachers and 70 for secondary school teachers; b) Primary school teachers are entitled to retire at 52 if they have completed 32 years of service or at 55 if they have 30 years of service.

United Kingdom (E/W, NI): The usual retirement age is 60 but early retirement is possible under certain circumstances. After the age of 65 and up to the age of 70, an annual employment agreement must be made with employers.

United Kingdom (SC): Teachers who stop working or leave the teaching profession before they are 60 do not receive their pension until they reach that age, irrespective of their years of service.

Iceland: Teachers taken on before 1997 can retire after 35 years' service if they have reached the age of 60, after 34 years' service at the age of 61, etc.

Bulgaria: The ages shown will probably be increased when the reform currently being implemented takes effect.

Czech Republic: The minimum age of retirement for women is 58.5 years (depending on the number of children, this limit can be reduced) and for men is 60.5 if they have completed 25 years of service. Since the law was changed in 1996, the retirement age is being raised so that by 2007 it will be 61 for women and 62 for men.

Estonia: A reform is currently under way. In the year 2016, the minimum retirement age for men and women will be 63.

Latvia: According to the 1995 legislation, the retirement age is 60, both for men and women. During the transition period, the retirement age increases every year by six months for women. Women can retire from 57. No maximum age has been set for retirement.

Lithuania: Since 1 January 1995, the retirement age has increased every year by a few months. On 1 January 2009, the retirement age will be 60 for women and 62.5 for men.

Hungary: The minimum retirement age depends on the number of years of service (at least 34 years for women and at least 37 years for men). The maximum retirement age is 62 for all.

Poland: Teachers can retire before the age of 55 provided they have completed a minimum of 30 years of service, including 20 years in teaching.

Romania: Teachers can retire earlier if they have completed 25 or 30 years of service respectively for women and men.

Slovenia: For women, the minimum retirement age is 53 if they have completed 35 years of service. There is no fixed upper limit, but women who have completed 20 (or 15) years of service can retire at the age of 58 (or 60). As for men, the minimum retirement age is 58 if they have completed 40 years of service. There is no fixed upper limit, but men who have completed at least 20 (or 15) years of service can retire at the age of 63 (or 65).

Slovakia: Women can retire at the age of 57 if they have completed 25 years of service. The minimum retirement age for women who have had three or more children is 54 (less one year per child). Men can retire at 60 if they have completed 25 years of service.

Cyprus: Teachers can retire after 33 years and 4 months of service with full benefits.

132

The retirement age is often independent of the level of education (except in Portugal and Finland). While the maximum compulsory retirement age is 65 in the majority of the countries of the European Union and the EFTA/EEA, the situation is less uniform as regards the minimum voluntary retirement age. Nonetheless, 60 is the minimum age in Belgium, Denmark, Spain, France, Luxembourg, Austria, Finland, Liechtenstein and is the normal age of retirement in the United Kingdom.

In two countries (Italy and Portugal), there is a considerable gap between the minimum and the maximum retirement age. In Portugal, this is due to the fact that, on the one hand, primary school teachers can retire at the age of 52 and, on the other hand, the maximum retirement age is 70 for secondary school teachers.

It should be pointed out that only Sweden has a universally applicable compulsory retirement age (65).

In the pre-accession countries, with the exception of Latvia, Poland and Cyprus, the retirement age differs according to sex. Thus, in Bulgaria, the Czech Republic, Estonia, Lithuania, Romania and Slovenia, two minimum ages are presented: one is the retirement age for women, the other applies to male teachers. In Slovakia, women who have had three or more children are entitled in addition to a reduction in the number of years of service. Similarly, in the Czech Republic the retirement age for women depends on how many children they have had.

Generally speaking, in these countries there is not a significant difference between the minimum and maximum retirement age. Only Poland and Slovenia have a relatively wide gap that is linked to the minimum number of years of service required for entitlement to retirement.

MORE THAN 1 IN 5 TEACHERS ———————— ARE NEARING THE END OF THEIR CAREERS ————————

As illustrated by figure G9, the time at which retirement is taken depends on a number of factors: the age of the teacher, the number of years' service, the teacher's sex and the level at which the teacher works (primary, secondary, etc.). Figure G10 presents the percentage of teachers who are within the last ten years of their careers.

In the majority of EU countries for which data are available more than one teacher in five will be retired within ten years. Italy has the highest percentage – more than one in three teachers will have retired within ten years – and Italy also has the earliest retirement age. The opposite applies in Austria and the United Kingdom, with only 12% being within the last ten years of their careers.

In pre-accession countries for which data are available the percentages are even higher than in EU countries, particularly in the Czech Republic, where more than 40% of teachers will have retired within ten years. The teaching population is generally younger in these countries than in EU countries, but retirement age is set at a younger age.

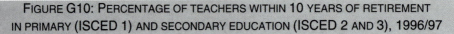

FIGURE G10: PERCENTAGE OF TEACHERS WITHIN 10 YEARS OF RETIREMENT
IN PRIMARY (ISCED 1) AND SECONDARY EDUCATION (ISCED 2 AND 3), 1996/97

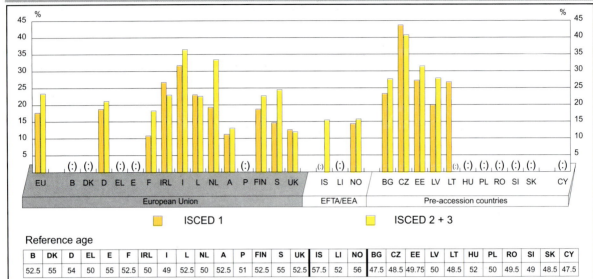

ISCED 1   ISCED 2 + 3

Reference age

B	DK	D	EL	E	F	IRL	I	L	NL	A	P	FIN	S	UK	IS	LI	NO	BG	CZ	EE	LV	LT	HU	PL	RO	SI	SK	CY
52.5	55	54	50	55	52.5	50	49	52.5	50	52.5	51	52.5	55	52.5	57.5	52	56	47.5	48.5	49.75	50	48.5	52	50	49.5	49	48.5	47.5

Source: Eurostat, UOE.

Additional notes

France: Data on ISCED 3 teachers include ISCED 5 teachers from upper grades of *lycées*.
Ireland and **Austria**: Headteachers without direct teaching duties are also included.
Luxembourg: 1997/98; only teachers from the public sector are included.
Netherlands: 1997/98; all heads (whether with teaching duties or not) are excluded.
Finland: ISCED 5 teachers and some ISCED 6 teachers from vocational and technical programmes are also included in ISCED 3.
Iceland: Only ISCED 3 teachers are included.
Norway: Data on ISCED 1 include ISCED 2 teachers, data on ISCED 2/3 teachers only include ISCED 3 teachers.
Slovakia: Headteachers without direct teaching duties are also included.

Explanatory note

The reference age for calculating this indicator is equal to the average age of retirement (i.e. the arithmetic mean between the minimum and maximum retirement ages given by indicator G19) minus 10 years. Data on teachers' ages were collected in age bands in the UOE Data Collection. The number of teachers in the age range containing the reference age was adjusted according to the following formula: [(upper limit of the age band – reference age) / interval in years]. All teachers in higher age bands were then added. (Taking Germany as an example, the number of teachers aged over 54 years = [(55-54)/5=20%] of the 50-54 age band + 100% of the 55-59 age band + 100% of the 60-64 age band + 100% of the ≥ 65 group.

Only teachers in post are taken into account (allowing for exceptions): staff allocated to duties other than teaching (inspectors, non-teaching heads, teachers on secondment, etc.) and trainee teachers in teaching practice in schools are excluded.

Teachers approaching retirement are proportionally more numerous in secondary than in primary education. This is the case for all countries that have provided data on teachers' ages, excluding Ireland, Luxembourg, the United Kingdom and the Czech Republic. The largest gap between the education levels is observed in Sweden (10%); on the contrary, in the United Kingdom the difference is slight.

The significant proportion of older teachers can certainly be partly explained by the fact that in the 1960s, in most European countries, there was a very high birth rate which led to an increase in pupil numbers and consequently to a wide recruitment of teachers. In the 1980s, there was a fall in pupil numbers and little need to recruit new staff. As a result, the number of younger teachers entering the profession was restricted, causing an imbalance in the age structure of the profession. As the cohort of teachers recruited in the 1960s reaches retirement age in the coming years, it will be important to ensure that planning the supply of teachers is managed effectively everywhere to avoid the risk of shortages.

MORE FEMALE TEACHERS
ESPECIALLY IN PRIMARY EDUCATION

Primary teaching is a predominantly female profession in the EU. In all Member States but Greece, women are clearly in the majority at this level of education, the largest proportion of all being found in Italy (94%). More equal proportions of men and women are observed in Denmark, with 60% of the staff at the most being women.

The percentage of women in the teaching population declines at higher levels of education. This can be said for all countries except Greece and the Netherlands.

In upper secondary education, the male/female ratio in the teaching staff is more balanced. Although women are in the majority, the percentage is around 50% in several countries. Two countries have a particularly low proportion of women teachers in upper secondary education: Denmark (30%) and Germany (36%).

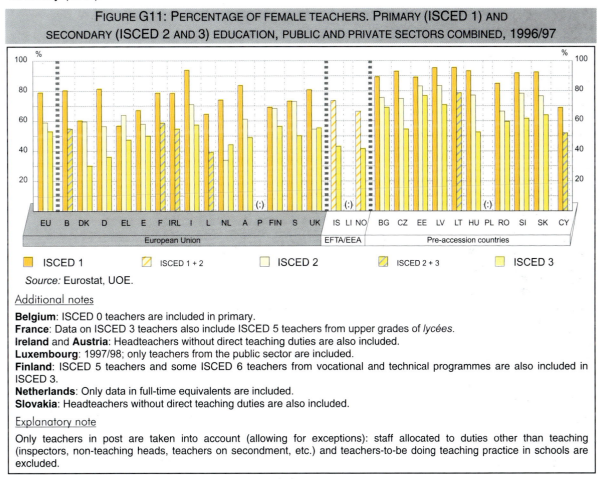

FIGURE G11: PERCENTAGE OF FEMALE TEACHERS. PRIMARY (ISCED 1) AND SECONDARY (ISCED 2 AND 3) EDUCATION, PUBLIC AND PRIVATE SECTORS COMBINED, 1996/97

Source: Eurostat, UOE.

Additional notes

Belgium: ISCED 0 teachers are included in primary.
France: Data on ISCED 3 teachers also include ISCED 5 teachers from upper grades of *lycées*.
Ireland and **Austria**: Headteachers without direct teaching duties are also included.
Luxembourg: 1997/98; only teachers from the public sector are included.
Finland: ISCED 5 teachers and some ISCED 6 teachers from vocational and technical programmes are also included in ISCED 3.
Netherlands: Only data in full-time equivalents are included.
Slovakia: Headteachers without direct teaching duties are also included.

Explanatory note

Only teachers in post are taken into account (allowing for exceptions): staff allocated to duties other than teaching (inspectors, non-teaching heads, teachers on secondment, etc.) and teachers-to-be doing teaching practice in schools are excluded.

In the EFTA/EEA countries women are in the majority in primary and lower secondary education taken together in Iceland and Norway, but are in the minority at the upper secondary level.

In the pre-accession countries for which data are available, women outnumber the men at the three levels of education considered. A particularly high proportion of female teachers is found in primary education — with over 85% in all countries, and over 95% in Latvia and Lithuania.

LENGTH OF SERVICE REMAINS THE MAIN SOURCE OF DIFFERENCES IN TEACHERS' SALARIES

In order to illustrate teachers' financial position relative to the average standard of living in their respective countries, Figures G12 to G14 show for each level of education, teachers' minimum and maximum salaries as a percentage of the **per capita gross domestic product** (GDP) – an index of the general standard of living in the country. This indicator is obtained by dividing the GDP, which reflects the country's wealth, by the total population of the country. By systematically comparing a teacher's salary (in national currency) to the per capita GDP (at current prices in national currency), it is possible to make comparisons both within each country and between countries. Analysis of this ratio provides an idea of the teacher's salary status.

FIGURE G12: MINIMUM AND MAXIMUM SALARIES OF PRIMARY TEACHERS RELATIVE TO PER CAPITA GDP, 1997/98

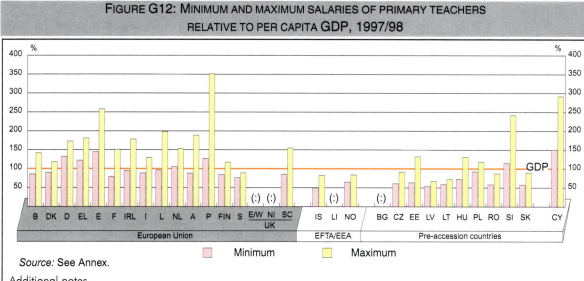

Source: See Annex.

Additional notes

Denmark: 1997 salaries.
Germany: because of the complexity and variety of situations, teachers' salaries have been calculated by taking the average age at the start of the career (it depends on the starting age and the length of studies) and by using the salaries of the West German *Länder* as the basis.
France: The data refer to *professeurs des écoles* and *professeurs certifiés*. A further category of teachers, *professeurs agrégés*, can teach in secondary schools. Their minimum salary is FRF 124 663 and their maximum is FRF 271 539.
United Kingdom: A considerable number of teachers have specific responsibilities and therefore receive higher salaries than those shown here.
Iceland: Only basic salaries are shown. Additional payments (for overtime, extra responsibility, etc.) are considerable.
Norway: The figures given are a weighted average of the salaries (minima and maxima) of each of the five categories of teachers. These categories depend on teachers' specialisation and length of training.
Hungary: Only basic salaries are shown. Additional payments can give rise to differences.

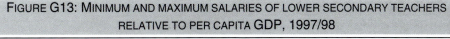

FIGURE G13: MINIMUM AND MAXIMUM SALARIES OF LOWER SECONDARY TEACHERS RELATIVE TO PER CAPITA GDP, 1997/98

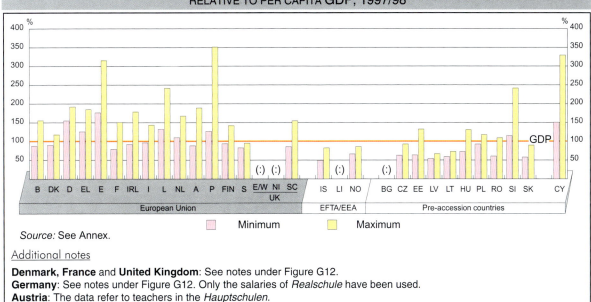

Source: See Annex.

Additional notes

Denmark, France and **United Kingdom**: See notes under Figure G12.
Germany: See notes under Figure G12. Only the salaries of *Realschule* have been used.
Austria: The data refer to teachers in the *Hauptschulen*.
Iceland and **Norway**: See notes under Figure G12.
Hungary: See notes under Figure G12.

FIGURE G14: MINIMUM AND MAXIMUM SALARIES OF UPPER SECONDARY TEACHERS RELATIVE TO PER CAPITA GDP, 1997/98

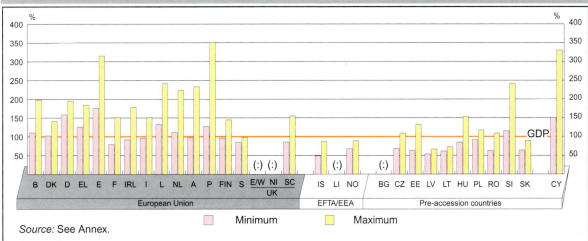

Source: See Annex.

Additional notes

Germany, France and **United Kingdom**: See notes under Figure G12.
Iceland and **Norway**: See notes under Figure G12.

Explanatory notes

The values appearing in this graph have been obtained by dividing the gross annual salary (minimum and maximum) in national currency by the per capita GDP (at current prices in national currency) of the country concerned.

Gross annual salary is defined as the amount paid by the employer in the year – including all bonuses, increases and allowances such as those for cost of living, end of year (if applicable), holiday pay, etc. – less the employer's social security and pension contributions. This salary does not include any other financial benefits in respect of additional functions, further qualifications or specific responsibilities.

The figures are based on the situation of a teacher who is (a) single and without children and (b) living in the capital.

Minimum salary is the salary received by teachers with the above profile who are starting teaching, having completed their education, initial training and trial period.

Maximum salary is the salary received by teachers with the above profile who are at the end of their career, i.e. during the last year prior to retirement.

Of the factors examined here, seniority is the main reason for differences between teacher salaries. As regards salaries, the maximum can be as much as twice the minimum. Among the EU and EFTA/EEA countries, the greatest difference between minimum and maximum salaries relative to per capita GDP occurs in Portugal, but there are also significant differences in France, Ireland, Luxembourg, Austria and the United Kingdom (Scotland). Conversely, in Germany, Sweden and Norway we find the least significant increase in salary between the start and the end of the teaching career.

In only a few countries can the differences be explained by the fact that the teachers work at different levels of education. In Spain, Luxembourg and Finland, primary level salaries are appreciably lower than secondary level salaries. In contrast, in Belgium, the Netherlands and Austria, upper secondary teachers' salaries are appreciably higher than those of their colleagues in primary or lower secondary. In this case, the differences are due – at least in part – to these teachers' level of training.

In Sweden, Iceland and Norway, at all levels of education, whether it is at the start or the end of their career, teachers receive a salary below the per capita GDP of the country.

In Greece and Portugal, teachers' minimum salaries are routinely more than 1.25 times the per capita GDP. This is also the case in Luxembourg, but only for secondary school teachers.

In the pre-accession countries seniority is also a determining factor as regards the differences in teachers' salaries. Estonia, Slovenia and Cyprus have the most significant increases between the salary at the start of a teacher's career and at the end. By contrast, the increase is less marked in Latvia, Lithuania and Poland.

There are also differences in salaries depending on the level at which the teacher works. In Romania and Cyprus, secondary school teachers have a higher salary than primary school teachers and the gap is even wider at the end of the teacher's career. In the Czech Republic and Hungary, there are marked differences between teachers' salaries at upper secondary level and at other levels.

In all countries, with the exception of Slovenia and Cyprus, minimum teachers' salaries are below the per capita GDP, regardless of the level of education at which the teacher works. In Poland, teachers' salaries at the start of their career are close to the per capita GDP.

SPECIAL EDUCATION

FROM SEGREGATION TO INTEGRATION

Special education was developed in the course of the nineteenth century in order to guarantee the right of all children to education. Structures separate from mainstream education were established in twelve Member States of the European Union for the education of 'handicapped' children – now referred to more commonly as children with special educational needs. These were followed by other structures. The current trend is towards the integration of these children in either special or ordinary classes in mainstream schools.

Generally speaking, the first form of integration consisted of the introduction of separate special classes in mainstream schools, with integration only coming later. This pattern of development has occurred in Denmark, Spain, France, Ireland, Austria, Portugal, Finland, Sweden and the United Kingdom.

The integration of some children with special needs started in the late 1940s in the United Kingdom (England, Wales and Northern Ireland), but has been more recent in the other countries of the EU.

During the century, Belgium, Denmark and the United Kingdom (Scotland) were the first countries to consider opening separate classes for children with special educational needs in mainstream schools. However, in Belgium this experiment was suspended in 1970, and at the present time integration is only practised on a very limited basis. In Italy, on the other hand, an increasingly integrated structure has gradually replaced the segregated structure.

In the EFTA/EEA countries, the development of education for children with special educational needs has been marked by the provision of separate classes within mainstream education and then the relatively recent appearance of integration. In Iceland, there are parallel separate schools for severely disabled pupils. In Norway, the closure of many special schools in 1992 has resulted in a reduction in the number of pupils attending separate schools. There are still separate classes in mainstream schools, for pupils with severe learning difficulties.

Among the pre-accession countries, in the Czech Republic, Latvia, Poland, Slovenia, Slovakia and Cyprus, the provision of special education has followed the same pattern of development as in most of the EU Member States. It was provided first in separate schools before moving to separate classes and has finally very recently been integrated into mainstream education.

In Estonia and Hungary, there have been separate special schools since the beginning of the century. Integration has been possible since 1991 and 1973 respectively.

Since 1920, Lithuanian pupils, depending on their educational needs, have attended either separate schools or separate classes. Since 1991, integration has also been practised in parallel with this type of segregated education.

In Bulgaria and Romania, education for children with special educational needs is provided exclusively in special schools, although special classes were introduced between 1960 and 1980 in Bulgarian schools. In Romania, the legislative framework offers the possibility of integration, but human and financial resources are insufficient.

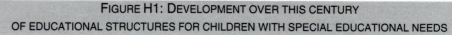

FIGURE H1: DEVELOPMENT OVER THIS CENTURY
OF EDUCATIONAL STRUCTURES FOR CHILDREN WITH SPECIAL EDUCATIONAL NEEDS

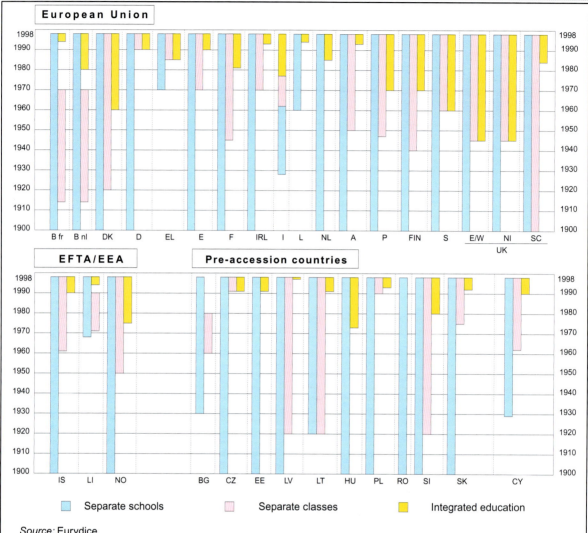

Source: Eurydice.

Additional notes

Belgium: There are some experiments with integration but they are limited in scope.

Germany: Since 1970, there have been experiments with integration in the form of pilot schemes.

Spain: An experimental programme of integration was introduced in 1985. The integration of pupils with special educational needs has been widespread since 1990 (LOGSE).

Netherlands: Since 1980, increasing numbers of children have been integrated into mainstream education.

Sweden: Since the end of the 1950s, increasing numbers of children have been integrated into mainstream education. Since 1 January 1996, the municipalities have been responsible for the education of children with severe learning difficulties. Nowadays, the aim is to achieve full integration, except for deaf children who remain in separate schools.

Bulgaria and **Romania**: Integration is being introduced.

THREE MAJOR ORGANISATIONAL MODELS OF EDUCATION FOR CHILDREN WITH SPECIAL EDUCATIONAL NEEDS: FROM SEPARATE EDUCATION TO INTEGRATION

Certain pupils are recognized as having special educational needs because they have either physical disabilities, sensory impairment (such as deafness or problems of vision) or severe learning or emotional problems. The current trend in the different countries of the EU, of the EFTA/EEA and of the pre-accession countries is towards the integration of children with special educational needs into mainstream schools, giving teachers varying degrees of support in terms of supplementary staff, materials and equipment.

Countries can be divided into three categories according to their policy on integrating children with special educational needs:

- The first category (referred to as the 'one-track' category) includes countries that develop a policy and practices geared towards the integration of almost all pupils within mainstream education. Generally speaking, this type of integration is supported by a wide range of services focusing on the mainstream school. The percentage of pupils attending special (i.e. separate) classes or schools is less than 1%, and the children considered as having special needs do not generally constitute a large percentage of the population (less than 2%). Among the countries of the EU and the EFTA/EEA, this approach can be found in Greece, Spain, Italy, Portugal, Sweden and Norway, and, among the pre-accession countries, in Cyprus.

- In the countries that belong to the second category (the 'two-track' category), there are two distinct education systems. These systems are (or at least were until very recently) under separate legislation, with different laws for mainstream and special education. In Belgium and the Netherlands (for the countries of the EU) and in Bulgaria, Latvia and Romania (for the pre-accession countries), special education is fairly well developed and is generally treated quite separately. These countries cater for over 3% of pupils in separate special education, and the percentage of pupils with special educational needs in mainstream schools is very small.

- The countries belonging to the third category (the 'multi-track') have a multiplicity of approaches to integration. They do not offer one single solution (integration in mainstream education with the support of many different services) or a choice between two options (mainstream or special education), but rather a variety of services between these two systems. These range from special multiple classes (full-time or part-time) to different forms of inter-school cooperation including 'exchange' activities (with teachers and pupils from mainstream and special schools arranging temporary or part-time exchanges). These countries sometimes have a considerable number of pupils with special educational needs and between 1 and 5% of pupils in separate schools. In the EU and the EFTA/EEA, the countries belonging to this category include Denmark, Germany, France, Ireland, Luxembourg, Austria, Finland, the United Kingdom, Iceland and Liechtenstein, and, among the pre-accession countries, the Czech Republic, Estonia, Lithuania, Hungary, Poland, Slovenia and Slovakia.

The situation is currently in the throes of change: the 'two-track' countries are tending to adopt a 'multi-track' approach. In these countries, a growing number of structures are appearing somewhere between mainstream education and special education. These same countries are adopting radical legislative measures to overcome the marked differences between mainstream schools and special education institutions.

In the 'one-track' countries, the general trend is towards the conversion of a number of the special schools that still operate into resource centres. This type of development is also found in the 'multi-track' category.

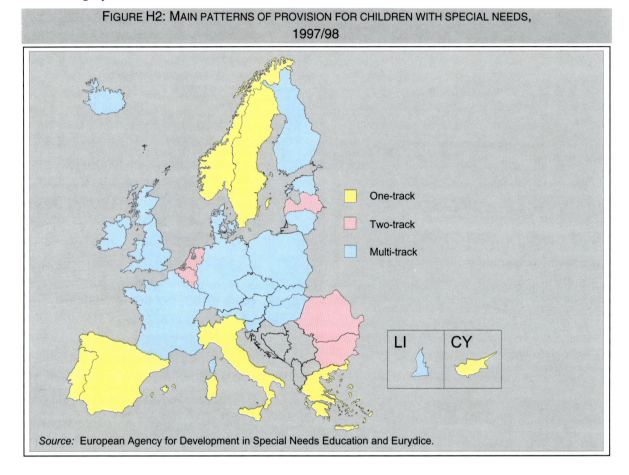

FIGURE H2: MAIN PATTERNS OF PROVISION FOR CHILDREN WITH SPECIAL NEEDS, 1997/98

One-track

Two-track

Multi-track

Source: European Agency for Development in Special Needs Education and Eurydice.

——————— CONDITIONS REQUIRED FOR INTEGRATION ———————

In most countries of the EU and the EFTA/EEA for which information is available, there are no legal limits on the integration of children with special needs. Whether integration is widespread or on an experimental basis, certain preconditions have to be met, including:

- the agreement of a board comprising psychologists and/or educationalists (Germany, Spain, France, United Kingdom – Scotland);

- the school's ability to cater for the needs of integrated pupils (Germany, Greece, Spain, Austria) but also concern that the education of the rest of the pupils in the class remains effective (Germany, United Kingdom – England, Wales and Northern Ireland);

- parents' views (Germany, Spain, France, Austria, United Kingdom, Liechtenstein).

In some countries the nature and degree of the need may play a part in deciding on integration. For instance, in the United Kingdom, many deaf children are integrated while in Greece, Sweden, Iceland and Norway they are in separate schools. Children with severe learning difficulties or emotional and behavioural difficulties are also in separate schools in Spain, Austria and Portugal.

In the pre-accession countries, integration is sometimes subject to certain conditions. For example, in the Czech Republic, Estonia, Poland, Slovakia and Cyprus, the approval of the competent authority and/or the parents is required.

PROVIDING SUPPORT FOR THE INTEGRATION OF CHILDREN WITH SPECIAL EDUCATIONAL NEEDS

In most countries, some of the children with special educational needs are integrated into mainstream education. Where this is the case, the class teacher teaches them like all the other pupils. In most countries where one or other form of integration is organized, **pedagogical support** is given to the teacher by various professionals, in most cases specialist teachers, who may for example give the child some separate tuition or advise the class teacher. The class teacher and the specialist teacher generally work together within the school, sometimes in the classroom and sometimes outside.

Of the EU and the EFTA/EEA countries, Greece and Italy regard specialist teachers as part of the staff of mainstream schools. In contrast, in the Flemish Community of Belgium, Denmark, the Netherlands, Sweden, and the United Kingdom (Scotland), the specialist teacher is attached to an external agency (for example a special school or a local support service). In Austria, Sweden, the United Kingdom (England, Wales, Northern Ireland), Iceland and Norway, specialist teachers can be part of the staff or attached to an external agency. In Luxembourg, teachers' assistants are not teachers as such but professionals such as social workers or therapists in various disciplines. In Germany and Spain, support for integrating children with special needs is provided by specialist teachers and other specialists. In the United Kingdom (England, Wales and Northern Ireland), learning support assistants provide help to teachers to enable some children with special educational needs to be educated within mainstream schools.

Likewise in the pre-accession countries, Lithuania, Hungary, Slovenia and Cyprus see specialist teachers as part of the educational team of mainstream schools, while in the Czech Republic, Latvia and Romania, specialist teachers are sent by centres outside the schools in which children with special educational needs are integrated.

Support for children with special educational needs and their teachers in mainstream education also involve services other than education services, mainly **health and social services**. The support provided and the degree of intervention vary considerably from country to country. For example, in France, specialist services under the auspices of the ministry of Health and Social Security, provide support for children in mainstream education, both within and out of school. In most pre-accession countries, as well as being taught (by specialists or otherwise), children with special educational needs receive support from the social and/or medical services.

SPECIAL EDUCATIONAL NEEDS
IN THE INITIAL TRAINING OF TEACHERS

Teachers are the main professionals involved in the education of children, whether they have special educational needs or not. It is therefore important for them to acquire the knowledge and skills required to cater for all children.

FIGURE H3: INITIAL TRAINING FOR SPECIAL EDUCATIONAL NEEDS.
PRIMARY AND SECONDARY LEVEL TEACHERS, 1997/98

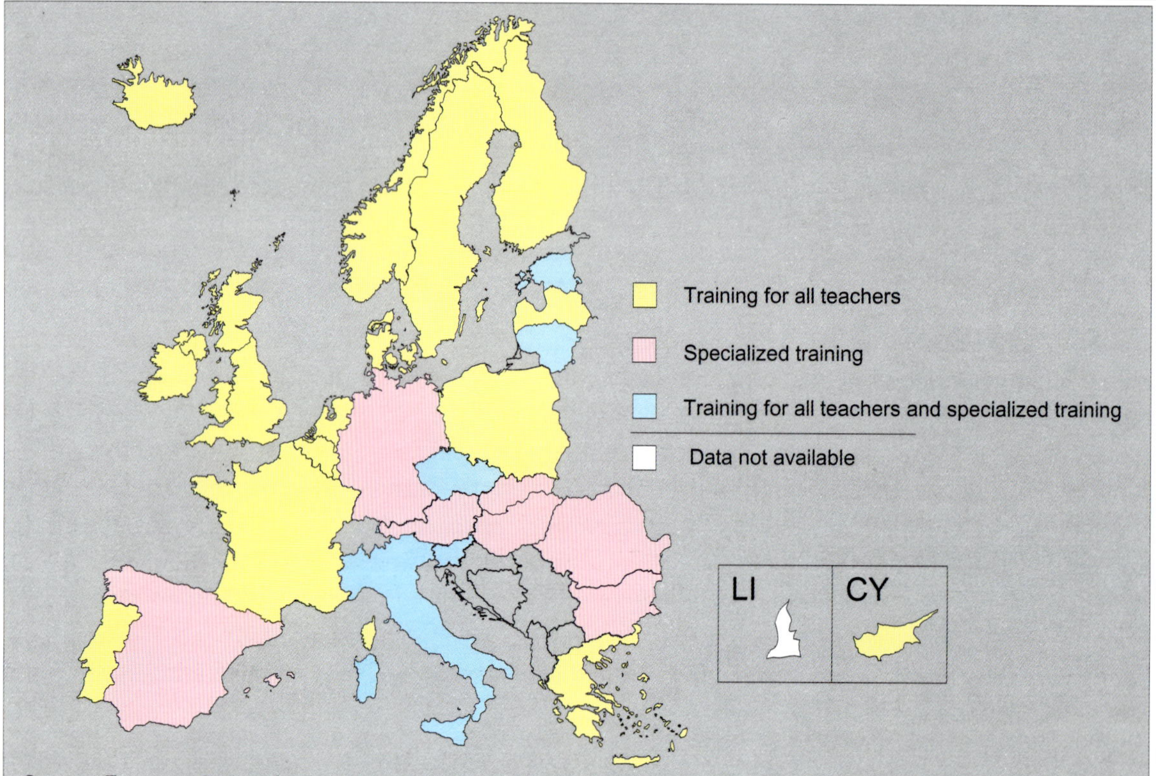

Training for all teachers

Specialized training

Training for all teachers and specialized training

Data not available

LI   CY

Source: European Agency for Development in Special Needs Education and Eurydice.

Additional notes

Sweden: Students may be offered training for special educational needs. When this training is offered, the length and focus of such training vary according to the university and the university college.
United Kingdom (E/W, NI): Additional training is needed for teachers who specialize in the education of children with significant sensory impairments.
Cyprus: The information given only covers pre-primary and primary school teachers.

In most EU and EFTA/EEA countries, part of the initial training of all teachers relates to special education. In certain countries (Belgium, Denmark, Greece, France, Ireland, Italy, Luxembourg, Portugal, United Kingdom, Iceland), this aspect of teacher training consists of general information on the different types of disabilities, on the need for differentiated education and on ways to adapt the curriculum to the needs of each pupil. In Belgium, Ireland and Luxembourg, this theoretical input is followed by practical training. In Greece, future teachers visit special schools during their period of training.

In a number of countries, student teachers receive more in-depth training. For example, in Finland all future teachers follow a course two hours a week for a year that provides them with theoretical and practical training on special educational needs. In Norway, a considerable proportion of the initial training of all teachers is devoted to special needs (half a year).

In most pre-accession countries, part of the initial training of all teachers concerns children with special educational needs. The purpose of the general information provided is to enable future teachers to cater for the educational needs of each pupil. In the Czech Republic and Poland, the duration and content of the information vary according to the teacher training institution attended. In Lithuania, the theory is followed by a period of practical training.

In addition to this basic training that forms an integral part of the initial training of all teachers, in certain countries student teachers can opt for one or other course or module devoted to special educational needs. This is the case, among EU and EFTA/EEA countries, in Denmark, Greece, Spain, Ireland, the Netherlands, Austria, Sweden, the United Kingdom, Iceland and Norway, and, among the pre-accession countries, in the Czech Republic, Estonia, Latvia, Lithuania, Poland and Cyprus.

Within the EU, in Germany, Spain, Italy and Austria, and, among the pre-accession countries, in the Czech Republic, Estonia, Lithuania, Hungary, Romania, Slovenia and Slovakia, one of the training programmes offered to future teachers is designed exclusively for those who wish to work with children with special educational needs. This programme is organized in parallel with the initial training followed by all student teachers. It is generally a long course of study, lasting between three and five years according to the country.

—— ADDITIONAL TRAINING FOR SPECIAL EDUCATIONAL NEEDS ——

Additional training is provided for teachers who wish to work with children with special educational needs, whether in special or mainstream education. This additional training is generally provided after the period of initial training. In a number of countries, to be eligible to follow this additional training course, the teacher must have worked in mainstream education. The professional experience required varies from country to country – one year in the United Kingdom and up to five years in Denmark (for certain qualifications) and Greece. In contrast, in a number of EU and EFTA/EEA countries (Belgium, Germany, Spain for primary teachers, France, Italy, Sweden and Norway) and in almost all pre-accession countries (except Lithuania), the additional training can be undertaken immediately following the period of initial training.

In more than half of the countries, the additional training is optional and is provided through in-service training. In the other countries (Germany, Greece for primary teachers only, Portugal, Finland, Bulgaria, Estonia, Poland, Romania, Slovenia and Slovakia), it is compulsory.

In a number of countries (Ireland, Italy, Austria, Finland, the United Kingdom, the Czech Republic and Lithuania), additional training is compulsory for teachers who wish to work with children with certain disabilities, such as visual or hearing impairment, or speech difficulties.

Participation in additional training and recognition as a specialist teacher are rewarded in different ways from country to country: a higher salary (the Flemish Community of Belgium, Germany in some *Länder*, Greece, France, the Netherlands, Norway, Lithuania and Poland) or priority status in recruitment procedures (Iceland, Norway, Lithuania and Poland).

In most countries, additional training provides not only general training but also specific training on certain categories of special educational needs. In Germany, Luxembourg and Lithuania teachers are given a considerable degree of specialisation.

THE STRUCTURES OF PRIMARY AND SECONDARY SPECIAL EDUCATION ── CLOSELY RELATED TO THOSE OF MAINSTREAM EDUCATION ──

Within each EU and EFTA/EEA country that has parallel special education provisions, the structure is similar to that of mainstream education. This structure is presented in Figure H4, which gives the names of the separate institutions providing special education. Divergence from the structure of mainstream education appears in the duration of compulsory education. In the French-speaking Community of Belgium (in full-time education) and in Finland (in some cases), compulsory education is longer for children with special educational needs. In the Flemish Community of Belgium, special primary education continues up to age 13 and secondary education to age 21, with the possibility of prolongation for a limited number of years.

In the pre-accession countries, the structures of special education provided in separate schools are very similar to those of mainstream education. The length of compulsory education is the same for all children, whether they have special educational needs or not, except for Cyprus where compulsory education for pupils with special educational needs extends to the age of 18, or 21 in some cases.

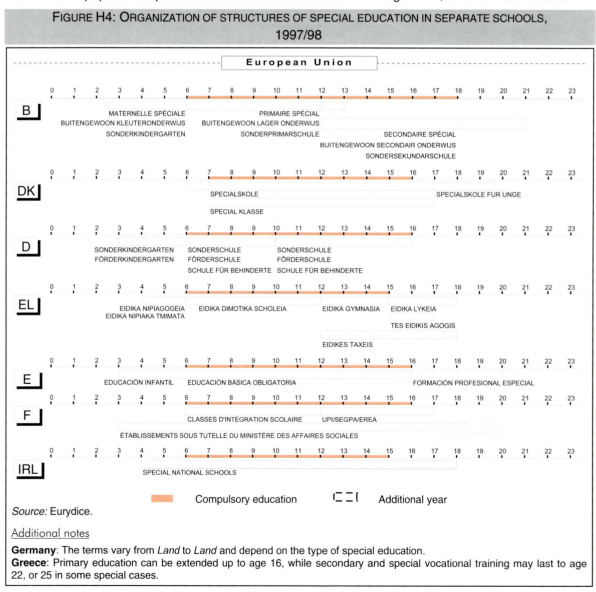

FIGURE H4: ORGANIZATION OF STRUCTURES OF SPECIAL EDUCATION IN SEPARATE SCHOOLS, 1997/98

Source: Eurydice.

Additional notes

Germany: The terms vary from *Land* to *Land* and depend on the type of special education.
Greece: Primary education can be extended up to age 16, while secondary and special vocational training may last to age 22, or 25 in some special cases.

FIGURE H4 (CONTINUED): ORGANIZATION OF STRUCTURES OF SPECIAL EDUCATION IN SEPARATE SCHOOLS, 1997/98

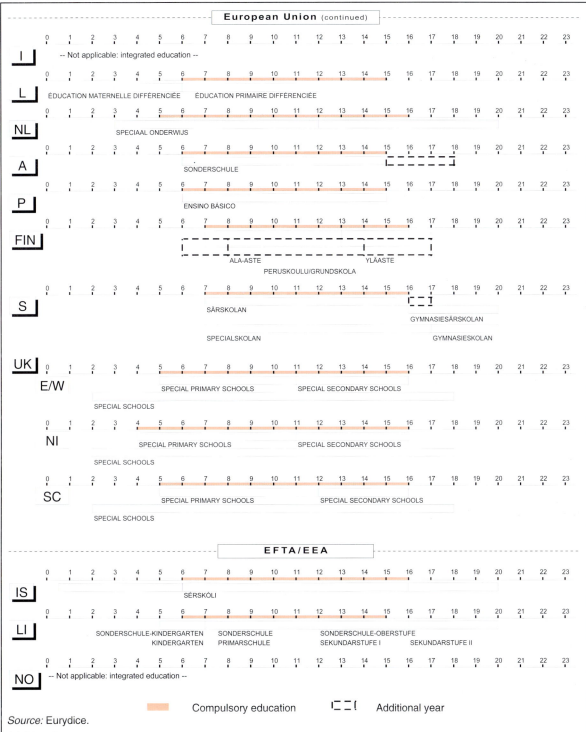

Source: Eurydice.

Additional notes

Finland: Special secondary education is also provided in special vocational institutions.
Sweden: All pupils in compulsory education follow the same curriculum. However, there are differences in the curricula designed for profoundly deaf children and those with severe learning difficulties. The *särskola* is often integrated with the *grundskola*.
United Kingdom (E/W, NI): Wherever possible, children with special educational needs must follow the statutory curriculum. However, the law allows modification of the National Curriculum, and related assessment arrangements, or exemption from the National Curriculum, for any child who has a statement of special educational needs.

FIGURE H4 (CONTINUED): ORGANIZATION OF STRUCTURES OF SPECIAL EDUCATION IN SEPARATE SCHOOLS, 1997/98

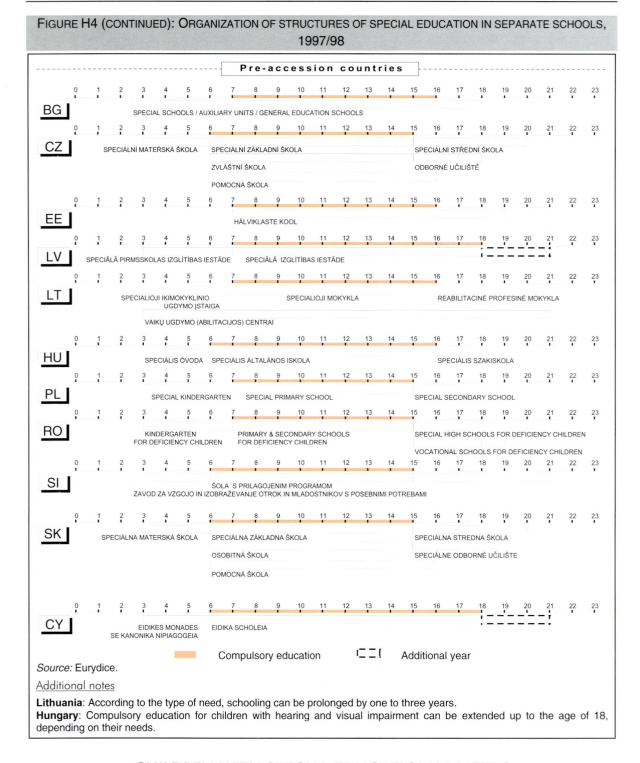

Source: Eurydice.

<u>Additional notes</u>

Lithuania: According to the type of need, schooling can be prolonged by one to three years.
Hungary: Compulsory education for children with hearing and visual impairment can be extended up to the age of 18, depending on their needs.

CHILDREN WITH SPECIAL EDUCATIONAL NEEDS
IN THE SCHOOL POPULATION

Each country applies its own criteria to determine whether or not a child has special educational needs. The definitions and categories therefore vary from country to country. Most countries use between six and ten categories, while some countries define only one or two. In the Netherlands, there are thirteen categories. In most countries these categories are assessed regularly. So it may happen that a child moves from one category to another, depending on his progress.

On the basis of these definitions, the different countries consider that a certain percentage of children in the overall school population has special needs. The percentage is less than 2% in some countries of the EU (Greece, Spain, Italy and the United Kingdom – Scotland) and in two pre-accession countries (Slovenia and Romania). In contrast, in Denmark, Finland and Iceland, over 10% of children are recognized as having special educational needs.

The differences observed between countries are determined not only by the type of categorisation adopted but also by the assessment procedures, the resources allocated to the education of these children and the structures set in place to cater for them.

When a child has been recognized as having special educational needs, one must then decide in which institution he will receive the education required to cater for his needs. Different countries adopt different approaches, ranging from integration in mainstream education to teaching in special schools, with a wide variety of intermediate solutions.

Figure H5 shows for each country the percentage of children who are recognized as having special educational needs and the percentage of these children who are educated within separate structures (special classes or schools).

It can be seen that in some countries the vast majority of children with special educational needs attend separate schools. This is the case in Belgium and the Netherlands (EU countries) and in Romania, Slovenia and Slovakia (pre-accession countries).

On the other hand, in Denmark, Greece, Spain, Portugal, Finland, Sweden, Iceland and Norway, for the EU and EFTA/EEA countries, and in Lithuania and Cyprus, for the pre-accession countries, most children with special educational needs are integrated into mainstream education. A small percentage of them attend special schools.

FIGURE H5: PERCENTAGE OF CHILDREN RECOGNIZED AS HAVING SPECIAL EDUCATIONAL NEEDS AND PERCENTAGE OF CHILDREN WITH SPECIAL NEEDS EDUCATED SEPARATELY (SPECIAL CLASSES AND SCHOOLS). COMPULSORY PRIMARY AND SECONDARY EDUCATION, 1997/98

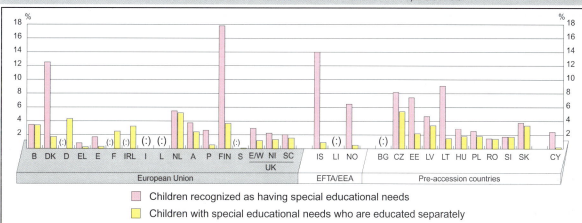

Children recognized as having special educational needs

Children with special educational needs who are educated separately

Source: European Agency for Development in Special Needs Education and Eurydice.

Additional notes

Belgium: 1995/96 for the French-speaking Community, 1996/97 for the Flemish Community.
Denmark and **France**: Estimate.
Germany: The statistics do not include the number of pupils with special educational needs in mainstream education for all *Länder*.
Netherlands: Estimate for children recognized as having special educational needs.
Austria, Portugal and **Sweden**: 1995/96.
Finland: 1998/99. The vast majority of pupils recognized as having special educational needs receive part-time special education; they are given special support for their minor learning or adjustment problems in conjunction with regular education.
United Kingdom (E/W, NI): 1996/97 for Wales. The statistics only refer to children with statements of special educational needs; those children at earlier stages of the process of the identification and assessment of special educational needs are not included. The figures for children educated separately do not include those in special classes or units of mainstream schools.
Norway: 1995/96.
Czech Republic, Slovakia and **Cyprus**: 1995/96.
Lithuania, Poland, Romania and **Slovenia**: 1997/98.
Slovenia: The percentage of children with special educational needs in mainstream education is estimated to be 1 or 2%.

FOREIGN LANGUAGES

In most countries of the European Union and of the EFTA/EEA, the teaching of foreign languages begins in earnest at the start of primary education. When the teaching of languages is compulsory, it is generally from the third or fourth year of primary education. Luxembourg and Norway are exceptional in this regard as they introduce the teaching of a foreign language at the start of the first year of primary level.

In the French and Flemish Communities of Belgium, Germany, France and the United Kingdom (except Scotland), a first foreign language is compulsory for all pupils from the start of secondary education. In these countries, during primary education or at least the final years of this level, schools are free to impose a foreign language as a compulsory subject on all their pupils.

In Luxembourg, the second compulsory foreign language is introduced from the second year of primary school. Two of the national languages, German and French, are considered as foreign languages. For this reason, they are used for the teaching of different subjects instead of the mother tongue, Letzeburgesch, as the pupils get older. A third foreign language is compulsory for all pupils before the end of lower secondary school.

In Sweden and Iceland, a second foreign language becomes compulsory before the end of primary level. In the Flemish Community of Belgium, Greece, the Netherlands, Finland and Liechtenstein, a second foreign language becomes compulsory at lower secondary level or before the end of the single-structure system. In some other EU and EFTA/EEA countries, a second language is offered as a compulsory option at this level of education (Spain, Portugal and Norway) or depends on the section or school attended by the pupil (Germany, France, Austria). In Italy, the *scuola media* may offer a second foreign language among their compulsory options.

Ireland is an exception: foreign languages are not among the compulsory subjects in the curriculum at any level. However, pupils take Irish and English throughout the period of compulsory education.

In most pre-accession countries, compulsory teaching of a foreign language starts in primary school or in the first years of the single-structure system.

In Slovenia, before becoming compulsory at secondary level or during the final years of the single-structure system, a foreign language is offered as an option.

The teaching of a second foreign language is compulsory from the end of primary school in Estonia and from the start of lower secondary school in Latvia, Lithuania, Romania and Cyprus. At this educational level, each school may offer a second foreign language among its compulsory options in the Czech Republic, Hungary, Poland and Slovenia.

In most countries, whether they be countries of the EU, the EFTA/EEA or pre-accession countries, after the end of compulsory education or the start of upper secondary level, the section or branch chosen by the student determines the number of languages taught and the status (compulsory or optional) of the subject. In some countries, the institutions are free to offer one or more foreign languages among their compulsory options.

In addition to the above, some countries have set up pilot projects either at pre-primary level (Spain, Italy, Austria), or at primary school (Germany, Ireland, Bulgaria, Poland). Most of the time, the aim of these projects is to teach a foreign language at a level of education at which it is not yet compulsory.

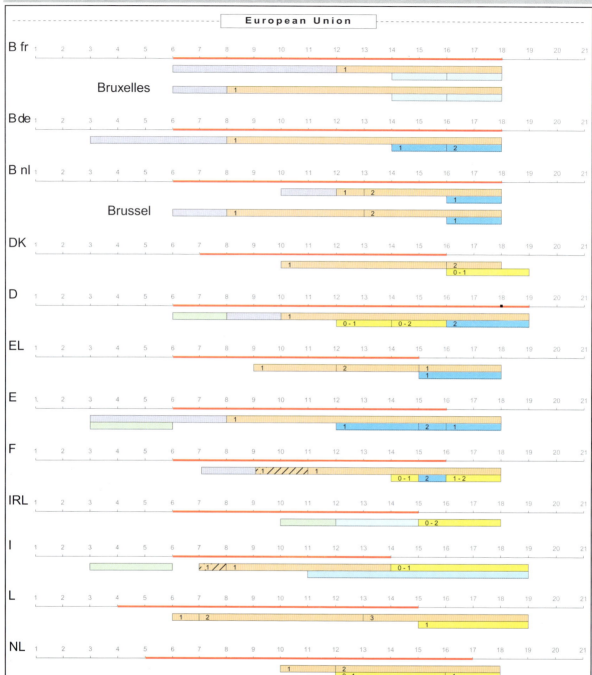

FIGURE I1: THE AVAILABILITY OF FOREIGN LANGUAGES AT PRE-PRIMARY, PRIMARY AND GENERAL SECONDARY LEVELS, 1997/98

Source: Eurydice.

Additional notes

Belgium (B fr): In 1998/99, it became compulsory to teach a foreign language to all pupils from the age of 10.

Denmark: Pupils may choose a second foreign language as an option from the 7th form. Instruction in the second language is furthermore a requirement for entry into general upper secondary education. It is not part of the compulsory curriculum but the vast majority of pupils take this language (primarily German).

France: In 1998/99, it became compulsory to teach a second foreign language to pupils from the age of 13. However, in certain regions pupils can choose a regional language. From 1999/2000 it became compulsory to teach a foreign language to all pupils from the age of 9.

Ireland: The teaching of foreign languages is not compulsory. Nonetheless, English and Irish are taught in Ireland.

Italy: In 1992/93, learning one compulsory foreign language has been phased in for all pupils aged 7 and over.

Luxembourg: In the '*classique*' section, the teaching of English starts at the age of 14 and not at the age of 13.

Netherlands: It is compulsory to teach one foreign language in primary school. In practice, this starts between the ages of 10 and 12.

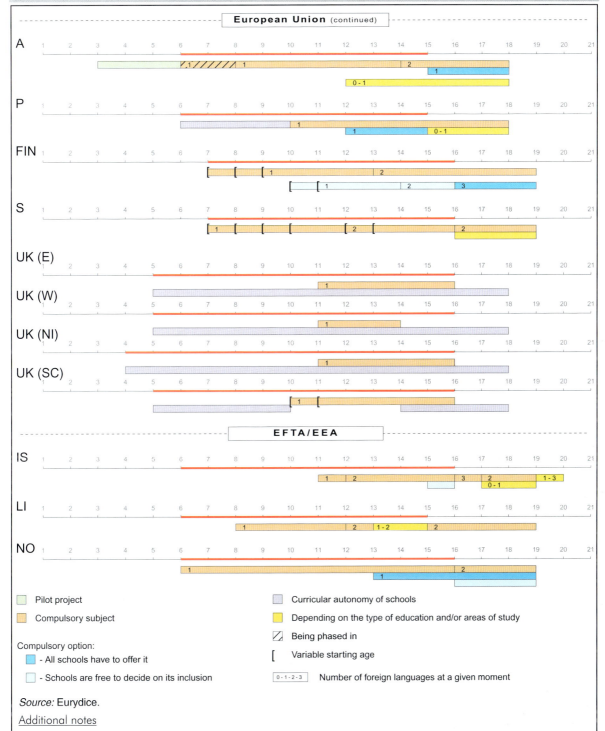

FIGURE I1 (CONTINUED): THE AVAILABILITY OF FOREIGN LANGUAGES AT PRE-PRIMARY, PRIMARY AND GENERAL SECONDARY LEVELS, 1997/98

	Legend
Pilot project	Curricular autonomy of schools
Compulsory subject	Depending on the type of education and/or areas of study
	Being phased in

Compulsory option:
- All schools have to offer it
- Schools are free to decide on its inclusion

[Variable starting age

0-1-2-3 Number of foreign languages at a given moment

Source: Eurydice.

Additional notes

Portugal: At upper secondary level, a second language is compulsory if the student has studied only one language during *ensino básico*.

Finland: The national curriculum encourages the schools to include foreign languages as optional subjects in the local curriculum.

Sweden: In 1997/98, around one third of Swedish schools offered English courses from the first year of *Grundskola* (7 years). Most pupils (i.e. around 80%) started learning English before the age of 10.

United Kingdom (E/W, NI): There is no compulsory curriculum for 16-18 year olds. Students are free to choose their subjects from those offered by the institution. Most schools would normally offer courses in foreign languages.

United Kingdom (SC): There are no Curriculum Guidelines for 16-18 year olds. Generally, students choose five subjects from those offered by the institution. Most schools would normally offer two foreign languages.

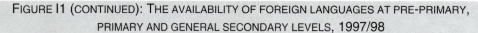

FIGURE I1 (CONTINUED): THE AVAILABILITY OF FOREIGN LANGUAGES AT PRE-PRIMARY, PRIMARY AND GENERAL SECONDARY LEVELS, 1997/98

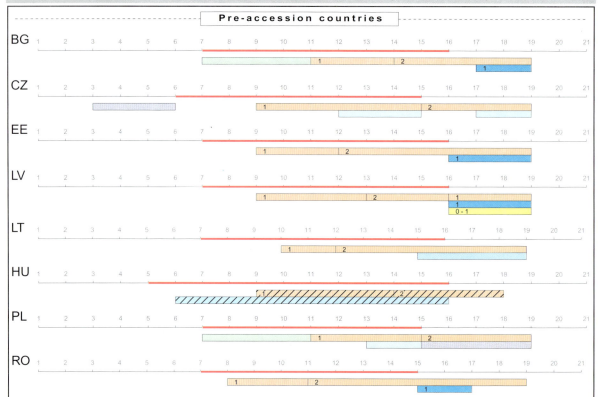

Source: Eurydice.

<u>Additional notes</u>

Estonia: Up till 1998 minority Russian medium schools had their own curricula. Since September 1998, a new Estonian curriculum has started in the Russian medium schools.

Latvia: The first foreign language starts at the age of 11 in the schools for linguistic minorities.

Lithuania: Schools for linguistic minorities follow the national curricula. The contents are the same as in the other schools, only the way the curricula are implemented differs.

Poland: From 1999/2000, it becomes compulsory to teach one foreign language from the age of 10.

Romania: The new primary school curriculum that was published in September 1998 provides for the teaching of foreign languages from age 9.

<u>Explanatory note</u>

These diagrams only deal with languages described as "foreign". Regional and/or ancient languages are only included when they are considered alternatives to choosing foreign languages by the curricula.

D e f i n i t i o n   o f   t h e   t e r m s   u s e d   i n   t h e   c a p t i o n :

Pilot project: A foreign language that is part of a pilot project, limited in time, set up and financed at least partly by the public authorities (the education authorities responsible).

Compulsory subject: A foreign language that is included among the compulsory subjects in the minimum curriculum developed centrally, which pupils are obliged to study.

Compulsory option: The centrally devised minimum curriculum intends that pupils have to choose a certain number of subjects from among those offered as compulsory options. Either the institution <u>is obliged</u> to offer a foreign language among the range of compulsory options (dark blue) or the institution <u>is free</u> to include a foreign language among the compulsory options (light blue).

Curricular autonomy: Institutions are at liberty to impose a foreign language as a compulsory subject or a compulsory option on all their pupils, in addition to the subjects that form part of the minimum curriculum.

Depending on the type of education and/or areas of study: Depending on the type of studies or the type of general education, the minimum curriculum may or may not contain foreign languages, either as compulsory subjects or compulsory options.

Being phased in: New legal requirements concerning the teaching of a foreign language cannot be put in place straight away in all schools. So institutions have a certain time to adapt to the provisions of the new law. Therefore teaching of this foreign language is being phased in.

Number of foreign languages at a given time: This number only refers to languages that are regarded as compulsory subjects or compulsory options in the minimum curriculum. In the yellow band, two numbers separated by a dash indicates the minimum and maximum number of foreign languages depending on the areas of studies.

Variable starting age: Education authorities do not impose a starting age for teaching a compulsory or a optional compulsory foreign language, but confine themselves to setting objectives to be attained in a certain level of education. Institutions therefore have the liberty to decide when they start to teach a foreign language.

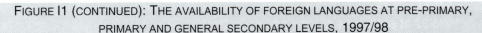

FIGURE I1 (CONTINUED): THE AVAILABILITY OF FOREIGN LANGUAGES AT PRE-PRIMARY, PRIMARY AND GENERAL SECONDARY LEVELS, 1997/98

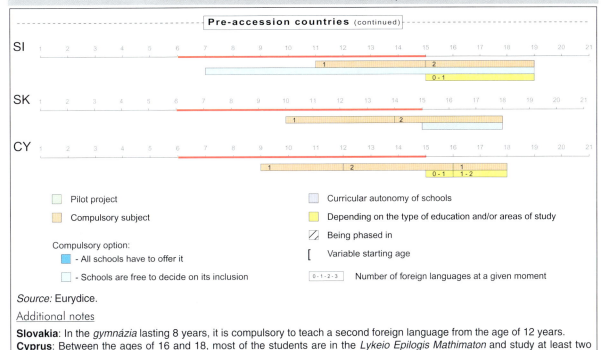

Pre-accession countries (continued)

SI

SK

CY

- Pilot project
- Compulsory subject

Compulsory option:
- - All schools have to offer it
- - Schools are free to decide on its inclusion

- Curricular autonomy of schools
- Depending on the type of education and/or areas of study
- Being phased in
- [Variable starting age
- 0-1-2-3 Number of foreign languages at a given moment

Source: Eurydice.

<u>Additional notes</u>

Slovakia: In the *gymnázia* lasting 8 years, it is compulsory to teach a second foreign language from the age of 12 years.
Cyprus: Between the ages of 16 and 18, most of the students are in the *Lykeio Epilogis Mathimaton* and study at least two compulsory foreign languages.

ONE FOREIGN LANGUAGE IS LEARNED
BY VARIABLE PROPORTIONS OF PRIMARY PUPILS

As seen in Figure I1, foreign language learning is either available to or compulsory for primary pupils in most European countries. In certain countries, it is even possible to learn two languages.

FIGURE I2: DISTRIBUTION OF PUPILS IN PRIMARY EDUCATION (ISCED 1)
ACCORDING TO THE NUMBER OF FOREIGN LANGUAGES LEARNED, 1996/97

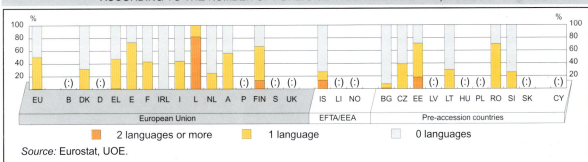

- 2 languages or more
- 1 language
- 0 languages

Source: Eurostat, UOE.

<u>Additional notes</u>

Belgium (B de): In the German-speaking Community, all ISCED 1 pupils learn one foreign language.
France: 1997/98.
Ireland: A pilot project, the Modern Languages Primary Project, was started in 1998 to support the introduction of one of French, German, Spanish or Italian in a few hundred primary schools.
Netherlands and **Portugal**: 1995/96.
Austria: 1997/98; pupils learning two languages are included in those learning one.
Finland: The national language taught in schools where it is not the teaching language is counted as a foreign language.
Czech Republic and **Slovenia**: Pupils learning two languages are included in those learning one.
Estonia: The national language taught in schools where it is not the teaching language is counted as a foreign language.

<u>Explanatory note</u>

These data refer to all primary pupils learning foreign languages, even if teaching the language does not start in the first years. Percentages do not indicate whether attendance of such courses is compulsory.

Irish, Letzeburgesch and regional languages are excluded, although provision may be made for them in certain Member States.

Allowing for exceptions, when one of the national languages is taught in schools where it is not the teaching language, it is not considered as a foreign language.

Figure I2 shows the percentage of pupils enrolled in primary education learning one, two or no foreign languages in 1996/97 at some time of their primary schooling. The most frequently learned languages differ from country to country and all foreign languages are therefore taken into account here (see Figure I5). The year in which a foreign language is started at primary level should be taken into account in the analysis.

In the EU countries for which data are available, on average, 50% of primary pupils follow foreign language courses. In Denmark, the Netherlands and Iceland, the proportion of pupils learning languages at this level is considerably smaller. In Ireland, foreign language teaching is not provided in primary schools. Conversely, in Spain and Finland, percentages are relatively high; in Luxembourg, all pupils are involved.

The most common situation is to learn one foreign language (49% of pupils on average in the EU). It is very much the exception to learn two; only 1% of EU pupils learn two foreign languages in primary school. Finland, Iceland and especially Luxembourg have the greatest proportions of pupils learning two languages (13%, 14% and 82% respectively).

Most pupils in pre-accession countries for which data are available do not learn any foreign languages at primary school. Only Estonia and Romania have a different profile: the percentage of pupils learning foreign languages exceeds 70%; in Estonia, 18% of pupils learn at least two languages.

ENGLISH: THE MOST TAUGHT FOREIGN LANGUAGE IN PRIMARY SCHOOLS

The foreign language most taught in primary schools in the EU is **English**: on average, more than one child in three learns English. The percentage is around 60% in Austria, Finland and Sweden. The countries with the highest percentages of primary pupils learning English are Spain (71%) and Portugal (84%). In Luxembourg, the English language is not taught at this level and, in Belgium, the number of children learning English at primary school is very low.

In Iceland, only 14% of primary pupils learn English.

In pre-accession countries, overall values are lower than in the EU. Nevertheless, at least some pupils are involved in learning English in each country. The highest percentages of pupils learning English are found in Estonia, Latvia and Cyprus, with 44%, 29% and 36% respectively.

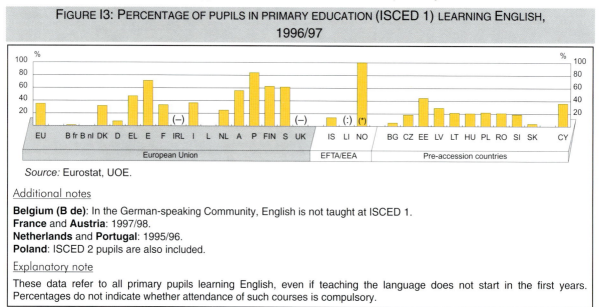

FIGURE I3: PERCENTAGE OF PUPILS IN PRIMARY EDUCATION (ISCED 1) LEARNING ENGLISH, 1996/97

Source: Eurostat, UOE.

Additional notes

Belgium (B de): In the German-speaking Community, English is not taught at ISCED 1.
France and **Austria**: 1997/98.
Netherlands and **Portugal**: 1995/96.
Poland: ISCED 2 pupils are also included.

Explanatory note

These data refer to all primary pupils learning English, even if teaching the language does not start in the first years. Percentages do not indicate whether attendance of such courses is compulsory.

Of all the other foreign languages taught at primary level **French** is in second place with an average of 3% learning it in the EU as a whole. Percentages are below 10%, except in Portugal, where 16% learn this language and in the Flemish Community of Belgium and Luxembourg, where all pupils learn French from the 5th and the 2nd year of primary school respectively. In both cases, French is one of the country's official languages.

In pre-accession countries, the percentage of primary pupils learning French is very small (approximately 1%). Romania is an exception, with 43%.

FIGURE I4: PERCENTAGE OF PUPILS IN PRIMARY EDUCATION (ISCED 1) LEARNING FRENCH, 1996/97

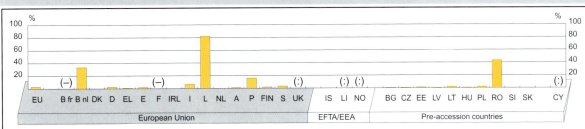

Source: Eurostat, UOE.

Additional notes

Belgium (B de): In the German-speaking Community, all pupils learn French from the first year of primary school.
France and **Austria**: 1997/98.
Ireland: A pilot project, the Modern Languages Primary Project, was started in 1998 to support the introduction of one of French, German, Spanish or Italian in a few hundred primary schools.
Netherlands and **Portugal**: 1995/96.
Poland: ISCED 2 pupils are also included.

Explanatory note

These data refer to all primary pupils learning French, even if teaching the language does not start in the first years. Percentages do not indicate whether attendance of such courses is compulsory.

APART FROM ENGLISH,
— THE MOST POPULAR FOREIGN LANGUAGES AT PRIMARY LEVEL VARY —

In some EU and EFTA/EEA countries, languages other than English and French are learned. Among the main ones are: German in the French-speaking Community of Belgium, France, Luxembourg, Finland and Sweden; Dutch in the French-speaking Community of Belgium; Swedish in Finland and Danish in Iceland.

In pre-accession countries, in addition to English, German is taught at this level in all countries and, in some countries, French and other languages from Eastern countries are learned (Russian, Estonian, Latvian, Hungarian and Slovakian).

FIGURE 15: FOREIGN LANGUAGES MOST LEARNED AT PRIMARY LEVEL (ISCED 1) AND PERCENTAGE OF PUPILS LEARNING THEM, BY COUNTRY, 1996/97

	European Union															
	B fr	B nl	DK	D	EL	E	F	IRL	I	L	NL	A	P	FIN	S	UK
1st foreign language	NL 15	● 33	● 32	● 8	● 47	● 71	● 33		● 36	● 100	● 25	● 56	● 93	● 63	● 62	
2nd foreign language	● 1			● 3		● 2	● 7	(-)	● 6	● 82		● 1	● 21	● 8	● 6	(:)
3rd foreign language	● 1						● 2		● 1					SV 4	● 3	

	EFTA/EEA			Pre-accession countries										
	IS	LI	NO	BG	CZ	EE	LV	LT	HU	PL	RO	SI	SK	CY
1st foreign language	DA 25			● 5	● 20	● 44	LV 34	● 21	● 21	● 22	● 43	● 19	SK 7	● 36
2nd foreign language	● 14	(:)	(:)	● 2		EE 27	● 29	● 7	● 20	● 16	● 21	● 6	● 4	
3rd foreign language				● 1		● 12	● 5	● 2	HU 5	● 13	● 3		● 3	

● German   ● English   ● Spanish   ● French   ● Russian

For the other codes, see the Glossary

Source: Eurostat, UOE.

Additional notes

France and **Austria**: 1997/98.
Ireland: A pilot project, the Modern Languages Primary Project, was started in 1998 to support the introduction of one of French, German, Spanish or Italian in a few hundred primary schools.
Netherlands and **Portugal**: 1995/96.
Finland: The national language taught in schools where it is not the teaching language (4%) is counted as a foreign language.
Estonia, Latvia, Hungary and **Slovakia**: The national language taught in schools where it is not the teaching language is counted as a foreign language.
Poland: ISCED 2 pupils are also included.

Explanatory note

The Figure shows, for each country, the languages (3 at the most) most frequently taught at primary level. They are classified according to the percentage of pupils learning them, in decreasing order. Marginal cases (less than 1%) are excluded.

Allowing for exceptions, when one of the national languages is taught in schools where it is not the teaching language, it is not considered as a foreign language.

These data refer to all primary pupils learning foreign languages, even if teaching the language does not start in the first years. Percentages do not indicate whether attendance of such courses is compulsory.

ALL PUPILS IN GENERAL SECONDARY EDUCATION
LEARN AT LEAST ONE FOREIGN LANGUAGE

Every young person enrolled in general secondary education learns at least one foreign language. In the EU as a whole, the average number of foreign languages studied per pupil during the course of general secondary education is 1.4. It ranges from 1 language in Ireland and Portugal to 2.5 in Finland and 2.9 in Luxembourg. Icelandic pupils enrolled in secondary education learn on average 1.7 languages.

In pre-accession countries, except in the Czech Republic, Hungary and Slovenia, the average number of foreign languages learned per pupil is equal to or above the EU average. However, the highest values observed in some EU countries are not reached.

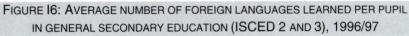

FIGURE 16: AVERAGE NUMBER OF FOREIGN LANGUAGES LEARNED PER PUPIL
IN GENERAL SECONDARY EDUCATION (ISCED 2 AND 3), 1996/97

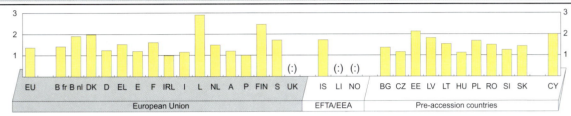

Source: Eurostat, UOE.

Additional notes

Belgium (B de): In the German-speaking Community, the average number is 1.4.
France: In ISCED 3, students from technological education are included in general education.
Ireland: Only full-time pupils are included.
Netherlands: 1995/96; only full-time pupils are included.
Austria: 1997/98.
Portugal: 1995/96; only ISCED 2 pupils are included, including pupils from the vocational stream.
Finland: The national language taught in schools where it is not the teaching language is counted as a foreign language.
Sweden: Only ISCED 2 pupils are included.
Iceland: In ISCED 3, students from the vocational stream are also included.
Czech Republic: Only full-time pupils are included.
Estonia, Hungary and **Latvia**: The national language taught in schools where it is not the teaching language is counted as a foreign language.
Poland: Only ISCED 3 students are included.
Slovenia: In ISCED 3, students from the vocational stream are also included.
Slovakia: Only ISCED 3 students are included; the national language taught in schools where it is not the teaching language is counted as a foreign language.

Explanatory note

The average number of foreign languages learned in general secondary education is obtained by dividing the total number of pupils learning languages by the number of pupils at that level.

Irish, Letzeburgesch and regional languages are excluded, although provision may be made for them in certain Member States.

Allowing for exceptions, when one of the national languages is taught in schools where it is not the teaching language, it is not considered as a foreign language.

ENGLISH IS THE MOST TAUGHT FOREIGN LANGUAGE
IN SECONDARY EDUCATION

English is by far the most popular foreign language at secondary level. Far fewer pupils learn other official EU languages. Thus, on average in the EU, 91% of pupils in general secondary education learn English whereas 34% study French, 15% German and only 10% Spanish. This phenomenon is also observed in EFTA/EEA and pre-accession countries.

The extent to which **English** is taught is largely comparable in all Member States where it is not the mother tongue and Iceland. In many countries, over 90% of pupils of general secondary education are taught English. Proportions are lower (between 68 and 83%) in Belgium, Greece, Italy, Luxembourg, Portugal and Iceland.

In pre-accession countries, the teaching of English is also widespread in general secondary education: at least 47% pupils learn it everywhere. In Estonia, the percentage is 82%. In Cyprus, all pupils enrolled in general secondary education learn English.

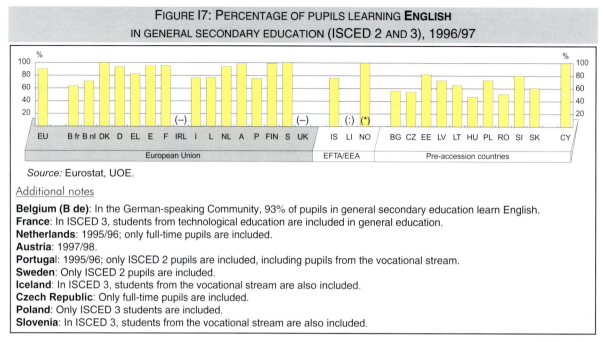

FIGURE I7: PERCENTAGE OF PUPILS LEARNING **ENGLISH**
IN GENERAL SECONDARY EDUCATION (ISCED 2 AND 3), 1996/97

Source: Eurostat, UOE.

Additional notes

Belgium (B de): In the German-speaking Community, 93% of pupils in general secondary education learn English.
France: In ISCED 3, students from technological education are included in general education.
Netherlands: 1995/96; only full-time pupils are included.
Austria: 1997/98.
Portugal: 1995/96; only ISCED 2 pupils are included, including pupils from the vocational stream.
Sweden: Only ISCED 2 pupils are included.
Iceland: In ISCED 3, students from the vocational stream are also included.
Czech Republic: Only full-time pupils are included.
Poland: Only ISCED 3 students are included.
Slovenia: In ISCED 3, students from the vocational stream are also included.

French is the second most taught foreign language in the EU as a whole, but with variations between member countries. Fewer than one pupil in five learns French in Denmark, the Netherlands, Austria, Finland and Iceland. On the other hand, percentages exceed 60% in Greece (63%), Ireland (70%), the Flemish Community of Belgium (95%) and Luxembourg (98%). In the three latter, French is the most taught language at this level; in the Flemish Community of Belgium and Luxembourg, French is one of the country's national languages.

French is taught in all pre-accession countries, although in small proportions. Romania and Cyprus are exceptions and show very high percentages of pupils learning French in general secondary education: 74% and 100%, respectively.

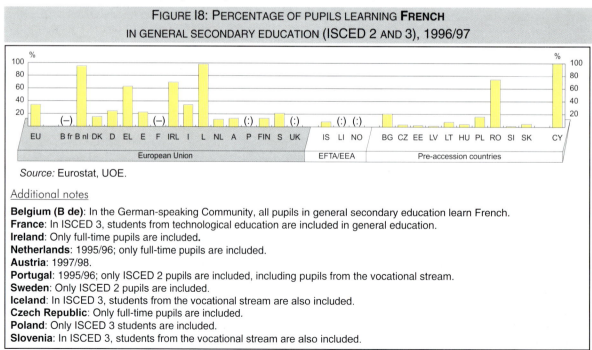

FIGURE I8: PERCENTAGE OF PUPILS LEARNING **FRENCH**
IN GENERAL SECONDARY EDUCATION (ISCED 2 AND 3), 1996/97

Source: Eurostat, UOE.

Additional notes

Belgium (B de): In the German-speaking Community, all pupils in general secondary education learn French.
France: In ISCED 3, students from technological education are included in general education.
Ireland: Only full-time pupils are included.
Netherlands: 1995/96; only full-time pupils are included.
Austria: 1997/98.
Portugal: 1995/96; only ISCED 2 pupils are included, including pupils from the vocational stream.
Sweden: Only ISCED 2 pupils are included.
Iceland: In ISCED 3, students from the vocational stream are also included.
Czech Republic: Only full-time pupils are included.
Poland: Only ISCED 3 students are included.
Slovenia: In ISCED 3, students from the vocational stream are also included.

German as a foreign language is taught in all Member States of which it is not the only national language. In Luxembourg, German is an official language and is obligatorily learned by all pupils. Of the four languages under consideration here, it is in second place in Denmark, Ireland, the Netherlands, Finland, Sweden and Iceland. The percentages of pupils learning German in general secondary education are particularly high in Denmark (76%) and Luxembourg (98%).

In pre-accession countries, German is taught in each country, usually to a higher percentage of pupils than the EU average. The percentage of pupils learning German in general secondary education ranges from 20 to 60%, except in Romania where it is below 10%. In some countries, German comes in second place as a foreign language.

FIGURE I9: PERCENTAGE OF PUPILS LEARNING **GERMAN**
IN GENERAL SECONDARY EDUCATION (ISCED 2 AND 3), 1996/97

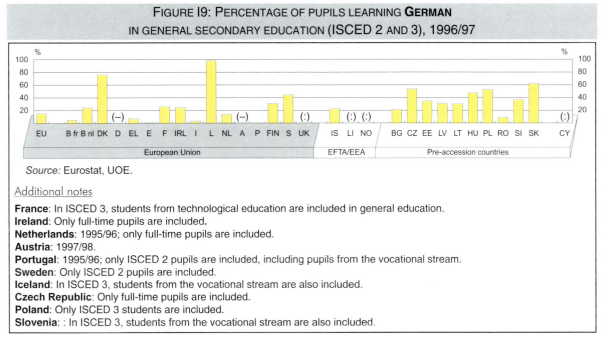

Source: Eurostat, UOE.

Additional notes

France: In ISCED 3, students from technological education are included in general education.
Ireland: Only full-time pupils are included.
Netherlands: 1995/96; only full-time pupils are included.
Austria: 1997/98.
Portugal: 1995/96; only ISCED 2 pupils are included, including pupils from the vocational stream.
Sweden: Only ISCED 2 pupils are included.
Iceland: In ISCED 3, students from the vocational stream are also included.
Czech Republic: Only full-time pupils are included.
Poland: Only ISCED 3 students are included.
Slovenia: : In ISCED 3, students from the vocational stream are also included.

While **Spanish** is taught in most EU Member States at secondary level, the proportion of pupils learning it in general secondary education does not exceed 5%; in many countries, only 1% are involved. In Luxembourg, there are 11%. France is an exception, with one third of pupils learning Spanish.

In pre-accession countries, the teaching of Spanish is even more marginal. The greatest proportion of pupils learning this language is found in Latvia (3%).

FIGURE I10: PERCENTAGE OF PUPILS LEARNING **SPANISH**
IN GENERAL SECONDARY EDUCATION (ISCED 2 AND 3), 1996/97

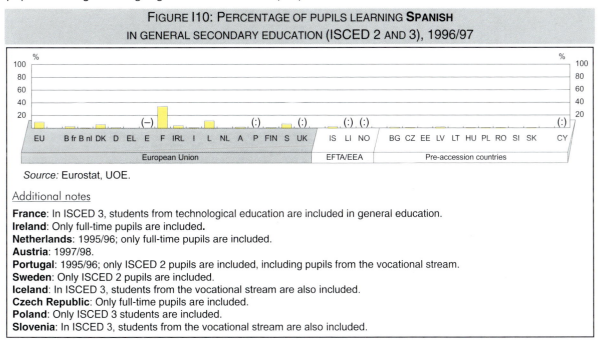

Source: Eurostat, UOE.

Additional notes

France: In ISCED 3, students from technological education are included in general education.
Ireland: Only full-time pupils are included.
Netherlands: 1995/96; only full-time pupils are included.
Austria: 1997/98.
Portugal: 1995/96; only ISCED 2 pupils are included, including pupils from the vocational stream.
Sweden: Only ISCED 2 pupils are included.
Iceland: In ISCED 3, students from the vocational stream are also included.
Czech Republic: Only full-time pupils are included.
Poland: Only ISCED 3 students are included.
Slovenia: In ISCED 3, students from the vocational stream are also included.

APART FROM ENGLISH, THE MOST POPULAR FOREIGN LANGUAGES —— IN GENERAL SECONDARY EDUCATION VARY ——

In some EU and EFTA/EEA countries, languages other than English, French, German and Spanish are learned: Dutch in the French-speaking Community of Belgium, Russian in Germany, Italian in France and Austria, Swedish in Finland and Iceland, and Danish in Iceland.

Among pre-accession countries, Russian is taught in most countries, as well as, in some countries, Estonian, Latvian, Hungarian and Italian.

FIGURE I11: FOREIGN LANGUAGES MOST LEARNED AT GENERAL SECONDARY LEVEL (ISCED 2 AND 3) AND PERCENTAGE OF PUPILS LEARNING THEM, BY COUNTRY, 1996/97

	European Union															
	B fr	B nl	DK	D	EL	E	F	IRL	I	L	NL	A	P	FIN	S	UK
1st foreign language	NL 70	95	100	94	83	96	95	70	76	98		98		99	100	
2nd foreign language	64	71	76	24	63	23	34	25	34	92	(:)	13	(:)	SV 93	44	(:)
3rd foreign language	5	24	15	3	7		26	4	3	77		IT 6		31	21	
4th foreign language	3		6	1			IT 4			11		2		13	6	

	EFTA/EEA			Pre-accession countries											
	IS	LI	NO	BG	CZ	EE	LV	LT	HU	PL	RO	SI	SK		CY
1st foreign language	76			56	55	82	73	65	48	73	74	80	62		100
2nd foreign language	DA 61	(:)	(:)	31	54	58	39	49	47	53	52	37	61		100
3rd foreign language	23			21	3	35	LV 37	31	HU 8	26	15	IT 5	9		
4th foreign language	8			21		EE 32	31								

● German   ● English   ● Spanish   ● French   ● Russian

For the other codes, see the Glossary

Source: Eurostat, UOE.

Additional notes

France: In ISCED 3, students from technological education are included in general education.
Ireland: Only full-time pupils are included.
Netherlands: 1995/96; only full-time pupils are included.
Austria: 1997/98.
Portugal: 1995/96; only ISCED 2 pupils are included, including pupils from the vocational stream.
Finland: The national language taught in schools where it is not the teaching language is counted as a foreign language (6%).
Sweden: Only ISCED 2 pupils are included.
Iceland: In ISCED 3, students from the vocational stream are also included.
Czech Republic: Only full-time pupils are included.
Estonia, Latvia, Hungary and **Slovakia**: The national language taught in schools where it is not the teaching language is counted as a foreign language.
Poland: Only ISCED 3 students are included.
Slovenia: In ISCED 3, students from the vocational stream are also included.

Explanatory note

The Figure shows, for each country, the languages most taught (4 at the most) in general secondary education. They are classified according to the percentage of pupils learning them, in decreasing order. Marginal cases (less than 1%) are excluded.

Allowing for exceptions, when one of the national languages is taught in schools where it is not the teaching language, it is not considered as a foreign language.

FOREIGN LANGUAGES ARE TAUGHT MORE IN GENERAL EDUCATION ——— THAN IN THE VOCATIONAL STREAM ———

In the EU Member States for which data are available, the percentage of pupils learning foreign languages is very similar in the vocational and general streams in Greece, France, Luxembourg, Austria and Sweden. Conversely, differences between streams are much larger in Spain and greatest in Denmark and Ireland.

FIGURE I12: PERCENTAGE OF PUPILS IN GENERAL AND VOCATIONAL SECONDARY EDUCATION (ISCED 2 AND 3) LEARNING FOREIGN LANGUAGES. DISTRIBUTION ACCORDING TO THE NUMBER OF LANGUAGES LEARNED, 1996/97

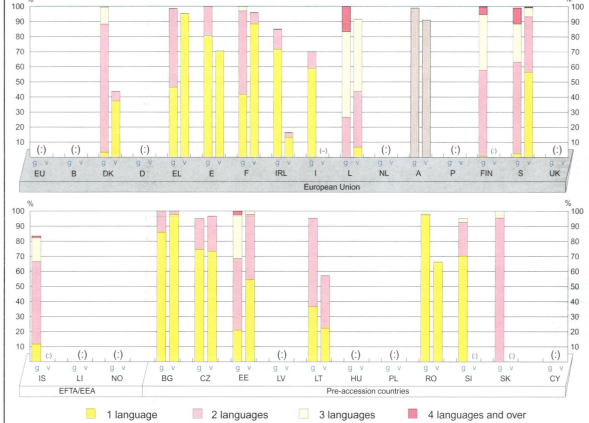

Source: Eurostat, UOE.

Additional notes

The vocational stream at ISCED level 2 exists only in Spain, France, Luxembourg and Austria.
France: In ISCED 3, students from technological education are included in general education.
Italy: Only ISCED 2 pupils are included.
Netherlands and **Portugal**: 1995/96.
Austria: 1997/98; the number of pupils learning two languages is included in those learning one.
Finland: The national language taught in schools where it is not the teaching language is counted as a foreign language.
Sweden: 1995/96; only ISCED 3 students are included.
Iceland: In ISCED 3, students from the vocational stream are also included.
Czech Republic: Only full-time pupils are included.
Estonia: The national language taught in schools where it is not the teaching language is counted as a foreign language.
Poland: Only ISCED 3 students are included.
Slovenia: In ISCED 3, students from the vocational stream are also included.
Slovakia: Only ISCED 3 students are included; the national language taught in schools where it is not the teaching language is counted as a foreign language.

Explanatory note

Irish, Letzeburgesch and regional languages are excluded, although provision may be made for them in certain Member States.

Allowing for exceptions, when one of the national languages is taught in schools where it is not the teaching language, it is not considered as a foreign language.

In pre-accession countries, two groups of countries can also be distinguished. In Bulgaria, the Czech Republic and Estonia, differences in enrolment in foreign language courses are negligible. They are larger in Lithuania and Romania.

In all EU countries, the proportion of young people learning more than one language is higher in the general stream.

In pre-accession countries, as in the EU, the teaching of two languages is more frequent in the general stream. Only the Czech Republic does not follow the pattern.

INFORMATION AND COMMUNICATION TECHNOLOGY

NATIONAL POLICY AND OFFICIAL DOCUMENTS ON THE USE —— OF INFORMATION AND COMMUNICATION TECHNOLOGY ——

During 1997/98, a national or official policy encouraging the use of information and communication technology in education has been in operation in almost all countries of the European Union, the EFTA/EEA and the pre-accession countries (except the Czech Republic and Slovakia).

This national policy has generally taken the form of one or more official documents (law, decree, circular, recommendation). In the majority of countries, the official documents on the use of ICT date from the 1990s, even the late 1990s.

In all countries, these official documents cover at least compulsory education (primary and secondary). In some countries, as illustrated in the Figure J1, they also cover tertiary education. Documents are also devoted to pre-primary education in the Flemish Community of Belgium, Spain, France, Italy, Luxembourg, Portugal, Finland and Sweden in the EU, and in Slovenia in the pre-accession countries.

FIGURE J1: EDUCATION LEVELS COVERED BY OFFICIAL DOCUMENTS ON THE USE OF ICT (IN FORCE DURING 1997/98)

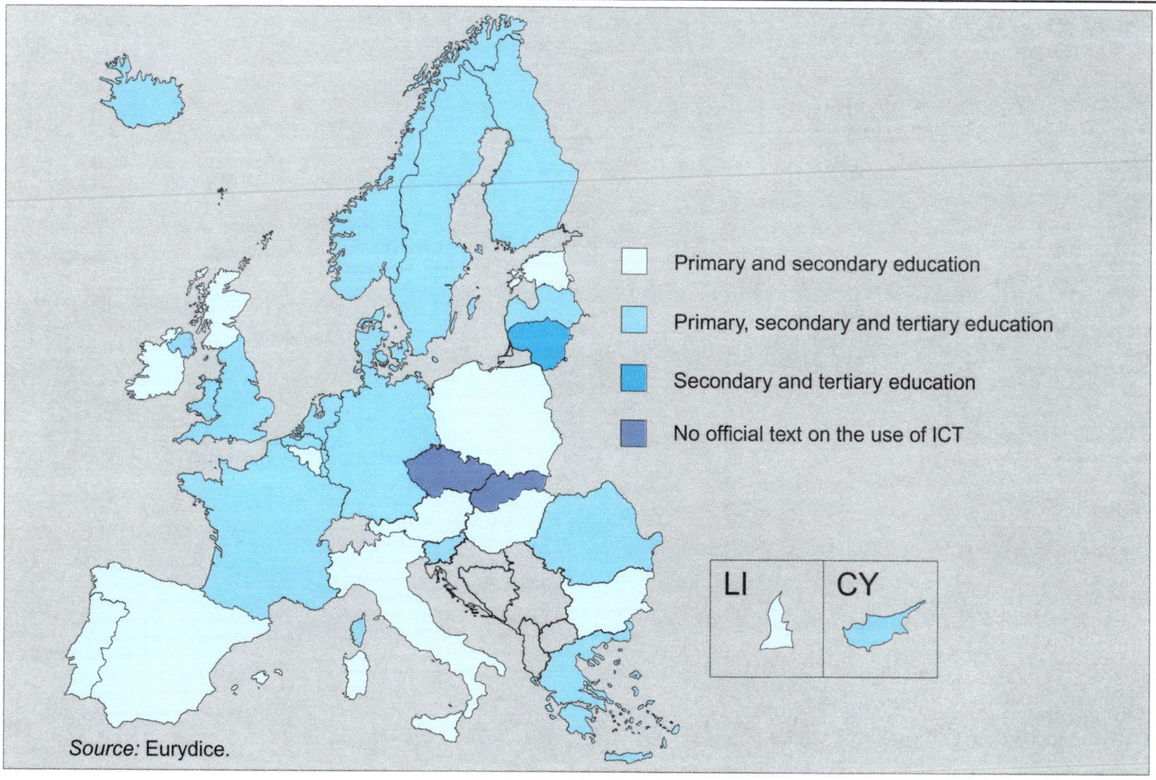

Legend:
- Primary and secondary education
- Primary, secondary and tertiary education
- Secondary and tertiary education
- No official text on the use of ICT

LI   CY

Source: Eurydice.

Additional notes

Netherlands: In tertiary education, only teacher-training institutes are involved in the national programme launched in 1997.
United Kingdom: The National Grid for Learning intends to support learners in all sectors of education.
Czech Republic: In 1999, the government approved the document 'Towards the information society' and has required the Ministry of Education, Youth and Sport to take account of it in formulating its national education policy.

NATIONAL OR OFFICIAL BODIES RESPONSIBLE
FOR SUPERVISING THE NATIONAL POLICY

In all the countries where official documents advocate the use of ICT in teaching, there are one or more national or official bodies that are entrusted with the task of applying them or promoting practical measures and centralising initiatives.

The number of such bodies varies from country to country, but their duties and responsibilities normally include some or all of the following: they define the objectives to be pursued; they select and/or supply the hardware and the software; they organize teacher training and the development of new software; they monitor and coordinate the various initiatives implemented in this area; they are responsible for the application of the decisions taken and the agreements concluded and they collect information to assess the impact of the projects and programmes set in place; etc.

FIGURE J2: NATIONAL OR OFFICIAL BODIES WITH A REMIT FOR
ICT IN EDUCATION, 1997/98

European Union	
B fr	Ministère de la Communauté française – Administration Générale de l'Enseignement et de la Recherche Scientifique
B de	Ministry: Organisation of the Unterrichtswesens
B nl	Department for Education Policy Co-ordination Division
DK	Undervisningsministeriet UNI*C Center for Teknologistøttet Uddannelse – CTU
D	Kultusministerien / Wissenschaftsministerien *(Länder)* Bundesministerium für Bildung und Forschung *(Bund)*
EL	Armodies Ypiresies YPEPTH Pedagogiko Instituto Instituto Technologias Ypologiston Tmimata Anotaton Ekpaideutikon Idrymaton Instituto Epexergasias Logou Ypeuthynoi Plhroforikis kai Neon Technologion (PLHNET) Dieuthynseon Protovathmias kai Deyterovathmias Ekpaideusis Nomon Periferiaka Epimorfotika Kentra Etairies systimaton pliroforikis
E	PNTIC (Ministerio de Educación y Cultura) Dirección General de Evaluación; Servicio de Renovación Pedagógica Dirección General de Ordenación e Innovación Educativa, etc (depending on the Autonomous Communities)
F	Ministère de l'éducation nationale, de la recherche et de la technologie Rectorats
IRL	Department of Education and Science – National centre for technology in education
I	Coordinatore del Programma di sviluppo delle tecnologie didattiche Comitato tecnico per il Programma di sviluppo delle tecnologie didattiche Gruppo di lavoro della Direzione Generale per l'Istruzione Tecnica Nucleo operativo del Programma di sviluppo delle tecnologie didattiche Nuclei di riferimento dei Provveditorati agli studi Ispettori tecnici
L	Centre de technologie de l'éducation – CTE Service de Coordination de la Recherche et de l'Innovation pédagogiques et technologiques – SCRIPT
NL	Procesmanagement ICT
A	Bundesministerium für Unterricht und kulturelle Angelegenheiten Landesschulräte Bezirksschulräte Schulleiter
P	Programa Nonio-Seculo XXI (Ministry of Education)
FIN	Opetusministeriö – Undervisningsminsteriet Opetushallitus – Utbildningsstyrelsen Opetuksen, tutkimuksen ja kulttuurin tietoyhteiskuntaneuvottelukunta – Delegationen för informationssamhället inom utbildningen, forskningen och kulturen Sitra
S	Statens skolverk
UK (E/W, NI)	British Educational Communications and Technology Agency – Becta Local Education Authorities (E/W) Strategic Management Group (NI) New Opportunities Fund Teacher Training Agency – TTA (E)
UK (SC)	Scottish Council for Educational Technology Scottish Office Superhighways Task Force

FIGURE J2 (CONTINUED): NATIONAL OR OFFICIAL BODIES WITH A REMIT FOR ICT IN EDUCATION, 1997/98	
EFTA/EEA	
IS	Ministry of Education, Science and Culture
LI	Schulamt Arbeitsgruppen P, Sek I und Sek II
NO	Kirke-, utdannings- og forskningsdepartementet Nasjonalt læremiddelsenter Forsknings- og kompetansenettverk for IT I utdanningen Statens utdanningskontor
Pre-accession countries	
BG	Ministry of Education and Science
CZ	Ministerstvo školství, mládeže a tělovýchovy
EE	Haridusministeerium Tiigrihüppe Sihtasutus PHARE 'Infosüsteemid hariduses' Programme EENet
LV	Izglītības un zinātnes ministrija Latvijas Universitāte Uzraudzības padome
LT	Švietimo ir Mokslo Ministerija Informatikos ir Prognozavimo Centras – IPC
HU	Oktatási Minisztérium Sulinet Iroda Megyei Pedagógiai Intézetek
PL	Ministerstwo Edukacji Narodowej
RO	Council for ICT of the ministry of National Education National Commission for ICT Council for Coordination of the Romanian Education Network
SI	SI/RO Programme Council Ministry of Education and Sport National Education Institute Centre for Vocational Education and Training
SK	Ministerstvo školstva SR, Metodické centrá
CY	Ypourgeio Paideias kai Politismou

Source: Eurydice.

Additional notes

Netherlands: Since 1999, the official body has been the *Directie ICT, Ministerie van Onderwijs, Cultuur en Wetenschappen*.
Sweden: A new project, *ITiS*, was set up in the autumn of 1998.
Bulgaria: Within the next two years Bulgaria expects to set up a central agency/unit.

NATIONAL PROJECTS FOR THE INTRODUCTION OF TECHNOLOGY
ARE ON THE INCREASE

One or more national or Community-wide projects aimed at introducing ICT into secondary education have been put in place in all the countries of the EU and the EFTA/EEA and in most pre-accession countries, with the exception of the Czech Republic and Cyprus (lower secondary education). Many countries also ran projects in primary education in 1997/98, with the exception of the German-speaking Community of Belgium for the countries of the EU, and in the Czech Republic, Latvia, Lithuania and Poland for the pre-accession countries.

In Spain, plans are being developed through the *Programme of New Information and Communication Technologies* (directly run by the ministry) and the different Autonomous Communities, covering three levels of education (primary, lower secondary, upper secondary).

These national or Community-wide plans go hand in hand with local initiatives. They are particularly numerous in Finland and Sweden.

SCHEDULE FOR IMPLEMENTING THE PROJECTS: OFTEN BEYOND THE YEAR 2000

Projects at all three levels of education generally started after 1995. The most long-standing initiatives were launched in the '80's; some involved the three levels of education (Spain and France) but they more often concerned the general upper secondary level (Luxembourg, Austria, Bulgaria, Lithuania and Cyprus).

In 1999, a project will get under way for primary education in the French community of Belgium and Iceland and for the three levels of education in Romania and Slovakia. When a date is fixed for completion, the full implementation of the projects is planned for 1999 or 2000 in most cases. The schedule for implementation extends beyond that in the Netherlands, Finland, Slovenia, and Slovakia. In Bulgaria, no decision has as yet been taken as regards the full implementation of the programme for compulsory education, and the schedule has not yet been decided.

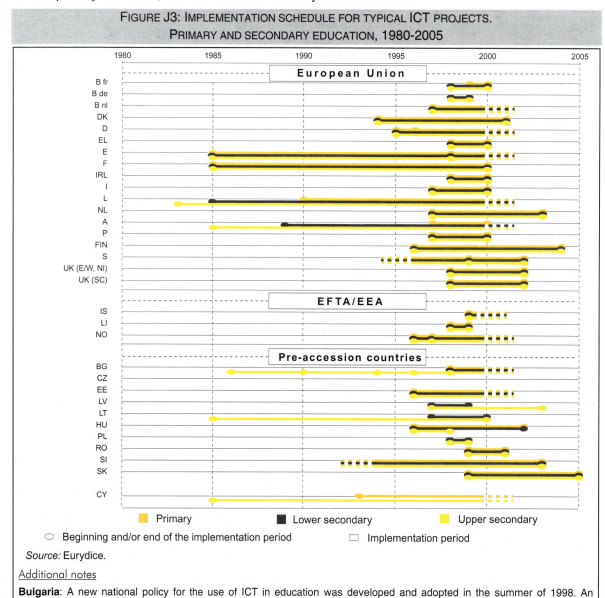

FIGURE J3: IMPLEMENTATION SCHEDULE FOR TYPICAL ICT PROJECTS. PRIMARY AND SECONDARY EDUCATION, 1980-2005

Source: Eurydice.

Additional notes

Bulgaria: A new national policy for the use of ICT in education was developed and adopted in the summer of 1998. An implementation programme has been drawn up with special attention being given to funding.
Czech Republic: A debate of national education programmes will be launched in 2000, covering among other things the place of ICT.

SHARING RESPONSIBILITY FOR THE PURCHASE AND MAINTENANCE OF HARDWARE

In some countries all the responsibility for the purchase and maintenance of equipment rests at one level of authority. But in most countries this function is undertaken by the local authority and/or at school level. In some countries it is centralized. For example, in the Flemish Community of Belgium and in upper secondary education in Austria, it is the ministry that handles the purchase and maintenance of hardware. In Romania, this is the responsibility of the ministry, assisted by a non-governmental organisation. In Luxembourg, at secondary level, the ministry is helped in this task by the *Centre de technologie de l'éducation*.

In several countries, depending on the level of education and on the type of expenditure (purchase of hardware, software, maintenance of equipment) the responsibilities differ and are sometimes shared by various levels of authority.

FIGURE J4: RESPONSIBILITY FOR THE PURCHASE AND MAINTENANCE OF HARDWARE. PRIMARY AND SECONDARY EDUCATION. PROJECTS UNDER WAY IN 1997/98

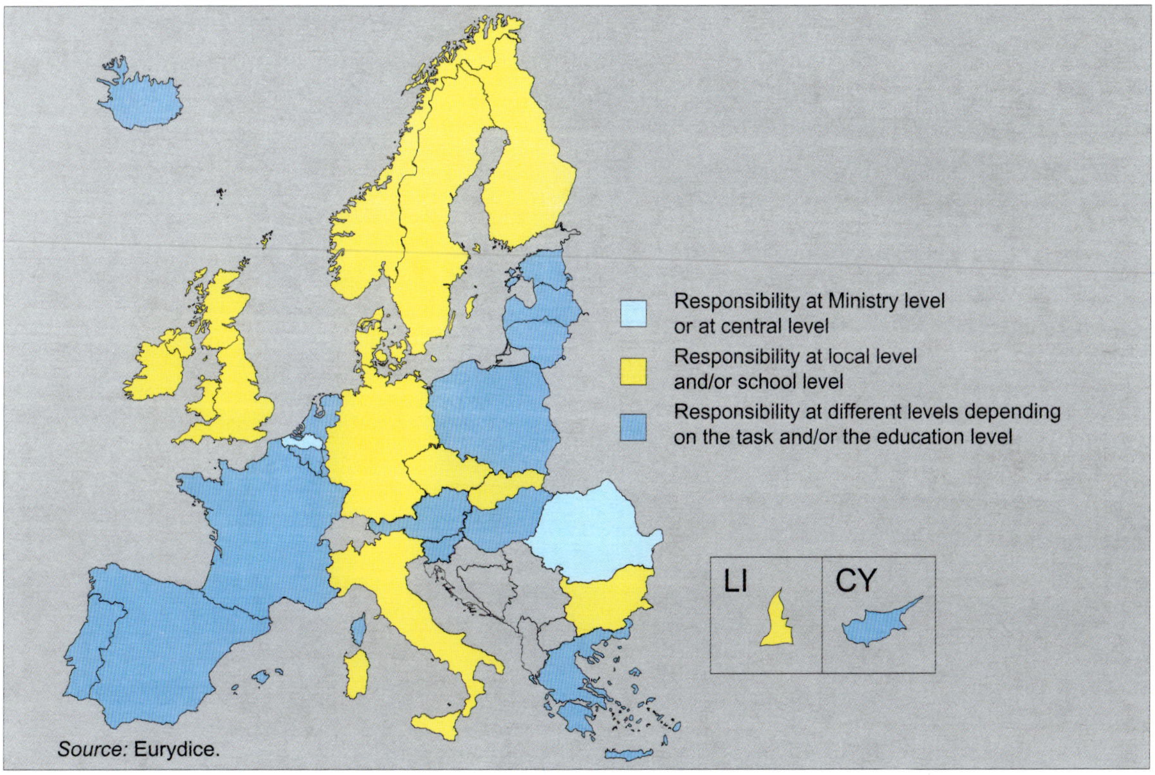

Responsibility at Ministry level or at central level

Responsibility at local level and/or school level

Responsibility at different levels depending on the task and/or the education level

Source: Eurydice.

Additional notes

Belgium (B de): The situation shown relates to secondary education. There is no ongoing project in primary education.
Belgium (B nl): The ministry defines the framework (PC/KD 1998-2002) and provides the additional finance available for infrastructure. The schools decide how to allocate the money between the purchase of hardware and software and in-service training.
Luxembourg: In primary education, responsibility for purchasing and maintenance is assumed at local level; in secondary education, the Minister is assisted in this task by the *Centre de technologie de l'éducation*.
Austria: In primary education, responsibility for purchasing and maintenance is assumed by different levels of authority; in lower secondary education, this is the local level; in upper secondary education, the ministry is responsible for school equipment.
Bulgaria: Over the next two years, the central level will play a significant role in providing equipment in schools.
Czech Republic: The situation shown relates to secondary education; there is no ongoing project in primary education.
Poland: In primary education, responsibility for purchasing and maintenance is assumed at local level; in secondary education, different levels of authority share it.
Slovakia: The situation shown relates to upper secondary education; there is no ongoing project in primary or lower secondary education.
Cyprus: The situation shown relates to primary and upper secondary education; there is no ongoing project in lower secondary education.

EXPENDITURE ON EQUIPMENT PREDOMINATES
IN SPECIFIC BUDGETS

All countries have allocated specific budgets to implementing the projects, with the exception of Bulgaria at primary level.

It is not always possible to ascertain the distribution among the various headings. For example, in Spain the *PNTIC* does not allocate a budget for human resources because the staff and the teachers specialising in ICT are civil servants and their pay comes out of a different budget. In France, teacher training and human resources are the responsibility of the State whereas equipment is the responsibility of the local authorities. In Italy, the distribution is different as it depends on the projects undertaken by the schools. In Norway, the subsidies cover expenditure on human resources, but not on equipment. In Luxembourg, at primary level, the equipment budget is the responsibility of the municipality. In Austria, at primary level, there is no national budget; the *Länder* and municipalities may or may not provide a budget.

Where it is possible to ascertain how the budget is distributed among the various headings, it can be seen that in general 60%-80% of the budget is devoted to the purchase of equipment and 20%-40% to human resources. However in Greece, at all education levels, these figures are reversed. In Luxembourg, throughout secondary level, in Bulgaria and Cyprus at upper secondary level, almost the entire budget (90-95%) is devoted to equipment.

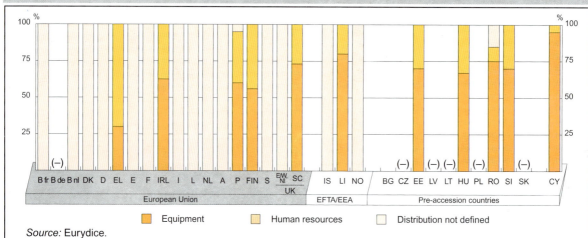

FIGURE J5: DISTRIBUTION OF THE SPECIFIC BUDGET BETWEEN THE PURCHASE OF EQUIPMENT AND EXPENDITURE ON HUMAN RESOURCES. PRIMARY EDUCATION. PROJECTS UNDER WAY IN 1997/98

Source: Eurydice.

(–): There is no national project on the use of ICT at this level of education.

<u>Additional notes</u>

Finland: The expenditure on human resources includes the cost of the development of teaching methods and environments.
United Kingdom (E/W, NI): The programme of £700 million for the *National Grid for Learning* up to 2002 includes provision for ICT infrastructure, services and content. Some of this funding is in the form of grants paid at a rate of 50% of expenditure. The £230 million fund available through the National Lottery from 1999 is specifically to train serving teachers and school librarians (at both primary and secondary level).

FIGURE J6: DISTRIBUTION OF THE SPECIFIC BUDGET BETWEEN THE PURCHASE OF EQUIPMENT AND EXPENDITURE ON HUMAN RESOURCES. LOWER SECONDARY EDUCATION. PROJECTS UNDER WAY IN 1997/98

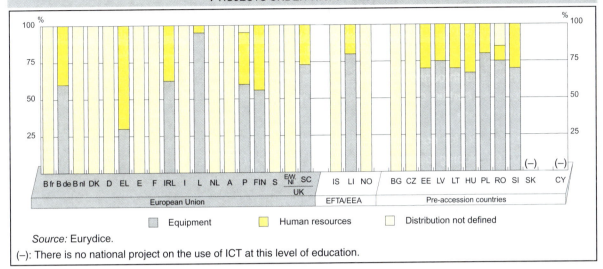

Source: Eurydice.

(–): There is no national project on the use of ICT at this level of education.

FIGURE J7: DISTRIBUTION OF THE SPECIFIC BUDGET BETWEEN THE PURCHASE OF EQUIPMENT AND EXPENDITURE ON HUMAN RESOURCES. GENERAL UPPER SECONDARY EDUCATION. PROJECTS UNDER WAY IN 1997/98

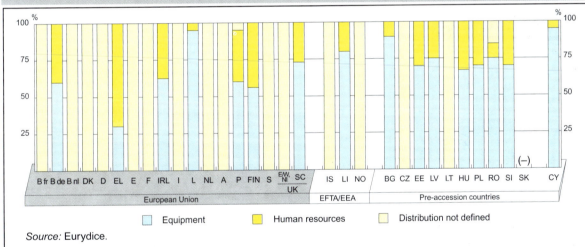

Source: Eurydice.

(–): There is no national project on the use of ICT at this level of education.

Additional notes

Finland: The expenditure on human resources includes the cost of the development of teaching methods and environments.
United Kingdom (E/W, NI): The programme of £700 million for the *National Grid for Learning* up to 2002 includes provision for ICT infrastructure, services and content. Some of this funding is in the form of grants paid at a rate of 50% of expenditure. The £230 million fund available through the National Lottery from 1999 is specifically to train serving teachers and school librarians (at both primary and secondary level).
Latvia: The expenditure on human resources includes an 'others' heading.

PROJECTS WITH A VARIETY OF AIMS

Objectives have been set in all existing projects. Six categories have been defined here. The objectives relate to equipment; the acquisition and construction of software; the skills of teachers and pupils and the use of the Internet.

In most countries, and throughout the three levels of education, the stated objectives cover the six categories. However certain countries have not set objectives for the acquisition, distribution and development of software.

However, in Denmark, for compulsory and general upper secondary education, the projects have concentrated on developing teachers' skills and on fostering the use of the Internet in general, through the creation of a common Internet service provider, the *Sektornet*, for all schools to further promote the development of pupils' skills. In the Netherlands a national education network, the *Kennisnet*, in which schools, libraries and museums are linked together, has been created in 1999.

In Austria (Hauptschule) and Bulgaria, the plan worked out for lower secondary education centres on developing the skills of teachers and pupils.

Several countries' projects also include objectives other than those cited in the above categories. They cover aspects such as the administration of the education system, monitoring the education system and/or innovations to it, training all citizens in the use of the new technologies, etc.

FIGURE J8: OBJECTIVES IN ICT.
PRIMARY EDUCATION. PROJECTS UNDER WAY IN 1997/98

	B fr	B de	B nl	DK	D	EL	E	F	IRL	I	L	NL	A	P	FIN	S	UK (E/W, NI)	UK (SC)
Equipment (availability, renewal, accessibility, etc.)	●	(–)	●	●	●	●	●	●	●	●	●	●	●	●		●	●	●
Acquisition and/or distribution of software		(–)	●	●	●	●	●	●		●	●	●	●	●		●	●	●
Development of teachers' skills	●	(–)	●	●	●	●	●	●	●	●	●	●	●	●	●	●	●	●
Development of pupils' skills	●	(–)		●	●	●	●	●	●	●	●	●	●	●	●	●	●	●
Help in the development of software/ educational software		(–)		●	●	●	●	●	●		●		●	●	●	●	●	●
Use of the Internet	●	(–)	●	●	●	●	●	●	●	●	●	●	●	●	●	●	●	●

	IS	LI	NO	BG	CZ	EE	LV	LT	HU	PL	RO	SI	SK	CY
Equipment (availability, renewal, accessibility, etc.)	●	●	●	(–)	●	(–)	(–)	●	(–)	●	●	(–)		●
Acquisition and/or distribution of software	●	●	●	●	(–)	●	(–)	(–)	●	(–)	●	●	(–)	●
Development of teachers' skills	●	●	●	●	(–)	●	(–)	(–)	●	(–)	●	●	(–)	●
Development of pupils' skills	●	●	●	●	(–)	●	(–)	(–)	●	(–)	●	●	(–)	●
Help in the development of software/ educational software	●		●		(–)	●	(–)	(–)	●	(–)		●	(–)	●
Use of the Internet	●	●	●	●	(–)	●	(–)	(–)	●	(–)	●	●	(–)	●

Source: Eurydice.

(–): There is no national project on the use of ICT at this level of education.

<u>Additional notes</u>

Belgium (B fr): Hardware is being supplied to all primary and secondary schools over a period of three years (1998-2000).
Sweden: From 1998/99, the *ITiS* project's objectives relate to equipment and distribution of software. In general, the municipalities have the overall responsibility for these areas.

FIGURE J9: OBJECTIVES IN ICT.
LOWER SECONDARY EDUCATION. PROJECTS UNDER WAY IN 1997/98

	B fr	B de	B nl	DK	D	EL	E	F	IRL	I	L	NL	A (a)	A (b)	P	FIN	S	UK (E/W, NI)	UK (SC)
Equipment (availability, renewal, accessibility, etc.)	○	○	○		○	○	○	○	○	○	○	○		○	○		○	○	
Acquisition and/or distribution of software		○	○		○	○	○			○	○	○		○	○			○	○
Development of teachers' skills	○	○	○	○	○	○	○	○	○	○	○	○	○	○	○	○	○	○	○
Development of pupils' skills	○	○			○	○	○	○	○	○	○	○	○	○	○	○	○	○	○
Help in the development of software/educational software		○			○	○	○	○	○	○		○		○	○	○	○	○	○
Use of the Internet	○	○	○	○	○	○	○	○	○	○	○	○	○	○	○	○	○	○	○

	IS	LI	NO	BG	CZ	EE	LV	LT	HU	PL	RO	SI	SK	CY
Equipment (availability, renewal, accessibility, etc.)	○	○	○	(–)	○	○	○	○	○	○	○	(–)		(–)
Acquisition and/or distribution of software	○	○	○	(–)	○	○	○	○	○	○	○	(–)		(–)
Development of teachers' skills	○	○	○	(–)	○	○	○	○	○	○	○	(–)		(–)
Development of pupils' skills	○	○	○	○	(–)	○	○	○		○	○	(–)		(–)
Help in the development of software/educational software	○		○	(–)	○	○	○	○			○	(–)		(–)
Use of the Internet	○	○	○	(–)	○	○	○	○	○	○	○	(–)		(–)

Source: Eurydice.

(–): There is no national project on the use of ICT at this level of education.

Additional notes

Belgium (B fr): Hardware is being supplied to all primary and secondary schools over a period of three years (1998-2000).
Austria: (a) *Hauptschulen*, (b) *Allgemeinbildende Höhere Schulen*.
Sweden: From 1998/99, the *ITiS* project's objectives relate to equipment and distribution of software. In general, the municipalities have the overall responsibility for these areas.

FIGURE J10: OBJECTIVES IN ICT.
GENERAL UPPER SECONDARY EDUCATION. PROJECTS UNDER WAY IN 1997/98

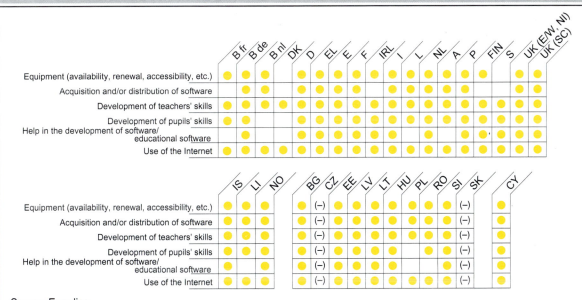

Source: Eurydice.

(–): There is no national project on the use of ICT at this level of education.

Additional notes

Belgium (B fr): Hardware is being supplied to all primary and secondary schools over a period of three years (1998-2000).
Sweden: From 1998/99, the *ITiS* project's objectives relate to equipment and distribution of software. In general, the municipalities have the overall responsibility for these areas.

MANY COUNTRIES INCLUDE ICT
IN THE PRIMARY LEVEL CURRICULUM

In primary education, ICT is included in the curriculum in the majority of EU, EFTA/EEA and pre-accession countries. Elsewhere, plans for its inclusion are ongoing. Depending on the country concerned, the presence of ICT in the curriculum is more or less recent. In the United Kingdom, ICT has been a statutory requirement in England and Wales since the introduction of the National Curriculum in 1988, and in Northern Ireland (as an educational theme woven through the main subjects) since the introduction of the Northern Ireland Curriculum from 1990.

In the United Kingdom, the curriculum does not specify the **number of hours** to be devoted to this compulsory subject as the schools are free to decide on the allocation of the hours of teaching. In Poland, 27 hours a year are allocated to this subject.

FIGURE J11: INCLUSION OF ICT IN THE CURRICULUM.
PRIMARY EDUCATION, 1997/98

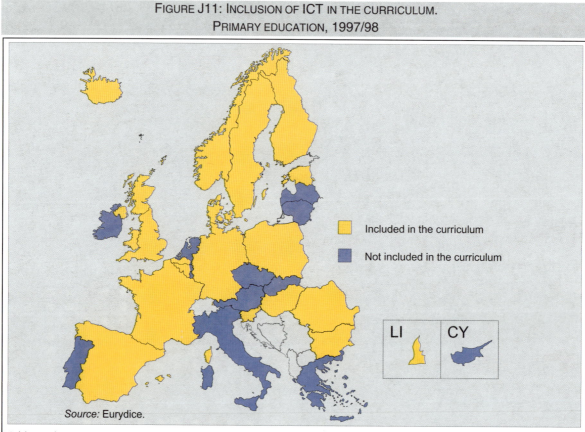

Included in the curriculum

Not included in the curriculum

Source: Eurydice.

Additional notes

Belgium (B fr): The decree on 'Missions' (1997) plans to integrate ICT into education by means of Skills Platforms. These platforms, under discussions since 1994, have been adopted and clearly defined in 1999.
Germany: The *Kultusministerkonferenz* and the legislation of the different *Länder* make recommendations on the use and the role of ICT in school life.
Greece: ICT was not part of the curriculum in 1997/1998, but a pilot project to investigate the use of ICT for teaching the other subjects is being carried out in 10 selected primary schools.
Italy: There are no recommendations on the use of ICT in the curriculum, but one of the aims of the *Programma di Sviluppo delle Tecnologie Didattiche* is to improve the effectiveness of the teaching-learning process and to improve didactic organization both for single subjects and for the acquisition of general skills through the use of ICT.
Netherlands: Since 1998/99, the new media have been part of the cross-curricular attainment targets for primary education.
Iceland: ICT is part of the curriculum since 1999/2000.
Bulgaria: ICT is included in the curriculum as an elective subject, schools are free to teach it.
Czech Republic: A debate of national education programmes will be launched in 2000, covering among other things the place of ICT.
Latvia and **Lithuania**: ICT is an extra-curricular subject (taught after class hours).

Explanatory note

By curriculum is meant any form of official recommendation regarding the subjects taught.

ICT is offered as an option in some countries, in some cases only recently (Liechtenstein, Bulgaria and Romania). In the case of an elective course, the number of hours to be devoted to it is seldom specified in the curriculum. It depends sometimes on the school, as is the case in Finland, Estonia and Hungary. Where a certain number of hours is specified, it varies: 26 hours a year in Slovenia, 28 hours in Romania and 40 hours in Liechtenstein.

Pupils' results in this subject are taken into account for **progression** to the next year in certain pre-accession countries: Estonia, Poland and Romania. A **certificate** is awarded on the basis of the knowledge and skills acquired in this subject at the end of primary school in Liechtenstein.

THE MOST COMMON APPROACH TO ICT IN PRIMARY EDUCATION IS TO USE IT AS A TOOL

When ICT is included in the curriculum, two main approaches may be distinguished. It may be taught either as a separate subject, or used as a tool and/or for carrying out interdisciplinary projects. The use of ICT as a tool or to carry out such projects is the most widespread approach in the EU countries that have brought it into the curriculum for primary education.

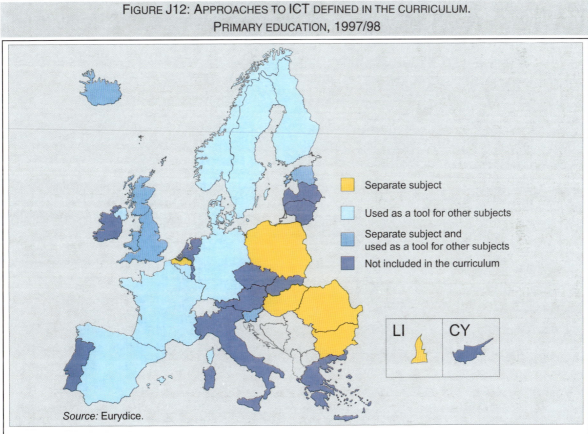

FIGURE J12: APPROACHES TO ICT DEFINED IN THE CURRICULUM. PRIMARY EDUCATION, 1997/98

- Separate subject
- Used as a tool for other subjects
- Separate subject and used as a tool for other subjects
- Not included in the curriculum

Source: Eurydice.

Additional notes

Germany: The *Kultusministerkonferenz* and the legislation of the different *Länder* make recommendations on the use and the role of ICT in school life.
Greece: ICT was not part of the curriculum in 1997/1998, but an experiment in using ICT for teaching other subjects is being carried out in 10 selected primary schools.
Spain: The curriculum merely issues recommendations on the use of ICT.
Luxembourg: ICT constitutes a learning tool increasingly incorporated in all subjects.
Netherlands: Since 1998/99, the new media have been part of the cross-curricular attainment targets for primary education.
Austria: The integrative use of ICT will soon be included in the curriculum.
Poland: Since 1998, ICT has been a compulsory subject in the schools equipped with it, in the 4th, 5th and 6th years.

ICT is a separate compulsory subject in only some countries: in the United Kingdom (with the exception of Northern Ireland), in Iceland and Liechtenstein and in several pre-accession countries. In the United Kingdom (England, Wales, Scotland), Estonia and Slovenia, ICT is used to carry out interdisciplinary projects as well as it being taught as a subject in its own right. In these three countries, the recommendations or regulations on the use of ICT for projects are dealt with in a **separate section** of the curriculum. This is also the case in Norway.

Whatever the approach advocated, the **objectives** pursued by the teaching or the use of ICT at primary level can cover various categories. Four major fields are distinguished here, namely programming, the use of software, information searches and communication via a network.

FIGURE J13: OBJECTIVES DEFINED IN THE CURRICULUM FOR THE TEACHING OR THE USE OF ICT. PRIMARY EDUCATION, 1997/98

	B fr	B de	B nl	DK	D	EL	E	F	IRL	I	L	NL	A	P	FIN	S	UK (E/W, NI)	UK (SC)
To develop programming skills	(−)				●	(−)	(−)		(−)	(−)	(−)	(−)	(−)	(−)			●	●
To learn correct use of a word processor, a spreadsheet, etc.	●	(−)		●	●	(−)	(−)	●	(−)	(−)	(−)	(−)	(−)	(−)	●	●	●	●
To learn to search for information on a CD-ROM, a network, etc.	●	(−)		●	●	(−)	(−)	●	(−)	(−)	(−)	(−)	(−)	(−)	●	●	●	●
To communicate via a network	●	(−)		●	●	(−)	(−)		(−)	(−)	(−)	(−)	(−)	(−)	●	●		

	IS	LI	NO	BG	CZ	EE	LV	LT	HU	PL	RO	SI	SK	CY
To develop programming skills		●		●	(−)		(−)	(−)		●	●	(−)		(−)
To learn correct use of a word processor, a spreadsheet, etc.	●	●	●	●	(−)	●	(−)	(−)		●	●	●	(−)	(−)
To learn to search for information on a CD-ROM, a network, etc.	●	●	●	●	(−)	●	(−)	(−)		●	●	●	(−)	(−)
To communicate via a network	●			●	(−)	●	(−)	(−)		●	●	●	(−)	(−)

Source: Eurydice.

(−): This subject is not included in the curriculum at this level of education.

Additional notes

Belgium (B nl): By the end of primary school pupils are required to be able to use ICT and to process data.
Germany: The *Kultusministerkonferenz* and the legislation of the different *Länder* make recommendations on the use and the role of ICT in school life.
Netherlands: Since 1998/99, the new media have been part of the cross-curricular attainment targets for primary education; objectives have been defined in all areas except programming skills.
Finland: The curricula are designed at the local level on the basis of the national core curriculum. The schools define the objectives and what is taught on the basis of the national guidelines.
Sweden: ICT is to be used as a tool in the classroom, although basic competencies required for it are not listed.
Bulgaria: Programming and communication via a network will appear only during the second part of the programme.

Of the EU and EFTA/EEA countries, at this level of education, Germany is the only country in which the recommendations of the *Kultusministerkonferenz* and the legislation of the different *Länder* cover the four categories of objectives, indicating their interest in using ICT for multidisciplinary purposes. The United Kingdom and Liechtenstein pursue all the categories of objectives, except for communication via a network. In England and Wales, the curriculum is deliberately not technically specific, in order to allow for technological change. The objectives are defined in terms of the skills to be acquired and functions to be accomplished through the use of ICT, rather than in terms of particular tools, techniques and applications to be used.

In the French Community of Belgium, Denmark, France, Finland, Sweden and Iceland, the development of programming skills is not an objective defined in the curriculum. In the other countries, the objectives pursued as regards the use of ICT to conduct projects includes in particular the use of software and/or learning to search for information.

In pre-accession countries, the range of cover is more broad-based. In Bulgaria, Romania and Slovenia, all the categories are mentioned. In Estonia and Poland, the development of programming skills is not an objective at this level of education. In Hungary, no specific objectives are defined, but the course aims to familiarize pupils with ICT and to enable them to acquire basic knowledge.

ICT IS IN ALMOST ALL CURRICULA
AT LOWER SECONDARY LEVEL

ICT is included in the lower secondary curriculum in a large majority of countries. Recommendations concerning ICT are more recent in some countries than in others: Germany was the first to introduce the subject into its curriculum in the late 1970s. Greece and Scotland included it in the early '80's, but it only became part of the curriculum in Ireland and Liechtenstein in 1998. In the United Kingdom, England and Wales have had a statutory requirement to teach ICT since the introduction of the National Curriculum in 1988, and it has also been compulsory (as an educational theme crossing subject boundaries) in Northern Ireland since the introduction of the Northern Ireland Curriculum in 1990. In some countries, ICT is offered as an option. ICT only recently appeared in the curriculum in the German-speaking Community of Belgium, Bulgaria and Romania.

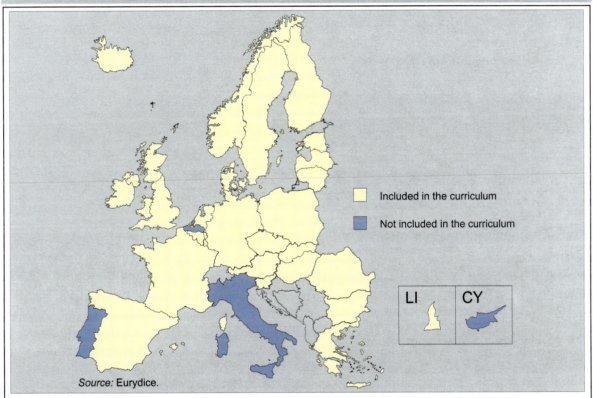

FIGURE J14: INCLUSION OF ICT IN THE CURRICULUM.
LOWER SECONDARY EDUCATION, 1997/98

Included in the curriculum

Not included in the curriculum

LI   CY

Source: Eurydice.

Additional notes

Italy: There are no recommendations on the use of ICT in the curriculum, but one of the aims of the *Programma di Sviluppo delle Tecnologie Didattiche* is to use it to improve the effectiveness of the teaching-learning process and to improve the didactic organization both for single subjects and for the acquisition of general skills.
Slovakia: ICT is a compulsory subject only in the classes specialized for Mathematics, Physics and IT.

Explanatory note

By curriculum is meant any form of official recommendation relating to the subjects to be taught.

In Germany, ICT is offered as a compulsory subject, as a compulsory option or as an elective subject. In the Czech Republic, it is an elective subject at the discretion of the head of school.

When ICT is a compulsory curriculum subject, the **number of hours** allocated is generally specified in the curriculum. It is 80 hours (maximum) a year in Liechtenstein. If it is an elective subject, the number of hours is sometimes specified. This varies from 14 hours in the Czech Republic to 100 hours in the German-speaking Community of Belgium. Whether the subject is compulsory or elective, the number of hours devoted to ICT may be decided at school level (Finland, the United Kingdom – England, Wales and Northern Ireland, Estonia and Latvia) or on the year during which it is taught (France).

The results obtained in this subject are taken into account for **progression** to the next year in the French Community of Belgium, Germany (when the subject is compulsory or a compulsory option), Spain, Luxembourg, Bulgaria, Estonia, Hungary, Poland, Romania, Slovenia and Slovakia.

An **external assessment** is organized for this subject in France (at the end of lower secondary education).

A grade on the annual pupil's school report or a **certificate** at the end of lower secondary education (or the single structure) is awarded on the basis of the knowledge and skills acquired in this subject in the German-speaking Community of Belgium, Germany, Luxembourg, Liechtenstein, the Czech Republic, Hungary, Slovenia and Slovakia.

A VARIETY OF APPROACHES TO ICT COEXIST IN LOWER SECONDARY EDUCATION

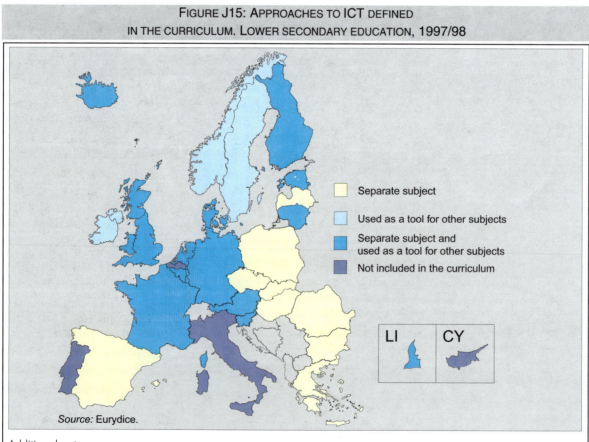

FIGURE J15: APPROACHES TO ICT DEFINED IN THE CURRICULUM. LOWER SECONDARY EDUCATION, 1997/98

Separate subject

Used as a tool for other subjects

Separate subject and used as a tool for other subjects

Not included in the curriculum

LI   CY

Source: Eurydice.

Additional notes

Finland: The curricula are prepared at the local level on the basis of the national core curriculum. Schools can decide to include ICT in the curriculum as an elective subject.

At this level of education, few curricula advocate the use of ICT solely in interdisciplinary projects. They exist in Ireland, Finland, Sweden, the United Kingdom (Northern Ireland) and Norway. Elsewhere, this approach is supplemented or replaced by ICT being a curriculum subject in its own right.

FIGURE J16: OBJECTIVES DEFINED IN THE CURRICULUM FOR THE TEACHING OR THE USE OF ICT. LOWER SECONDARY EDUCATION, 1997/98

	B fr	B de	B nl	DK	D	EL	E	F	IRL	I	L	NL	A	P	FIN	S	UK (E/W, NI)	UK (SC)
To develop programming skills	○	(−)	○	○	○				○	(−)			○	(−)			○	○
To learn correct use of a word processor, a spreadsheet, etc.	○	○	(−)	○	○	○	○	○	○	○	(−)	○	○	○	(−)	○	○	○
To learn to search for information on a CD-ROM, a network, etc.		○	(−)	○	○	○	○	○		○	(−)	○	○	○	(−)	○	○	○
To communicate via a network		○	(−)	○	○	○	○	○		○	(−)	○	○	○	(−)	○		○

	IS	LI	NO	BG	CZ	EE	LV	LT	HU	PL	RO	SI	SK	CY
To develop programming skills		○		○	○		○	○	○		○	○	○	(−)
To learn correct use of a word processor, a spreadsheet, etc.	○	○	○	○	○	○	○	○	○	○	○	○	○	(−)
To learn to search for information on a CD-ROM, a network, etc.	○	○	○	○	○	○	○	○	○	○	○	○	○	(−)
To communicate via a network	○		○		○	○	○	○		○	○	○	○	(−)

Source: Eurydice.

(−): This subject is not included in the curriculum at this level of education.

Additional notes

Finland: The curricula are designed at the local level on the basis of the national core curriculum. The schools define the objectives and what is taught on the basis of the national guidelines.
Sweden: ICT is to be used as a tool in the classroom, although basic competencies required for it are not listed.
United Kingdom (E/W): The National Curriculum Programme of Study at Key Stage 3 includes communicating and handling information, but does not make specific mention of communication via a network. However, this is becoming increasingly important in view of the development of the National Grid for Learning.

In general, the **objectives** of the courses in ICT at lower secondary level concern the four categories presented in the Figure J16. However, the development of programming skills is not specified at this level of education in the German-speaking Community of Belgium, Spain, France, Luxembourg, the Netherlands, Finland, Sweden, Iceland and Norway among the EU and the EFTA/EEA countries. Among the pre-accession countries, the development of programming skills is not included in the curriculum in Estonia and Poland. Communication via a network is not one of the objectives or key skills of the French Community of Belgium, Ireland, Liechtenstein, Bulgaria or Hungary. In the United Kingdom (England and Wales), the objectives for the curriculum are defined in terms of the skills to be acquired and functions to be accomplished through the use of ICT, rather than in terms of particular tools, techniques and applications to be used.

In addition to the objectives belonging to these categories, the German curriculum includes courses to build awareness of the history of technologies, the problems of intellectual property and the role of the computer in the world of work. In Spain, the Netherlands, the United Kingdom (England, Wales and Northern Ireland), Liechtenstein and the Czech Republic, the curriculum also emphasizes the value of information and the role of ICT within society.

ICT IN MOST CURRICULA
AT GENERAL UPPER SECONDARY LEVEL

With the exception of the Flemish Community of Belgium, Italy and the Netherlands, all the countries have included, in 1997/98, ICT in the curriculum of general upper secondary education, in some cases for a long time. Germany was the first to put the subject on its curriculum in the late 1970s; in Slovenia it has been offered since 1974. In Luxembourg ICT was introduced for certain streams in 1983. In 1998, the subject became part of the curriculum in Ireland, Sweden, and Liechtenstein.

FIGURE J17: INCLUSION OF ICT IN THE CURRICULUM.
GENERAL UPPER SECONDARY EDUCATION, 1997/98

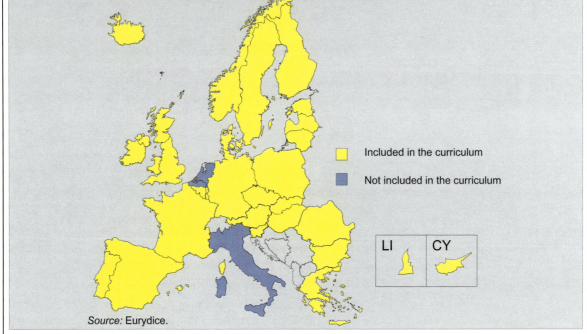

☐ Included in the curriculum

■ Not included in the curriculum

LI   CY

Source: Eurydice.

Additional notes

Belgium (B nl): ICT does not yet form part of the curriculum, but the skills to be acquired by the end of secondary education are currently being defined.
Denmark: *Gymnasium* and *HF* courses.
France, Austria, Czech Republic, Slovakia and **Cyprus**: 1st year of general upper secondary education.
Italy: There are no recommendations on the use of ICT in the curriculum, but one of the aims of the *Programma di Sviluppo delle Tecnologie Didattiche* is to use it to improve the effectiveness of the teaching-learning process and to improve the didactic organization both for single subjects and for the acquisition of general skills.
Netherlands: In the new examination programmes introduced in 1998/99, ICT is considered an optional examination subject.
United Kingdom: ICT is compulsory during Key Stage 4 (first two years of compulsory upper secondary education) in England and, as an education theme woven through the main subjects, in Northern Ireland. In Wales, ICT is elective during Key Stage 4. In post-compulsory secondary education, ICT is an elective subject in England, Wales and Northern Ireland.
Poland: 1st or 2nd year of general upper secondary education.

Explanatory note

By curriculum is meant any form of official recommendation regarding subjects to be taught.

In several countries, ICT is offered as an elective subject. In Germany and Bulgaria, ICT is offered as a compulsory subject, as a compulsory option and/or as an elective subject.

When ICT is included in the curriculum as a compulsory subject, the **number of hours** allocated is generally specified in the curriculum. This varies from 24 hours in Cyprus to 80 hours (maximum) a year in Liechtenstein. If it is an optional subject, the number of hours is sometimes specified. This varies from 60 hours in Slovakia to 143 hours in Norway. Whether the subject is compulsory or optional, the number of hours devoted to it sometimes depends on the school or on the course option chosen (in the German-speaking Community of Belgium, Luxembourg, Finland, Estonia and Slovenia).

The results obtained in this subject are taken into account for **progression** to the next year in the French Community of Belgium, Germany (when the subject is compulsory or compulsory optional), Spain, Italy, Luxembourg, Austria and Portugal, for the UE countries, and in all the pre-accession countries with the exception of Latvia and Cyprus. An **external assessment** is organized for this subject in Luxembourg (for certain course options), the United Kingdom (Scotland), Norway, Bulgaria (in some specialized secondary schools) and Hungary. In the United Kingdom (England, Wales and Northern Ireland), students who study ICT in the first two years of upper secondary education (i.e. last two years of compulsory education) may take an externally certificated qualification (for example a GCSE) in this subject, but this is not compulsory. Some schools in Northern Ireland offer an alternative external accreditation in ICT. Students who choose to study ICT in post-compulsory upper secondary education normally take an externally certificated qualification (for example GCE A level) in this subject.

A grade on the student's annual school report or a **certificate** at the end of general upper secondary education is awarded on the basis of the knowledge and skills acquired in this subject in the German-speaking Community of Belgium, Denmark, Germany, Luxembourg, Austria, Finland, Portugal, the United Kingdom (Scotland), Liechtenstein, the Czech Republic, Lithuania, Hungary, Romania (in upper secondary specialising in ICT), Slovenia and Slovakia.

ICT IS USUALLY TAUGHT AS A SEPARATE SUBJECT
—— IN GENERAL UPPER SECONDARY EDUCATION ——

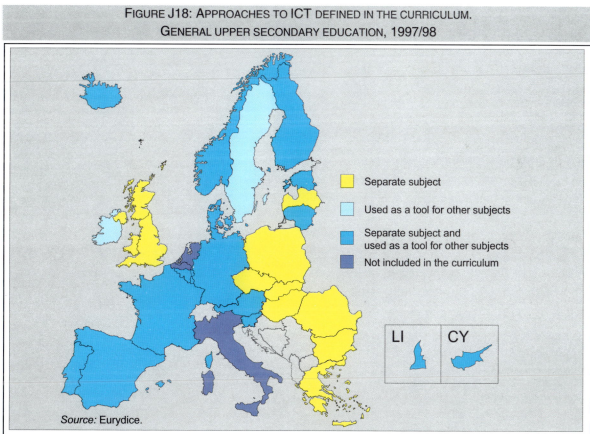

FIGURE J18: APPROACHES TO ICT DEFINED IN THE CURRICULUM.
GENERAL UPPER SECONDARY EDUCATION, 1997/98

Separate subject

Used as a tool for other subjects

Separate subject and used as a tool for other subjects

Not included in the curriculum

Source: Eurydice.

Additional notes

Denmark: *Gymnasium* and *HF* courses.
Netherlands: Since 1998/99, ICT has been introduced a subject with an optional examination.
Finland: The curricula are prepared at the local level on the basis of the national core curriculum. The school can decide to include ICT in the curriculum as an optional subject.
United Kingdom: ICT is compulsory during Key Stage 4 (first two years of upper secondary education) in England and, as an education theme woven through the main subjects, in Northern Ireland. In Wales, ICT is elective during Key Stage 4. In post-compulsory secondary education, ICT is an optional subject in England, Wales and Northern Ireland.

In general upper secondary education, ICT is a separate curriculum subject in nearly all countries, except Ireland, the Netherlands, Portugal and Sweden. It is a compulsory subject during the first year(s) of general upper secondary education in France, Austria, England (Key Stage 4), the Czech Republic, Poland, and Cyprus, and throughout general upper secondary education in Luxembourg, Iceland, Liechtenstein, Bulgaria, Lithuania, Hungary and Slovenia.

In several countries, the general upper secondary curriculum recommends or requires the syllabus to be supplemented by the use of ICT to tackle other subjects or carry out interdisciplinary projects.

FIGURE J19: OBJECTIVES DEFINED IN THE CURRICULUM FOR THE TEACHING OR THE USE OF ICT.
GENERAL UPPER SECONDARY EDUCATION, 1997/98

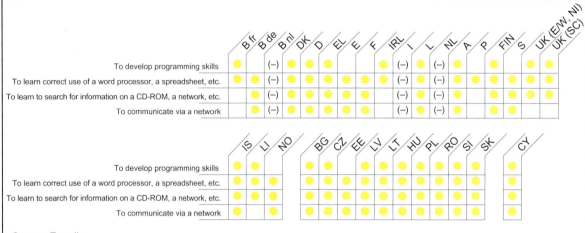

Source: Eurydice.

(–): This subject is not included in the curriculum at this level of education.

Additional notes

Denmark: *Gymnasium* and *HF* courses.
Finland: The curricula are designed at the local level on the basis of the national core curriculum. The schools define the objectives and what is taught on the basis of the national guidelines.
Sweden: ICT is to be used as a tool in the classroom, although basic competencies required for it are not listed.
United Kingdom: In England, Wales and Northern Ireland, students in post-compulsory secondary education electing to study ICT would also be expected to communicate using networks.

Among the EU countries that have incorporated ICT into the curriculum of general upper secondary education, most pursue all categories of **objectives** shown in Figure J19. However, the development of programming skills is not specified at this level of education in the German-speaking Community of Belgium, Spain, France, Portugal and Sweden, and in the EFTA/EEA countries, in Norway. Communication via a network is not one of the objectives or key skills in the French Community of Belgium, Ireland and Liechtenstein. In Portugal, the use of software is the only specific objective targeted.

All the pre-accession countries have fully incorporated ICT into this level of education, and pursue all the aims referred to here, except in Estonia where programming is not included.

SPECIALIST ICT TEACHERS ARE MOSTLY FOUND
AT SECONDARY LEVEL

At primary level, there are **specialist** teachers for the subject information and communication technology in Liechtenstein, and among the pre-accession countries, in Estonia, Hungary, Poland and Romania.

At lower secondary level, teachers are trained as specialists in ICT in a majority of countries. At upper secondary level, there are few countries (the French Community of Belgium, France, Ireland, the Netherlands and Sweden) where there are no specialist ICT teachers.

Their initial training is generally provided at university level. Specialist teachers in Liechtenstein are trained at upper secondary level. Depending on the level of education at which they are to teach, some specialist teachers in the German-speaking and Flemish Communities of Belgium, Austria, Latvia, Hungary and Poland may be trained in non-university tertiary education. The duration of the training of specialist ICT teachers varies from 1.5 - 2 years in Austria (*Hauptschule*) to 7 years in Luxembourg.

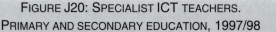

FIGURE J20: SPECIALIST ICT TEACHERS.
PRIMARY AND SECONDARY EDUCATION, 1997/98

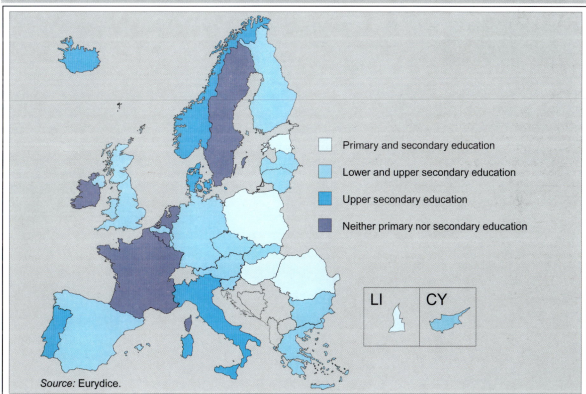

Source: Eurydice.

Additional notes

Belgium (B nl): There are specialist ICT teachers in lower secondary education.
Netherlands: In the 1997 ICT programme, ICT coordinators are required to achieve a standard of ICT competence. No initial teacher training is provided for ICT. In secondary education, ICT as a subject is taught by teachers, qualified to teach on the basis of other teaching qualifications.

For **general class teachers** or **specialist teachers in other subjects,** training in ICT is optional during their initial training in some countries of the Union (Germany, Spain, Ireland, Italy and Portugal) and in some pre-accession countries (Bulgaria, Estonia, Hungary, Romania and Slovenia).

On the other hand, training in ICT forms an integral part of compulsory courses for teachers in the French and Flemish Communities of Belgium, Denmark, France, Luxembourg, the Netherlands, Austria, Finland, Sweden, the United Kingdom, Iceland, Norway, Latvia and Cyprus.

In Lithuania, Poland and Slovakia, the universities decide whether this course is compulsory or optional for initial teacher training.

FIGURE J21: ICT COURSES DURING INITIAL TRAINING OF GENERAL CLASS TEACHERS
(OR SPECIALISTS IN OTHER SUBJECTS). PRIMARY EDUCATION, 1997/98

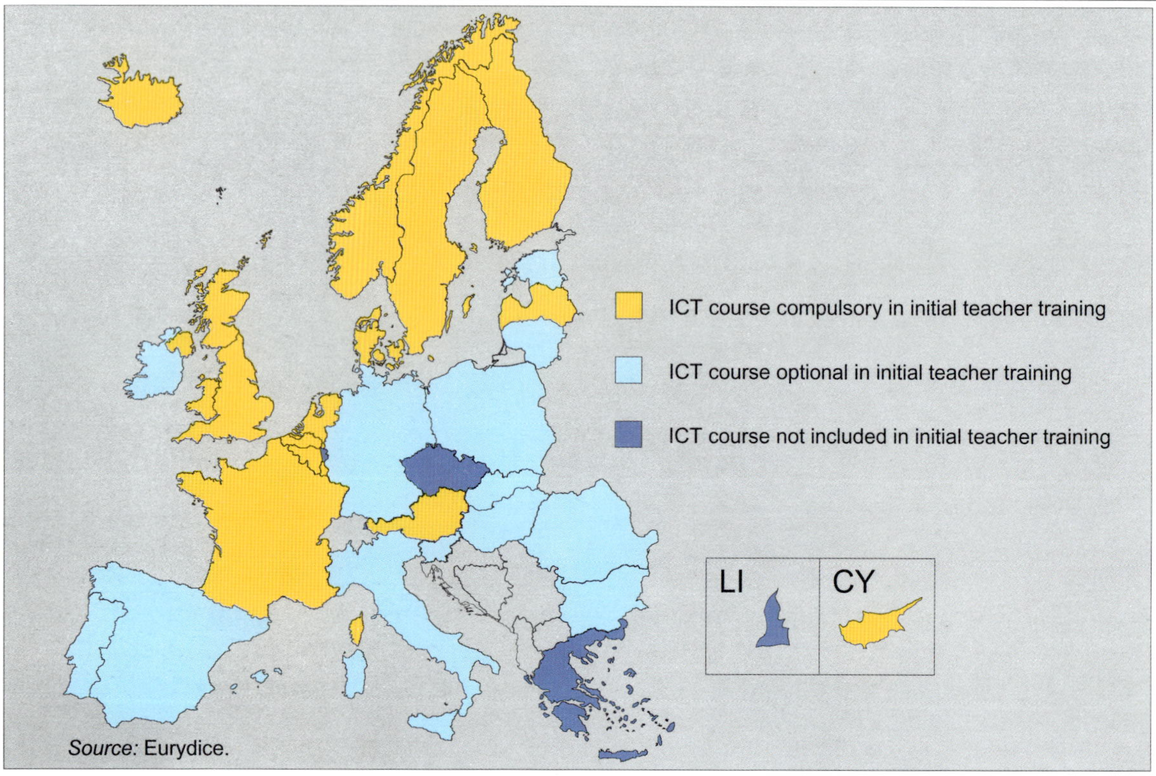

ICT course compulsory in initial teacher training

ICT course optional in initial teacher training

ICT course not included in initial teacher training

LI   CY

Source: Eurydice.

Additional notes

Belgium (B nl) and **Netherlands**: The use of ICT is compulsory in initial teaching training, focussing on general basic competencies.

Germany: More and more universities are offering ICT courses as part of initial teacher training.

Ireland: From 1999, ICT course will be compulsory in initial teacher training.

United Kingdom (E/W, NI): An Initial Teacher Training National Curriculum for the use of ICT in subject teaching was introduced in England in September 1998. In Wales, similar arrangements are currently under consultation. There are no plans for statutory requirements in Northern Ireland, but ITT providers are implementing a strategy to achieve equivalent teacher competence.

Bulgaria: Depending on the teacher's specialisation, ICT may or may not be part of initial teacher training.

Depending on the country, at secondary level, the initial training of general class teachers or specialist teachers in other subjects may or may not include training in ICT. This training is compulsory in the French Community of Belgium (for lower secondary school teachers), the Flemish Community of Belgium, Denmark, France, Luxembourg, the Netherlands, Austria (for teachers in *Hauptschulen),* Finland, Sweden, the United Kingdom, Iceland (at lower secondary level), Norway, the Czech Republic and Latvia. It is optional in the German-speaking Community of Belgium, Germany, Spain, Ireland, Italy, Austria (for teachers in *Allgemeinbildenden Höheren Schulen),* Portugal, Estonia, Hungary, Romania and Slovenia.

In Lithuania, Poland, Slovakia and Cyprus, the universities decide whether this course is compulsory or optional for initial training of secondary school teachers.

FIGURE J22: ICT COURSES DURING INITIAL TRAINING OF GENERAL CLASS TEACHERS (OR SPECIALISTS IN OTHER SUBJECTS). LOWER SECONDARY EDUCATION, 1997/98

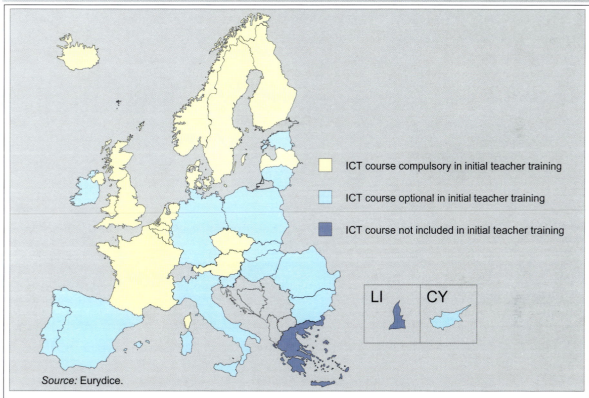

ICT course compulsory in initial teacher training

ICT course optional in initial teacher training

ICT course not included in initial teacher training

Source: Eurydice.

Additional notes

Belgium (B nl) and **Netherlands**: The use of ICT is compulsory in initial teaching training, focussing on general basic competencies.

Germany: More and more universities are offering ICT courses as part of initial teacher training.

Ireland: Since 1999, an ICT course has been compulsory in initial teacher training.

United Kingdom (E/W, NI): An Initial Teacher Training National Curriculum for the use of ICT in subject teaching was introduced in England in September 1998. In Wales, similar arrangements are currently under consultation. There are no plans for statutory requirements in Northern Ireland, but ITT providers are implementing a strategy to achieve equivalent teacher competence.

Bulgaria: Depending on the teacher's specialisation, ICT may or may not be part of initial teacher training.

FIGURE J23: ICT COURSES DURING INITIAL TRAINING OF SPECIALISTS IN OTHER SUBJECTS.
GENERAL UPPER SECONDARY EDUCATION, 1997/98

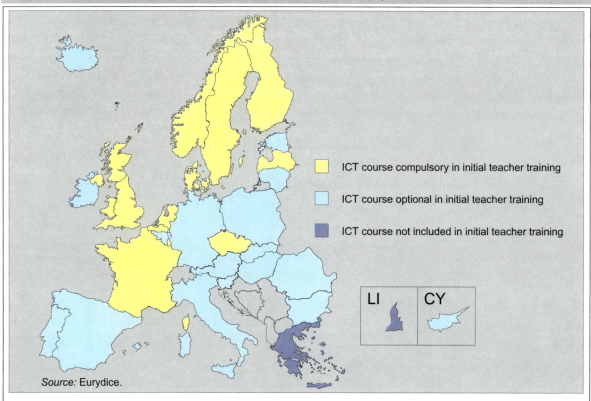

ICT course compulsory in initial teacher training

ICT course optional in initial teacher training

ICT course not included in initial teacher training

LI CY

Source: Eurydice.

Additional notes:

Belgium (B nl) and **Netherlands**: The use of ICT is compulsory in initial teaching training, focussing on general basic competencies.

Denmark: Depending on the teacher's specialisation, ICT may or may not be part of initial teacher training.

Germany: In several universities, ICT training is compulsory for future teachers of mathematics. More and more ICT courses are being offered to teachers training to be specialists in other subjects, at many universities.

Ireland: Since 1999, an ICT course has been compulsory in initial teacher training.

United Kingdom (E/W, NI): An Initial Teacher Training National Curriculum for the use of ICT in subject teaching was introduced in England in September 1998. In Wales, similar arrangements are currently under consultation. There are no plans for statutory requirements in Northern Ireland, but ITT providers are implementing a strategy to achieve equivalent teacher competence.

Bulgaria: Depending on the teacher's specialisation, ICT may or may not be part of initial teacher training.

IN-SERVICE TRAINING:
OFTEN AVAILABLE, RARELY COMPULSORY

All countries that train their teachers in the new technologies have defined policies on in-service training in this field. Most countries have an official plan for in-service training in which updating ICT skills is a priority. In Germany, Latvia and Poland, updating ICT skills is part of an official plan but it is not a priority. Portugal, Bulgaria, the Czech Republic, Estonia, Romania and Cyprus are the exceptions, as they do not have official plans in this area.

At primary level, in-service training in the new technologies is a right and not an obligation for all teachers, whether they be general or specialist teachers. In the United Kingdom, the New Opportunities Fund ICT training programme (funded by the National Lottery) is intended to increase the expertise of all serving teachers in the use of ICT in their teaching, to the level of newly qualified teachers.

At secondary level, in-service training in ICT is compulsory in Germany, Greece, Bulgaria and Latvia, but only for those teachers who specialise in technology. The same applies to specialist teachers at upper secondary level in the German-speaking Community of Belgium, and in Cyprus.

In Sweden, at the different levels of education, there is a government initiative to give teachers support in acquiring and exploiting the opportunities provided by ICT. It starts from school year 1999/2000 and involves 40% of teachers.

Annexes

In order to make the presentation of data tables easier, the 'other countries taking part in the PHARE programme' was shortened into 'other PHARE countries', although this expression is less correct.

CONTEXT

CHANGE IN THE NUMBER OF YOUNG PEOPLE IN THE 0-9, 10-19 AND 20-29 AGE GROUPS IN THE EUROPEAN UNION, FROM 1975 TO 1997.

(FIGURE A1)   (1 000)

	0 TO 9 YEARS	10 TO 19 YEARS	20 TO 29 YEARS	0 TO 29 YEARS
1975	54 225.9	55 647.7	50 497.3	160 370.9
1980	48 516.4	58 047.7	52 192.0	158 756.1
1985	44 711.2	54 868.4	55 812.5	155 392.1
1990	43 568.0	49 133.5	58 414.9	151 116.4
1995	42 866.8	46 003.9	56 558.2	145 428.9
1997	42 407.0	45 409.9	54 311.2	142 128.1

Source: Eurostat, population statistics.

NUMBER OF THE POPULATION IN THE 0-9, 10-19 AND 20-29 AGE GROUPS, 1997.

(FIGURE A2)   (1 000)

	0 TO 9 YEARS	10 TO 19 YEARS	20 TO 29 YEARS	TOTAL POPULATION
European Union				
EU	42 407.0	45 409.9	54 311.2	373 716.7
B	1 215.0	1 219.6	1.380.0	10 170.2
DK	660.3	582.1	758.2	5 275.1
D	8 652.2	9 021.8	10 969.4	82 012.2
EL	1 051.9	1 393.8	1 595.8	10 486.6
E	3 919.0	5 329.3	6 572.1	39 298.6
F	7 383.3	7 775.4	8 309.4	58 491.6
IRL	529.1	662.7	562.6	3 652.2
I	5 516.9	6 302.2	8 897.8	57 461.0
L	54.3	46.4	57.9	418.3
NL	1 950.0	1 837.4	2 316.5	15 567.1
A	927.2	939.2	1 194.0	8 067.8
P	1 098.1	1 365.8	1 627.4	9 934.1
FIN	641.1	652.8	645.2	5 132.3
S	1 150.9	1 014.0	1 174.7	8 844.5
UK	7 657.8	7 267.3	8 250.3	58 905.0
EFTA/EEA				
IS	44.5	41.6	40.4	269.9
LI	3.9	3.9	5.0	31.1
NO	600.8	527.8	647.9	4 392.7
Pre-accession countries				
BG	888.6	1 152.6	1 201.3	8 340.9
CZ	1 171.7	1 481.8	1 597.4	10 309.1
EE	178.7	214.8	208.4	1 462.1
LV	301.0	357.1	343.7	2 479.9
LT	504.7	544.4	553.0	3 707.2
HU	1 178.4	1 392.7	1 554.8	10 174.4
PL	5 107.0	6 583.9	5 479.5	38 639.3
RO	2 790.9	3 549.3	3 911.0	22 581.9
SI	215.7	282.8	290.9	1 987.0
SK	726.5	907.3	825.6	5 378.9
CY	120.4	117.6	103.1	741.0

Source: Eurostat, population statistics.

NUMBER AND PERCENTAGE IN THE 0-29 AGE GROUP BY NUTS 1 AND NUTS 2 REGIONS, 1997

(FIGURE A3)

		TOTAL POPULATION (1 000)	POPULATION 0 TO 29 YEARS (1 000)	0 TO 29 YEARS (%)
EUROPEAN UNION				
BE	**BELGIQUE-BELGIË***	10 170.2	3 814.6	38
BE1	RÉG. BRUXELLES-CAP.-BRUSSELS HFDST. GEWEST	950.6	366.5	39
BE2	VLAAMS GEWEST	5 898.8	2 174.7	37
BE3	RÉGION WALLONNE	3 320.8	1 273.3	38
DK	**DANMARK**	5 275.1	2 000.6	38
DE	**DEUTSCHLAND**	82 012.2	28 643.5	35
DE1	BADEN-WURTTEMBERG	10 374.5	3 761.2	36
DE2	BAYERN	12 043.9	4 282.9	36
DE3	BERLIN	3 458.8	1 171.8	34
DE4	BRANDENBURG	2 554.4	896.2	35
DE5	BREMEN	677.8	222.0	33
DE6	HAMBURG	1 708.0	559.4	33
DE7	HESSEN	6 027.3	2 062.9	34
DE8	MECKLENBURG-VORPOMMERN	1 817.2	666.0	37
DE9	NIEDERSACHSEN	7 815.1	2 770.4	35
DEA	NORDRHEIN-WESTFALEN	17 947.7	6 254.6	35
DEB	RHEINLAND-PFALZ	4 000.6	1 391.1	35
DEC	SAARLAND	1 084.2	354.8	33
DED	SACHSEN	4 545.7	1 515.0	33
DEE	SACHSEN-ANHALT	2 723.6	926.7	34
DEF	SCHLESWIG-HOLSTEIN	2 742.3	945.5	34
DEG	THURINGEN	2 491.1	862.8	35
GR	**ELLADA**	10 486.6	4 041.7	39
GR1	VOREIA ELLADA	3 387.8	1 313.4	39
GR2	KENTRIKI ELLADA	2 638.3	985.6	37
GR3	ATTIKI	3 447.6	1 338.3	39
GR4	NISIA AIGAIOU, KRITI	1 012.9	404.2	40
ES	**ESPAÑA**	39 298.6	15 820.4	40
ES1	NOROESTE	4 317.4	1 585.6	37
ES2	NORESTE	4 032.0	1 465.0	36
ES3	COMUNIDAD DE MADRID	5 019.4	2 018.4	40
ES4	CENTRO (E)	5 280.7	2 033.0	38
ES5	ESTE	10 713.6	4 208.4	39
ES6	SUR	8 365.5	3 794.7	45
ES7	CANARIAS	1 570.0	715.2	46
FR	**FRANCE***	60 025.5	24 281.2	41
FR1	ÎLE DE FRANCE	11 041.4	4 720.5	43
FR2	BASSIN PARISIEN	10 492.4	4 254.2	41
FR3	NORD-PAS-DE-CALAIS	4 004.1	1 784.0	45
FR4	EST	5 136.1	2 094.4	41
FR5	OUEST	7 661.1	3 007.7	39
FR6	SUD-OUEST	6 114.5	2 210.2	36
FR7	CENTRE-EST	6 942.1	2 803.0	40
FR8	MEDITERRANEE	6 983.1	2 594.3	37
FR9	DEPARTEMENTS D'OUTRE-MER	1 650.7	813.0	49
IE	**IRELAND**	3 652.2	1 754.4	48
IT	**ITALIA**	57 461.0	20 716.8	36
IT1	NORD OVEST	6 064.1	1 847.1	30
IT2	LOMBARDIA	8 958.7	3 029.6	34
IT3	NORD EST	6 557.8	2 221.3	34
IT4	EMILIA-ROMAGNA	3 937.9	1 163.9	30
IT5	CENTRO (I)	5 802.2	1 807.3	31
IT6	LAZIO	5 217.2	1 858.6	36
IT7	ABRUZZI-MOLISE	1 604.4	579.5	36
IT8	CAMPANIA	5 785.4	2 577.3	45
IT9	SUD	6 769.7	2 842.5	42
ITA	SICILIA	5 100.8	2 129.7	42
ITB	SARDEGNA	1 663.0	659.8	40
LU	**LUXEMBOURG**	418.3	158.6	38
NL	**NEDERLAND**	15 567.1	6 103.9	39
NL1	NOORD-NEDERLAND	1 634.0	639.3	39
NL2	OOST-NEDERLAND	3 225.5	1 308.5	41
NL3	WEST-NEDERLAND	7 267.3	2 844.9	39
NL4	ZUID-NEDERLAND	3 440.3	1 311.1	38

Source: Eurostat, population statistics.

* : National statistics.

** : Data 1995.

Number and Percentage in the 0-29 Age Group by NUTS 1 and NUTS 2 Regions, 1997

(Figure A3)

		Total Population (1 000)	Population 0 to 29 years (1 000)	0 to 29 years (%)
EUROPEAN UNION (CONTINUED)				
AT	**ÖSTERREICH (AUSTRIA)**	8 067.8	3 060.4	38
AT1	OSTÖSTERREICH	3 404.0	1 222.5	36
AT2	SÜDÖSTERREICH	1 770.6	671.9	38
AT3	WESTÖSTERREICH	2 893.2	1 165.9	40
PT	**PORTUGAL**	9 934.1	4 091.3	41
PT1	CONTINENTE	9 433.4	3 847.2	41
PT11	NORTE	3 544.8	1 588.9	45
PT12	CENTRO (P)	1 710.1	671.3	39
PT13	LISBOA E VALE DO TEJO	3 313.5	1 272.4	38
PT14	ALENTEJO	519.0	185.4	36
PT15	ALGARVE	346.1	129.1	37
PT2	ACORES	242.6	120.0	49
PT3	MADEIRA	258.0	124.2	48
FI	**SUOMI (FINLAND)**	5 132.3	1 939.1	38
FI1	MANNER-SUOMI	5 107.1	1 929.7	38
FI13	ITÄ-SUOMI	701.4	254.8	36
FI14	VÄLI-SUOMI	705.8	273.0	39
FI15	POHJOIS-SUOMI	559.1	233.4	42
FI16	UUSIMAA	1 327.2	515.4	39
FI17	ETELÄ-SUOMI	1 813.5	653.1	36
FI2	AHVENANMAA/°ALAND	25.3	9.4	37
SE	**SVERIGE**	8 844.5	3 339.5	38
SE01	STOCKHOLM	1 744.3	666.8	38
SE02	ÖSTRA MELLANSVERIGE	1 498.0	573.5	38
SE04	SYDSVERIGE	1 266.3	473.5	37
SE06	NORRA MELLANSVERIGE	857.1	308.6	36
SE07	MELLERSTA NORRLAND	391.1	140.2	36
SE08	ÖVRE NORRLAND	524.2	201.7	38
SE09	SMÅLAND MED ÖARNA	(:)	(:)	37*
SE0A	VÄSTSVERIGE	(:)	(:)	38*
UK	**UNITED KINGDOM* ***	58 500.2	23 533.7	40
UKC	NORTH EAST	2 607.4	1 039.1	40
UKD	NORTH WEST (INCLUDING MERSEYSIDE)	6 901.1	2 795.9	41
UKE	YORKSHIRE AND THE HUMBER	5 027.2	2 030.2	40
UKF	EAST MIDLANDS	4 113.1	1 637.3	40
UKG	WEST MIDLANDS	5 300.7	2 150.7	41
UKH	EASTERN	5 240.3	2 072.3	40
UKI	LONDON	6 987.4	2 958.3	42
UKJ	SOUTH EAST	7 815.7	3 057.8	39
UKK	SOUTH WEST	4 812.6	1 811.7	38
UKL	WALES	2 914.9	1 140.1	39
UKM	SCOTLAND	5 134.5	2 068.6	40
UKN	NORTHERN IRELAND	1 645.3	771.7	47
EFTA/EEA				
IS	**ÍSLAND**	269.9	126.6	47
LI	**LIECHTENSTEIN**	31.1	12.8	41
NO	**NORGE**	4 392.7	1 776.6	40
PRE-ACCESSION COUNTRIES				
BG	**BĂLGARIJA**	8 340.9	3 242.6	39
CZ	**ČESKÁ REPUBLIKA**	10 309.1	4 251.0	41
EE	**EESTI**	1 462.1	601.9	41
LV	**LATVIJA**	2 479.9	1 001.8	40
LT	**LIETUVA**	3 707.2	1 602.0	43
HU	**MAGYARORSZÁG**	10 174.4	4 125.9	41
PL	**POLSKA**	38 639.3	17 170.4	44
RO	**ROMÂNIA**	22 581.9	10 251.2	45
SI	**SLOVENIJA**	1 987.0	789.4	40
SK	**SLOVENSKÁ REPUBLIKA**	5 378.9	2 459.3	46
CY	**KYPROS**	741.0	341.1	46

Source: Eurostat, population statistics.

* : National statistics.
** : Data 1995.

Additional note

Portugal, Finland and **Sweden**: NUTS 2.

PERCENTAGE OF PEOPLE WHO DO NOT HAVE A QUALIFICATION OF UPPER SECONDARY EDUCATION BY AGE GROUP, 1997

(FIGURE A4)   (%)

AGE	EU	B	DK	D	EL	E	F	IRL	I	L	NL	A	P	FIN	S	UK
20-29 YEARS	31	21	21	19	26	39	24	27	42	47	28	18	55	13	14	37
30-39 YEARS	35	31	19	15	40	56	31	40	51	49	29	19	71	16	16	43
40-49 YEARS	42	44	18	17	54	71	40	56	60	53	36	28	79	30	25	44
50-59 YEARS	53	56	26	25	71	84	52	66	76	60	45	35	87	45	35	53

	EFTA/EEA				Pre-accession countries											
	IS*	LI	NO		BG*	CZ	EE	LV*	LT*	HU	PL	RO	SI	SK*		CY*
20-29 YEARS	44	(:)	8		(:)	8	15	(:)	(:)	22	13	15	16	(:)		20
30-39 YEARS	33	(:)	10		24	9	6	6	8	22	13	17	21	11		35
40-49 YEARS	35	(:)	18		30	15	12	13	14	30	20	33	31	18		55
50-59 YEARS	42	(:)	28		48	21	24	32	37	54	40	60	39	36		70

Source: Eurostat, Labour force survey.

* National statistics.

PERCENTAGE OF PEOPLE IN EDUCATION OR TRAINING AMONG YOUNG PEOPLE AGED 15 TO 24, 1987 AND 1997

(FIGURE A5)   (%)

	EU	B	DK	D	EL	E	F	IRL	I	L	NL	A	P	FIN	S	UK
1987	49	56	61	57	51	49	51	46	45	44	61	(:)	35	38*	34*	39
1997	61	67	68	67	59	62	69	60	55	62	66	57	57	72	65	49

Source: Eurostat, Labour force survey.

* : National statistics.

PUPILS AND STUDENTS AGED 0 TO 29 YEARS IN THE POPULATION OF 0- TO 29-YEAR-OLDS, 1996/97

(FIGURE A7)   (1 000)

	European Union							
	EU	B	DK	D	EL	E	F	IRL
STUDENTS 0-29	69 013.3	2 392.7	1 117.6	16 371.6	1 955.9	9 026.0	14 405.0	991.7
POPULATION 0-29	121 252.6	3 814.6	2 000.7	28 643.4	4 041.5	15 820.4	23 468.2	1 754.4

	I	L	NL	A	P	FIN	S	UK
STUDENTS 0-29	(:)	(:)	3 388.0	1 640.5	2 088.1	1 096.1	1 941.1	12 599.0
POPULATION 0-29	(:)	(:)	6 103.9	3 060.3	4 091.2	1 939.1	3 339.6	23 175.4

	EFTA/EEA				Pre-accession countries			
	IS	LI	NO		BG	CZ	EE	LV
STUDENTS 0-29	79.7	5.9	1 014.0		1 651.0	2 249.6	338.0	512.1
POPULATION 0-29	126.6	12.8	1 776.6		3 242.6	4 251.0	601.9	1 001.8

	Pre-accession countries (continued)							
	LT	HU	PL	RO	SI	SK		CY
STUDENTS 0-29	768.768	2 106.8	9 565.0	4 672.2	409.0	(:)		(:)
POPULATION 0-29	1 602.0	4 125.9	17 170.4	10 251.2	789.4	2 459.3		(:)

Source: Eurostat, UOE.

CHANGE IN THE UNEMPLOYMENT RATES BY AGE GROUP, IN THE EUROPEAN UNION, 1987-1997

(FIGURE A9)   (%)

	1987	1988	1989	1990	1991	1992	1993	1994	1995	1996	1997
15-59 ANS	11	10	9	9	9	9	11	12	11	11	11
15-24 ANS	22	20	18	16	17	18	21	22	21	22	21
25-34 ANS	11	11	10	9	10	10	12	13	12	12	12

Source: Eurostat, Labour force survey.

CHANGE IN THE UNEMPLOYMENT RATES BY AGE GROUP, BY MEMBER STATE, 1987-1997

(FIGURE A10)   (%)

B

1987	1988	1989	1990	1991	1992	1993	1994	1995	1996	1997	
11	10	8	7	7	7	8	10	10	10	9	15-59 YEARS
21	18	16	15	14	13	19	22	22	21	21	15-24 YEARS
12	11	9	8	8	7	9	10	10	10	9	25-34 YEARS

DK

1987	1988	1989	1990	1991	1992	1993	1994	1995	1996	1997
6	7	8	9	9	9	11	8	7	7	6
9	9	12	12	12	12	15	10	10	11	8
7	8	10	10	11	11	13	9	8	7	6

D

1987	1988	1989	1990	1991	1992	1993	1994	1995	1996	1997	
7	6	6	5	5	6	8	9	8	9	10	15-59 YEARS
8	7	6	5	6	6	8	9	9	10	11	15-24 YEARS
8	7	6	5	6	6	8	9	8	8	9	25-34 YEARS

EL

1987	1988	1989	1990	1991	1992	1993	1994	1995	1996	1997
8	8	8	8	8	8	9	10	10	10	10
25	26	25	23	25	25	27	28	28	31	31
9	9	9	9	9	9	10	11	11	12	12

E

1987	1988	1989	1990	1991	1992	1993	1994	1995	1996	1997	
22	21	18	17	17	18	23	25	23	23	22	15-59 YEARS
44	41	34	32	31	33	42	45	42	42	39	15-24 YEARS
21	21	19	18	18	20	25	28	26	26	24	25-34 YEARS

F

1987	1988	1989	1990	1991	1992	1993	1994	1995	1996	1997
11	10	10	10	9	10	12	13	12	13	13
23	22	20	20	20	22	26	29	27	28	29
11	10	10	10	10	11	13	14	13	14	14

IRL

1987	1988	1989	1990	1991	1992	1993	1994	1995	1996	1997	
19	18	17	15	16	16	16	15	13	12	11	15-59 YEARS
26	25	22	20	23	23	25	23	19	18	16	15-24 YEARS
18	16	15	14	15	15	15	14	11	11	10	25-34 YEARS

I

1987	1988	1989	1990	1991	1992	1993	1994	1995	1996	1997
11	12	12	10	11	10	11	12	12	13	13
34	33	32	29	28	27	30	32	33	34	34
11	12	13	12	12	10	12	14	14	15	15

L

1987	1988	1989	1990	1991	1992	1993	1994	1995	1996	1997	
3	2	2	2	2	2	2	4	3	3	3	15-59 YEARS
5	5	3	4	3	4	4	8	7	9	7	15-24 YEARS
2	2	2	2	2	3	2	4	3	4	3	25-34 YEARS

NL

1987	1988	1989	1990	1991	1992	1993	1994	1995	1996	1997
10	10	9	8	7	6	6	7	7	7	6
17	14	13	11	11	8	10	11	12	11	10
10	9	9	8	7	5	6	8	7	6	5

A

1987	1988	1989	1990	1991	1992	1993	1994	1995	1996	1997	
(:)	(:)	(:)	(:)	(:)	(:)	(:)	(:)	4	5	5	15-59 YEARS
5	5	4	4	4	4	5	(:)	6	7	8	15-24 YEARS
(:)	(:)	(:)	(:)	(:)	(:)	(:)	(:)	4	5	5	25-34 YEARS

P

1987	1988	1989	1990	1991	1992	1993	1994	1995	1996	1997
8	6	6	5	4	4	6	7	8	8	7
18	14	12	10	9	10	12	15	16	17	14
8	7	6	5	5	5	6	8	8	8	7

FIN

1987	1988	1989	1990	1991	1992	1993	1994	1995	1996	1997	
5	5	4	4	8	13	18	19	18	16	15	15-59 YEARS
10	8	6	7	15	25	33	34	41	42	35	15-24 YEARS
5	4	3	3	8	14	19	19	17	14	16	25-34 YEARS

S

1987	1988	1989	1990	1991	1992	1993	1994	1995	1996	1997
2	2	2	2	3	6	10	10	8	10	10
5	4	4	5	8	14	23	23	19	22	22
3	2	2	2	4	8	12	12	9	11	12

UK

1987	1988	1989	1990	1991	1992	1993	1994	1995	1996	1997	
11	9	7	7	9	10	10	10	9	8	7	15-59 YEARS
16	13	10	10	14	16	18	16	16	15	14	15-24 YEARS
12	10	8	7	9	11	11	10	9	9	7	25-34 YEARS

Source: Eurostat, Labour force survey.

Additional note

Austria, Finland and **Sweden**: Data for 1987-94 are from the national statistical offices.

UNEMPLOYMENT RATES OF 15- TO 24-YEAR-OLDS WHO HAVE LEFT SCHOOL AND OF 25- TO 59 YEAR OLDS, 1997

(FIGURE A11) (%)

	European Union															
	EU	B	DK	D	EL	E	F	IRL	I	L	NL	A	P	FIN	S	UK
15 TO 24 YEARS NO LONGER ATTENDING SCHOOL	23.5	21.0	8.5	16.1	29.9	36.3	32.9	16.6	32.4	6.8	7.2	7.9	13.1	23.0	22.1	14.6
25 TO 59 YEARS	9.4	7.7	4.9	9.9	7.3	18.0	11.0	9.2	9.3	2.0	4.8	4.8	5.8	12.4	8.9	6.0

	EFTA/EEA				Pre-accession countries											
	IS*	LI	NO		BG*	CZ	EE	LV*	LT*	HU	PL	RO	SI	SK*		CY*
15 TO 24 YEARS NO LONGER ATTENDING SCHOOL	7.1	(:)	(:)		(:)	7.0**	14.0	(:)	(:)	28.4	22.8**	10.7	17.3	10.4		(:)
25 TO 59 YEARS	3.0	(:)	3.1		(:)	3.8	9.9	(:)	(:)	7.8	9.9	4.2	5.5	8.0		(:)

Source: Eurostat, Labour force survey.

* : National statistics.

** : All 15-24 years.

PERCENTAGE OF EMPLOYEES WITH INSECURE JOBS BY AGE GROUP, 1997

(FIGURE A12) (%)

	European Union															
	EU	B	DK	D	EL	E	F	IRL	I	L	NL	A	P	FIN	S	UK
15 TO 24 YEARS NO LONGER ATTENDING SCHOOL	18.4	16.4	17.2	5.3	19.8	64.6	18.9	9.3	10.1	(:)	21.8	3.3	25.2	36.6	35.0	10.6
25 TO 59 YEARS	7.1	5.7	6.2	3.8	8.3	25.2	6.9	6.1	5.5	1.0	5.7	2.2	9.3	14.3	12.7	4.9

	EFTA/EEA				Pre-accession countries											
	IS*	LI	NO		BG*	CZ	EE	LV*	LT*	HU	PL	RO	SI	SK*		CY*
15 TO 24 YEARS NO LONGER ATTENDING SCHOOL	19.3	(:)	(:)		(:)	2.1	4.3	(:)	(:)	5.6	2.9	9.0	14.0	4.3		(:)
25 TO 59 YEARS	6.5	(:)	4.3		(:)	1.0	3.6	(:)	(:)	3.7	1.3	1.6	2.6	1.6		(:)

Source: Eurostat, Labour force survey.

* : National statistics.

UNEMPLOYMENT RATES AMONG IN THE 25-59 AGE BAND, BY LEVEL OF EDUCATION, 1997

(FIGURE A13) (%)

	European Union															
	EU	B	DK	D	EL	E	F	IRL	I	L	NL	A	P	FIN	S	UK
ISCED 0-2	12.5	12.9	8.2	16.8	6.8	19.9	15.3	15.0	10.7	3.2	7.3	7.5	6.3	16.9	12.0	7.9
ISCED 3	8.8	7.1	4.7	10.0	9.1	17.6	9.9	6.6	8.2	(:)	4.1	4.3	6.5	13.4	10.2	5.9
ISCED 5-7	5.8	3.4	3.4	5.8	5.7	13.6	6.7	3.5	7.0	(:)	3.3	2.7	2.4	5.7	4.2	3.1

	EFTA/EEA				Pre-accession countries											
	IS*	LI	NO		BG*	CZ	EE	LV*	LT*	HU	PL	RO	SI	SK*		CY*
ISCED 0-2	5.0	(:)	(:)		13.5	12.4	15.5	14.6	16.1	13.1	15.1	3.9	8.7	6.6		(:)
ISCED 3	(:)	(:)	3.4		9.7	3.0	11.6	14.4	16.3	7.2	10.1	5.0	5.0	2.4		(:)
ISCED 5-7	(:)	(:)	(:)		5.2	1.9	6.9	7.6	8.9	1.7	3.0	2.1	2.7	0.3		(:)

Source: Eurostat, Labour force survey.

* : National statistics.

UNEMPLOYMENT RATES AMONG HIGHER EDUCATION GRADUATES (ISCED 5-7), BY AGE GROUP, 1997

(FIGURE A14) (%)

	European Union															
	EU	B	DK	D	EL	E	F	IRL	I	L	NL	A	P	FIN	S	UK
25-34	8.6	4.7	5.3	5.2	11.1	22.2	9.4	3.9	18.8	(:)	3.7	4.2	4.2	8.6	4.1	3.3
35-44	4.2	2.3	2.2	5.0	2.2	7.8	5.3	2.9	2.4	(:)	3.2	(:)	(:)	4.3	5.1	2.6
45-54	3.7	2.6	2.6	5.1	2.5	4.6	4.5	(:)	0.7	(:)	3.0	(:)	(:)	5.2	3.3	2.9
25-54	5.7	3.4	3.3	5.1	5.8	14.0	6.8	3.5	7.4	(:)	3.4	2.4	2.3	6.0	4.2	3.0

	EFTA/EEA				Pre-accession countries											
	IS*	LI	NO		BG*	CZ	EE	LV*	LT*	HU	PL	RO	SI	SK*		CY*
25-34	(:)	(:)	(:)		(:)	2.7	7.6	(:)	(:)	2.5	3.5	4.7	4.3	3.2		(:)
35-44	(:)	(:)	(:)		(:)	1.6	6.7	(:)	(:)	1.3	2.6	0.9	1.7	1.6		(:)
45-54	(:)	(:)	(:)		(:)	1.6	8.2	(:)	(:)	1.1	2.9	1.6	2.2	1.1		(:)
25-54	(:)	(:)	(:)		(:)	1.9	7.4	(:)	(:)	1.5	3.0	2.2	2.8	(:)		(:)

Source: Eurostat, Labour force survey.

* : National statistics.

Unemployment rates by education level and sex (25-59 age range), 1997

(Figure A15) (%)

		European Union														
		EU	B	DK	D	EL	E	F	IRL	I	L	NL	A	P	FIN	S	UK
ISCED 0-3	Men	9.3	7.4	4.5	10.7	4.9	14.9	10.4	11.5	7.6	1.6	3.9	5.0	5.7	14.6	11.0	8.0
	Women	12.1	13.4	6.7	12.0	12.4	27.5	14.4	11.6	13.1	3.6	7.4	5.1	7.1	14.5	10.4	5.7
ISCED 5-7	Men	5.1	2.8	3.2	5.1	4.3	9.9	6.2	3.0	5.3	(:)	2.8	2.2	2.3	5.4	5.2	3.4
	Women	6.9	4.1	3.7	7.0	7.5	18.2	7.3	4.0	9.2	(:)	4.0	3.4	2.5	6.0	3.3	2.7

		EFTA/EEA				Pre-accession countries										
		IS*	LI	NO		BG*	CZ	EE	LV*	LT*	HU	PL	RO	SI	SK*		CY*
ISCED 0-3	Men	(:)	(:)	2.9		(:)	4.1	12.8	(:)	(:)	9.6	9.0	4.4	6.1	4.6		(:)
	Women	(:)	(:)	4.0		(:)	6.7	11.8	(:)	(:)	7.9	13.9	4.9	5.9	3.4		(:)
ISCED 5-7	Men	(:)	(:)	(:)		5.3	1.2	6.9	8.1	8.7	1.2	2.6	1.8	2.9	1.5		(:)
	Women	(:)	(:)	(:)		5.0	2.6	7.0	7.3	8.9	2.2	3.3	2.4	2.4	2.4		(:)

Source: Eurostat, Labour force survey.

* : National statistics.

Occupations of people in the 25-34 and 35-59 age ranges, with higher education qualifications, 1997

(Figure A16)

Professionals and managers

	EU	B	DK	D	EL	E	F	IRL	I	L	NL	A	P	FIN	S	UK
25-34	52.1	57.5	44.6	46.7	55.6	41.7	41.2	56.1	60.1	69.2	58.3	82.2	61.8	67.5	46.3	65.2
35-59	64.7	70.6	55.9	54.1	73.5	65.6	59.2	71.1	78.8	79.8	76.5	90.9	62.6	75.6	55.7	74.5

Technicians and associate professionals

	EU	B	DK	D	EL	E	F	IRL	I	L	NL	A	P	FIN	S	UK
25-34	23.7	15.3	39	25.6	17.3	16.8	38.3	7.6	20.8	23.4	24	11.7	27.7	17.1	39.7	15
35-59	19	12.1	32.9	21.8	10.2	12.3	31.4	5.4	12.7	16.8	14	6.3	32.7	15.1	32.5	10.8

Clerks, service and sales workers

	EU	B	DK	D	EL	E	F	IRL	I	L	NL	A	P	FIN	S	UK
25-34	15	22.3	13	11.8	16.5	26	14.8	24.1	17.1	-	13.9	-	10.6	4.9	9.4	12.7
35-59	8.6	14.1	6.5	9.5	9.8	12.3	5.5	13.3	6.8	-	7.1	-	4.7	3.7	7.4	9.2

Craft workers and machine operators

	EU	B	DK	D	EL	E	F	IRL	I	L	NL	A	P	FIN	S	UK
25-34	7.7	3.8	-	13.5	5.5	14.4	3.7	-	-	-	3.2	-	-	-	-	6.2
35-59	6.5	2.1	4.2	12.9	4	8.6	2.5	7.8	1.7	-	2	-	-	-	-	4.8

Source: Eurostat, Labour force survey.

- : Non reliable data.

Percentage of employees aged 25-59 with insecure jobs, by education level, 1997

(Figure A17) (%)

	European Union															
	EU	B	DK	D	EL	E	F	IRL	I	L	NL	A	P	FIN	S	UK
ISCED 0-2	10.2	7.0	9.5	5.0	13.3	30.0	9.8	9.3	7.1	1.2	5.7	3.4	9.8	11.8	11.3	5.5
ISCED 3-7	5.7	5.2	5.5	3.6	5.8	19.7	5.5	4.3	4.2	0.8	5.7	1.9	8.2	15.0	13.1	4.5

	EFTA/EEA				Pre-accession countries										
	IS*	LI	NO		BG*	CZ	EE	LV*	LT*	HU	PL	RO	SI	SK*		CY*
ISCED 0-2	6.9	(:)	(:)		(:)	2.4	(:)	(:)	(:)	6.6	2.7	3.8	3.0	2.2		(:)
ISCED 3-7	6.2	(:)	4.1		(:)	0.9	3.4	(:)	(:)	2.9	1.1	1.3	2.5	1.0		(:)

Source: Eurostat, Labour force survey.

* : National statistics.

Average gross monthly earnings by education level, in Euros, 1995

(Figure A18) (EUR)

	European Union														
	B	DK	D (1)	D (2)	EL	E	F	IRL	I	L	NL	A	P	FIN	S	UK
ISCED 0-2	1 840	2 349	2 117	1 549	933	1 012	1 630	1 653	1 291	2 190	1 821	1 620	564	1 723	1 828	1 456
ISCED 3	2 044	2 761	2 620	1 774	968	1 295	1 744	1 677	1 627	3 085	2 050	2 103	812	1 786	2 072	1 752
ISCED 5-7	2 885	3 885	3 946	2 667	1 386	1 705	2 744	2 438	2 526	3 930	3 030	3 862	1 660	2 567	2 593	2 447

Source: Eurostat, Structure of earnings statistics.

Additional note

Germany: (1) Former republic of Germany prior to 3.10.1990; (2) New *Länder* and East-Berlin.

STRUCTURES AND SCHOOLS

DISTRIBUTION OF PUPILS AND STUDENTS BY LEVEL OF EDUCATION, IN THOUSANDS, 1996/97

(FIGURE B2)   (1 000)

	TOTAL IN THE EDUCATIONAL SYSTEM (ISCED 0-7)	PUPILS IN PRE-PRIMARY EDUCATION (ISCED 0)	PUPILS IN PRIMARY EDUCATION (ISCED 1)	PUPILS IN LOWER SECONDARY EDUCATION (ISCED 2)	STUDENTS IN UPPER SECONDARY EDUCATION (ISCED 3)	STUDENTS IN TERTIARY EDUCATION (ISCED 5-7)
European Union						
EU	83 419.3	10 818.8	23 655.8	17 153.9	19 369.3	12 265.7
B	2 589.4	421.1	750.7	353.4	703.3	360.9
DK	1 176.1	221.5	346.5	201.1	226.7	180.4
D	16 784.2	2 343.5	3 859.5	5 340.3	3 042.1	2 131.9
EL	1 965.5	132.7	652.0	407.1	410.5	363.2
E	9 356.4	1 117.3	2 702.6	1 126.6	2 725.5	1 684.5
F	14 582.0	2 451.2	4 004.7	3 362.3	2 617.4	2 062.5
IRL	1 002.1	115.6	358.8	199.6	189.8	134.6
I	10 882.6	1 577.1	2 810.2	1 851.8	2 751.0	1 892.5
L	70.2	9.9	28.4	14.6	14.2	1.8
NL	3 510.0	394.4	1 231.0	750.7	665.1	469.0
A	1 641.1	225.0	381.9	380.1	413.4	240.6
P	2 284.1	198.7	824.8	460.7	449.1	350.9
FIN	1 192.0	114.7	380.9	205.4	264.6	226.5
S	2 159.3	345.0	690.6	329.9	518.5	275.2
UK	14 224.3	454.3	5 329.8	2 170.6	4 378.2	1 891.5
EFTA/EEA						
IS	82.2	14.3	29.3	12.9	17.8	7.9
LI	5.9	0.9	2.1	1.6	1.1	0.1
NO	1 067.6	183.5	330.6	155.6	212.5	185.3
Pre-accession countries						
BG	1 674.9	247.0	431.8	373.3	360.1	262.8
CZ	2 233.4	324.8	661.1	539.2	512.5	195.7
EE	341.3	57.0	126.8	58.6	59.8	39.0
LV	516.5	62.7	146.7	160.5	85.0	61.6
LT	772.3	87.1	222.7	251.4	127.3	83.6
HU	2 204.7	395.5	502.6	504.1	599.8	202.8
PL	9 662.5	983.5	5 021.4	(:)	2 730.1	927.5
RO	4 688.3	659.2	1 405.3	1 140.9	1 128.4	354.5
SI	425.7	49.9	98.9	106.7	116.8	53.5
SK	1 299.9	170.2	331.8	351.8	344.3	101.8
CY	162.0	26.0	64.8	33.2	28.1	10.0
Other countries taking part in the PHARE programme						
AL	772.5	84.2	303.6	257.1	93.1	34.5
BA	578.4	(:)	191.8	197.3	144.2	45.1
MK	407.6	32.5	133.0	127.9	83.8	30.4

Source: Eurostat, UOE.

Additional notes

Germany, France, Ireland and **Luxembourg**: The sum of the values in the different ISCED levels differs from the total because a certain number of students cannot be allocated by ISCED level.
Germany: ISCED 7 is excluded.
Spain: Data on the old and the new educational system are presented jointly. As the duration of ISCED levels 2 and 3 varies from one system to another, a statistical adjustment has been made in the two levels concerned.
Luxembourg: There is no complete system of tertiary education at university; non subsidised private education is excluded.
Iceland: Only full-time students are included in ISCED levels 3 to 7.
Liechtenstein: 1995/96. There is no complete system of tertiary education at university.
Poland, Romania, and Slovenia: ISCED 7 is excluded.
Poland: ISCED 2 is included in ISCED 1, some ISCED 5/6 education programmes are included in ISCED 3.
Slovenia: Only the first stage of the single structure is considered as ISCED 1.
Bosnia & Herzegovina: ISCED 0 and ISCED 7 are excluded.
Former Yugoslav Rep. of Makedonia: ISCED 7 is excluded.

DISTRIBUTION OF PRIMARY AND SECONDARY STUDENTS ACCORDING TO THE TYPE OF SCHOOL THEY ATTEND, 1996/97
(FIGURE B3)   (1 000)

	PUBLIC	PRIVATE TOTAL			TOTAL
		TOTAL OF WHICH	SUBSIDISED PRIVATE	NON SUBSIDISED PRIVATE	
European Union					
B	744.3	1 063.1	1 063.1	-	1 807.4
DK	688.3	86.0	86.0	-	774.2
D	11 663.8	578.0	(:)	(:)	12 241.8
EL	1 392.7	77.0	-	77.0	1 469.6
E	4 624.5	1 930.1	1 505.9	424.2	6 554.7
F	7 924.4	2 060.0	1 692.5	367.5	9 984.4
IRL	741.4	6.8	-	6.8	748.2
I	6 989.3	423.7	-	423.7	7 413.0
L	53.9	3.3	3.3	-	57.2
NL	579.3	2 026.4	2 009.7	16.7	2 605.7
A	1 088.8	86.6	86.6	-	1 175.4
P	1 569.5	165.0	(:)	(:)	1 734.5
FIN	816.6	34.3	34.3	-	850.9
S	1 507.0	32.1	32.1	-	1 539.0
UK	8 825.6	616.1	15.3	600.8	9 441.7
EFTA/EEA					
IS	41.6	0.6	0.6	0	42.3
LI	4.9	0.1	-	0.1	5.0
NO	672.8	25.9	(:)	(:)	698.7
Pre-accession countries					
BG	1 159.3	5.9	-	5.9	1 165.2
CZ	1 627.5	85.4	85.4	-	1 712.9
EE	242.0	3.2	-	3.2	245.2
LV	389.4	2.8	-	2.8	392.2
LT	595.7	1.4	-	1.5	597.1
HU	1 532.4	74.0	74.0	-	1 606.5
PL	7 598.3	153.2	-	153.2	7 751.5
RO	3 640.5	34.1	34.1	-	3 674.6
SI	321.0	1.3	1.3	-	322.4
SK	980.7	47.2	47.2	-	1 027.9
CY	117.9	8.9	-	8.9	126.8
Other countries taking part in the PHARE programme					
AL	653.8	(:)	(:)	(:)	653.8
BA	533.3	(:)	(:)	(:)	533.3
MK	344.7	(:)	(:)	(:)	344.7

Source: Eurostat, UOE.

Additional notes

Luxembourg: Non subsidised private education is excluded.
Netherlands: Equal funding of public and subsidised private schools is a constitutional right.
United Kingdom: Figures do not include further education institutions that provide post-compulsory general and vocational education.
Iceland: Only full-time students are included.
Liechtenstein: 1995/96.

PRE-PRIMARY EDUCATION

PARTICIPATION RATES OF 4-YEAR-OLDS IN EDUCATION-ORIENTED PRE-PRIMARY INSTITUTIONS, FROM 1960 TO 1997

(FIGURE C1)   (%)

	1960	1970	1980	1990	1996	1997
European Union						
B	92	100	100	99	100	100
DK	(:)	36 (1973)	54	74	79	80
D	(:)	(:)	65	71	71	81
EL	(:)	(:)	38	51	54	56
E	34	43	69	95	100	99
F	63	87	100	100	100	100
IRL	(:)	(:)	54	55	54	54
I	(:)	(:)	(:)	(:)	(:)	93
L	43	65	94	94	100*	100*
NL	71	86	96	98	97	99
A	(:)	29	57	66	71	72
P	(:)	(:)	18	46	55	55
FIN	(:)	16 (1975)	18	26	29	36
S	(:)	(:)	28	48	57	63
UK	(:)	(:)	83	91	93	94
EFTA/EEA						
IS	(:)	(:)	(:)	(:)	(:)	86
LI	(:)	(:)	(:)	(:)	(:)	36
NO	(:)	(:)	(:)	(:)	(:)	70
Pre-accession countries						
BG	(:)	(:)	(:)	(:)	(:)	66
CZ	(:)	(:)	(:)	(:)	(:)	83
EE	(:)	(:)	(:)	(:)	(:)	69
LV	(:)	(:)	(:)	(:)	(:)	52
LT	(:)	(:)	(:)	(:)	(:)	38
HU	(:)	(:)	(:)	(:)	(:)	96
PL	(:)	(:)	(:)	(:)	(:)	28
RO	(:)	(:)	(:)	(:)	(:)	57
SI	(:)	(:)	(:)	(:)	(:)	(:)
SK	(:)	(:)	(:)	(:)	(:)	(:)
CY	(:)	(:)	(:)	(:)	(:)	(:)
Other countries taking part in the PHARE programme						
AL	(:)	(:)	(:)	(:)	(:)	39
BA	(:)	(:)	(:)	(:)	(:)	(:)
MK	(:)	(:)	(:)	(:)	(:)	14

Source: Eurostat, UOE and population statistics.

Additional notes

Belgium: The data prior to 1980 are shown as a dotted line because they are available only for all children enrolled in nursery schools (*écoles maternelles/kleuteronderwijs*) regardless of their age.
Greece: Only children between 3½ and 4½ years old in public sector nursery schools are included.
Ireland: Pupils attending certain private schools are not included.
Luxembourg: The data are shown as a dotted line as the percentages include enrolment of both 4- and 5-year-olds.
United Kingdom (E): The data cover children in nursery schools, nursery and infant classes in primary schools, special schools and independent schools.
Liechstenstein: 1995/96.
Hungary: Only full-time students are included.
Albania: Only full-time students are included.

PARTICIPATION RATES IN EDUCATION-ORIENTED PRE-PRIMARY INSTITUTIONS AND PRIMARY INSTITUTIONS BY AGE, 1996/97

(FIGURE C3)
(1 000)

		PRE-PRIMARY LEVEL	PRIMARY LEVEL	TOTAL POPULATION		PRE-PRIMARY LEVEL	PRIMARY LEVEL	TOTAL POPULATION		PRE-PRIMARY LEVEL	PRIMARY LEVEL	TOTAL POPULATION
European Union												
3 YEARS	B	119.4	(–)	121.1	DK	43.1	(–)	68.5	D	470.9	(–)	811.5
4 YEARS		125.2	(–)	125.8		55.1	(–)	69.1		676.4	(–)	832.1
5 YEARS		125.2	1.7	127.7		57.7	(–)	66.0		722.7	(–)	865.1
6 YEARS		5.4	120.3	126.4		59.4	2.8			449.6	425.5	950.9
7 YEARS		0.2	123.1	123.8		5.9	56.5	63.2		24.0	910.1	938.5
3 YEARS	EL	13.6	(–)	102.3	E	256.7	(–)	384.3	F	701.2	0.2	700.5
4 YEARS		57.6	(–)	103.4		391.7	(–)	394.6		709.2	0.2	703.0
5 YEARS		61.6		104.2		400.1	(–)	394.0		733.0	10.0	737.5
6 YEARS		(–)	104.0	106.6		0.5	410.3	390.3		9.7	747.4	754.3
7 YEARS		(–)	103.5	108.3		0.2	419.9	397.5		0.5	762.0	758.9
3 YEARS	IRL	1.6	(–)	49.9	I	503.5	(–)	554.3	L	(:)	(–)	5.7
4 YEARS		27.7	(–)	51.8		537.9	(–)	578.9		(:)	(–)	5.5
5 YEARS		53.4	0.1	54.1		535.8	2.7	554.4		9.9*	(–)	5.3
6 YEARS		31.9	24.1	55.41		(–)	562.5	558.9		(–)	5.5*	5.5
7 YEARS		1.0	53.6	55.4		(–)	568.3	562.1		(–)	5.2*	5.2
3 YEARS	NL	0	0.2	196.2	A	30.2	(–)	95.4	P	43.8	(–)	113.0
4 YEARS		195.2	0.9	198.1		69.2	(–)			62.0	(–)	113.7
5 YEARS		197.4	1.5	200.9		87.4	(–)	95.1		80.1	(–)	114.6
6 YEARS		1.6	197.0	201.0		36.0	57.0	93.5		0	106.9	108.0
7 YEARS		0.2	192.0	192.9		1.0	92.3	92.0		(–)	108.4	110.4
3 YEARS	FIN	20.8	(–)	64.8	S	69.0	(–)	117.4	UK	332.5	35.6	760.9
4 YEARS		23.8	(–)	66.8		78.3	(–)	123.4		84.8	644.4	775.4
5 YEARS		27.2	(–)	65.7		86.0	(–)	125.8		(–)	788.9	794.0
6 YEARS		42.5	0.6*	66.1		111.8	10.1	126.9		(–)	780.9	789.0
7 YEARS		0.4	63.2*	64.1		(–)	115.1	120.0		(–)	769.7	778.5
EFTA/EEA												
3 YEARS	IS	3.8	(–)	4.6	LI	-	(–)	0.4	NO	36.6	(–)	60.3
4 YEARS		3.9	(–)	4.5		0.1	(–)	0.4		42.7	(–)	61.1
5 YEARS		4.0	0	4.5		0.4	(–)	0.4		46.6	(–)	61.9
6 YEARS		(–)	4.6	4.7		0.3	0.1	0.4		57.1	0.5	61.9
7 YEARS		(–)	4.4	4.5		0	0.4	0.4		0.5	59.6	60.2
Pre-accession countries												
3 YEARS	BG	45.2	(–)	82.8	CZ	53.0	(–)	120.0	EE	9.9	(–)	14.7
4 YEARS		57.0	(–)	86.5		90.0	(–)	120.6		11.9	(–)	17.2
5 YEARS		62.8	0.5	89.4		115.0	(–)	128.4		13.1	0	18.1
6 YEARS		70.7	9.9	97.3		58.9	68.8	127.7		12.6		20.7
7 YEARS		3.9	98.4	102.4		5.5	120.7	125.9		(–)		22.3
3 YEARS	LV	12.2	(–)	26.1	LT	16.2	(–)	45.8	HU	102.1	(–)	115.5
4 YEARS		15.7	(–)	30.1		19.9	(–)	52.2		115.1	(–)	119.8
5 YEARS		16.9	(–)	32.3		22.4	0	55.3		128.4	2.4	125.0
6 YEARS		17.9	1.5	34.8		24.8	5.9	55.5		19.1	105.9	123.5
7 YEARS		-	30.5	36.0		3.3	48.0	55.9		0.7	120.4	120.8
3 YEARS	PL	96.0	(–)	485.8	RO	86.1	(–)	242.2	SI	(:)	(–)	19.9
4 YEARS		140.6	(–)	505.4		144.7	(–)	251.9		(:)	(–)	20.1
5 YEARS		195.3	(–)	536.7		187.4	(–)	257.6		30.2*	(–)	21.7
6 YEARS		533.1	3.9	535.7		241.0	55.6	283.6		19.7	1.7	22.4
7 YEARS		10.0	541.7	552.1		-	311.6	351.6		(–)	22.6	23.3
3 YEARS	SK	(:)	(:)	72.5					CY	4.0	(–)	(:)
4 YEARS		(:)	(:)	73.7						8.0	(–)	(:)
5 YEARS		(:)	(:)	77.4						11.8	1.8	(:)
6 YEARS		(:)	(:)	77.3						0.3	10.8	(:)
7 YEARS		(:)	(:)	77.5						-	10.4	(:)
Other countries taking part in the PHARE programme												
3 YEARS	AL	20.2	(–)	70.9	BA	(:)	(:)	(:)	MK	3.2	(–)	29.0
4 YEARS		29.6	(–)	75.2		(:)	(:)	(:)		4.2	(–)	30.2
5 YEARS		34.5	(–)	77.2		(:)	(:)	(:)		9.8	0.0	31.8
6 YEARS		(–)	63.2	76.3		(:)	(:)	(:)		15.2	7.9	31.2
7 YEARS		(–)	68.3	76.3		(:)	(:)	(:)		0.1	31.2	31.5

Source: Eurostat, UOE and population statistics.

Additional notes

Greece: Only children attending the *nipiagogeia* (public sector nursery schools) are included.
France: 1997/98.
Ireland: Pupils attending certain private schools are not included.
Luxembourg: Early entry into pre-primary education (for 3-year-olds) will be provided from the 1998/99 school year onwards. In ISCED 0, children aged 4 are included with 5-year-olds.
Netherlands: 4-year-olds attend the non-compulsory year of *basisonderwijs*. Compulsory primary education starts at age 5, but for the purposes of international statistics, 5-year-olds are included under ISCED 0.
United Kingdom: The data are presented for the United Kingdom as a whole; disparities between the component parts are therefore concealed. ISCED 1 data include reception classes and 4-year-olds in Northern Ireland (compulsory education starts at age 4). The data cover pupils in nursery schools and nursery and infant classes in primary schools.
Liechtenstein: 1995/96.
Norway: As of 1997/98, compulsory schooling starts at 6.
Slovenia: Data for children aged 3 and 4 at ISCED 0 are included with those aged 5.

DISTRIBUTION OF CHILDREN ATTENDING EDUCATION-ORIENTED PRE-PRIMARY PROVISION ACCORDING TO THE TYPE OF INSTITUTIONS THEY ATTEND, 1996/97

(FIGURE C4)   (%)

	European Union										
	B	DK	D	EL	E	F	IRL	I	L	NL	A
SCHOOL INSTITUTIONS	100	28	4	100	100	100	100	100	100	100	4
EDUCATION-ORIENTED NON-SCHOOL INSTITUTIONS	(−)	72	96	(−)	(:)	(−)	(−)	(−)	(−)	(−)	96

	European Union (continued)						EFTA/EEA		
	P	FIN	S	UK			IS	LI	NO
SCHOOL INSTITUTIONS	(:)	5	20*	(:)			100	(:)	(−)
EDUCATION-ORIENTED NON-SCHOOL INSTITUTIONS	(:)	95	80*	(:)			(−)	(:)	100

Source: Eurostat, UOE.

PARTICIPATION RATES OF 3-YEAR-OLDS IN EDUCATION-ORIENTED PRE-PRIMARY INSTITUTIONS, BY NUTS 1 AND NUTS 2 REGIONS, 1996/97

(FIGURE C5)

	RATE (%)	NUMBER OF 3-YEAR-OLDS IN EDUCATION-ORIENTED PRE-PRIMARY PROVISION (1 000)	TOTAL NUMBER OF 3-YEAR-OLDS IN THE POPULATION (1 000)			RATE (%)	NUMBER OF 3-YEAR-OLDS IN EDUCATION-ORIENTED PRE-PRIMARY PROVISION (1 000)	TOTAL NUMBER OF 3-YEAR-OLDS IN THE POPULATION (1 000)
EUROPEAN UNION				**FRANCE**		100	701.3	700.5
BELGIQUE-BELGIË	99	119.4	121.1	fr1	Île de France	100	148.9	147.4
be1 Bruxelles-Brussel		(:)	11.6	fr2	Bassin Parisien	97	123.1	126.4
be2 Vlaams Gewest	98	67.4	69.0	fr3	Nord - Pas-de-Calais	100	53.1	52.9
be3 Région Wallonne		(:)	40.5	fr4	Est	98	60.4	61.6
DANMARK	63	43.1	68.5	fr5	Ouest	100	88.5	86.5
DEUTSCHLAND	58	470.9	811.5	fr6	Sud-Ouest	100	62.5	62.2
de1 Baden-Württemberg		(:)	118.7	fr7	Centre-Est	100	83.9	83.8
de2 Bayern		(:)	135.6	fr8	Méditerranée	100	80.9	79.8
de3 Berlin		(:)	27.8	fr9	dép. d'Outremer	95	29.0	30.5
de4 Brandenburg		(:)	13.4	**IRELAND**		3	1.6	49.9
de5 Bremen		(:)	6.2	**ITALIA**		91	503.5	554.3
de6 Hamburg		(:)	15.1	it1	Nord Ovest	94	42.7	45.2
de7 Hessen		(:)	62.7	it2	Lombardia	99	75.9	76.6
de8 Mecklenburg-Vorpommern		(:)	9.9	it3	Nord Est	99	56.2	56.7
de9 Niedersachsen		(:)	88.0	it4	Emilia-Romagna	97	27.2	28.2
dea Nordrhein-Westfalen		(:)	196.8	it5	Centro (I)	99	44.4	44.7
deb Rheinland-Pfalz		(:)	44.0	it6	Lazio	90	44.6	49.8
dec Saarland		(:)	10.8	it7	Abruzzo-Molise	97	15.3	15.8
ded Sachsen		(:)	24.0	it8	Campania	79	61.2	77.3
dee Sachsen-Anhalt		(:)	14.9	it9	Sud	96	75.9	79.2
def Schleswig-Holstein		(:)	29.7	ita	Sicilia	69	44.7	65.3
deg Thüringen		(:)	13.7	itb	Sardegna	98	15.5	15.7
ELLADA	13	13.6	102.3	**LUXEMBOURG**			(:)	5.3
gr1 Voreia Ellada		(:)	33.5	**NEDERLAND**			(−)	196.2
gr2 Kentriki Ellada		(:)	22.8	nl1	Noord-Nederland		(−)	19.6
gr3 Attiki		(:)	35.2	nl2	Oost-Nederland		(−)	42.6
gr4 Nisia Aigaiou. Kriti		(:)	10.9	nl3	West-Nederland		(−)	92.0
ESPANA	67	256.7	384.3	nl4	Zuid-Nederland		(−)	42.0
es1 Noroeste	82	26.7	32.6	**ÖSTERREICH**		32	30.2	95.4
es2 Noreste	97	31.1	32.1	at1	Ostösterreich		(:)	38.1
es3 Comunidad de Madrid	75	36.7	48.9	at2	Südösterreich		(:)	19.8
es4 Centro (E)	82	41.0	49.7	at3	Westösterreich		(:)	37.4
es5 Este	77	79.3	102.6	**PORTUGAL**		39	43.8	113.0
es6 Sur	31	30.7	100.5	pt1	Portugal (Continente)		(:)	105.9
es7 Canarias	63	11.3	17.9	pt11	Norte		(:)	44.3
				pt12	Centro (P)		(:)	17.4
				pt13	Lisboa e Vale do Tejo		(:)	35.6
				pt14	Alentejo		(:)	4.7
				pt15	Algarve		(:)	3.9
				pt2	Açores		(:)	3.7
				pt3	Madeira		(:)	3.4

Source: Eurostat, UOE and population statistics.

Additional notes

France: 1997/98.
Ireland: Pupils attending certain private schools are not included.

PARTICIPATION RATES OF 3-YEAR-OLDS IN EDUCATION-ORIENTED PRE-PRIMARY INSTITUTIONS, BY NUTS 1 AND NUTS 2 REGIONS, 1996/97

(FIGURE C5)

		RATE (%)	NUMBER OF 3-YEAR-OLDS IN EDUCATION-ORIENTED PRE-PRIMARY PROVISION (1 000)	TOTAL NUMBER OF 3-YEAR-OLDS IN THE POPULATION (1 000)			RATE (%)	NUMBER OF 3-YEAR-OLDS IN EDUCATION-ORIENTED PRE-PRIMARY PROVISION (1 000)	TOTAL NUMBER OF 3-YEAR-OLDS IN THE POPULATION (1 000)
EUROPEAN UNION (continued)					**UNITED KINGDOM (continued)**				
SUOMI (FINLAND)		32	20.8	64.8	uk8	North West (UK)	63	52.3	83.2
fi1	Manner-Suomi	32	20.6	64.5	uk9	Wales	76	27.8	36.3
fi11	Uusimaa (suuralue)	41	7.6	18.3	ukA	Scotland	20	13.4	65.8
fi12	Etelä-Suomi	30	6.3	21.3	ukB	Northern Ireland	43	11.0	25.8
fi13	Itä-Suomi	29	2.3	8.0	**EFTA/EEA**				
fi14	Väli-Suomi	26	2.3	9.0	**ÍSLAND**		83	3.8	4.6
fi15	Pohjois-Suomi	26	2.0	7.9	**LIECHTENSTEIN**			-	0.4
fi2	Ahvenanmaa	53	0.2	0.3	**NORGE**		61	36.6	60.3
SVERIGE		59	68.9	117.4	**PRE-ACCESSION COUNTRIES**				
se1	Stockholm	70	17.4	24.6	**BĂLGARIJA**		55	45.2	82.8
se2	Östra Mellansverige	56	11.2	20.0	**ČESKÁ REPUBLIKA**		44	53.0	120.0
se3	Småland med öarna	52	5.4	10.4	**EESTI**		67	9.9	14.7
se4	Sydsverige	57	9.2	16.1	**LATVIJA**		47	12.2	26.1
se5	Västsverige	54	13.2	24.3	**LIETUVA**		35	16.2	45.8
se6	Norra Mellansverige	55	5.8	10.6	**MAGYARORSZÁG**		88	102.1	115.5
se7	Mellersta Norrland	62	2.9	4.7	**POLSKA**		20	96.0	485.8
se8	Övre Norrland	57	3.8	6.7	**ROMÂNIA**		36	86.1	242.2
UNITED KINGDOM		48	368.1	763.8	**SLOVENIJA**		(–)	(:)	19.9
uk1	North	84	32.1	38.3	**SLOVENSKÁ REPUBLIKA**		(–)	(:)	72.5
uk2	Yorkshire and Humberside	68	44.3	65.0	**KYPROS**		:	(:)	(:)
uk3	East Midlands	48	25.2	52.6	**OTHER COUNTRIES TAKING PART IN THE PHARE PROGRAMME**				
uk4	East Anglia	27	7.3	26.9	**ALBANIA**		29	20.2	70.9
uk5	South East (UK)	41	99.2	242.4	**BOSNA I HERZEGOVINA**			(:)	(:)
uk6	South West (UK)	23	13.2	58.0	**FORMER YUGOSLAV REPUBLIC OF MACEDONIA**		11	3.2	29.0
uk7	West Midlands	61	42.4	69.6					

Source: Eurostat, UOE and population statistics.

Additional notes

United Kingdom: The data cover children in nursery schools and nursery and infant classes in primary schools.
Population data 1995/96 is used for NUTS regions UKA and UKB as well as parts of NUTS UK5 and UK6.
Liechtenstein: 1995/96.
Hungary: Only full-time pupils are included.
Slovenia: Data for children aged 3 and 4 at ISCED 0 are included with those aged 5.
Albania: Only full-time pupils are included.

ENROLMENT OF 3-YEAR-OLDS IN EDUCATION-ORIENTED PRE-PRIMARY INSTITUTIONS, IN THOUSANDS, IN COMPARISON TO PERCENTAGE OF MOTHERS WITH A 3-YEAR-OLD CHILD AND IN EMPLOYMENT, 1996/97

(FIGURE C6)

	European Union										
	B	DK	D	EL	E	F	IRL	I	L	NL	A
NUMBER OF 3-YEAR-OLDS IN EDUCATION-ORIENTED PRE-PRIMARY PROVISION	119.4	43.1	470.9	13.6	256.7	701.2	1.6	503.5	(:)	(–)	30.2
TOTAL NUMBER OF 3-YEAR-OLDS IN THE POPULATION	121.1	68.5	811.5	102.3	384.3	700.5	49.9	554.3	5.7	196.2	95.4
NUMBER OF MOTHERS OF 3-YEAR-OLD CHILD IN EMPLOYMENT	65	(:)	43	47	37	54	46	41	40	54	60

	European Union (continued)					**EFTA/EEA**		
	P	FIN	S	UK		IS	LI	NO
NUMBER OF 3-YEAR-OLDS IN EDUCATION-ORIENTED PRE-PRIMARY PROVISION	43,8	20,8	68,9	332,5		3,8	-	36,6
TOTAL NUMBER OF 3-YEAR-OLDS IN THE POPULATION	113	64,8	117,4	760,9		4,6	0,4	60,3
NUMBER OF MOTHERS OF 3-YEAR-OLD CHILD IN EMPLOYMENT	68	62	66	57		74	(:)	(:)

Source: Eurostat, UOE, Labour force survey and population statistics.

Additional notes

France: 1997/98.
Ireland: Pupils attending certain private schools are not included.
Luxembourg: Early entry into pre-primary education (for 3-year-olds) will be offered from 1998/99 onwards.
Sweden and **Iceland**: National estimates are used in percentages of mothers with a job.
United Kingdom: The data cover children in nursery schools and nursery classes in primary schools.

AVERAGE DURATION OF ATTENDANCE BY CHILDREN AGED 3-7 AT AN EDUCATION-ORIENTED PRE-PRIMARY INSTITUTION IN COMPARISON TO DURATION OF OFFICIAL PROVISION, 1996/97

(FIGURE C7)

		PARTICI-PATION RATES (FIG. C3) (%)	DURATION OF ATTENDANCE AVERAGE (YEARS)	THEORE-TICAL (YEARS)			PARTICI-PATION RATES (FIG. C3) (%)	DURATION OF ATTENDANCE AVERAGE (YEARS)	THEORE-TICAL (YEARS)			PARTICI-PATION RATES (FIG. C3) (%)	DURATION OF ATTENDANCE AVERAGE (YEARS)	THEORE-TICAL (YEARS)
European Union														
3 YEARS	B	99			DK		63			D		58		
4 YEARS		100					80					81		
5 YEARS		98					87					84		
6 YEARS		4					91					47		
7 YEARS		0					9					3		
TOTAL		300	3.0	3			330	3.3	4			273	2.7	3
3 YEARS	EL	13			E		67			F		100		
4 YEARS		56					99					100		
5 YEARS		59					100					99		
6 YEARS		(–)					0					1		
7 YEARS		(–)					0					0		
TOTAL		128	1.3	2			266	2.7	3			301	3.0	4
3 YEARS	IRL	3			I		91			L		(:)		
4 YEARS		54					93					100		
5 YEARS		99					97					100		
6 YEARS		57					(–)					(–)		
7 YEARS		2					(–)					(–)		
TOTAL		215	2.1	2			280	2.8	3			200	2.0	2.5
3 YEARS	NL	0			A		32			P		39		
4 YEARS		99					72					55		
5 YEARS		98					92					70		
6 YEARS		1					38					0		
7 YEARS		0					1					(–)		
TOTAL		198	2.0	2			236	2.4	3			163	1.6	3
3 YEARS	FIN	32			S		59			UK		42		
4 YEARS		36					63					11		
5 YEARS		41					68					0		
6 YEARS		64					88					0		
7 YEARS		1					(–)					0		
TOTAL		174	1.7	4			279	2.8	4			53	0.5	2
EFTA/EEA														
3 YEARS	IS	83			LI		-			NO		61		
4 YEARS		86					36					70		
5 YEARS		88					100					75		
6 YEARS		(–)					79					92		
7 YEARS		(–)					3					1		
TOTAL		257	2.6	3			218	2.2	2			299	3.0	4
Pre-accession countries														
3 YEARS	BG	55			CZ		44			EE		67		
4 YEARS		66					75					69		
5 YEARS		70					90					72		
6 YEARS		73					46					61		
7 YEARS		4					4					-		
TOTAL		267	2.7	4			259	2.6	3			270	2.7	4
3 YEARS	LV	47			LT		35			HU		88		
4 YEARS		52					38					96		
5 YEARS		52					40					100		
6 YEARS		52					45					15		
7 YEARS		-					6					1		
TOTAL		203	2.0	4			165	1.6	4			301	3.0	3
3 YEARS	PL	20			RO		36			SI		(:)		
4 YEARS		28					57					(:)		
5 YEARS		36					73					49		
6 YEARS		100					85					88		
7 YEARS		2					-					-		
TOTAL		185	1.9	4			251	2.5	4			137	1.4	4

Source: Eurostat, UOE et Eurydice.

Additional notes

Greece: Only children enrolled in the public sector nursery schools (*nipiagogeia*) are included. An educational structure is only in place for children aged 4 and over.

France: 1997/98.

Ireland: Children aged 6 and 7 who are of compulsory school age but who are in the infant classes are included. There is no genuine theoretical duration of attendance at an education-oriented pre-primary institution: policy is being written for the pre-primary level.

Luxembourg: Early entry into pre-primary education (for 3-year-olds) will be provided from school year 1998/99 onwards.

Netherlands: Are classified in ISCED 0 the 4- and 5-year-olds from the *basisonderwijs*.

United Kingdom: The data cover children in nursery schools and nursery classes in primary schools.

Liechtenstein: 1995/96.

Norway: From school year 1997/98 onwards. the single structure starts at age 6. and no longer at age 7.

Slovenia: Data for children aged 3 and 4 at ISCED 0 are included with those aged 5.

AVERAGE DURATION OF ATTENDANCE BY CHILDREN AGED 3-7 AT AN EDUCATION-ORIENTED PRE-PRIMARY INSTITUTION IN COMPARISON TO DURATION OF OFFICIAL PROVISION, 1996/97

(FIGURE C7)

		PARTICI-PATION RATES (FIG. C3) (%)	DURATION OF ATTENDANCE				PARTICI-PATION RATES (FIG. C3) (%)	DURATION OF ATTENDANCE				PARTICI-PATION RATES (FIG. C3) (%)	DURATION OF ATTENDANCE	
			AVERAGE (YEARS)	THEORE-TICAL (YEARS)				AVERAGE (YEARS)	THEORE-TICAL (YEARS)				AVERAGE (YEARS)	THEORE-TICAL (YEARS)
Pre-accession countries (continued)														
3 YEARS	SK	(:)								CY		(:)		
4 YEARS		(:)										(:)		
5 YEARS		(:)										(:)		
6 YEARS		(:)										(:)		
7 YEARS		(:)										(:)		
TOTAL		(:)	(:)	3								(:)	(:)	3
Other countries taking part in the PHARE programme														
3 YEARS	AL	29			BA	(:)				MK		0		
4 YEARS		39				(:)						49		
5 YEARS		45				(:)						31		
6 YEARS		-				(:)						14		
7 YEARS		-				(:)						11		
TOTAL		112	1.1			(:)	(:)					105	1.0	

Source: Eurostat, UOE and Eurydice.

PRESCRIBED OR RECOMMENDED MAXIMUM NUMBERS OF 4-YEAR-OLD CHILDREN PER ADULT IN SCHOOLS AND OTHER EDUCATION-ORIENTED PRE-PRIMARY INSTITUTIONS, 1997/98

(FIGURE C9)

	European Union															
	B	DK	D	EL	E	F	IRL	I	L	NL	A	P	FIN	S	UK (E/W)	UK (SC)
MAXIMUM NUMBER OF CHILDREN	(−)	(−)	30	30	25	(−)	35	25	26	(−)	25	25	7	(−)	26	20
NUMBER OF ADULTS			2	1	1		1	1	1		1	1	1		2	2

	EFTA/EEA				Pre-accession countries											
	IS	LI	NO		BG	CZ	EE	LV	LT	HU	PL	RO	SI	SK		CY
MAXIMUM NUMBER OF CHILDREN	8	20	18		16	20	18	16	15	25	25	20	24	25		26
NUMBER OF ADULTS	1	1	2		2	1	1	1	1	1	1	1	1	1		1

(−): No regulations.

Source: Eurydice.

CLASS SIZE REGULATIONS OR RECOMMENDATIONS, 1997/98

(FIGURE D2)

	European Union															
	B	DK	D	EL	E	F	IRL	I	L	NL	A	P	FIN	S	UK (E/W, NI)	UK (SC)
MINIMA				15				15	18		10	20				
MAXIMA	(–)	28	28	30	25	(–)	35	25	26	(–)	30	34	(–)	(–)	(–)	33

	EFTA/EEA				Pre-accession countries										
	IS	LI	NO		BG	CZ	EE	LV	LT	HU	PL	RO	SI	SK	CY
MINIMA		12			17	10					25	10			
MAXIMA	(–)	24	28		26	30	36	36	24	26	35	25	28	35	34

Source: Eurydice.

(–): No recommendations.

ANNUAL NUMBER OF HOURS OF TAUGHT TIME (AROUND AGE 7), 1997/98

(FIGURE D4)

	WEEKLY LOAD	NUMBER OF DAYS PER WEEK	DAILY LOAD	NUMBER OF DAYS PER YEAR	ANNUAL LOAD
European Union					
B	min. 28 x 50' = 1 400'	5	280'	182	min. 50 960' = 849h
DK	20 x 45' = 900'	5	180'	200	min. 36 000' = 600h max. 720h
D	981'	5	196'	188	36 886' = 615h
EL	min. 23 x 45' = 1 035' max. 25 x 45' = 1 125'	5	min. 207' max. 225'	175	min. 31 500' = 525h max. 39 375' = 656h
E	(25 x 60') - (5 x 30') = 1 350'	5	270'	180	48 600' = 810h
F	(26 x 60') - (5 x 30') = 1 410'	5	282'	180	50 760' = 846h
IRL	23h20' = 1 400'	5	280'	183	min. 51 240' = 854h
I	(30 x 60') - (6 x 30') = 1 620'	6	270'	min. 200	min. 54 000' = 900h
L	(18 x 55') + (12 x 50') = 1 590'	6	265'	212	56 180'=936h
NL	22h = 1 320'	5	264'	200	52 800' = 880h
A	21 x 50' = 1 050'	5/6	210'/175'	180/214	37 800' = 630h
P	(25 x 60') - (5 x 30') = 1 350'	5	270'	175	47 250' = 788 h
FIN	min. 19 x 45' = 855' max. 21 x 45' = 945'	5	min. 171' max. 189'	190	min. 32 490' = 542h max. 35 910' = 599h
S				min. 178 max. 190	
UK E/W NI SC	22h = 1 320' 15h = 900' 25h = 1 500'	5 5 5	264' 180' 300'	190 190 190	50 160' = 836h 34 200' = 570h 57 000' = 950h
EFTA/EEA					
IS	28 x 40'= 1 120'	5	224'	170	38 080' = 635h
LI	26 x 45' = 1 170'	5	234'	200	46 800' = 780h
NO	min. 20 x 45' = 900'	5	min.180'	190	min. 34 200' = 570h
Pre-accession countries					
BG	min. 22 (ou 25) x 40'= 880'/1 000' max. 22 (ou 25) x 45' = 990'/1 125'	5 5	min.176'/200' max.198'/225'	160 160	min. 28 160'= 470h/ 32 000'= 533h max. 31 680'= 528h/ 36 000' = 600h
CZ	22 x 45'= 990'	5	198'	193	38 214' = 637h
EE	20 x 45'= 900'	5	180'	175	31 500' = 525h
LV	min. 19 x 35' = 665' max. 20 x 35' = 700'	5 5	133' 140'	170 170	min. 22 610' = 377h max. 23 800' = 397h
LT	22 x 35'= 770'	5	154'	170	26 180' = 436h
HU	20 x 45'= 900'	5	180'	185	33 300' = 555h
PL	19 x 45' = 855'	5	171'	184	31 464' = 524h
RO	min. 20 x 50' = 1 000' max. 24 x 50' = 1 200'	5 5	200' 240'	170 170	min. 34 000' = 567h max. 40 800' = 680h
SI	min. 20.5 x 45' = 923' max. 22.5 x 45' = 1 013'	5 5	185' 203'	175 175	min. 34 988' = 583h max. 38 138' = 636h
SK	22 x 45'= 990'	5	198'	186	36 828' = 614h
CY	31 x 40'= 1 240'	5	248'	174	43 152' = 719h

Source: Eurydice.

ANNUAL NUMBER OF HOURS OF TAUGHT TIME (AROUND AGE 10), 1997/98

(FIGURE D5)

	WEEKLY LOAD	NUMBER OF DAYS PER WEEK	DAILY LOAD	NUMBER OF DAYS PER YEAR	ANNUAL LOAD
European Union					
B	min. 28 x 50' = 1400'	5	280'	182	min. 50 960' = 849h
DK	24 x 45' = 1080'	5	216'	200	43 200' = 720h
D	1 139'	5	228'	188	42 808' = 713h
EL	min. 29 x 45' = 1305' max. 30 x 45' = 1350'	5	min. 261' max. 270'	175	min. 45 675' = 761h max. 47 250' = 788h
E	(25 x 60') - (5 x 30') = 1 350'	5	270'	180	48 600' = 810h
F	(26 x 60') - (5 x 30') = 1 410'	5	282'	180	50 760' = 846h
IRL	23h20' = 1 400'	5	280'	min. 183	min. 51 240' = 854h
I	(30 x 60') - (6 x 30') = 1 620'	6	270'	min. 200	min. 54 000' = 900h
L	(18 x 55') + (12 x 50') = 1 590'	6	265'	212	56 180' = 936h
NL	25h = 1 500'	5	300'	200	60 000' = 1 000h
A	25 x 50' = 1 250'	5/6	250'/208'	180/214	45 000' = 750h
P	min. 30 x 50' = 1 500' max. 31 x 50' = 1 550'	5/6	min. 300' max. 310'	175	min. 52 500' = 875h max. 54 250' = 904h
FIN	min. 23 x 45' = 1 035' max. 25 x 45' = 1 125'	5	min. 207' max. 225'	190	min. 39 330' = 656h max. 42 750' = 713h
S				min. 178 max. 190	
UK E/W NI SC	24h = 1 440' 22h30' = 1 350' 25h = 1 500'	5 5 5	288' 270' 300'	190 190 190	54 720' = 912h 51 300' = 855h 57 000' = 950h
EFTA/EEA					
IS	31 x 40' = 1 240'	5	248'	170	42 160' = 703h
LI	30 x 45' = 1 350'	5	270'	200	54 000' = 900h
NO	27 x 45' = 1 215'	5	243'	190	46 170' = 770h
Pre-accession countries					
BG	min.25 (ou 29) x 40'= 1 000'/1 160' max. 25 (ou 29) x 45' = 1 125'/1 305'	5 5	min. 200'/232' max. 225'/261'	165 165	min. 33 000' = 550h/ 38 280' = 638h max. 37 125' = 619h/ 43 065' = 718h
CZ	25 x 45' = 1 125'	5	225'	193	43 425' = 724h
EE	25 x 45' = 1 125'	5	225'	175	39 375' = 656h
LV	min. 21 x 40'= 840' max. 24 x 40' = 960'	5 5	168' 192'	175 175	min. 29 400' = 490h max. 33 600' = 560h
LT	min. 23 x 45'= 1 035' max. 25 x 45' = 1 125'	5 5	207' 225'	170 170	min. 35 190' = 587h max. 38 250' = 638h
HU	22.5 x 45'= 1 013'	5	203'	185	37 463' = 624h
PL	23 x 45' = 1 035'	5	207'	184	38 088' = 635h
RO	min. 23 x 50'= 1 150' max. 32 x 50' = 1 600'	5 5	230' 320'	170 170	min. 39 100' = 652h max. 54 400' = 907h
SI	min. 23.5 x 45'= 1 058' max. 25.5 x 45' = 1 148'	5 5	212' 230'	175 175	min. 39 713' = 662h max. 42 863' = 714h
SK	26 x 45' = 1 170'	5	234'	186	43 524' = 725h
CY	35 x 40' = 1 400'	5	280'	174	48 720' = 812h

Source: Eurydice.

RECOMMENDATIONS ON THE DISTRIBUTION OF ANNUAL HOURS OF TEACHING OF COMPULSORY SUBJECTS AT AROUND AGE 7, 1997/98

(FIGURE D7)

	MOTHER TONGUE	MATHEMATICS	HUMAN AND NATURAL SCIENCES	FOREIGN LANGUAGES	SPORT	ARTISTIC ACTIVITIES	RELIGION AND ETHICS	FLEXIBLE TIMETABLE	TOTAL
European Union									
B fr	272 32%	153 18%	110 13%		59 7%	136 16%	59 7%	59 7%	848 100%
B de	272 32%	153 18%	110 13%	59 7%	59 7%	136 16%	59 7%		848 100%
B nl								849 100%	849 100%
DK	270 45%	120 20%	30 5%		30 5%	60 10%	60 10%	30 5%	600 100%
D	152 25%	138 22%	80 13%		75 12%	102 17%	55 9%	13 2%	615 100%
EL	236 36%	131 20%	83 13%		52 8%	105 16%	22 3%	26 4%	629 100%
E	175 22%	87 11%	87 11%		70 9%	70 9%	52 6%	269 33%	810 100%
F	293 35%	163 19%	130 15%		98 11%	98 11%		65 8%	846 100%
IRL	342 40%	145 17%	94 11%		43 5%	137 16%	94 11%		854 100%
I	121 13%	90 10%	149 17%	90 10%	60 7%	119 13%	60 7%	211 23%	900 100%
L	38 4%	187 20%	92 10%	251 27%	92 10%	92 10%	92 10%	92 10%	936 100%
NL								880 100%	880 100%
A	210 33%	120 19%	90 14%		60 10%	90 14%	60 10%		630 100%
P								788 100%	788 100%
FIN	152 24%	105 17%	86 14%	38 6%	57 9%	95 15%	38 6%	57 9%	628 100%
S								100%	100%
UK (EW)								836 100%	836 100%
UK (NI)								570 100%	570 100%
UK (SC)	143 15%	143 15%	237 25%			143 15%	95 10%	190 20%	950 100%
EFTA/EEA									
IS	158 25%	68 11%	46 7%		68 11%	113 18%	23 4%	158 25%	634 100%
LI	320 41%	164 21%	62 8%		101 13%	101 13%	31 4%		779 100%
NO	171 30%	100 18%	71 12%	18 3%	43 8%	71 12%	50 9%	46 8%	570 100%
Pre-accession countries									
BG	150 32%	75 16%	47 10%		65 14%	75 16%		56 12%	468 100%
CZ	290 45%	145 23%	58 9%		58 9%	87 14%			638 100%
EE	163 31%	84 16%	58 11%		73 14%	147 28%			525 100%
LV	159 42%	79 21%	40 11%		40 11%	40 11%		20 5%	378 100%
LT	159 36%	79 18%	40 9%		59 14%	80 18%	20 5%		437 100%
HU								555 100%	555 100%
PL	179 34%	124 24%	28 5%		83 16%	110 21%			524 100%
RO	255 45%	114 20%			85 15%	85 15%	28 5%		567 100%
SI	131 23%	131 23%	88 15%		94 16%	91 16%		48 8%	583 100%
SK	251 41%	140 23%	56 9%		84 14%	84 14%			615 100%
CY	302 42%	116 16%	70 10%		46 6%	139 19%	46 6%		719 100%

Source: Eurydice.

Additional note

Finland: The required number for artistic activities and sport is 209. The figures given refer to the absolute minimum per subject.

RECOMMENDATIONS ON THE DISTRIBUTION OF ANNUAL HOURS OF TEACHING OF COMPULSORY SUBJECTS AT AROUND AGE 10, 1997/98

(FIGURE D8)

	MOTHER TONGUE	MATHE-MATICS	HUMAN AND NATURAL SCIENCES	FOREIGN LANGUAGES	SPORT	ARTISTIC ACTIVITIES	RELIGION AND ETHICS	ICT	FLEXIBLE TIMETABLE	TOTAL
European Union										
B fr	212 / 25%	152 / 18%	196 / 23%		61 / 7%	91 / 11%	61 / 7%		75 / 9%	848 / 100%
B de	212 / 25%	151 / 18%	184 / 22%	90 / 11%	61 / 7%	91 / 11%	61 / 7%			850 / 100%
B nl									849 / 100%	849 / 100%
DK	180 / 23%	120 / 15%	90 / 12%	60 / 8%	90 / 12%	180 / 23%	30 / 4%		30 / 4%	780 / 100%
D	164 / 23%	135 / 19%	120 / 17%		81 / 11%	130 / 18%	60 / 8%		23 / 4%	713 / 100%
EL	211 / 28%	105 / 14%	184 / 24%	79 / 10%	52 / 7%	52 / 7%	52 / 7%		26 / 3%	761 / 100%
E	138 / 17%	85 / 11%	85 / 11%	85 / 11%	53 / 6%	53 / 6%	53 / 6%		258 / 32%	810 / 100%
F	293 / 35%	179 / 21%	130 / 15%		89 / 10%	89 / 10%			65 / 8%	845 / 100%
IRL	342 / 40%	145 / 17%	94 / 11%		43 / 5%	137 / 16%	94 / 11%			854 / 100%
I	121 / 13%	90 / 10%	149 / 17%	90 / 10%	60 / 7%	119 / 13%	60 / 7%		211 / 23%	900 / 100%
L	29 / 3%	159 / 17%	93 / 10%	374 / 40%	93 / 10%	93 / 10%	93 / 10%			936 / 100%
NL									1 000 / 100%	1 000 / 100%
A	210 / 28%	120 / 16%	90 / 12%	30 / 4%	90 / 12%	150 / 20%	60 / 8%			750 / 100%
P	145,8 / 17%	116,6 / 13%	175 / 20%	116,6 / 13%	58,3 / 7%	233,3 / 27%	29,1 / 3%			875 / 100%
FIN	152 / 24%	105 / 17%	86 / 14%	38 / 6%	57 / 9%	95 / 15%	38 / 6%		57 / 9%	628 / 100%
S									100%	100%
UK (E/W)									912 / 100%	912 / 100%
UK (NI)									855 / 100%	855 / 100%
UK (SC)	143 / 15%	143 / 15%	237 / 25%			143 / 15%	95 / 10%		190 / 20%	950 / 100%
EFTA/EEA										
IS	136 / 19%	91 / 13%	113 / 16%		68 / 10%	136 / 19%	23 / 3%		136 / 19%	703 / 100%
LI	180 / 20%	149 / 17%	248 / 28%	58 / 6%	90 / 10%	117 / 13%	58 / 6%			900 / 100%
NO	147 / 19%	109 / 14%	161 / 21%	67 / 9%	67 / 9%	152 / 20%	67 / 9%			770 / 100%
Pre-accession countries										
BG	152 / 28%	76 / 14%	114 / 21%		57 / 10%	76 / 14%			76 / 14%	551 / 100%
CZ	203 / 28%	145 / 20%	116 / 16%	87 / 12%	58 / 8%	116 / 16%				725 / 100%
EE	138 / 21%	118 / 18%	164 / 25%	98 / 15%	59 / 9%	79 / 12%				656 / 100%
LV	163 / 33%	93 / 19%	47 / 10%	70 / 14%	47 / 10%	70 / 14%				490 / 100%
LT	179 / 31%	102 / 17%	51 / 9%	51 / 9%	51 / 9%	102 / 17%	25 / 4%		25 / 4%	586 / 100%
HU									624 / 100%	624 / 100%
PL	166 / 26%	138 / 22%	110 / 17%		83 / 13%	56 / 9%		27 / 4%	55 / 9%	635 / 100%
RO	198 / 30%	114 / 17%	113 / 17%	57 / 9%	57 / 9%	85 / 13%	28 / 4%			652 / 100%
SI	131 / 20%	131 / 20%	143 / 22%		94 / 14%	114 / 17%			48 / 7%	661 / 100%
SK	140 / 19%	140 / 19%	167 / 23%	112 / 15%	56 / 8%	84 / 12%	28 / 4%			727 / 100%
CY	233 / 29%	139 / 17%	139 / 17%	46 / 6%	46 / 6%	139 / 17%	46 / 6%		24 / 3%	812 / 100%

Source: Eurydice.

Additional note

Finland: The required number for artistic activities and sport is 209. The figures given refer to the absolute minimum per subject.

SECONDARY EDUCATION

DISTRIBUTION OF STUDENTS IN GENERAL AND VOCATIONAL LOWER SECONDARY EDUCATION (ISCED 2), 1996/97

(FIGURE E3)   (1 000)

	European Union											
	EU	B	DK	D	EL	E	F	IRL	I	L	NL	A
GENERAL	16 714.4	257.7	201.1	5340.3	407.1	1120.6	3169.4	199.6	1851.8	4.8	616.5	380.1
VOCATIONAL	439.5	95.7	(–)	(–)	0	5.9	192.9	(–)	-	9.8	134.1	-

	European Union (continued)					EFTA/EEA				Pre-accession countries		
	P	FIN	S	UK		IS	LI	NO		BG	CZ	EE
GENERAL	459.6	205.4	(:)	2170.6		12.9	(:)	155.6		373.3	538.9	58
VOCATIONAL	1	(–)	(:)	(–)		(–)	(:)	(:)		(–)	.0.3	0.5

	Pre-accession countries (continued)								Other PHARE countries		
	LV	LT	HU	PL	RO	SI	SK	CY	AL	BA	MK
GENERAL	158.9	244.8	504.1	(:)	1 140.9	106.7	351.7	33.2	257.1	197.3	127.9
VOCATIONAL	1.6	6.6	(–)	(:)	(–)	(–)	0.1	(–)	(–)	(–)	(–)

Source: Eurostat, UOE.

Additional notes

Belgium: Pupils in (transitional) secondary technical and art education are included with pupils in vocational education. The high percentage of pupils in lower secondary vocational education is explained by pupils in social advancement education.

France: Pupils in technological education are included with pupils in vocational education.

Luxembourg: Pupils in technical secondary education are considered as pupils in the vocational stream.

United Kingdom: For international statistical purposes, all pupils in secondary schools are classified as following general programmes.

Bulgaria: A small number of pupils enrolled in vocational programmes at ISCED 2 are included in ISCED 3.

Poland: ISCED 2 pupils are included in ISCED 1.

Slovakia: Data are given in full-time equivalents, special education is excluded.

DISTRIBUTION OF STUDENTS IN GENERAL AND VOCATIONAL UPPER SECONDARY EDUCATION (ISCED 3), 1996/97

(FIGURE E4)   (1 000)

	European Union											
	EU	B	DK	D	EL	E	F	IRL	I	L	NL	A
GENERAL	8 227.4	224.3	107.6	721.6	275.1	1 825.6	1 163.9	153.7	791.2	4.7	215.3	100.9
VOCATIONAL	11 122.8	479	119.1	2 320.5	135.4	900	1 453.5	36.1	1 959.8	9.5	449.8	312.5

	European Union (continued)					EFTA/EEA				Pre-accession countries		
	P	FIN	S	UK		IS	LI	NO		BG	CZ	EE
GENERAL	334.7	123.9	242	1 942.9		12.1	0.2	87.8		153.5	75.9	37.8
VOCATIONAL	114.4	140.6	257.3	2 435.3		5.7	0.9	124.7		206.6	436.6	22

	Pre-accession countries (continued)								Other PHARE countries		
	LV	LT	HU	PL	RO	SI	SK	CY	AL	BA	MK
GENERAL	49.6	81.7	194.5	793.2	334.6	26.4	65.6	23.5	76.4	25.9	25.4
VOCATIONAL	35.4	45.6	405.3	1 936.9	793.8	90.4	278.7	4.6	16.6	118.3	58.4

Source: Eurostat, UOE.

Additional notes

Belgium: Students in (transitional) secondary technical and art education are included with students in vocational education. The high percentage of students in upper secondary vocational education is explained by students in social advancement education.

France: Students in technological education are included with students in vocational education.

Luxembourg: Students in technical secondary education are considered as students in the vocational stream.

Sweden: Adult education (mature students) is included. Some students (in adult and special education) cannot be split into general and vocational education.

United Kingdom: For international statistical purposes, all students in secondary schools are classified as following general programmes. All students on further education courses, some of which are academic, are classified as following vocational programmes. The majority of these students are also over theoretical school age.

Iceland: Only full-time students are included.

Liechtenstein: Only the *Gymnasium (Oberstufe)* are regarded as providing general education. Vocational courses alternate between school and workplace – pupils participate in practical in-company training in Liechtenstein and attend theory courses in a neighbouring country. 1995/96.

Bulgaria: A small number of students enrolled in vocational programmes at ISCED 2 are included in ISCED 3.

Hungary: Students in pre-vocational education are included in vocational.

Slovakia: Data are given in full-time equivalents, special education is excluded.

DISTRIBUTION OF STUDENTS BETWEEN GENERAL AND VOCATIONAL STREAMS AT UPPER SECONDARY LEVEL (ISCED 3), BY GENDER, 1996/97

(FIGURE E5)   (1 000)

		European Union										
		B	DK	D	EL	E	F	IRL	I	L	NL	A
GENERAL	Men	103.5	46.9	328.8	123.1	873.8	515.6	74.0	344.3	2.1	100.9	48.8
	Women	120.8	60.8	392.8	152.0	951.8	648.3	79.7	446.9	2.6	114.4	52.1
VOCATIONAL	Men	250.0	65.5	1 296.2	81.7	449.8	820.9	16.2	1 039.2	4.9	251.1	172.4
	Women	229.0	53.6	1 024.3	53.7	450.2	632.6	19.9	920.6	4.6	198.7	140.1

		European Union (continued)				**EFTA/EEA**			**Pre-accession countries**		
		P	FIN	S	UK	IS	LI	NO	BG	CZ	EE
GENERAL	Men	151.8	51.8	94.3	980.3	5.2	0.1	38.8	51.0	31.0	15.6
	Women	182.9	72.2	147.7	962.6	6.9	0.1	49.0	102.5	44.9	22.2
VOCATIONAL	Men	63.2	68.6	129.4	1 052.0	3.9	0.5	73.6	128.4	223.4	12.8
	Women	51.2	72.0	127.9	1 383.3	1.8	0.3	51.1	78.1	213.2	9.2

		Pre-accession countries (continued)								**Other PHARE countries**		
		LV	LT	HU	PL	RO	SI	SK	CY	AL	BA	MK
GENERAL	Men	19.5	33.6	79.5	273.2	108.6	10.4	27.3	10.0	36.9	8.6	(:)
	Women	30.1	48.1	115.0	520.1	226.0	16.0	38.3	13.0	39.6	17.3	(:)
VOCATIONAL	Men	19.5	26.2	216.9	1 086.1	453.4	47.3	143.7	4.0	11.5	67.0	(:)
	Women	16.0	19.4	188.4	850.8	340.3	43.1	135.0	1.0	5.1	51.3	(:)

Source: Eurostat, UOE.

Additional notes

Belgium: Students in (transitional) secondary technical and art education are included with students in vocational education. The high percentage of students in upper secondary vocational education is explained by students in social advancement education.

France: Students in technological education are included with students in vocational education.

Luxembourg: Students in technical secondary education are considered as students in the vocational stream.

Sweden: Some students (in adult and special education) cannot be split into general and vocational education.

United Kingdom: For international statistical purposes, all students in secondary schools are classified as following general programmes. All students on further education courses, some of which are academic, are classified as following vocational programmes. The majority of these students are also over theoretical school age.

Iceland: Only full-time students are included.

Liechtenstein: 1995/96. Only the *Gymnasium (Oberstufe)* are regarded as providing general education. Vocational courses alternate between school and workplace – students participate in practical in-company training in Liechtenstein and attend theory courses in a neighbouring country.

Bulgaria: A small number of pupils enrolled in vocational programmes at ISCED 2 are included in ISCED 3.

Hungary: Students in pre-vocational education are included in vocational.

Slovakia: Data are given in full-time equivalents, special education is excluded.

NUMBER OF UPPER SECONDARY PUPILS (ISCED 3) IN GENERAL EDUCATION BY NUTS 1 AND NUTS 2 REGIONS, 1996/97

(FIGURE E6)

		RATE	TOTAL NUMBER OF STUDENTS IN UPPER SECONDARY EDUCATION	TOTAL NUMBER OF STUDENTS IN GENERAL UPPER SECONDARY EDUCATION
		%	(1 000)	(1 000)
EUROPEAN UNION				
BE	**BELGIQUE-BELGIË***	32	703.2	224.2
BE1	RÉG. BRUXELLES-CAP.-BRUSSELS HFDST. GEWEST	35	84.1	29.5
BE2	VLAAMS GEWEST	30	376.6	112.6
BE3	RÉGION WALLONNE	34	242.5	82.2
DK	**DANMARK**	47	226.7	107.6
DE	**DEUTSCHLAND**	24	3 042.1	721.6
DE1	BADEN-WURTTEMBERG	19	401.7	75.8
DE2	BAYERN	19	410.5	80.0
DE3	BERLIN	35	120.9	42.0
DE4	BRANDENBURG	33	106.3	35.0
DE5	BREMEN	25	31.2	7.7
DE6	HAMBURG	27	67.0	17.9
DE7	HESSEN	26	221.2	56.7
DE8	MECKLENBURG-VORPOMMERN	18	82.6	14.9
DE9	NIEDERSACHSEN	22	296.4	65.0

Source: Eurostat, UOE.

Additional note

Belgium: Pupils in (transitional) secondary technical and art education are included with pupils in vocational education.

NUMBER OF UPPER SECONDARY PUPILS (ISCED 3) IN GENERAL EDUCATION
BY NUTS 1 AND NUTS 2 REGIONS, 1996/97

(FIGURE E6)

		RATE %	TOTAL NUMBER OF STUDENTS IN UPPER SECONDARY EDUCATION (1 000)	TOTAL NUMBER OF STUDENTS IN GENERAL UPPER SECONDARY EDUCATION (1 000)
EUROPEAN UNION (CONTINUED)				
DE	**DEUTSCHLAND** (continued)	24	3 042.1	721.6
DEA	NORDRHEIN-WESTFALEN	29	647.2	188.0
DEB	RHEINLAND-PFALZ	24	135.9	32.2
DEC	SAARLAND	21	39.6	8.2
DED	SACHSEN	20	177.2	36.3
DEE	SACHSEN-ANHALT	21	102.5	21.3
DEF	SCHLESWIG-HOLSTEIN	21	98.2	20.4
DEG	THURINGEN	20	103.7	20.3
GR	**ELLADA**	67	410.5	275.1
GR1	VOREIA ELLADA	(:)	(:)	(:)
GR2	KENTRIKI ELLADA	(:)	(:)	(:)
GR3	ATTIKI	(:)	(:)	(:)
GR4	NISIA AIGAIOU, KRITI	(:)	(:)	(:)
ES	**ESPAÑA**	67	2 725.5	1 825.5
ES1	NOROESTE	65	312.8	202.9
ES2	NORESTE	63	287.1	180.8
ES3	COMUNIDAD DE MADRID	74	360.8	266.0
ES4	CENTRO (E)	70	353.0	246.1
ES5	ESTE	63	690.3	436.6
ES6	SUR	69	598.0	415.2
ES7	CANARIAS	63	123.6	77.9
FR	**FRANCE***	44	2 703.4	1 198.9
FR1	ÎLE DE FRANCE	50	455.9	225.7
FR2	BASSIN PARISIEN	42	487.7	205.9
FR3	NORD-PAS-DE-CALAIS	40	212.6	85.2
FR4	EST	41	236.2	97.3
FR5	OUEST	43	377.4	161.6
FR6	SUD-OUEST	44	257.0	113.8
FR7	CENTRE-EST	46	310.5	143.5
FR8	MEDITERRANEE	47	280.2	130.8
FR9	DEPARTEMENTS D'OUTRE-MER	41	86.0	34.9
IE	**IRELAND**	81	189.8	153.7
IT	**ITALIA**	29	2 751.0	791.2
IT1	NORD OVEST	30	236.2	70.3
IT2	LOMBARDIA	28	369.7	103.7
IT3	NORD EST	25	288.9	73.0
IT4	EMILIA-ROMAGNA	25	154.6	38.9
IT5	CENTRO (I)	28	257.7	73.3
IT6	LAZIO	36	267.2	95.5
IT7	ABRUZZI-MOLISE	29	87.8	25.0
IT8	CAMPANIA	29	319.2	93.6
IT9	SUD	29	384.3	110.9
ITA	SICILIA	28	280.7	79.3
ITB	SARDEGNA	26	104.6	27.6
LU	**LUXEMBOURG**	33	14.2	4.7
NL	**NEDERLAND**	32	665.1	215.3
NL1	NOORD-NEDERLAND	(:)	(:)	(:)
NL2	OOST-NEDERLAND	(:)	(:)	(:)
NL3	WEST-NEDERLAND	(:)	(:)	(:)
NL4	ZUID-NEDERLAND	(:)	(:)	(:)
AT	**ÖSTERREICH (AUSTRIA)**	24	413.4	100.9
AT1	OSTÖSTERREICH	26	158.8	40.6
AT2	SÜDÖSTERREICH	25	94.1	23.3
AT3	WESTÖSTERREICH	23	160.4	37.0
PT	**PORTUGAL**	74	477.2	354.0
PT1	CONTINENTE	74	456.2	336.4
PT11	NORTE	70	140.2	98.6
PT12	CENTRO (P)	72	80.7	58.0
PT13	LISBOA E VALE DO TEJO	77	192.9	149.2
PT14	ALENTEJO	72	23.7	17.0
PT15	ALGARVE	72	18.8	13.6
PT2	ACORES	82	10.3	8.5
PT3	MADEIRA	85	10.7	9.1

Source: Eurostat, UOE.

NUMBER OF UPPER SECONDARY PUPILS (ISCED 3) IN GENERAL EDUCATION BY NUTS 1 AND NUTS 2 REGIONS, 1996/97

(FIGURE E6)

		RATE %	TOTAL NUMBER OF STUDENTS IN UPPER SECONDARY EDUCATION (1 000)	TOTAL NUMBER OF STUDENTS IN GENERAL UPPER SECONDARY EDUCATION (1 000)
EUROPEAN UNION (CONTINUED)				
FI	**SUOMI (FINLAND)**	47	264.6	123.9
FI1	MANNER-SUOMI	47	263.4	123.6
FI13	ITÄ-SUOMI	53	64.7	34.3
FI14	VÄLI-SUOMI	46	88.7	40.5
FI15	POHJOIS-SUOMI	44	37.7	16.8
FI16	UUSIMAA	45	39.2	17.7
FI17	ETELÄ-SUOMI	43	33.1	14.4
FI2	AHVENANMAA/°ALAND	33	1.2	0.4
SE	**SVERIGE**	48	503.8	242.0
SE01	STOCKHOLM	51	102.4	52.7
SE02	ÖSTRA MELLANSVERIGE	48	85.2	40.6
SE04	SYDSVERIGE	45	44.7	20.1
SE06	NORRA MELLANSVERIGE	49	71.4	34.8
SE07	MELLERSTA NORRLAND	47	103.2	48.3
SE08	ÖVRE NORRLAND	46	45.2	20.6
SE09	SMÅLAND MED ÖARNA	46	21.4	9.8
SE0A	VÄSTSVERIGE	50	30.2	15.1
UK	**UNITED KINGDOM**	44	4 378.2	1 942.9
UK1	NORTH	42	228.4	96.2
UK2	YORKSHIRE AND HUMBERSIDE	39	398.1	157.2
UK3	EAST MIDLANDS	42	321.3	134.6
UK4	EAST ANGLIA	52	135.0	69.6
UK5	SOUTH EAST	47	1236.2	576.0
UK6	SOUTH WEST	44	359.8	157.6
UK7	WEST MIDLANDS	37	463.2	170.3
UK8	NORTH WEST	37	529.0	196.2
UK9	WALES	47	207.1	97.7
UKa	SCOTLAND	61	347.0	212.0
UKb	NORTHERN IRELAND	49	153.2	75.4
EFTA/EEA				
IS	**ÍSLAND**	68	17.8	12.1
LI	**LIECHTENSTEIN**	22	1.1	0.2
NO	**NORGE**	41	212.5	87.8
PRE-ACCESSION COUNTRIES				
BG	**BĂLGARIJA**	43	360.1	153.5
CZ	**ČESKÁ REPUBLIKA**	15	512.5	75.9
EE	**EESTI**	63	59.8	37.8
LV	**LATVIJA**	58	85.0	49.6
LT	**LIETUVA**	64	127.3	81.7
HU	**MAGYARORSZÁG**	32	599.8	194.5
PL	**POLSKA**	29	2 730.1	793.2
RO	**ROMÂNIA**	30	1 128.4	334.6
SI	**SLOVENIJA**	23	116.8	26.4
SK	**SLOVENSKÁ REPUBLIKA**	19	344.3	65.6
CY	**KYPROS**	84	28.1	23.5
OTHER COUNTRIES TAKING PART IN THE PHARE PROGRAMME				
AL	**ALBANIA**	82	93.1	76.4
BA	**BOSNIA HERZEGOVINA**	18	144.2	25.9
MK	**FORMER YUGOSLAV REPUBLIC OF MACEDONIA**	30	83.7	25.4

Source: Eurostat, UOE.

Additional notes

Sweden: Adult education and distance learning are excluded.
United Kingdom: For international statistical purposes, all students in secondary schools are classified as following general programmes. All students on further education courses, some of which are academic, are classified as following vocational programmes. The majority of these students are also over theoretical school age.
Iceland: Only full-time students only are included.
Bulgaria: A small number of students enrolled in vocational programmes at ISCED 2 are included in ISCED 3.
Hungary: Students in pre-vocational education are included in vocational.
Slovakia: Data is given in full-time equivalents, special education is excluded.

ANNUAL NUMBER OF HOURS OF TAUGHT TIME IN GENERAL LOWER SECONDARY EDUCATION, 1997/98

(FIGURE E7)

	WEEKLY LOAD		NUMBER OF DAYS PER WEEK	DAILY LOAD (MINUTES)	NUMBER OF DAYS PER YEAR	ANNUAL LOAD		
	(A)		(B)	(A) / (B) = (C)	(F)	= (C) X (F)		
European Union								
B fr, B de	min. 28 x 50'	= 1 400'	5	280'	182	min.	50 960'	= 849h
	max. 34 x 50'	= 1 700'	5	340'	182	max.	61 880'	= 1 031h
B nl	min. 28 x 50'	= 1 400'	5	280'	182	min.	50 960'	= 849h
	max. 33 x 50'	= 1 650'	5	330'	182	max.	60 060'	= 1 001h
DK	min. 26 x 45'	= 1 170'	5	234'	200	min.	46 800'	= 780h
	max. 40 x 45'	= 1 800'	5	360'	200	max.	72 000'	= 1 200h
D	min. 28 x 45'	= 1 260'	5	252'	188	min.	47 376'	= 790h
	max. 34 x 45'	= 1 530'	5	306'	188	max.	57 528'	= 959h
EL	35 x 45'	= 1 575'	5	315'	175	max.	55 125'	= 919h
E	min. 27 x 55'	= 1 485'	5	297'	175	min.	51 975'	= 866h
	max. 32 x 55'	= 1 760'	5	352'	175	max.	61 600'	= 1 027h
F	min. 25.5 x 55'	= 1 402.5'	5	280.5'	180	min.	50 490'	= 841.5h
	max. 30 x 55'	= 1 650'	5	330'	180	max.	59 400'	= 990h
IRL	45 x 40'	= 1 800'	5	360'	167	min.	60 120'	= 1 002h
I	min. (30 x 60') - (6 j x 20') = 1 680'		6	280'	(min.) 200		56 000'	= 933h
	max. (40 x 60') - (6 j x 20') = 2 280'		6	380'	(min.) 200		76 000'	= 1 266h
L	30 x 50'	= 1 500'	6	250'	216	min.	54 000'	= 900h
NL	theoritical average 32 x 50'=	1 600'	5	320'	200		64 000'	= 1 067h
A	min. 29 x 50'	= 1 450'	5	290'	180	min.	52 200'	= 870h
	max. 34 x 50'	= 1 700'	5	340'	180	max.	61 200'	= 1 020h
P	min. 30 x 50'	= 1 500'	5/6	300'/250'	175/210	min.	52 500'	= 875h
	max. 31 x 50'	= 1 550'	5/6	310'/258'	175/210	max.	54 250'	= 904h
FIN	30 x 45'	= 1 350'	5	270'	190		51 300'	= 855h
S								
UK (E/W)	average actual taught time 25h =	1 500'	5	300'	190		57 000'	= 950h
UK (NI)	min. 22.5h	= 1 350'	5	270'	190		51 300'	= 855h
UK (SC)	27.5h	= 1 650'	5	330'	190		62 700'	= 1 045h
EFTA/EEA								
IS	35 x 40'	= 1 400'	5	280'	170		47 600'	= 793h
LI	min. 34 x 45'	= 1 530'	5	306'	200		61 200'	= 1 020h
	max. 38 x 45'	= 1 710'	5	342'	200		68 400'	= 1 140h
NO	30 x 45'	= 1 350'	5	270'	190		51 300'	= 855h

Source: Eurydice.

Additional notes

Germany: The annual number of class hours is an average, calculated using the recommendations for different schools and courses at lower secondary level made by the Standing Conference of the Ministers of Education and Cultural Affairs of the *Länder* on 3 December 1993. The annual hours of teaching varies between a set minimum and maximum as secondary education can last either 8 or 9 years, according to the *Land*.

Spain: Data are approximate. They may vary slightly from one Autonomous Community to another. A five-minute deduction is made per hour to allow for changing classes.

Ireland: Secondary schools must be open for a minimum of 179 days a year of which they devote a maximum of 12 days to certificate examinations. The statistics presented here have been calculated on the basis of the minimum of 167 days of education.

Italy: A deduction of twenty minutes per day is made to allow for changing classes.

Austria: The data reflect the situation in *Hauptschulen*. Lower secondary schools can follow a set timetable. An increasing number of schools, however, are making use of autonomy in changing the curricula in a given frame.

Finland: This is an average based on 30 weekly periods of 45 minutes each. The law also authorizes 50-minute periods.

Sweden: Since the 1995 reform, schools can freely distribute the 6 665 compulsory periods over the nine years of the *Grundskola*. There is no fixed annual or weekly distribution.

United Kingdom: There is no legal requirement for minimum taught lesson time in England and Wales. School governing bodies and headteachers in state schools are, however, required to ensure that there is sufficient time to deliver the whole curriculum. The figures for England and Wales are based on average taught lesson time per week in 1996. Time spent on registration, the daily act of collective worship and all breaks is excluded. For Northern Ireland, figures are based on the set minimum of 22.5 hours per week. For Scotland, figures represent the maximum taught time that teachers are contractually required to provide; the actual time pupils spend in school is more.

Iceland: The municipalities are free to add hours to this minimum.

ANNUAL NUMBER OF HOURS OF TAUGHT TIME IN GENERAL LOWER SECONDARY EDUCATION, 1997/98

(FIGURE E7)

	WEEKLY LOAD			NUMBER OF DAYS PER WEEK	DAILY LOAD (MINUTES)	NUMBER OF DAYS PER YEAR	ANNUAL LOAD		
	(A)			(B)	(A) / (B) = (C)	(F)	= (C) X (F)		
Pre-accession countries									
BG	min. 30 x 45'	=	1 350'	5	270'	170	min.	45 900'	=	765h
	max. 34 x 45'	=	1 530'		306'		max.	52 020'	=	867h
CZ	min. 27 x 45'	=	1 215'	5	243'	193	min.	46 899'	=	782h
	max. 30 x 45'	=	1 350'		270'		max.	52 110'	=	869h
EE	min. 30 x 45'	=	1 350'	5	270'	175	min.	47 250'	=	788h
	max. 34 x 45'	=	1 530'		306'		max.	53 550'	=	893h
LV	min. 31 x 40'	=	1 240'	5	248'	175	min.	43 400'	=	723h
	max. 32 x 40'	=	1 280'	5	256'	175	max.	44 800'	=	747h
LT	min. 30 x 45'	=	1 350'	5	270'	195	min.	52 650'	=	878h
	max. 33 x 45'	=	1 485'	5	297'	195	max.	57 915'	=	965h
HU	25 x 45'	=	1 125'	5	225'	185		41 625'	=	694h
PL	28 x 45'	=	1 260'	5	252'	184		46 368'	=	773h
RO	min. 31 x 50'	=	1 550'	5	310'	170	min.	52 700'	=	878h
	max. 40 x 50'	=	2 000'		400'		max.	68 000'	=	1 133h
SI	min. 26.4 x 45'	=	1 188'	5	238'	175	min.	46 980'	=	783h
	max. 30.4 x 45'	=	1 368'		274'		max.	53 505'	=	892h
SK	min. 26 x 45'	=	1 170'	5	234'	186	min.	43 524'	=	725h
	max. 31 x 45'	=	1 395'	5	279'		max.	51 894'	=	865h
CY	35 x 45'	=	1 575'	5	315'	166		52 290'	=	872h

Source: Eurydice.

Additional notes

Estonia: The minimum number of hours is that for the seventh year and the maximum that for the last year of the single structure system.
Cyprus: The number of days per year refers to regular working days. To these another 2 weeks of examinations should be added.

ANNUAL NUMBER OF HOURS OF TAUGHT TIME IN GENERAL UPPER SECONDARY EDUCATION, 1997/98

(FIGURE E8)

	WEEKLY LOAD			NUMBER OF DAYS PER WEEK	DAILY LOAD (MINUTES)	NUMBER OF DAYS PER YEAR	ANNUAL LOAD		
	(A)			(B)	(A) / (B) = (C)	(F)	= (C) X (F)		
European Union									
B fr, B de	min.	28 x 50'	= 1 400'	5	280'	182	min.	50 960'	=	849h
	max.	34 x 50'	= 1 700'	5	340'	182	max.	61 880'	=	1 031h
B nl	min.	28 x 50'	= 1 400'	5	280'	182	min.	50 960'	=	849h
	max.	33 x 50'	= 1 650'	5	330'	182	max.	60 060'	=	1 001h
DK	min.	30 x 45'	= 1 350'	5	270'	200	min.	54 000'	=	900h
	max.	32 x 45'	= 1 440'	5	288'	200	max.	57 600'	=	960h
D	min.	30 x 45'	= 1 350'	5	270'	188	min.	50 760'	=	846h
	max.	33 x 45'	= 1 485'	5	297'	188	max.	55 836'	=	931h
EL	min.	30 x 45'	= 1 350'	5	270'	175	min.	47 250'	=	788h
	max.	34 x 45'	= 1 530'	5	306'	175	max.	53 550'	=	893h
E	min.	29 x 55'	= 1 595'	5	319'	175	min.	55 825'	=	930h
	max.	33 x 55'	= 1 815'	5	363'	175	max.	63 525'	=	1 059h
F	min.	29 x 55'	= 1 595'	5	319'	180	min.	57 420'	=	957h
	max.	31 x 55'	= 1 705'	5	341'	180	max.	61 380'	=	1 023h
IRL		45 x 40'	= 1 800'	5	360'	167	min.	60 120'	=	1 002h
I	min. (25 x 60') - (6 j x 20') = 1 380'			6	230'	(min.) 200	min.	46 000'	=	767h
	max. (30 x 60') - (6 j x 20') = 1 680'			6	280'	(min.) 200	max.	56 000'	=	933h

Source: Eurydice.

Additional notes

Germany: The annual number of class hours was calculated on the basis of the 'Agreement on the reorganisation of the *Gymnasiale Oberstufe*' made by the Standing Conference of the Ministers of Education and Cultural Affairs of 7 July 1972, as amended on 28 February 1997. The annual hours of teaching vary between a set minimum and maximum as secondary education can last either 8 or 9 years, according to the *Land*.
Greece: Data only refer to the general *Lykeio*.
Spain: Data are approximate. They may vary slightly from one Autonomous Community to another. A five-minute deduction is made per hour to allow for changing classes.
Ireland: Secondary schools must be open for a minimum of 179 days a year of which they devote a maximum of 12 days to certificate examinations. The statistics presented here have been calculated on the basis of the minimum of 167 days of education.
Italy: A deduction of twenty minutes per day is made to allow for changing classes.

215

ANNUAL NUMBER OF HOURS OF TAUGHT TIME IN GENERAL UPPER SECONDARY EDUCATION, 1997/98

(FIGURE E8)

	WEEKLY LOAD			NUMBER OF DAYS PER WEEK	DAILY LOAD (MINUTES)	NUMBER OF DAYS PER YEAR	ANNUAL LOAD		
	(A)			(B)	(A) / (B) = (C)	(F)	= (C) X (F)		
European Union (continued)									
L	min.	30 x 50'	= 1 500'	6	250'	216	min.	54 000'	= 900h
	max.	31 x 50'	= 1 550'	6	258'	216	max.	55 800'	= 930h
NL	theoritical average	30 x 50'	= 1 500'	5	300'	200		60 000'	= 1 000h
A	min.	32 x 50'	= 1 600'	5	320'	180	min.	57 600'	= 960h
	max.	38 x 50'	= 1 900'	5	380'	180	max.	68 400'	= 1 140h
P	min.	23 x 50'	= 1 150'	5/6	230'/192'	160/192	min.	36 800'	= 613h
	max.	33 x 50'	= 1 650'	5/6	330'/275'	160/192	max.	52 800'	= 880h
FIN		28,5 x 45'	= 1 283'	5	257'	190		48 735'	= 812h
S	theoritical average	20 x 60'	= 1 200'	5	240'	178		42 720'	= 712h
UK (E/W)	average actual taught time	25 x 60'	= 1 500'	5	300'	190		57 000'	= 950h
UK (NI)	min.	22.5 x 60'	= 1 350'	5	270'	190		51 300'	= 855h
UK (SC)		27.5 x 60'	= 1 650'	5	330'	190		62 700'	= 1 045h
EFTA/EEA									
IS		35 x 40'	= 1 400'	5	280'	145		40 600'	= 677h
LI	min.	34 x 45'	= 1 530'	5	306'	200	min.	61 200'	= 1 020h
	max.	38 x 45'	= 1 710'	5	342'	200	max.	68 400'	= 1 140h
NO		30 x 45'	= 1 350'	5	270'	190		51 300'	= 855h
Pre-accession countries									
BG	min.	31 x 45'	= 1 395'	5	279'	180	min.	50 220'	= 837h
	max.	35 x 45'	= 1 575'		315'		max.	56 700'	= 945h
CZ	min.	30 x 45'	= 1 350'	5	270'	193	min.	52 110'	= 869h
	max.	31 x 45'	= 1 395'		279'		max.	53 847'	= 897h
EE		35 x 45'	= 1 575'	5	315'	175		55 125'	= 919h
LV	min.	30 x 45'	= 1 350'	5	270'	175	min.	47 250'	= 788h
	max.	36 x 45'	= 1 620'	5	324'		max.	56 700'	= 945h
LT	min.	32 x 45'	= 1 440'	5	288'	195	min.	56 160'	= 936h
	max.	35 x 45'	= 1 575'	5	315'	195	max.	61 425'	= 1 024h
HU		30 x 45'	= 1 350'	5	270'	185		49 950'	= 833h
PL		29 x 45'	= 1 305'	5	261'	184		48 024'	= 800h
RO	min.	30 x 50'	= 1 500'	5	300'	170	min.	51 000'	= 850h
	max.	34 x 50'	= 1 700'		340'		max.	57 800'	= 963h
SI	min.	32 x 45'	= 1 440'	5	288'	190	min.	54 720'	= 912h
	max.	34 x 45'	= 1 530'	5	306'	190	max.	57 870'	= 965h
SK	min.	30 x 45'	= 1 350'	5	270'	186	min.	50 220'	= 837h
	max.	37 x 45'	= 1 665'	5	333'	186	max.	61 938'	= 1 032h
CY		35 x 45'	= 1 575'	5	315'	161		50 715'	= 845h

Source: Eurydice.

Additional notes

Portugal: In 1995/96, a new system of evaluation was established. Final tests and examinations introduced by this system effectively lead to a three-week reduction in taught time.

Finland: Data refer to a theoretical average. In practice, there are considerable differences between individual pupils and between the three years of upper secondary education.

Sweden: The theoretical average is based on the equal distribution of 2 150 periods over three years.

United Kingdom (E/W, NI): Data are for the last two years of compulsory education (14- to 16-year-olds). For **England** and **Wales**, they are based on statistics of average taught lesson time per week in 1996. For **Northern Ireland**, figures are based on the prescribed minimum of 22.5 hours per week. In post-compulsory education (16- to 18-year-olds), there is no prescribed annual number of taught hours as each pupil has an individual programme. Individual examining bodies may, however, provide guidance on the number of lessons which might be required to cover the syllabus. Attendance requirements are determined by the individual institution. In **Scotland**, the number of hours for post-compulsory education (16- to 18-year-olds) is the same as for compulsory secondary education but pupils have the choice of a number and kinds of courses.

Iceland: Examination days are not taken into account. For a normal four-year course, the average is 677 hours per year, but each student's number of hours can vary from one semester to another.

Cyprus: The number of days per year refers to regular working days. To these another 2 weeks of examinations should be added.

NUMBER AND PERCENTAGES OF MINIMUM ANNUAL TIMETABLE ALLOCATED TO COMPULSORY SUBJECTS AROUND AGE 13 IN GENERAL LOWER SECONDARY EDUCATION, 1997/98

(FIGURE E10)

	MOTHER TONGUE	MATHE-MATICS	NATURAL SCIENCES	HUMAN SCIENCES	FOREIGN LANGUA-GES	PHYSICAL EDUCA-TION	ARTISTIC ACTIVITIES	ICT	COM-PULSORY OPTIONS	FLEXIBLE TIMETABLE	OTHER	TOTAL
European Union												
B fr, B de	152 18%	152 18%	61 7%	121 14%	121 14%	91 11%	30 4%		121 14%			849 100%
B nl	121 14%	121 14%	30 4%	61 7%	121 14%	61 7%	61 7%		152 18%		121 14%	849 100%
DK	180 20%	120 13%	120 13%	120 13%	180 20%	60 7%	90 10%				30 3%	900 100%
D	114 13%	114 13%	115 13%	106 12%	210 24%	74 8%	66 8%			75 9%		874 100%
EL	105 11%	105 11%	79 9%	105 11%	131 14%	79 9%	53 6%				266 29%	923 100%
E	105 12%	70 8%	70 8%	70 8%	105 12%	35 4%	70 8%			226 26%	115 13%	866 100%
F	153 16%	136 15%	119 13%	119 13%	102 11%	102 11%	68 7%	68 7%	68 7%			935 100%
IRL									1 074 100%			1 074 100%
I	187 20%	93 10%	93 10%	156 17%	93 10%	63 7%	124 13%				124 13%	933 100%
L		90 10%	30 3%	90 10%	480 53%	60 7%	90 10%				60 7%	900 100%
NL	111 10%	111 10%	89 8%	144 14%	144 14%	100 9%	78 7%	6 1%	233 22%		50 5%	1 067 100%
A	120 12%	165 16%	180 18%	120 12%	90 9%	90 9%	90 9%				165 16%	1 020 100%
P	117 13%	117 13%	117 13%	175 20%	87 10%	58 7%	87 10%		87 10%		29 3%	874 100%
FIN	76 9%	86 10%	124 14%	57 7%	133 16%	57 7%	29 3%		190 22%		105 12%	857 100%
S										807 100%		807 100%
UK (E/W)										950 100%		950 100%
UK (NI)										855 100%		855 100%
UK (SC)	157 15%	157 15%	261 25%				157 15%			209 20%	104 10%	1 045 100%

Source: Eurydice.

Additional notes

Belgium (B fr): The number of hours for mathematics, sciences, a foreign language and other subjects are the minima which pupils can complete according to their chosen options. The time can rise to four times the set minimum once these options have been added.

Denmark: The distribution of hours per subject are only set by Ministry guidelines based on an estimated 30 periods per week. However, in practice, the municipalities and the schools decide on the minimum and maximum number of hours per week.

Germany: The annual number of hours per subject is an average based upon the number of lesson hours per week for a class in the eighth year of education in the various types of school and different *Länder*. The category 'Other' groups together religious education and other subjects, according to the *Land*.

Greece: This corresponds to the curriculum for the second year of the *gymnasio*.

Spain: In the autonomous communities with two official languages (the community's language and Spanish), the flexible portion of the timetable is 45%, which provides a means of including the second official language in the curriculum.

Ireland: Curricula and directives give full school autonomy for allocating the time spent on each subject. Mother tongue includes English and Irish. Civil, social and political education is included under 'Human sciences'.

Netherlands: Greek and Latin, in *VWO*, and a third foreign language in *HAVO* and *VWO*, are included under compulsory options.

Austria: Refers to the fourth year of the *Hauptschule*. Information and communication technologies are taught on an integrated basis.

Portugal: The number of hours attributed to sport depends on the available human resources and infrastructure in each school. It can rise to 105 hours.

Finland: Within the limits of the national core curriculum, schools can decide how to distribute the subjects over the 3 years of the 2nd stage of *peruskoulu*. The figures show a theoretical average based on the minima given for the whole 2nd stage and assuming that the subjects are spread equally throughout the 3 years.

Sweden: The 1995 reform also establishes the number of lesson hours per subject throughout compulsory education and schools are free to decide at what moment they introduce a discipline and how the hours for this subject are distributed over the nine years. As the reform is implemented, the situation will tend towards a flexible timetable.

United Kingdom: Schools are substantially free to decide the amount of time to allocate to each subject.

United Kingdom (SC): The category "environmental studies" also includes "human sciences" and "ICT". The category "artistic activities" includes "physical education". These categories are specified in advice to schools which is provided by the *Scottish Executive*.

NUMBER AND PERCENTAGES OF MINIMUM ANNUAL TIMETABLE ALLOCATED TO COMPULSORY SUBJECTS AROUND AGE 13 IN GENERAL LOWER SECONDARY EDUCATION, 1997/98

(FIGURE E10)

	MOTHER TONGUE	MATHE-MATICS	NATURAL SCIENCES	HUMAN SCIENCES	FOREIGN LANGUA-GES	PHYSICAL EDUCA-TION	ARTISTIC ACTIVITIES	ICT	COM-PULSORY OPTIONS	FLEXIBLE TIMETABLE	OTHER	TOTAL
EFTA/EEA												
IS	113 / 14%	90 / 11%	69 / 9%	46 / 6%	136 / 17%	68 / 9%	158 / 20%			90 / 11%	23 / 3%	793 / 100%
LI	150 / 15%	150 / 15%	60 / 6%	120 / 12%	120 / 12%	120 / 12%	120 / 12%				180 / 18%	1 020 / 100%
NO	133 / 16%	104,5 / 12%	85,5 / 10%	95 / 11%	85,5 / 10%	76 / 9%	85,5 / 10%		76 / 9%		114 / 13%	855 / 100%
Pre-accession countries												
BG	128 / 17%	102 / 13%	153 / 20%	102 / 13%	102 / 13%	51 / 7%	102 / 13%				26 / 3%	765 / 100%
CZ	116 / 13%	116 / 13%			87 / 10%	58 / 7%				492 / 57%		869 / 100%
EE	102 / 13%	110 / 14%	134 / 17%	173 / 22%	134 / 17%	55 / 7%	55 / 7%		24 / 3%			787 / 100%
LV	117 / 16%	140 / 19%	47 / 7%	117 / 16%	140 / 19%	47 / 7%	46 / 6%	23 / 3%			47 / 7%	724 / 100%
LT	146 / 17%	117 / 13%	29 / 3%	117 / 13%	146 / 17%	59 / 7%	117 / 13%			117 / 13%	29 / 3%	878 / 100%
HU										694 / 100%		694 / 100%
PL	138 / 18%	110 / 14%	179 / 23%	41 / 5%	55 / 7%	83 / 11%	84 / 11%	27 / 4%		55 / 7%		772 / 100%
RO	113 / 13%	113 / 13%	227 / 26%	85 / 10%	113 / 13%	57 / 6%	57 / 6%		28 / 3%		85 / 10%	878 / 100%
SI	99 / 13%	99 / 13%	158 / 20%	99 / 13%	50 / 6%	65 / 8%	62 / 8%		37 / 5%		116 / 15%	783 / 100%
SK	112 / 13%	112 / 13%	167 / 19%	167 / 19%	84 / 10%	56 / 6%	84 / 10%		28 / 3%	56 / 6%		866 / 100%
CY	199 / 23%	75 / 9%	75 / 9%	100 / 11%	112 / 13%	75 / 9%	175 / 20%				62 / 7%	872 / 100%

Source: Eurydice.

Additional notes

Norway: the 76 hours of optional subject time may be devoted either to learning another foreign language or practical project work.

Czech Republic: The flexible hours concern the following subjects: geography, history, civics, family education, biology, music, arts, physics, chemistry, practical work and other options. The headteacher, in co-operation with the advisory body, sets the number of taught hours per subject, as long as all the curriculum subjects are taught, the minimum number of hours is adhered to and the set maximum is not exceeded.

Estonia: The hours of teaching are allocated by subject for pupils who speak Estonian. Those whose mother tongue is not Estonian follow a timetable that has more hours of Estonian as a foreign language.

Lithuania: Depending on the choice of the school or on the special needs of a class, 4 of the 30 weekly periods, indicated as flexible timetable, are allocated either to a foreign language, mathematics, biology or physical education.

Hungary: Within certain limits (minimum and maximum), schools are free to decide how to allocate time to the different subjects.

Poland: 'Natural sciences' includes geography. Flexible timetables contain these options.

NUMBER AND PERCENTAGES OF MINIMUM ANNUAL TIMETABLE ALLOCATED TO COMPULSORY SUBJECTS AROUND AGE 16 IN THE SCIENCE SECTION OF GENERAL UPPER SECONDARY EDUCATION, 1997/98

(FIGURE E11)

	MOTHER TONGUE	MATHE-MATICS	NATURAL SCIENCES	HUMAN SCIENCES	FOREIGN LANGUA-GES	PHYSICAL EDUCA-TION	ARTISTIC ACTIVITIES	ICT	COM-PULSORY OPTIONS	FLEXIBLE TIMETABLE	OTHER	TOTAL
European Union												
B fr, B de	152 18%	121 14%	152 18%	91 11%	182 21%	61 7%			30 4%		61 7%	850 100%
B nl	121 14%	91 11%	61 7%	91 11%	152 18%	61 7%			212 25%		61 7%	850 100%
DK	90 10%	120 13%	270 29%	90 10%	210 23%	60 6%	90 10%					930 100%
D									282 33%	564 67%		846 100%
EL	105 13%	131 17%	184 23%	53 7%	53 7%	39 5%					223 28%	788 100%
E	105 11%	70 8%	140 15%	70 8%	105 11%	18 2%			70 8%	318 34%	35 4%	931 100%
F	132 14%	198 21%	231 24%	99 10%	99 10%	66 7%			99 10%	33 3%		957 100%
IRL										1 002 100%		1 002 100%
I	133 14%	100 11%	167 18%	134 14%	100 11%	67 7%	67 7%				165 18%	933 100%
L		120 13%	150 17%	90 10%	420 47%	30 3%	30 3%		30 3%		30 3%	900 100%
NL	100 10%			22 2%	89 9%	33 3%	22 2%		734 73%			1 000 100%
A	90 9%	120 11%	210 20%	180 17%	180 17%	60 6%	60 6%		90 9%		60 6%	1 050 100%
P	80 10%	107 13%	213 27%	80 10%	80 10%	53 7%					187 23%	800 100%
FIN										812 100%		812 100%
S										712 100%		712 100%
UK (E/W)										950 100%		950 100%
UK (NI)										855 100%		855 100%
UK (SC)	209 20%	105 10%	105 10%	105 10%		52 5%	105 10%	105 10%		209 20%	52 5%	1 045 100%
EFTA/EEA												
IS	116 17%	116 17%			193 29%	39 6%				213 32%		677 100%
LI	120 11%	120 11%	210 20%	90 8%	240 23%	60 6%	60 6%				160 15%	1 060 100%
NO	119 14%	147 17%	147 17%		265 31%	59 7%					119 14%	855 100%
Pre-accession countries												
BG	81 10%	81 10%	162 19%	216 26%	108 13%	54 6%			135 16%			837 100%
CZ	87 10%	87 10%	174 20%	116 13%	145 17%	58 7%	58 7%			145 17%		870 100%

Source: Eurydice.

Additional notes

Denmark: ICT is integrated into the teaching of the different compulsory subjects.

Germany: Compulsory subjects (564 hours a year) are grouped into three fields (languages, literature and arts; human sciences; mathematics, natural sciences and technology) to which religion and sport are added. Amongst these subjects, emphasis is placed on mother tongue, mathematics and a foreign language. Each of these subjects is allocated 10% of the weekly timetable. The compulsory optional subjects (282 hours a year) are intended for individual specialization in these fields.

Spain: In the autonomous communities with two official languages (the community's language and Spanish), the flexible portion of the timetable is 45%, which provides a means of including the second official language in the curriculum.

Ireland: Curricula and directives give full school autonomy for allocating the time spent on each subject.

Luxembourg: This timetable shows the scientific branch of general secondary education within the 'modern humanities' section.

Finland: The curriculum gives schools and pupils considerable autonomy, but there are still compulsory subjects at this level of education.

United Kingdom: Schools are substantially free to decide the amount of time to allocate to each subject.

United Kingdom (SC): Figure given for mother tongue should also include foreign languages. Figure given for ICT should also include other technology subjects. These categories are specified in advice to schools which is provided by the *Scottish Executive.*

Czech Republic: The flexible hours concern following subjects: Latin, social sciences, descriptive geometry, computer science. The headteacher, in co-operation with the advisory body, sets the number of taught hours per subject as long as all the curriculum subjects are taught, the minimum number of hours is adhered to and the set maximum is not exceeded.

NUMBER AND PERCENTAGES OF MINIMUM ANNUAL TIMETABLE ALLOCATED TO COMPULSORY SUBJECTS AROUND AGE 16 IN THE SCIENCE SECTION OF GENERAL UPPER SECONDARY EDUCATION, 1997/98

(FIGURE E11)

	MOTHER TONGUE	MATHE-MATICS	NATURAL SCIENCES	HUMAN SCIENCES	FOREIGN LANGUA-GES	PHYSICAL EDUCA-TION	ARTISTIC ACTIVITIES	ICT	COM-PULSORY OPTIONS	FLEXIBLE TIMETABLE	OTHER	TOTAL
					Pre-accession countries (continued)							
EE	119 13%	92 10%	140 15%	156 17%	119 13%	64 7%	64 7%		165 18%			919 100%
LV	175 20%	140 16%	93 11%	93 11%	210 24%	105 12%	47 6%					863 100%
LT	117 13%	88 9%	146 16%	117 13%	117 13%	59 6%	59 6%	29 3%		176 19%	29 3%	936 100%
HU										833 100%		833 100%
PL	110 14%	83 10%	179 22%	41 5%	138 17%	83 10%		54 7%		83 10%	28 4%	799 100%
RO	85 10%	142 17%	255 30%	113 13%	113 13%	57 7%			57 7%		28 3%	850 100%
SI	105 12%	105 12%	158 17%	158 17%	158 17%	79 9%			72 8%	79 9%		913 100%
SK	84 8%	84 8%	195 19%	56 6%	167 17%	84 8%			167 17%	167 17%		1 004 100%
CY	97 11%	169 20%	205 24%	73 9%	97 11%	48 6%			48 6%		109 13%	845 100%

Source: Eurydice.

Additional notes

Estonia: The hours of teaching are allocated by subject for pupils who speak Estonian. Those whose mother tongue is not Estonian follow a timetable that has more hours of Estonian as a foreign language.
Lithuania: Depending on the choice of the school or on the special needs of a class, 6 of the 32 weekly periods, indicated as flexible timetable, are allocated either to mother tongue, foreign languages, mathematics, computer science, physics, chemistry, biology, history, artistic activities or physical education.
Hungary: Within certain limits (minimum and maximum), schools are free to decide how to allocate time to the different subjects.

PERCENTAGE OF THOSE AGED 22 WHO HAVE SUCCESSFULLY COMPLETED AT LEAST UPPER SECONDARY EDUCATION (ISCED 3), 1997

(FIGURE E12)   (%)

EU	B	DK	D	EL	E	F	IRL	I	L	NL	A	P	FIN	S	UK
71.2	81.2	80.0	78.5	77.8	63.7	75.1	76.9	65.5	57.8	73.2	82.6	51.6	90.1	90.2	66.7

Source: Eurostat, Labour force survey.

Additional notes

Luxembourg: Most young people taking higher education courses are abroad. All of them have completed at least the upper secondary education level. The percentage is therefore under-estimated.
United Kingdom: The GCSE and equivalent qualifications taken at the end of compulsory schooling at the age of 16 are considered as lower secondary qualifications.

NUMBER OF GIRLS PER 100 BOYS OBTAINING A GENERAL UPPER SECONDARY EDUCATION QUALIFICATION, 1996/97

(FIGURE E13)   (1 000)

	European Union											
	EU	B	DK	D	EL	E	F	IRL	I	L	NL	A
GIRLS AND BOYS	1317.8	25.5	33.8	220.2	82.4	271.3	257.4	59.6	148.7	(:)	67.8	14.1
GIRLS	702.8	14.2	20.1	120.8	45.6	148.8	150	31.6	84.4	(:)	(:)	8.1
BOYS	541.7	11.3	13.7	99.5	36.8	122.4	107.4	28	64.2	(:)	(:)	6.1

	European Union (continued)					EFTA/EEA				Pre-accession countries		
	P	FIN	S	UK		IS	LI	NO		BG	CZ	EE
GIRLS AND BOYS	76.3	34.8	26	(:)		2	(:)	26.7		39.5	24	10.8
GIRLS	43.4	20.2	15.7	(:)		1.2	(:)	15.5		26.4	14.5	6.4
BOYS	32.9	14.5	10.2	(:)		0.8	(:)	11.2		13	9.5	4.3

	Pre-accession countries (continued)								Other PHARE countries		
	LV	LT	HU	PL	RO	SI	SK	CY	AL	BA	MK
GIRLS AND BOYS	14.6	23	88.2	171.1	78.6	5.7	16.3	(:)	12.6	(:)	(:)
GIRLS	9.2	13.8	50.5	115.8	53.6	3.6	9.9	(:)	7.6	(:)	(:)
BOYS	5.3	9.3	37.6	55.2	25	2.1	6.4	(:)	5	(:)	(:)

Source: Eurostat, UOE.

Additional notes

Belgium: Only data fom the Flemish Community are included.
Germany, Italy, Netherlands, Austria and **Portugal**: 1995/96.
Estonia, Hungary and **Slovakia**: 1995/96.

PARTICIPATION RATES, OVERALL AND BROKEN DOWN BY SEX, AT THE END OF COMPULSORY EDUCATION, 1996/97

(FIGURE E18)   (%)

European Union

	B (x= 18)			DK (x= 16)			D (x= 18)			EL (x= 15)			E (x= 16)		
	M	W	TOTAL	M	W	TOTAL	M	W	TOTAL	M	W	TOTAL	M	W	TOTAL
x-1	95.1	98.4	96.7	96.9	98.5	97.7	94.4	92.5	93.5	95.3	96.1	95.7	95.7	94.6	95.1
x	83.6	87.8	85.7	92.5	94.4	93.4	86.0	84.9	85.5	86.6	91.4	88.9	84.8	87.2	86.0
x+1	70.7	77.2	73.9	80.7	82.9	81.8	64.7	68.1	66.4	87.4	91.8	89.5	75.3	80.7	77.9
x+2	57.8	67.6	62.7	72.5	75.5	74.0	43.6	49.5	46.5	63.2	68.0	65.5	62.6	71.4	66.9

	F (x= 16)			IRL (x= 15)			I (x= 14)			L (x= 15)			NL (x= 18)		
	M	W	TOTAL	M	W	TOTAL	M	W	TOTAL	M	W	TOTAL	M	W	TOTAL
x-1	98.2	98.1	98.1	99.1	100.0	99.9	100.0*	99.5	100.0*	81.3	89.2	85.2	91.4	90.2	90.8
x	95.9	95.4	95.6	95.3	97.5	96.3	94.7	90.5	92.7	81.5	87.0	84.1	80.6	79.0	79.8
x+1	91.9	92.2	92.0	89.0	95.1	91.9	86.3	87.6	86.9	90.1	88.0	89.0	70.8	66.1	68.5
x+2	81.3	84.5	82.9	75.8	86.5	81.0	78.0	83.8	80.8	71.5	82.8	77.0	61.4	55.3	58.4

	A (x= 15)			P (x= 15)			FIN (x= 16)			S (x= 16)			UK (x= 16)		
	M	W	TOTAL	M	W	TOTAL	M	W	TOTAL	M	W	TOTAL	M	W	TOTAL
x-1	99.6	100.0	99.8	95.5	92.9	94.2	99.9	100.0	100.0	95.6	98.1	96.8	100.0	100.0	100.0
x	91.8	92.3	92.1	59.0	45.3	52.3	89.6	92.1	90.8	97.5	97.7	97.6	77.4	83.4	80.3
x+1	91.1	86.5	88.9	38.2	29.1	33.7	94.8	94.3	94.5	97.0	97.0	97.0	65.8	71.1	68.4
x+2	92.0	83.0	87.7	32.7	25.3	29.1	81.0	87.2	84.0	94.8	94.4	94.6	48.8	50.6	49.7

EFTA/EEA

	IS (x= 16)			LI (x= 15)			NO (x= 16)			Pre-acc. countries BG (x= 16)		
	M	W	TOTAL	M	W	TOTAL	M	W	TOTAL	M	W	TOTAL
x-1	100.0	100.0	100.0	(:)	(:)	(:)	99.1	100.0	99.7	88.2	94.3	91.0
x	87.7	90.9	89.3	(:)	(:)	(:)	95.3	95.4	95.3	85.1	88.6	87.0
x+1	73.3	80.2	76.6	(:)	(:)	(:)	93.6	93.4	93.5	78.9	80.9	79.9
x+2	65.0	69.6	67.3	(:)	(:)	(:)	87.2	89.9	88.5	66.2	67.8	67.0

Pre-accession countries (continued)

	CZ (x= 15)			EE (x= 16)			LV (x= 16)			LT (x= 16)			HU (x= 16)		
	M	W	TOTAL	M	W	TOTAL	M	W	TOTAL	M	W	TOTAL	M	W	TOTAL
x-1	100.0	100.0	100.0	95.0	96.1	96.0	88.7	93.4	91.0	93.8	92.7	93.0	84.0	85.0	85.0
x	99.2	100.0	99.6	90.3	92.9	92.0	80.8	89.1	85.0	84.4	87.5	86.0	86.8	87.5	87.1
x+1	98.4	99.7	99.0	76.4	84.0	80.1	71.7	82.3	76.9	69.4	78.9	75.1	69.4	73.0	71.2
x+2	82.0	88.8	85.3	56.2	64.0	60.1	49.9	63.4	56.6	48.1	59.2	53.6	40.4	39.6	40.0

	PL (x= 15)			RO (x= 15)			SI (x= 15)			SK (x= 15)			CY (x= 15)		
	M	W	TOTAL	M	W	TOTAL	M	W	TOTAL	M	W	TOTAL	M	W	TOTAL
x-1	97.2	97.0	97.0	92.7	92.3	95.5	97.0	97.7	97.0	(:)	(:)	(:)	(:)	(:)	(:)
x	95.3	96.0	96.0	77.7	79.6	78.6	95.6	98.7	97.0	(:)	(:)	(:)	(:)	(:)	(:)
x+1	92.0	94.0	92.8	71.1	70.8	70.9	93.8	94.2	94.0	(:)	(:)	(:)	(:)	(:)	(:)
x+2	90.0	92.0	89.7	58.2	64.1	61.1	84.3	89.9	87.0	(:)	(:)	(:)	(:)	(:)	(:)

M   Men   W   Women x Age at which compulsory education ends

Source: Eurostat, UOE.

Additional notes

Luxembourg: Data do not include students enrolled in non subsidised private education, international schools nor residents studying abroad.

TERTIARY EDUCATION

TRENDS IN THE NUMBER OF STUDENTS IN TERTIARY EDUCATION (ISCED 5, 6, 7), FROM 1975/76 TO 1996/97.
(FIGURES F1, F2 AND F12)

MEN AND WOMEN (1 000)

	European Union										
	EU	B	DK	D	EL	E	F	IRL	I	L	NL
1975/76	5 647	176	97	1 334	117	548	1 053	46	977	(:)	291
1980/81	6 543	217	115	1 515	121	698	1 176	55	1 126	(:)	364
1985/86	7 991	248	125	1 842	182	934	1 358	70	1 192	(:)	405
1990/91	9 655	276	151	2 082	195	1 222	1 699	90	1 452	(:)	479
1995/96	11 933	358	167	2 144	329	1 592	2 092	128	1 775	2	492
1996/97	12 266	361	180	2 132	363	1 684	2 063	135	1 893	2	469

	European Union (continued)						EFTA/EEA		
	A	P	FIN	S	UK		IS	LI	NO
1975/76	97	89	90	(:)	733		3	(:)	(:)
1980/81	125	90	113	(:)	828		4	(:)	(:)
1985/86	173	118	128	183	1 033		5	(:)	73
1990/91	206	186	166	193	1 258		5	(:)	114
1995/96	239	320	214	261	1 821		7	(:)	180
1996/97	241	351	226	275	1 891		8	0.1	185

Source: Eurostat, UOE.

WOMEN (1 000)

	European Union										
	EU	B	DK	D	EL	E	F	IRL	I	L	NL
1975/76	2 298	69	45	569	43	198	500	16	381	(:)	94
1980/81	2 878	93	54	680	50	305	594	22	482	(:)	144
1985/86	3 777	113	60	829	89	458	709	30	551	(:)	166
1990/91	4 683	133	77	880	98	624	902	41	720	(:)	212
1995/96	6 084	179	92	956	159	841	1 147	65	940	1	233
1996/97	6 343	182	98	975	174	890	1 134	69	1 022	1	226

	European Union (continued)						EFTA/EEA		
	A	P	FIN	S	UK		IS	LI	NO
1975/76	37	42	41	(:)	264		1	(:)	(:)
1980/81	53	44	53	(:)	303		2	(:)	(:)
1985/86	79	65	62	96	470		2	(:)	38
1990/91	94	103	86	104	607		3	(:)	60
1995/96	116	181	113	144	919		4	(:)	100
1996/97	117	200	120	154	980		5	(:)	104

Source: Eurostat, UOE.

MEN (1 000)

	European Union										
	EU	B	DK	D	EL	E	F	IRL	I	L	NL
1975/76	3 350	107	52	765	74	350	553	30	596	(:)	197
1980/81	3 666	124	61	835	71	393	582	33	644	(:)	220
1985/86	4 214	135	65	1 013	93	476	649	40	641	(:)	239
1990/91	4 971	143	74	1 201	97	598	797	49	732	(:)	266
1995/96	5 849	179	75	1 188	170	751	944	63	835	1	258
1996/97	5 923	179	82	1 156	189	794	929	65	871	1	243

	European Union (continued)						EFTA/EEA		
	A	P	FIN	S	UK		IS	LI	NO
1975/76	60	47	49	(:)	469		2	(:)	(:)
1980/81	72	46	60	(:)	525		2	(:)	(:)
1985/86	95	53	66	87	563		2	(:)	35
1990/91	112	82	79	89	651		2	(:)	54
1995/96	123	139	101	117	902		3	(:)	81
1996/97	123	151	107	122	912		3	(:)	81

Source: Eurostat, UOE.

<u>Additional notes</u>

Germany: Figures prior to 1990 refer to the former *Länder*.
United Kingdom: Data for years prior to 1982 do not include nursing and paramedic students.
Iceland: Only full-time students are included.

TERTIARY EDUCATION STUDENTS (ISCED 5, 6, 7) BY NUTS 1 AND NUTS 2 REGIONS, 1996/97

(FIGURE F3)

		RATE (%)	ISCED 5 TO 7 (1 000)	TOTAL (1 000)
EUROPEAN UNION				
EU	**EUROPEAN UNION**	**14.5**	**12 148.1**	**83 845.0**
BE	**BELGIQUE-BELGIË***	**13.9**	**360.9**	**2 588.6**
BE1	RÉG. BRUXELLES-CAP.-BRUSSELS HFDST. GEWEST	25.1	81.5	324.8
BE2	VLAAMS GEWEST	12.0	166.2	1 385.6
BE3	RÉGION WALLONNE	12.9	113.2	878.2
DK	**DANMARK**	**15.3**	**180.4**	**1 176.1**
DE	**DEUTSCHLAND**	**12.7**	**2 131.9**	**16 784.2**
DE1	BADEN-WURTTEMBERG	11.6	254.8	2 193.5
DE2	BAYERN	12.1	284.1	2 344.4
DE3	BERLIN	20.1	149.8	743.6
DE4	BRANDENBURG	5.1	28.7	557.4
DE5	BREMEN	19.7	27.3	138.5
DE6	HAMBURG	22.1	75.0	339.5
DE7	HESSEN	13.6	161.0	1 184.2
DE8	MECKLENBURG-VORPOMMERN	5.6	23.3	413.7
DE9	NIEDERSACHSEN	11.8	183.7	1 556.0
DEA	NORDRHEIN-WESTFALEN	16.1	605.9	3 757.2
DEB	RHEINLAND-PFALZ	12.4	99.5	802.5
DEC	SAARLAND	13.1	27.1	207.2
DED	SACHSEN	9.3	88.3	945.4
DEE	SACHSEN-ANHALT	6.5	36.5	560.2
DEF	SCHLESWIG-HOLSTEIN	10.3	53.0	516.3
DEG	THURINGEN	6.4	33.8	524.4
GR	**ELLADA**	**18.5**	**363.2**	**1 965.5**
GR1	VOREIA ELLADA	(:)	(:)	(:)
GR2	KENTRIKI ELLADA	(:)	(:)	(:)
GR3	ATTIKI	(:)	(:)	(:)
GR4	NISIA AIGAIOU, KRITI	(:)	(:)	(:)
ES	**ESPAÑA**	**16.9**	**1 555.6**	**9 227.6**
ES1	NOROESTE	17.4	164.4	943.1
ES2	NORESTE	19.3	169.9	880.2
ES3	COMUNIDAD DE MADRID	22.6	284.1	1 254.3
ES4	CENTRO (E)	14.9	177.2	1 189.8
ES5	ESTE	16.2	385.6	2 387.1
ES6	SUR	14.8	320.4	2 159.4
ES7	CANARIAS	13.1	54.1	413.8
FR	**FRANCE**	**13.9**	**2 091.9**	**15 094.0**
FR1	ÎLE DE FRANCE	18.6	534.5	2 866.5
FR2	BASSIN PARISIEN	10.5	273.4	2 597.1
FR3	NORD-PAS-DE-CALAIS	12.8	146.5	1 145.6
FR4	EST	13.4	174.3	1 297.8
FR5	OUEST	12.9	247.8	1 926.7
FR6	SUD-OUEST	15.8	218.4	1 384.3
FR7	CENTRE-EST	14.2	246.5	1 731.9
FR8	MEDITERRANEE	13.5	221.1	1 632.2
FR9	DEPARTEMENTS D'OUTRE-MER	5.7	29.4	512.0
IE	**IRELAND**	**13.5**	**134.6**	**998.3**
IT	**ITALIA**	**17.4**	**1 892.5**	**10 889.8**
IT1	NORD OVEST	17.0	153.3	899.0
IT2	LOMBARDIA	17.8	265.3	1 486.6
IT3	NORD EST	16.3	180.0	1 102.4
IT4	EMILIA-ROMAGNA	26.8	171.6	639.4
IT5	CENTRO (I)	23.3	236.9	1 015.3
IT6	LAZIO	23.7	257.7	1 087.5
IT7	ABRUZZI-MOLISE	16.5	53.4	323.1
IT8	CAMPANIA	14.4	199.0	1 377.7
IT9	SUD	10.6	153.7	1 453.7
ITA	SICILIA	14.3	163.7	1 140.7
ITB	SARDEGNA	15.9	58.0	364.4
LU	**LUXEMBOURG**	**2.5**	**1.8**	**68.9**
NL	**NEDERLAND**	**13.4**	**469.0**	**3 510.0**
NL1	NOORD-NEDERLAND	(:)	(:)	(:)
NL2	OOST-NEDERLAND	(:)	(:)	(:)
NL3	WEST-NEDERLAND	(:)	(:)	(:)
NL4	ZUID-NEDERLAND	(:)	(:)	(:)
AT	**ÖSTERREICH (AUSTRIA)**	**15.2**	**252.0**	**1 652.4**
AT1	OSTÖSTERREICH	20.2	139.8	690.7
AT2	SÜDÖSTERREICH	14.6	52.0	356.4
AT3	WESTÖSTERREICH	9.9	60.1	605.4
PT	**Portugal (1995/96)**	**13.7**	**319.5**	**2 327.5**
PT1	CONTINENTE	14.3	314.5	2 205.3
PT11	NORTE	12.0	96.7	806.8
PT12	CENTRO (P)	13.9	55.2	398.1
PT13	LISBOA E VALE DO TEJO	17.8	143.4	808.0
PT14	ALENTEJO	10.3	11.4	110.9
PT15	ALGARVE	9.4	7.7	81.6
PT2	ACORES	4.4	2.7	61.9
PT3	MADEIRA	3.8	2.3	60.3

TERTIARY EDUCATION STUDENTS (ISCED 5, 6, 7) BY NUTS 1 AND NUTS 2 REGIONS, 1996/97

(FIGURE F3)

		RATE (%)	ISCED 5 TO 7 (1 000)	TOTAL (1 000)
EUROPEAN UNION (CONTINUED)				
FI	**SUOMI (FINLAND)**	**19.0**	**226.5**	**1 192.0**
FI1	MANNER-SUOMI	19.1	226.3	1 187.0
FI13	UUSIMAA	22.8	73.8	323.4
FI14	ETELÄ-SUOMI	19.1	74.8	392.5
FI15	ITÄ-SUOMI	15.2	24.2	158.7
FI16	VÄLI-SUOMI	16.7	27.9	166.6
FI17	POHJOIS-SUOMI	17.6	25.6	145.8
FI2	AHVENANMAA/ÅLAND	3.0	0.2	5.0
SE	**SVERIGE**	**12.9**	**277.0**	**2 145.7**
SE01	STOCKHOLM	13.3	56.7	425.8
SE02	ÖSTRA MELLANSVERIGE	15.6	58.9	378.1
SE03	SMÅLAND MED ÖARNA	9.2	17.1	186.4
SE04	SYDSVERIGE	13.5	41.2	305.2
SE05	VÄSTSVERIGE	11.6	49.8	428.6
SE06	NORRA MELLANSVERIGE	8.8	16.9	191.9
SE07	MELLERSTA NORRLAND	11.1	10.1	90.6
SE08	ÖVRE NORRLAND	19.0	26.5	139.1
UK	**UNITED KINGDOM**	**13.3**	**1 891.4**	**14 224.3**
UK1	NORTH	11.2	83.9	749.8
UK2	YORKSHIRE AND HUMBERSIDE	12.7	160.2	1 263.8
UK3	EAST MIDLANDS	12.0	119.5	997.5
UK4	EAST ANGLIA	9.3	41.1	441.5
UK5	SOUTH EAST	15.7	669.8	4 278.4
UK6	SOUTH WEST	10.4	111.6	1 074.6
UK7	WEST MIDLANDS	11.2	154.4	1 374.3
UK8	NORTH WEST	11.3	186.7	1 649.2
UK9	WALES	13.1	92.9	710.2
UKa	SCOTLAND	18.6	224.4	1 206.1
UKb	NORTHERN IRELAND	9.8	46.9	478.8
EFTA/EEA				
IS	**ÍSLAND**	**9.6**	**7.9**	**82.2**
LI	**LIECHTENSTEIN**	**1.8**	**0.1**	**5.9**
NO	**NORGE**	**17.4**	**185.3**	**1 067.6**
PRE-ACCESSION COUNTRIES				
BG	**BĂLGARIJA**	**15.7**	**262.8**	**1 674.9**
CZ	**ČESKÁ REPUBLIKA**	**8.8**	**195.7**	**2 233.4**
EE	**EESTI**	**11.4**	**39.0**	**341.3**
LV	**LATVIJA**	**11.9**	**61.6**	**516.5**
LT	**LIETUVA**	**10.8**	**83.6**	**772.3**
HU	**MAGYARORSZÁG**	**9.2**	**202.8**	**2 204.7**
PL	**POLSKA**	**9.6**	**927.5**	**9 662.5**
RO	**ROMÂNIA**	**7.6**	**354.5**	**4 688.3**
SI	**SLOVENIJA**	**12.6**	**53.5**	**425.7**
SK	**SLOVENSKÁ REPUBLIKA**	**7.8**	**101.8**	**1 299.9**
CY	**KYPROS**	**6.2**	**10.0**	**162.0**

Source: Eurostat, UOE.

FIGURE F4: HIGHER EDUCATION ENTRANCE REQUIREMENTS, 1997/98

(FIGURE F4)

	LIMITS ON THE NUMBER OF PLACES AT NATIONAL/ REGIONAL LEVEL	LIMITS IMPOSED BY INSTITUTIONS IN THE LIGHT OF THEIR CAPACITY	SELECTION ON THE BASIS OF ABILITY	UNRESTRICTED ADMISSION
European Union				
B fr			Civil engineering (selection: examination set by the institution)	Most courses
B nl			Some courses: Civil engineering, architecture and, since 1997, dentistry, medicine, nautical science and some art courses (selection: examination set by the institution or the government)	Most courses
DK	Medicine and education	Most courses (selection: by the institution; specific requirements in relation to prior knowledge and, if the number of applicants exceeds the number of places, selection on the basis of school results and previous relevant work experience)	Journalism, photo-journalism, film studies, music	

FIGURE F4: HIGHER EDUCATION ENTRANCE REQUIREMENTS, 1997/98

(FIGURE F4)

	LIMITS ON THE NUMBER OF PLACES AT NATIONAL/ REGIONAL LEVEL	LIMITS IMPOSED BY INSTITUTIONS IN THE LIGHT OF THEIR CAPACITY	SELECTION ON THE BASIS OF ABILITY	UNRESTRICTED ADMISSION
	European Union (continued)			
D	Generally no *numerus clausus*, but a supraregional selection procedure for some disciplines (such as medicine) based on an inter-state agreement between the *Länder* (selection: average mark in the *Abitur*, the period spent waiting between the *Abitur* and the application, and social criteria)	Almost all *Fachhochschulen* (selection: by the institution, generally on the basis of the average mark in the *Abitur*, and the period spent waiting between the *Abitur* and the application) In courses to which admission is limited at federal level, around 20% of the places may be allocated by the universities themselves. (selection: on the basis of ability, motivation or specific conditions)	Art and sports courses (selection: aptitude test)	Most university courses
EL	All courses (selection: national examination)			
E		All courses (selection: on the basis of results in the national examination)	Some courses in art, translation or interpreting and physical education (selection: aptitude test in addition to the national examination)	
F	Medicine, paramedical subjects (selection: competitive examinations organised by each institution)	Applicable to some general courses in certain institutions (selection: priority to students resident in the *académie*, with a *numerus clausus* for the rest).	Certain courses (IUT, CPGE, etc.) (selection: by the institution, based on school record and interviews)	General university courses
IRL	Medicine, dentistry, veterinary medicine and teacher training courses including those leading to a Bachelor of Education (places limited on the basis of course capacity with an additional *numerus clausus* for medicine and education)	All courses (selection: by the institution, based on results in upper secondary school)		
I	Courses in medicine and surgery, dentistry, veterinary medicine, architecture. All university *Diploma* (D.U.). All specialisation courses. (number of places and selection criteria determined by the government; selection organised by the institution)	Certain university courses		Certain university courses
L	Teacher training (pre-primary and primary teachers)			Other courses
NL	Certain courses as decided by the government each year (6 university courses and 26 non-university) and certain courses according to the labour-market related quota	Certain courses (selection: by the institution)	Certain courses (selection: study of two specific subjects at secondary level – national decision)	In principle, all courses
A		All non-university courses (for example, *Fachhochschulen-Studiengänge*) and some other institutions of the post-secondary education sector	All *Universitäten der Künste* courses (selection: aptitude test) and university courses in sport	Most university courses
P		All courses have a *numerus clausus* fixed by each institution according to its capacity. Furthermore, institutions have to specify a minimum entrance requirement for their various courses (selection: national competitive examination for candidates with satisfactory school and exam results: candidates' marks to be above a minimum set by each institution)	Some courses (music and PE teachers) (selection: exam set by the institution).	
FIN	Graduate quotas fixed by the government for each discipline	All courses (selection: in the case of universities, on the basis of school results and/or an entrance exam; in the case of AMK institutions, on the basis of school results, work experience, an entrance exam or an aptitude test)		

FIGURE F4: HIGHER EDUCATION ENTRANCE REQUIREMENTS, 1997/98

(FIGURE F4)

	LIMITS ON THE NUMBER OF PLACES AT NATIONAL/ REGIONAL LEVEL	LIMITS IMPOSED BY INSTITUTIONS IN THE LIGHT OF THEIR CAPACITY	SELECTION ON THE BASIS OF ABILITY	UNRESTRICTED ADMISSION
European Union (continued)				
S	No maximum limitation for the number of registrations, but maximum limitation for financial support. Graduate quotas fixed by the government	All courses (selection: by the institution; specific requirements in relation to prior knowledge and, if the number of applicants exceeds the number of places, selection on the basis of school results, the results of a national university aptitude test, other tests, work experience)		
UK	Target number set for each institution	All courses (selection: by the institution)		
EFTA/EEA				
IS		All non-university courses (selection: by the institution on the basis of final upper secondary school exam results, or an entrance exam) Some university courses (selection: open competition, final results of upper secondary school and/or work experience)		Most university courses
LI		Some courses: *Fachhochschule Liechtenstein*		
NO	Most courses (selection: school results, age, and work experience). Number of places fixed by the government (for the majority of courses)		Some courses (generally university)	Some university courses
Pre-accession countries				
BG	Number of places fixed at central level (selection: by the institution, depending on the number of places allowed centrally)			
CZ		All courses (selection: by the institution on the basis of the upper secondary examination results and on an entrance examination)		
EE	Number of places, subsidised by the State, decided at central level	All courses (selection: on the basis of the results at upper secondary State examination and/or admission procedure set by the institution)		
LV	Number of places subsidised by the State, decided at central level	All courses (selection: by the institution, on the basis of the results of upper secondary examinations)	Certain courses in art and music (selection: on the basis of an entrance examination and an aptitude test)	
LT	Number of places fixed at central level (university and non university level education)	All courses (selection: on the basis of the results of upper secondary examinations and, for university education, an entrance examination)		
HU		All courses (selection: by the institution)		
PL	Courses in medicine (number of places limited by the Ministry of Health and Social Welfare)	All courses (selection: by the institution, on the basis of an entrance examination (written and/or oral), an interview, an aptitude test, results in final upper secondary school leaving certificate)		
RO	Number of places subsidised by the State decided at central level	All courses (selection: by the institution, on the basis of an entrance examination)		
SI	Number of places determined by the institutions and approved by the Government	All courses (selection: by the institution, on the basis of final upper secondary school exam results, upper secondary school results, or results in specific subjects)	Some courses (selection: by the institution, on the basis of an aptitude test)	
SK		All courses (selection: by the institution, on the basis of an entrance examination)		
CY		All university courses (selection: entrance examination set by the Ministry of Education and Culture)		

Source: Eurydice.

(FIGURE F5)

TERTIARY EDUCATION STUDENTS (ISCED 5, 6, 7) STUDYING IN ANOTHER EU MEMBER STATE OR EFTA/EEA COUNTRY, 1996/97

	EU	B	DK	D	EL	E	F	IRL	I	L	NL	A	P	FIN	S	UK	IS	LI	NO
EU	232 073	18 667	1 888	45 562	(:)	15 227	29 308	2 995	10 644	480	3 067	14 077	1 146	900	5 088	83 024	95	(:)	2 311
B	6 554		17	1 015	(:)	825	1 673	59	108	66	660	80	26	9	19	1 997	-	(:)	15
DK	3 860	52		691	(:)	275	396	26	34	-	58	65	2	40	. 672	1 549	38	(:)	629
D	30 600	531	561		(:)	3 044	5 468	392	1 099	17	843	5 394	204	195	635	12 217	13	(:)	286
EL	42 020	863	19	8 492		219	2 799	37	8 067	3	102	364	3	17	166	20 869	-	(:)	15
E	17 479	1 464	60	4 919	(:)		3 436	190	183	6	278	285	203	29	107	6 319	3	(:)	44
F	29 297	5 972	102	6 164	(:)	3 368		312	535	248	156	352	537	66	216	11 269	4	(:)	76
IRL	16 211	63	42	606	(:)	263	497		13	1	29	53	3	18	38	14 585	1	(:)	14
I	28 355	3 913	74	6 537	(:)	2 516	3 582	80		44	238	6 402	60	44	140	4 725	1	(:)	28
L	4 733	1 682	2	1 227	(:)	4	1 044	17	20		6	289	11	0	0	431	-	(:)	1
NL	10 184	3 127	99	2 466	(:)	695	809	44	123	2		97	21	28	152	2 521	2	(:)	109
A	8 836	43	35	6 674	(:)	514	395	27	86	2	62		5	15	109	869	1	(:)	21
P	9 346	569	19	1 589	(:)	725	4 364	14	25	86	84	34		15	33	1 789	-	(:)	14
FIN	6 072	49	92	1 086	(:)	156	286	62	67	1	47	157	4		2 347	1 718	11	(:)	135
S	5 505	52	377	1 046	(:)	351	680	54	102	-	86	265	8	318		2 166	14	(:)	530
UK	13 021	287	389	3 050	(:)	2 272	3 879	1 681	182	4	418	240	59	106	454		7	(:)	394
IS	1 617	6	622	288	(:)	3	74	4	11	1	10	16	-	33	351	198		(:)	194
LI	7	(:)	(:)	(:)	(:)	-	6	(:)	(:)	-	-	(:)	-	1	(:)	(:)	(:)		(:)
NO	7 449	34	1 030	1 160	(:)	195	504	51	37	1	93	85	4	42	1 002	3 211	23	(:)	

Source: Eurostat, UOE.

PARTICIPATION IN TERTIARY EDUCATION (ISCED 5, 6, 7) BY AGE AND BY GENDER, 1996/97

(FIGURE F11)

MEN (1 000)

	European Union											
	EU	B	DK	D	EL	E	F	IRL	I	L	NL	A
16 YEARS	1.1	0	0	0	-	-	0.1	0	(:)	-	-	-
17 YEARS	22.4	0.5	0	0.8	-	0	6.2	2.0	(:)	-	2.2	0.1
18 YEARS	297.6	17.5	0.1	3.2	31.1	55.9	79.4	9.9	(:)	0	11.5	1.8
19 YEARS	454.2	24.3	1.0	14.2	38.6	81.3	128.7	11.3	(:)	0	20.7	4.9
20 YEARS	526.4	25.1	3.3	44.7	31.6	95.5	141.6	9.8	(:)	0.04	26.7	8.1
21 YEARS	519.2	22.8	6.4	68.2	27.9	93.1	132.7	7.8	(:)	0.09	28.8	9.4
22 YEARS	471.6	19.0	8.0	83.1	18.5	88.1	114.4	5.0	(:)	0.12	29.3	10.0
23 YEARS	401.3	13.1	8.6	92.5	12.9	74.9	84.6	3.0	(:)	0.10	25.9	9.5
24 YEARS	339.3	8.6	8.8	105.3	7.8	60.2	50.0	2.1	(:)	0.06	21.9	10.0
25 YEARS	306.8	5.6	7.9	112.3	6.4	46.6	38.2	9.2	(:)	0.05	16.3	9.3
26 YEARS	242.3	3.9	6.1	105.0	4.5	31.0	26.7	(:)	(:)	0.02	11.3	8.7
27 YEARS	208.3	3.1	5.1	99.8	2.4	24.0	18.5	(:)	(:)	0.01	8.2	8.1
28 YEARS	175.7	2.4	4.2	86.3	1.5	19.0	14.7	(:)	(:)	0.01	5.7	6.8
29 YEARS	170.9	1.9	3.6	95.0	0.6	15.1	11.9	(:)	(:)	0.01	4.8	5.6

	European Union (continued)				EFTA/EEA			Pre-accession countries		
	P	FIN	S	UK	IS	LI	NO	BG	CZ	EE
16 YEARS	-	0	0	1.0	-	(:)	0	0	-	0
17 YEARS	2.9	0	0	7.7	-	(:)	0	1.1	0	0.2
18 YEARS	10.8	0.3	0.1	76.1	-	(:)	0.1	5.0	8.3	2.2
19 YEARS	17.6	4.6	4.1	103.0	0	(:)	3.9	8.4	14.6	2.5
20 YEARS	20.0	6.6	8.6	104.8	0.2	(:)	6.0	10.8	15.2	2.4
21 YEARS	18.7	9.4	11.6	82.4	0.4	(:)	8.0	12.3	14.4	2.1
22 YEARS	16.6	9.9	13.0	56.6	0.4	(:)	8.5	13.3	13.9	1.7
23 YEARS	13.0	9.0	12.0	42.2	0.5	(:)	8.8	10.1	11.1	1.4
24 YEARS	9.2	8.9	10.6	35.9	0.4	(:)	7.9	8.6	7.7	1.1
25 YEARS	6.6	7.8	9.1	31.4	0.3	(:)	6.5	7.1	5.4	0.9
26 YEARS	4.8	6.6	6.9	26.6	0.2	(:)	4.9	4.9	3.8	1.6
27 YEARS	3.5	5.5	5.6	24.5	0.1	(:)	4.0	3.6	3.0	(:)
28 YEARS	2.6	4.8	4.9	22.7	0.1	(:)	3.3	2.9	2.5	(:)
29 YEARS	2.3	4.0	4.4	21.8	0.1	(:)	2.6	2.1	2.0	(:)

	Pre-accession countries (continued)								Other PHARE countries		
	LV	LT	HU	PL	RO	SI	SK	CY	AL	BA	MK
16 YEARS	-	-	-	-	-	-	(:)	0	-	(:)	-
17 YEARS	0.1	0.1	-	-	-	0	(:)	0.1	-	(:)	0
18 YEARS	2.9	5.0	6.1	1.2	16.4	0.7	(:)	0.4	0.9	(:)	2.4
19 YEARS	4.1	6.5	12.2	38.9	22.8	4.0	(:)	0.8	1.1	(:)	5.4
20 YEARS	2.8	5.2	14.9	63.4	24.7	3.9	(:)	1.0	1.1	(:)	5.1
21 YEARS	2.8	4.2	14.1	64.0	23.6	3.3	(:)	0.7	1.1	(:)	4.3
22 YEARS	2.5	3.4	11.8	59.4	21.6	2.7	(:)	0.5	1.1	(:)	3.6
23 YEARS	1.6	2.5	7.8	52.7	16.8	1.8	(:)	0.2	0.9	(:)	2.7
24 YEARS	2.7	2.0	5.7	37.9	13.3	1.2	(:)	0.2	0.5	(:)	2.0
25 YEARS	1.3	1.2	13.2	22.6	9.5	1.0	(:)	0	0.2	(:)	1.4
26 YEARS	1.3	0.9	(:)	14.8	6.8	0.7	(:)	-	0.1	(:)	0.9
27 YEARS	0.5	0.6	(:)	8.3	5.4	0.6	(:)	-	0.1	(:)	0.7
28 YEARS	0.4	0.5	(:)	6.3	4.4	0.4	(:)	-	0	(:)	0.4
29 YEARS	0.3	0.4	(:)	5.4	2.5	0.3	(:)	-	0	(:)	0.3

Source: Eurostat, UOE.

Additional notes

Germany: The '29-year-olds' category includes people aged 29 and over.
Ireland: The '25-year-olds' category includes people aged 25 and over.
Iceland: Only full-time students are included.
Estonia: The '26-year-olds' category includes people aged 26 and over.
Hungary: The '25-year-olds' category includes people aged 25 and over.
Poland: Only ISCED 6 students are included.
Romania and **Slovenia**: ISCED 7 students are excluded.
Albania: ISCED 7 students are excluded.

PARTICIPATION IN TERTIARY EDUCATION (ISCED 5, 6, 7) BY AGE AND BY GENDER, 1996/97

(FIGURE F11)

WOMEN (1 000)

	EU	B	DK	D	EL	E	F	IRL	I	L	NL	A
European Union												
16 YEARS	1.5	0	0	0	-	-	0.1	0	(:)	-	-	-
17 YEARS	35.0	0.8	0	7.7	-	0	9.4	2.4	(:)	-	3.5	0.1
18 YEARS	403.1	25.2	0.1	24.1	40.0	76.9	110.7	11.8	(:)	0	15.2	4.2
19 YEARS	586.0	31.1	0.9	61.7	33.2	108.2	164.1	12.6	(:)	0.02	25.1	8.8
20 YEARS	655.9	30.8	3.4	87.2	31.5	125.4	170.8	10.8	(:)	0.12	29.5	10.7
21 YEARS	602.0	24.2	7.4	87.7	25.7	115.8	157.9	7.8	(:)	0.14	29.6	10.9
22 YEARS	509.3	17.5	10.2	82.3	14.3	106.5	135.0	4.5	(:)	0.14	26.3	10.4
23 YEARS	404.0	11.2	11.2	76.6	10.0	81.1	102.0	2.7	(:)	0.07	20.7	9.4
24 YEARS	323.4	6.9	11.2	76.4	5.4	59.6	69.9	1.8	(:)	0.04	16.5	9.1
25 YEARS	264.8	4.3	9.4	73.6	3.9	41.4	45.5	9.4	(:)	0.02	11.6	7.9
26 YEARS	195.2	3.0	7.1	62.8	3.1	27.7	29.7	(:)	(:)	0.01	8.0	6.8
27 YEARS	158.4	2.2	5.4	55.9	1.2	20.9	20.6	(:)	(:)	0.00	5.6	5.7
28 YEARS	132.1	1.7	4.3	47.1	1.0	16.7	15.6	(:)	(:)	0.01	4.1	4.9
29 YEARS	146.5	1.2	3.6	75.2	0.4	13.4	12.2	(:)	(:)	0.01	3.4	3.9

	P	FIN	S	UK		IS	LI	NO		BG	CZ	EE
	European Union (continued)					**EFTA/EEA**				**Pre-accession countries**		
16 YEARS	-	-	0	1.4		-	(:)	-		0.1	-	0
17 YEARS	1.9	0	0	9.2		-	(:)	0		2.4	0	0.2
18 YEARS	11.6	0.3	0.1	83.0		0	(:)	0.1		12.9	7.7	3.2
19 YEARS	19.6	6.1	6.7	107.8		0	(:)	6.0		20.8	14.5	3.3
20 YEARS	22.7	10.4	12.1	110.5		0.2	(:)	9.4		21.8	15.1	3.2
21 YEARS	23.4	12.0	14.6	84.8		0.4	(:)	10.4		21.1	13.4	2.6
22 YEARS	21.2	12.2	15.2	53.4		0.5	(:)	10.8		18.7	12.4	2.1
23 YEARS	17.2	9.7	13.0	39.2		0.6	(:)	9.8		14.5	10.2	1.6
24 YEARS	14.1	8.6	10.7	33.1		0.5	(:)	8.5		10.5	7.5	1.2
25 YEARS	11.3	7.5	8.8	30.3		0.4	(:)	6.7		8.3	5.2	1.0
26 YEARS	8.5	6.2	6.6	25.7		0.3	(:)	5.0		6.2	3.6	1.8
27 YEARS	6.4	4.9	5.4	24.3		0.2	(:)	4.0		4.9	2.6	(:)
28 YEARS	5.1	4.3	4.8	22.6		0.1	(:)	3.3		3.6	2.0	(:)
29 YEARS	4.0	3.7	4.3	21.3		0.1	(:)	2.6		2.8	1.6	(:)

	LV	LT	HU	PL	RO	SI	SK		CY	AL	BA	MK
	Pre-accession countries (continued)									**Other PHARE countries**		
16 YEARS	-	-	-	-	-	-	(:)		0	-	(:)	-
17 YEARS	0.1	0.1	-	-	-	0	(:)		0.3	-	(:)	0
18 YEARS	4.2	8.1	7.9	2.2	17.2	1.0	(:)		1.3	1.7	(:)	1.4
19 YEARS	5.9	9.1	15.5	71.7	24.5	5.8	(:)		1.2	2.1	(:)	3.1
20 YEARS	4.4	8.5	17.6	76.6	25.9	5.8	(:)		1.0	2.0	(:)	3.0
21 YEARS	4.0	6.3	16.7	74.2	24.5	4.8	(:)		0.7	1.7	(:)	2.5
22 YEARS	3.4	4.3	13.4	67.8	22.0	3.5	(:)		0.3	1.4	(:)	2.0
23 YEARS	3.0	3.4	8.0	58.8	18.0	2.2	(:)		0.1	0.6	(:)	1.3
24 YEARS	2.6	2.5	5.7	34.9	13.2	1.4	(:)		0.1	0.2	(:)	1.0
25 YEARS	1.7	1.6	13.1	22.0	8.6	0.9	(:)		0	0.1	(:)	0.6
26 YEARS	1.7	1.2	(:)	16.0	5.9	0.6	(:)		-	0	(:)	0.4
27 YEARS	1.1	0.9	(:)	11.4	4.8	0.5	(:)		-	0	(:)	0.3
28 YEARS	0.9	0.8	(:)	9.9	3.9	0.4	(:)		-	0	(:)	0.2
29 YEARS	0.7	0.6	(:)	9.6	2.3	0.3	(:)		-	0	(:)	0.1

Source: Eurostat, UOE.

Additional notes

Germany: The '29-year-olds' category includes people aged 29 and over.
Ireland: The '25-year-olds' category includes people aged 25 and over.
Iceland: Only full-time students are included.
Estonia: The '26-year-olds' category includes people aged 26 and over.
Hungary: The '25-year-olds' category includes people aged 25 and over.
Poland: Only ISCED 6 students are included.
Romania and **Slovenia**: ISCED 7 students are excluded.
Albania: ISCED 7 students are excluded.

PARTICIPATION RATE OF STUDENTS AGED 19 TO 24 (LIVING WITH THEIR PARENTS) IN TERTIARY EDUCATION (ISCED 5, 6, 7) BY EDUCATIONAL LEVEL OF PARENTS, 1997

(FIGURE F13)   (%)

EDUCATIONAL LEVEL OF PARENTS:	European Union															
	EU	B	DK	D	EL	E	F	IRL	I	L	NL	A	P	FIN	S	UK
ISCED 1 or 2	19	29	(:)	11	10	23	24	12	18	13	22	6	22	19	14	8
ISCED 3	27	42	(:)	14	27	49	37	33	44	27	30	15	63	21	23	9
ISCED 5 to 7	48	67	(:)	33	52	62	68	46	66	56	48	42	78	34	47	20

Source: Eurostat, Labour force survey.

PROPORTION OF PEOPLE BETWEEN THE AGES OF 30 AND 60 WITH TERTIARY EDUCATION QUALIFICATIONS (ISCED 5, 6 7), BY AGE GROUP, 1997

(FIGURES F14 AND F15)   (%)

AGE	European Union															
	EU	B	DK	D	EL	E	F	IRL	I	L	NL	A	P	FIN	S	UK
30-34	22	32	29	25	23	26	22	28	10	22	26	11	14	26	30	26
35-39	21	29	29	26	20	22	19	25	11	21	26	10	13	25	30	25
40-44	21	25	30	27	18	18	19	22	12	20	26	11	12	22	32	25
45-49	19	25	28	26	15	15	17	17	10	21	23	8	11	19	28	24
50-54	17	22	25	24	11	12	15	15	8	20	21	7	9	19	24	20
55-59	14	17	22	20	9	9	11	13	5	15	17	6	8	16	22	17

Source: Eurostat, Labour force survey.

GRADUATES FROM TERTIARY EDUCATION (ISCED 5, 6, 7), BY GENDER, 1997

(FIGURE F16)   (1 000)

	European Union											
	EU	B	DK	D	EL	E	F	IRL	I	L	NL	A
MEN	969.7	18.6	14.0	182.8	14.0	94.3	239.4	17.1	77.5	(:)	43.2	10.3
WOMEN	1 120.9	21.1	16.8	153.7	13.9	128.8	310.9	18.3	98.0	(:)	44.0	11.1

	European Union (continued)				EFTA/EEA				Pre-accession countries		
	P	FIN	S	UK	IS	LI	NO		BG	CZ	EE
MEN	15.5	12.0	14.7	216.3	0.7	(:)	22.6		13.3	13.5	2.2
WOMEN	27.3	16.6	20.5	239.9	1.0	(:)	30.4		25.7	16.6	3.9

	Pre-accession countries (continued)								Other PHARE countries		
	LV	LT	HU	PL	RO	SI	SK	CY	AL	BA	MK
MEN	4.0	6.9	13.2	43.8	36.9	3.6	5.9	(:)	1.8	(:)	1.4
WOMEN	6.0	10.5	18.2	72.1	44.1	5.4	6.9	(:)	2.0	(:)	1.9

Source: Eurostat, UOE.

Additional notes

Belgium: 1995/96. Only graduates from the Flemish Community are included.
Germany and **Netherlands**: 1995/96.
Ireland: Some students with a vocational qualification at ISCED level 5 are excluded. Students in private independent colleges are also excluded, as are those in nursing schools who obtained their qualification after three or four years of in-hospital training.
Czech Republic, Hungary, Poland and **Slovakia**: 1995/96.
Poland: Only graduates from ISCED 6 programmes are included.
Romania: Only graduates from the first degree of ISCED 6 are included.

GRADUATES IN TERTIARY EDUCATION (ISCED 5, 6, 7) BY FIELD OF STUDY, BY GENDER, 1996/97
(FIGURES F17 AND F18)

HUMANITIES, APPLIED ARTS, THEOLOGY (1 000)

	European Union											
	EU	B	DK	D	EL	E	F	IRL	I	L	NL	A
MALES	79.5	1.1	0.7	9.9	(:)	6.3	18.4	2.2	4.2	(:)	2.4	1.0
FEMALES	171.8	1.9	2.2	19.3	(:)	12.4	52.5	3.8	19.6	(:)	4.5	1.7
TOTAL	251.3	3.0	2.9	29.3	(:)	18.7	70.9	5.9	23.8	(:)	7.0	2.7

	European Union (continued)				EFTA/EEA			Pre-accession countries		
	P	FIN	S	UK	IS	LI	NO	BG	CZ	EE
MALES	1.3	0.7	0.9	30.3	0.1	(:)	4.2	0.7	1.1	0.2
FEMALES	3.4	1.7	1.4	47.6	0.2	(:)	7.2	1.9	1.5	0.4
TOTAL	4.7	2.4	2.2	77.8	0.3	(:)	11.4	2.6	2.6	0.6

	Pre-accession countries (continued)								Other PHARE countries		
	LV	LT	HU	PL	RO	SI	SK	CY	AL	BA	MK
MALES	0.3	(:)	0.8	(:)	2.9	0.2	0.5	(:)	0.1	(:)	0.1
FEMALES	0.8	(:)	1.5	(:)	5.7	0.4	0.5	(:)	0	(:)	0.3
TOTAL	1.1	1.7	2.3	13.2	8.6	0.5	1.0	(:)	0.1	(:)	0.4

Source: Eurostat, UOE.

SOCIAL SCIENCE (1 000)

	European Union											
	EU	B	DK	D	EL	E	F	IRL	I	L	NL	A
MALES	260.2	4.3	5.0	39.6	(:)	23.6	76.1	4.8	17.2	(:)	15.6	2.2
FEMALES	337.4	5.0	3.1	33.6	(:)	34.7	129.4	6.1	18.4	(:)	16.8	2.4
TOTAL	597.6	9.3	8.2	73.1	(:)	58.3	205.5	10.9	35.6	(:)	32.4	4.5

	European Union (continued)				EFTA/EEA			Pre-accession countries		
	P	FIN	S	UK	IS	LI	NO	BG	CZ	EE
MALES	5.7	1.5	3.0	61.6	0.1	(:)	7.8	3.5	3.8	0.5
FEMALES	9.4	2.7	4.0	71.9	0.1	(:)	8.7	8.4	5.1	1.4
TOTAL	15.0	4.2	6.9	133.5	0.3	(:)	16.6	11.8	8.8	1.9

	Pre-accession countries (continued)								Other PHARE countries		
	LV	LT	HU	PL	RO	SI	SK	CY	AL	BA	MK
MALES	0.9	(:)	1.9	(:)	9.3	1.2	0.9	(:)	0.3	(:)	0.3
FEMALES	1.4	(:)	2.8	(:)	14.9	2.4	1.3	(:)	0.3	(:)	0.4
TOTAL	2.4	3.5	4.7	28.0	24.1	3.6	2.2	(:)	0.6	(:)	0.7

Source: Eurostat, UOE.

EDUCATION SCIENCE AND TEACHER TRAINING (1 000)

	European Union											
	EU	B	DK	D	EL	E	F	IRL	I	L	NL	A
MALES	46.1	1.7	1.3	3.1	(:)	6.5	9.1	0.5	0.4	(:)	3.8	0.8
FEMALES	124.6	4.1	4.4	9.1	(:)	20.1	20.1	1.5	3.5	(:)	8.5	2.8
TOTAL	170.7	5.8	5.7	12.2	(:)	26.6	29.1	2.0	3.9	(:)	12.3	3.6

	European Union (continued)				EFTA/EEA			Pre-accession countries		
	P	FIN	S	UK	IS	LI	NO	BG	CZ	EE
MALES	1.1	0.7	1.6	15.5	0.1	(:)	1.6	1.0	1.2	0.1
FEMALES	5.1	2.3	6.2	36.9	0.3	(:)	5.3	5.8	3.5	0.5
TOTAL	6.2	3.0	7.8	52.4	0.4	(:)	7.0	6.8	4.7	0.6

	Pre-accession countries (continued)								Other PHARE countries		
	LV	LT	HU	PL	RO	SI	SK	CY	AL	BA	MK
MALES	0.5	(:)	2.7	(:)	0.8	0.1	0.6	(:)	(:)	(:)	(:)
FEMALES	1.8	(:)	9.3	(:)	1.3	0.9	2.0	(:)	(:)	(:)	0.3
TOTAL	2.3	2.8	12.0	32.0	2.1	1.1	2.6	(:)	(:)	(:)	(:)

Source: Eurostat, UOE.

(Additional notes   (See page 234))

GRADUATES IN TERTIARY EDUCATION (ISCED 5, 6, 7) BY FIELD OF STUDY, BY GENDER, 1996/97
(FIGURES F17 AND F18)

LAW (1 000)

| | European Union | | | | | | | | | | | |
	EU	B	DK	D	EL	E	F	IRL	I	L	NL	A
MALES	57.8	0.7	0.5	7.6	(:)	11.6	15.6	0.4	8.8	(:)	2.0	1.1
FEMALES	81.6	0.8	0.7	5.6	(:)	19.1	28.1	0.6	10.8	(:)	2.4	0.8
TOTAL	139.4	1.5	1.2	13.2	(:)	30.7	43.7	1.0	19.6	(:)	4.3	1.9

| | European Union (continued) | | | | EFTA/EEA | | | Pre-accession countries | | |
	P	FIN	S	UK	IS	LI	NO	BG	CZ	EE
MALES	0.8	0.2	0.5	7.9	0	(:)	1.3	0.6	0.7	0.1
FEMALES	1.5	0.2	0.6	10.5	0	(:)	1.5	1.1	1.3	0.2
TOTAL	2.3	0.4	1.1	18.4	0	(:)	2.7	1.7	2.0	0.4

| | Pre-accession countries (continued) | | | | | | | CY | Other PHARE countries | | |
	LV	LT	HU	PL	RO	SI	SK		AL	BA	MK
MALES	0.2	(:)	0.7	(:)	4.6	0.1	0.2	(:)	(:)	(:)	0.1
FEMALES	0.2	(:)	0.9	(:)	5.7	0.2	0.2	(:)	0.1	(:)	0.1
TOTAL	0.4	0.7	1.5	4.0	10.4	0.3	0.4	(:)	0.3	(:)	0.2

Source: Eurostat, UOE.

NATURAL SCIENCES (1 000)

| | European Union | | | | | | | | | | | |
	EU	B	DK	D	EL	E	F	IRL	I	L	NL	A
MALES	71.5	0.4	0.4	13.7	(:)	5.2	22.5	2.0	4.5	(:)	2.1	0.7
FEMALES	64.3	0.3	0.3	6.3	(:)	5.5	23.4	2.9	5.4	(:)	1.0	0.5
TOTAL	135.8	0.8	0.7	20.0	(:)	10.7	45.9	4.8	9.8	(:)	3.2	1.2

| | European Union (continued) | | | | EFTA/EEA | | | Pre-accession countries | | |
	P	FIN	S	UK	IS	LI	NO	BG	CZ	EE
MALES	0.3	0.4	0.8	18.5	0	(:)	0.4	0.3	0.5	0.1
FEMALES	0.7	0.4	0.8	16.8	0	(:)	0.4	0.6	0.4	0.1
TOTAL	1.1	0.8	1.6	35.3	0.1	(:)	0.8	0.9	0.9	0.2

| | Pre-accession countries (continued) | | | | | | | CY | Other PHARE countries | | |
	LV	LT	HU	PL	RO	SI	SK		AL	BA	MK
MALES	0.2	(:)	0.5	(:)	1.0	0.1	0.2	(:)	0	(:)	0.0
FEMALES	0.2	(:)	0.3	(:)	3.3	0.1	0.2	(:)	0	(:)	0.1
TOTAL	0.4	0.3	0.8	3.3	4.3	0.2	0.3	(:)	0	(:)	0.1

Source: Eurostat, UOE.

MATHEMATICS, COMPUTER SCIENCE (1 000)

| | European Union | | | | | | | | | | | |
	EU	B	DK	D	EL	E	F	IRL	I	L	NL	A
MALES	55.1	0.8	0.3	8.8	(:)	6.5	9.2	1.2	2.6	(:)	2.3	0.7
FEMALES	23.8	0.2	0.2	3.4	(:)	3.2	4.8	0.7	2.5	(:)	0.3	0.2
TOTAL	78.9	1.0	0.5	12.2	(:)	9.7	14.0	1.9	5.1	(:)	2.6	0.9

| | European Union (continued) | | | | EFTA/EEA | | | Pre-accession countries | | |
	P	FIN	S	UK	IS	LI	NO	BG	CZ	EE
MALES	0.6	1.2	1.1	19.7	0	(:)	0.6	0.2	0.3	0.0
FEMALES	0.7	0.3	0.3	7.1	0	(:)	0.2	0.2	0.0	0.0
TOTAL	1.3	1.5	1.4	26.8	0.1	(:)	0.7	0.4	0.3	0.1

| | Pre-accession countries (continued) | | | | | | | CY | Other PHARE countries | | |
	LV	LT	HU	PL	RO	SI	SK		AL	BA	MK
MALES	0.1	(:)	0.0	(:)	1.5	0.1	0.1	(:)	0	(:)	0
FEMALES	0.1	(:)	0.0	(:)	1.9	0.0	0.0	(:)	0	(:)	0
TOTAL	0.2	0.4	0.1	2.3	3.4	0.2	0.1	(:)	0	(:)	0

Source: Eurostat, UOE.

(Additional notes (See page 234))

GRADUATES IN TERTIARY EDUCATION (ISCED 5, 6, 7) BY FIELD OF STUDY, BY GENDER, 1996/97
(FIGURES F17 AND F18)

MEDICAL SCIENCES (1 000)

	EU	B	DK	D	EL	E	F	IRL	I	L	NL	A
	European Union											
MALES	64.4	1.4	0.5	19.3	(:)	6.0	8.4	0.5	9.3	(:)	3.3	0.7
FEMALES	152.6	3.5	3.6	34.6	(:)	16.4	21.9	0.9	10.9	(:)	7.3	1.6
TOTAL	217.0	4.9	4.1	53.9	(:)	22.4	30.3	1.5	20.2	(:)	10.5	2.3

	European Union (continued)				EFTA/EEA			Pre-accession countries		
	P	FIN	S	UK	IS	LI	NO	BG	CZ	EE
MALES	1.0	1.1	1.6	11.3	0	(:)	1.0	1.1	0.9	0.2
FEMALES	3.3	6.8	5.6	36.4	0.2	(:)	4.0	3.5	2.9	0.7
TOTAL	4.2	7.9	7.2	47.6	0.2	(:)	4.9	4.6	3.8	0.8

	Pre-accession countries (continued)							CY	Other PHARE countries		
	LV	LT	HU	PL	RO	SI	SK		AL	BA	MK
MALES	0.2	(:)	0.8	(:)	2.1	0.2	0.4	(:)	0.2	(:)	0.1
FEMALES	0.9	(:)	1.3	(:)	3.5	0.6	1.2	(:)	0.2	(:)	0.3
TOTAL	1.1	2.3	2.1	6.6	5.6	0.8	1.6	(:)	0.4	(:)	0.4

Source: Eurostat, UOE.

ENGINEERING, ARCHITECTURE (1 000)

	EU	B	DK	D	EL	E	F	IRL	I	L	NL	A
	European Union											
MALES	259.7	2.8	3.8	65.2	(:)	22.7	70.4	4.7	16.5	(:)	9.1	2.5
FEMALES	55.7	1.0	0.9	9.2	(:)	7.4	15.5	0.7	5.5	(:)	1.3	0.6
TOTAL	315.4	3.7	4.7	74.3	(:)	30.1	85.9	5.3	22.0	(:)	10.4	3.0

	European Union (continued)				EFTA/EEA			Pre-accession countries		
	P	FIN	S	UK	IS	LI	NO	BG	CZ	EE
MALES	3.7	5.3	5.0	48.1	0.2	(:)	3.1	3.6	4.3	0.5
FEMALES	1.8	1.0	1.4	9.7	0	(:)	0.8	2.3	1.4	0.2
TOTAL	5.5	6.3	6.4	57.8	0.2	(:)	4.0	6.0	5.8	0.7

	Pre-accession countries (continued)							CY	Other PHARE countries		
	LV	LT	HU	PL	RO	SI	SK		AL	BA	MK
MALES	1.4	(:)	4.0	(:)	11.1	1.3	2.9	(:)	0.2	(:)	0.5
FEMALES	0.4	(:)	1.3	(:)	4.4	0.4	1.0	(:)	0.1	(:)	0.3
TOTAL	1.8	3.4	5.4	16.5	15.5	1.6	3.9	(:)	0.4	(:)	0.8

Source: Eurostat, UOE.

OTHER (1 000)

	EU	B	DK	D	EL	E	F	IRL	I	L	NL	A
	European Union											
MALES	50.8	5.2	1.5	15.5	(:)	5.8	9.7	0.8	3.3	(:)	2.6	0.6
FEMALES	76.4	4.3	1.4	32.7	(:)	10.2	15.4	1.2	2.6	(:)	2.0	0.7
TOTAL	127.2	9.5	2.9	48.2	(:)	16.0	25.0	2.0	5.9	(:)	4.5	1.3

	European Union (continued)				EFTA/EEA			Pre-accession countries		
	P	FIN	S	UK	IS	LI	NO	BG	CZ	EE
MALES	1.0	0.9	0.3	3.5	0	(:)	2.4	2.3	0.7	0.5
FEMALES	1.4	1.3	0.3	3.1	0.1	(:)	2.2	2.0	0.5	0.5
TOTAL	2.5	2.2	0.6	6.6	0.1	(:)	4.6	4.2	1.2	0.9

	Pre-accession countries (continued)							CY	Other PHARE countries		
	LV	LT	HU	PL	RO	SI	SK		AL	BA	MK
MALES	0.2	(:)	1.8	(:)	3.5	0.2	0.2	(:)	(:)	(:)	(:)
FEMALES	0.1	(:)	0.7	(:)	3.4	0.4	0.4	(:)	0.1	(:)	0.2
TOTAL	0.4	2.3	2.5	9.9	7.0	0.6	0.6	(:)	0.6	(:)	0.4

Source: Eurostat, UOE.

(Additional notes   (See page 234))

GRADUATES IN TERTIARY EDUCATION (ISCED 5, 6, 7) BY FIELD OF STUDY, BY GENDER, 1996/97
(FIGURES F17 AND F18)

TOTAL (1 000)

	European Union											
	EU	B	DK	D	EL	E	F	IRL	I	L	NL	A
MALES	944.9	18.6	14.0	182.8	(:)	94.3	239.4	17.1	66.9	(:)	43.2	10.3
FEMALES	1 088.2	21.1	16.8	153.7	(:)	128.8	310.9	18.3	79.1	(:)	44.0	11.1
TOTAL	2 033.2	39.6	30.8	336.5	(:)	223.1	550.4	35.4	145.9	(:)	87.3	21.4

	European Union (continued)					EFTA/EEA				Pre-accession countries		
	P	FIN	S	UK		IS	LI	NO		BG	CZ	EE
MALES	15.5	12.0	14.7	216.3		0.7	(:)	22.4		13.3	13.5	2.2
FEMALES	27.3	16.6	20.5	239.9		1.0	(:)	30.3		25.7	16.6	3.9
TOTAL	42.8	28.6	35.2	456.2		1.7	(:)	52.6		39.0	30.1	6.1

	Pre-accession countries (continued)									Other PHARE countries		
	LV	LT	HU	PL	RO	SI	SK		CY	AL	BA	MK
MALES	4.0	6.9	13.2	43.8	36.9	3.6	5.9		(:)	1.8	(:)	1.4
FEMALES	6.0	10.5	18.2	72.1	44.1	5.4	6.9		(:)	2.0	(:)	1.9
TOTAL	10.0	17.4	31.3	115.9	81.0	8.9	12.8		(:)	4.0	(:)	3.3

Source: Eurostat, UOE.

Additional notes

Belgium: 1995/96. Only graduates from the Flemish Community are included.
Germany, Italy and **Netherlands**: 1995/96.
Ireland: The total number of those with tertiary education qualifications is included here, including those with two qualifications (about 4 000). Some students with a vocational qualification at ISCED level 5 are excluded. Students in private independent colleges are also excluded, as are those in nursing schools who obtained their qualification after three or four years of in-hospital training.
Czech Republic, Hungary, Poland and **Slovakia**: 1995/96
Poland: Only graduates from ISCED 6 programmes are included.
Romania: Only graduates from the first degree of ISCED 6 are included.

TEACHERS

TEACHERS IN RELATION TO THE TOTAL ACTIVE POPULATION. PRIMARY AND SECONDARY LEVELS (ISCED 1, 2 AND 3), PUBLIC AND PRIVATE SECTORS COMBINED, 1996

(FIGURE G5)

	TEACHERS (FULL-TIME AND PART-TIME) (1 000)	TEACHERS (FTE) (1 000)	NUMBER OF PRIMARY AND SECONDARY PUPILS (1 000)	PRIMARY AND SECONDARY PUPILS/ TOTAL POPULATION (%)	TOTAL ACTIVE POPULATION (1 000)	TOTAL POPULATION (1 000)
European Union						
EU*	4 458.4	3 137.0	60 874.1	16.3	168 212.8	373 716.7
B	214.1	188.2	1 807.4	17.8	4 215.3	10 170.2
DK*	83.7	73.7	774.2	14.7	2 827.8	5 275.1
D	766.9	649.8	12 241.8	14.9	39 162.0	82 012.2
EL	117.5	65.3	1 469.6	14.0	4 261.5	10 486.6
E	444.9	424.0	6 554.7	16.7	16 066.3	39 298.6
F	694.7	657.0	9 984.4	17.1	25 359.8	58 491.6
IRL	43.5	40.7	748.2	20.5	1 529.0	3 652.2
I	727.4	(:)	7 413.0	12.9	22 859.5	57 461.0
L	5.0	(:)	57.2	13.7	173.4	418.3
NL	(:)	153.9	2 646.7	17.0	7 605.1	15 567.1
A	111.1	106.4	1 175.4	14.6	3 804.7	8 067.8
P	145.7	(:)	1 734.5	17.5	4 841.6	9 934.1
FIN	65.3	63.6	850.9	16.6	2 493.4	5 132.3
S	137.1	104.4	1 539.0	17.4	4 369.4	8 844.5
UK	747.6	609.9	11 877.0	20.2	28 644.0	58 905.0
EFTA/EEA						
IS	4.9	4.8	60.0	22.2	144.7	269.9
LI	(:)	(:)	4.9	15.7	(:)	31.1
NO	85.5	(:)	698.7	15.9	2 277.8	4 392.7
Pre-accession countries						
BG	92.9	92.9	1 165.2	14.0	(:)	8 340.9
CZ	138.5	119.2	1 712.9	16.6	5 124.4	10 309.1
EE	19.3	18.3	245.2	16.8	696.9	1 462.1
LV	40.0	33.7	392.2	15.8	(:)	2 479.9
LT	55.5	(:)	601.5	16.2	(:)	3 707.2
HU	150.0	142.3	1 606.5	15.8	3 933.1	10 174.4
PL	451.8	(:)	7 751.5	20.1	16 996.4	38 639.3
RO	250.6	147.0	3 674.6	16.3	11 853.6	22 581.9
SI	23.9	21.5	322.4	16.2	956.8	1 987.0
SK	70.9	67.1	1 027.9	19.1	2 444.6	5 378.9
CY	10.1	9.9	126.0	17.0	306.1	741.0
Other countries taking part in the PHARE programme						
AL	37.0	37.0	653.8	19.8	(:)	3 297.7
BA	26.8	18.4	533.3	14.3	(:)	3 727.4
MK	18.7	(:)	344.7	17.3	(:)	1 991.4

Source: Eurostat, UOE et Labour force survey.

<u>Additional notes</u>

Belgium: ISCED 0 teachers are included as well.
Ireland and **Austria**: Non-teaching heads are included.
Luxembourg: 1997/98, only teachers from the public sector are included.
Netherlands: Only data in full-time equivalents are included.
Portugal: 1995/96
Finland: ISCED 5 teachers and some ISCED 6 teachers from vocational and technical programmes are also included in ISCED 3.
Iceland: In ISCED 3, only teachers from the public sector are included.
Liechtenstein: 1995/96.
Lithuania: Only full-time teachers are included.
Slovakia: Non-teaching heads are included.

TEACHERS WORKING FULL-TIME OR PART-TIME, IN PRIMARY (ISCED 1) AND SECONDARY EDUCATION (ISCED 2 AND 3), 1996/97

(FIGURES G6 AND G11)   (1 000)

ISCED 1						
FULL-TIME				PART-TIME		
MEN	WOMEN	TOTAL		MEN	WOMEN	TOTAL
European Union						
279.9	945.0	1224.9	EU	40.0	247.8	287.7
14.8	49.7	64.6	B	2.6	21.5	24.1
12.1	18.1	30.2	DK*	1.7	2.6	4.2
30.6	73.6	104.2	D	11.5	108.9	120.3
20.3	26.5	46.8	EL	-	-	-
50.8	102.0	152.8	E	4.2	8.9	13.1
42.7	153.9	196.5	F	2.5	12.2	14.7
3.5	12.6	16.1	IRL	0	0.1	0.1
15.7	234.7	250.5	I	0	0	0
0.9	1.4	2.3	L	0	0.2	0.2
21.7	24.5	46.2	NL	4.6	49.7	54.2
5.0	24.0	29.0	A	0.1	2.1	2.2
(:)	(:)	(:)	P	(:)	(:)	(:)
6.6	14.6	21.2	FIN	0.1	0.2	0.3
10.4	29.3	39.7	S	5.3	13.4	18.7
44.9	180.0	224.9	UK	9.9	48.6	58.6
EFTA/EEA						
0.8	1.7	2.5	IS	0.2	1.0	1.2
(:)	(:)	(:)	LI	(:)	(:)	(:)
16.2	23.2	39.4	NO	2.7	14.3	17.0
Pre-accession countries						
2.8	23.1	25.9	BG	-	-	-
2.5	33.0	35.5	CZ	(:)	(:)	(:)
0.6	6.1	6.7	EE	0.1	0.3	0.4
0.3	6.9	7.3	LV	0.2	3.4	3.6
0.8	17.6	18.4	LT	(:)	(:)	(:)
2.4	36.3	38.7	HU	0.2	0.4	0.7
(:)	(:)	325.7	PL	(:)	(:)	(:)
10.2	58.0	68.2	RO	0.5	3.1	3.6
0.5	5.8	6.3	SI	0.2	1.2	1.3
1.3	15.6	16.9	SK	-	-	-
1.3	2.9	4.1	CY	0	0	0.1
Other countries taking part in the PHARE programme						
3.6	9.7	13.3	AL	-	-	-
7.0	11.4	18.4	BA	-	-	-
2.0	3.8	5.8	MK	-	-	-

ISCED 2						
FULL-TIME				PART-TIME		
MEN	WOMEN	TOTAL		MEN	WOMEN	TOTAL
European Union						
345.0	427.2	772.2	EU	53.8	145.0	198.8
(:)	(:)	(:)	B	(:)	(:)	(:)
7.4	10.8	18.2	DK*	1.1	1.5	2.6
133.9	109.2	243.0	D	23.1	93.1	116.2
10.5	18.9	29.4	EL	2.3	3.7	6.1
27.5	37.9	65.5	E	2.7	3.6	6.4
(:)	(:)	(:)	F	(:)	(:)	(:)
(:)	(:)	(:)	IRL	(:)	(:)	(:)
54.0	131.4	185.3	I	0	0	0
(:)	(:)	(:)	L	(:)	(:)	(:)
27.0	3.4	30.4	NL	11.6	16.4	28.0
16.3	22.6	38.9	A	0.5	4.0	4.5
(:)	(:)	(:)	P	(:)	(:)	(:)
6.2	13.4	19.6	FIN	0.2	0.5	0.8
5.2	14.7	19.9	S	3.1	7.6	10.7
57.0	64.9	121.9	UK	9.2	14.5	23.7
EFTA/EEA						
(:)	(:)	(:)	IS	(:)	(:)	(:)
(:)	(:)	(:)	LI	(:)	(:)	(:)
(:)	(:)	(:)	NO	(:)	(:)	(:)
Pre-accession countries						
8.4	26.2	34.6	BG	-	-	-
11.6	34.7	46.3	CZ	(:)	(:)	(:)
0.8	4.6	5.4	EE	0.2	0.4	0.6
2.1	10.6	12.7	LV	1.0	5.2	6.2
(:)	(:)	(:)	LT	(:)	(:)	(:)
11.2	39.3	50.5	HU	1.0	1.9	2.9
(:)	(:)	(:)	PL	(:)	(:)	(:)
28.7	56.8	85.5	RO	6.1	12.0	18.1
1.3	5.4	6.7	SI	0.4	0.9	1.3
6.2	20.5	26.8	SK	0.1	0.1	0.2
(:)	(:)	(:)	CY	(:)	(:)	(:)
Other countries taking part in the PHARE programme						
8.5	9.1	17.6	AL	-	-	-
(:)	(:)	(:)	BA	-	-	-
3.9	3.2	7.1	MK	0.3	0.3	0.6

Source: Eurostat, UOE.

Additional notes

Belgium: ISCED 0 teachers are included with ISCED 1 teachers.
Ireland and **Austria**: Non-teaching heads are included.
Luxembourg: 1997/98, only teachers from the public sector are included.
Netherlands: Part-time teachers are defined as any teachers whose workload is lower than the full-time workload; all heads (whether with teaching duties or not) are excluded; ISCED 0 teachers are included in ISCED 1.
Iceland and **Norway**: All the teachers teaching in the single structure are regrouped in ISCED 1.
Czech Republic: Part-time teachers are included with full-time teachers.
Poland: All the teachers teaching in the single structure are regrouped in ISCED 1.
Bosnia & Herzegovina: All the teachers teaching in the single structure are regrouped in ISCED 1.

Source: Eurostat, UOE.

Additional notes

Belgium, France, Ireland and **Luxembourg**: ISCED 2 teachers are included with ISCED 3 teachers.
Ireland and **Austria**: Non-teaching heads are included.
Luxembourg: 1997/98, only teachers from the public sector are included.
Netherlands: Part-time teachers are defined as any teachers whose workload is lower than the full-time workload; all heads (whether with teaching duties or not) are excluded.
Iceland and **Norway**: All the teachers teaching in the single structure are regrouped in ISCED 1.
Czech Republic: Part-time teachers are included with full-time teachers.
Lithuania and **Cyprus**: ISCED 2 teachers are included with ISCED 3 teachers.
Poland: All the teachers teaching in the single structure are regrouped in ISCED 1.
Bosnia & Herzegovina: All the teachers teaching in the single structure are regrouped in ISCED 1.

TEACHERS WORKING FULL-TIME OR PART-TIME, IN PRIMARY (ISCED 1) AND SECONDARY EDUCATION (ISCED 2 AND 3), 1996/97

(FIGURES G6 AND G11)   (1 000)

ISCED 3						
FULL-TIME				PART-TIME		
MEN	WOMEN	TOTAL		MEN	WOMEN	TOTAL
European Union						
692.5	698.6	1391.2	EU	155.8	257.3	413.2
43.0	39.2	82.2	B	13.6	29.6	43.2
11.9	5.0	16.9	DK*	8.1	3.6	11.7
93.2	29.2	122.4	D	24.3	36.4	60.8
15.8	13.5	29.3	EL	2.7	3.1	5.9
92.0	92.8	184.8	E	11.9	10.5	22.4
177.2	221.0	398.2	F	23.1	62.2	85.3
9.6	11.8	21.4	IRL	2.7	3.1	5.9
124.5	167.2	291.7	I	0	0	0
1.7	1.0	2.7	L	0	0.1	0.2
10.2	1.7	11.9	NL	6.1	11.3	17.5
(:)	(:)	(:)	A	(:)	(:)	(:)
(:)	(:)	(:)	P	(:)	(:)	(:)
9.1	12.0	21.1	FIN	1.1	1.3	2.4
7.2	5.2	12.3	S	16.8	19.0	35.8
97.0	99.2	196.3	UK	45.2	77.0	122.3
EFTA/EEA						
0.6	0.4	1.0	IS	0.1	0.1	0.2
(:)	(:)	(:)	LI	(:)	(:)	(:)
13.8	7.2	20.9	NO	3.3	4.9	8.1

ISCED 3 (CONTINUED)						
FULL-TIME				PART-TIME		
MEN	WOMEN	TOTAL		MEN	WOMEN	TOTAL
Pre-accession countries						
10.1	22.3	32.4	BG	-	-	-
25.8	30.9	56.7	CZ	(:)	(:)	(:)
1.1	4.1	5.2	EE	0.3	0.6	0.9
2.2	5.2	7.5	LV	0.8	2.0	2.8
7.9	29.1	37.0	LT	(:)	(:)	(:)
21.4	23.9	45.4	HU	5.7	6.2	11.9
(:)	(:)	126.1	PL	(:)	(:)	(:)
24.2	35.7	59.9	RO	6.2	9.1	15.3
2.4	3.8	6.2	SI	0.8	1.3	2.1
7.1	14.0	21.1	SK	2.7	3.3	6.0
2.8	3.0	5.7	CY	0.1	0.1	0.1
Other countries taking part in the PHARE programme						
2.9	3.2	6.1	AL	-	-	-
3.4	2.9	6.4	BA	1.2	0.9	2.1
1.9	2.0	3.9	MK	0.6	0.6	1.2

Source: Eurostat, UOE.

Additional notes

Belgium, France, Ireland and **Luxembourg**: ISCED 2 teachers are included with ISCED 3 teachers.
France: ISCED 2 and ISCED 5 teachers from upper grades of *lycées* are included with ISCED 3 teachers.
Ireland and **Austria**: Non-teaching heads are included.
Luxembourg: 1997/98, only teachers from the public sector are included.
Netherlands: Part-time teachers are defined as any teachers whose workload is lower than the full-time workload; all heads (whether with teaching duties or not) are excluded.
Austria: Only data in full-time equivalents are included.
Finland: ISCED 5 teachers and some ISCED 6 teachers from vocational and technical programmes are also included in ISCED 3.
Czech Republic: Part-time teachers are included with full-time teachers.
Lithuania and **Cyprus**: ISCED 2 teachers are included with ISCED 3 teachers.
Poland: All the teachers teaching in the single structure are regrouped in ISCED 1.
Slovakia: Non-teaching heads are included.

237

DISTRIBUTION OF TEACHERS BY AGE BAND, IN THOUSANDS. PRIMARY EDUCATION (ISCED 1), PUBLIC AND PRIVATE SECTORS COMBINED, 1996/97

(FIGURE G7) (1 000)

	European Union											
	EU	B	DK	D	EL	E	F	IRL	I	L	NL	A
<30	149.6	(:)	(:)	11.8	(:)	(:)	39.7	1.7	12.4	0.5	15.4	4.3
30 - 39	308.9	(:)	(:)	34.3	(:)	(:)	95.4	4.6	65.5	0.5	27.5	10
40 - 49	538.8	(:)	(:)	103.6	(:)	(:)	123.6	5.3	103.4	0.7	42.5	11.8
> = 50	313.1	(:)	(:)	74.8	(:)	(:)	59.1	4.2	68.2	0.7	20.5	5.1
Age unknown	47.9	(:)	(:)	0	46.8	(:)	-	0.3	0.8	-	-	-

	European Union (continued)				EFTA/EEA				Pre-accession countries		
	P	FIN	S	UK	IS	LI	NO		BG	CZ	EE
<30	(:)	3.2	6.2	54.5	(:)	(:)	6.5		5.4	5.6	1.4
30 - 39	(:)	6.6	8.4	56.2	(:)	(:)	10.3		9.7	9.6	2.1
40 - 49	(:)	6.2	24	117.7	(:)	(:)	19.2		6.4	5.7	1.6
> = 50	(:)	5.4	19.8	55.1	(:)	(:)	19.3		4.4	14.6	1.9
Age unknown	(:)	-	-	-	(:)	(:)	1.1		-	-	-

	Pre-accession countries (continued)								Other PHARE countries		
	LV	LT	HU	PL	RO	SI	SK	CY	AL	BA	MK
<30	2.6	4.1	(:)	(:)	(:)	(:)	(:)	(:)	(:)	(:)	(:)
30 - 39	3.6	5.9	(:)	(:)	(:)	(:)	(:)	(:)	(:)	(:)	(:)
40 - 49	2.5	4.1	(:)	(:)	(:)	(:)	(:)	(:)	(:)	(:)	(:)
> = 50	2.2	4.4	(:)	(:)	(:)	(:)	(:)	(:)	(:)	(:)	(:)
Age unknown	-	-	39.4	325.7	71.8	7.6	16.9	(:)	13.3	18.4	5.8

Source: Eurostat, UOE.

Additional notes

Germany, Ireland, Italy and **Norway**: Teachers whose age is unknown are not included.
France: ISCED 0 teachers are included as well.
Ireland and **Austria**: Non-teaching heads are included.
Luxembourg: Data 1997/98, only teachers from the public sector are included.
Netherlands: 1997/98, all heads (whether with teaching duties or not) are excluded.
Norway: Data on ISCED 1 teachers include ISCED 2 teachers from the public sector.
Poland: All the teachers teaching in the single structure are regrouped in ISCED 1.
Slovakia: Non-teaching heads are included.

DISTRIBUTION OF TEACHERS BY AGE BAND. SECONDARY EDUCATION (ISCED 2 AND 3), PUBLIC AND PRIVATE SECTORS COMBINED, 1996/97

(FIGURE G8) (1 000)

	European Union											
	EU	B	DK	D	EL	E	F	IRL	I	L	NL	A
<30	115.9	(:)	(:)	13.2	(:)	(:)	56.9	3.9	1.9	0.2	4.7	5.2
30 - 39	393.6	(:)	(:)	90.4	(:)	(:)	108.4	7.5	82.2	0.7	17.7	29.6
40 - 49	813.7	(:)	(:)	247.8	(:)	(:)	191	9.4	196.5	0.9	36.6	30
> = 50	574.6	(:)	(:)	190.9	(:)	(:)	127.2	6.2	125.5	0.9	29.6	14.9
Age unknown	130	(:)	(:)	0.1	58.7	(:)	-	0.2	70.9	-	-	-

	European Union (continued)				EFTA/EEA				Pre-accession countries		
	P	FIN	S	UK	IS	LI	NO		BG	CZ	EE
<30	(:)	3.2	3.6	23.1	0.1	(:)	2		10.3	13.6	1.9
30 - 39	(:)	11	12.3	33.8	0.3	(:)	5.3		20.8	25.3	3.4
40 - 49	(:)	16	23.7	61.8	0.5	(:)	10		22.9	26	3.1
> = 50	(:)	13.7	38.8	26.9	0.4	(:)	9.8		13.1	38.1	3.8
Age unknown	(:)	-	-	-	-	-	2.1		-	-	-

	Pre-accession countries (continued)								Other PHARE countries		
	LV	LT	HU	PL	RO	SI	SK	CY	AL	BA	MK
<30	4.9	(:)	(:)	(:)	(:)	(:)	(:)	(:)	(:)	(:)	(:)
30 - 39	8.5	(:)	(:)	(:)	(:)	(:)	(:)	(:)	(:)	(:)	(:)
40 - 49	7.6	(:)	(:)	(:)	(:)	(:)	(:)	(:)	(:)	(:)	(:)
> = 50	8.1	(:)	(:)	(:)	(:)	(:)	(:)	(:)	(:)	(:)	(:)
Age unknown	-	37	110.6	126.1	178.8	16.4	54	(:)	23.7	8.4	12.8

Source: Eurostat, UOE.

Additional notes

Germany, Ireland, Italy and **Norway**: Teachers whose age is unknown are not included.
Ireland and **Austria**: Non-teaching heads are included.
Luxembourg: 1997/98, only teachers from the public sector are included.
Netherlands: 1997/98, all heads (whether with teaching duties or not) are included.
Finland: ISCED 5 teachers and some ISCED 6 teachers from vocational and technical programmes are also included in ISCED 3.
Iceland and **Norway**: Only ISCED 3 teachers from the public sector are included.
Slovakia: Non-teaching heads are included.

TEACHERS WITHIN 10 YEARS OF RETIREMENT IN PRIMARY (ISCED 1) AND SECONDARY EDUCATION (ISCED 2 AND 3), IN THOUSANDS, 1996/97

(FIGURE G10)

	PRIMARY		SECONDARY			REFERENCE AGE USED IN THE FIGURE
	TEACHERS WITHIN 10 YEARS OF RETIREMENT	TOTAL NUMBER OF TEACHERS	TEACHERS WITHIN 10 YEARS OF RETIREMENT	TOTAL NUMBER OF TEACHERS		
European Union						
EU	232.7	1310.4	444.6	1897.8		(-)
B	(:)	(:)	(:)	(:)		62.5
DK	(:)	(:)	(:)	(:)		65.0
D	42.2	224.5	114.7	542.2		64.0
EL	(:)	(:)	(:)	58.7		60.0
E	(:)	(:)	(:)	(:)		65.0
F	34.4	317.8	88.4	483.5		62.5
IRL	4.2	15.8	6.2	27.0		60.0
I	79.2	249.6	148.1	406.0		59.0
L	0.5	2.3	0.6	2.7		62.5
NL	20.5	105.9	29.6	88.5		60.0
A	3.5	31.3	10.4	79.8		62.5
P	(:)	(:)	(:)	(:)		61.0
FIN	4.0	21.5	10.0	43.9		62.5
S	8.5	58.3	19.2	78.4		65.0
UK	35.6	283.5	17.4	145.6		62.5
EFTA/EEA						
IS	(:)	(:)	0.2	1.2		67.5
LI	(:)	(:)	(:)	(:)		62.0
NO	8.0	55.3	4.3	27.0		66.0
Pre-accession countries						
BG	6.0	25.9	18.6	67.1		57.5
CZ	15.5	35.5	42.0	103.0		58.5
EE	1.9	7.1	3.8	12.2		59.8
LV	2.2	10.9	8.1	29.1		60.0
LT	4.9	18.4	(:)	37.0		58.5
HU	(:)	39.4	(:)	110.6		62.0
PL	(:)	325.7	(:)	126.1		60.0
RO	(:)	71.8	(:)	178.8		59.5
SI	(:)	7.6	(:)	16.4		59.0
SK	(:)	16.9	(:)	54.0		58.5
CY	(:)	(:)	(:)	(:)		57.5

Source: Eurostat, UOE.

Additional notes

France: Data on ISCED 3 teachers includes ISCED 5 teachers from upper grades of *lycées*.
Ireland and **Austria**: Non-teaching heads are included.
Luxembourg: 1997/98, only teachers from the public sector are included.
Netherlands: 1997/98, all heads (whether with teaching duties or not) are excluded.
Finland: ISCED 5 teachers and some ISCED 6 teachers from vocational and technical programmes are also included in ISCED 3.
Iceland: Only ISCED 3 teachers are included.
Norway: Data on ISCED 1 include ISCED 2 teachers, data on secondary teachers only include ISCED 3 teachers.
Poland: All the teachers teaching in the single structure are regrouped in ISCED 1.
Slovakia: Non-teaching heads are included.

GDP PER CAPITA 1998

(FIGURES G12, G13 AND G14)

	GDP IN NATIONAL CURRENCY AT CURRENT PRICES, (000 MILLION), 1998	NUMBER OF INHABITANTS, 1998 (1 000)
European Union		
B	9 051.9	10 192.3
DK	1 166.6	5 294.9
D	3 758.1	82 057.4
EL	35 735.0	10 511.0
E	82 650.3	39 347.9
F	8 464.3	58 726.9
IRL	57 513	3 694.0
I	2 031 579.2	57 563.3
L	631.3	423.7
NL	750.0	15 654.2
A	2 622.6	8 075.4
P	19 298.7	9 957.3
FIN	675.7	5 147.3
S	1 803.7	8 847.6
UK	837.6	59 089.6

Source: Eurostat, National Accounts ESA and population statistics.

EFTA/EEA		
IS	652.9	272.4
LI		31.3
NO	1 308.0	4 417.6
Pre-accession countries		
BG		8 341.0
CZ	1 776.7	10 309.1
EE	73 213.4	1 462.1
LV	3 773.5	2 480.0
LT	42 767.9	3 707.2
HU	6 125.0	10 174.4
PL	469 372.1	38 639.3
RO	338.7	22 582.0
SI	3.2	1 987.0
SK	717.4	5 378.9
CY	4 650.1	741.0

Source: Eurostat, population statistics.

Additional notes

Ireland and **Iceland**: GDP in national currency and at current prices, in millions, 1998.
Iceland and **Norway**: OECD data.
Czech Republic, Lithuania, Romania, Slovenia and **Cyprus**: National statistics.
Estonia, Latvia, Hungary and **Slovakia**: IMF data.
Poland: 1997.

**Teachers' gross annual salaries in national currency,
primary, lower and upper secondary levels, 1997/98**

(Figures G12, G13 and G14)

	PRIMARY		LOWER SECONDARY		UPPER SECONDARY	
	MINIMUM	MAXIMUM	MINIMUM	MAXIMUM	MINIMUM	MAXIMUM
European Union						
B	761 689	1 256 891	780 472	1 381 402	983 412	1 761 324
DK	197 924	259 932	197 924	259 932	226 118	310 264
D	60 486	79 022	71 046	87 901	72 634	89 489
EL	4 158 780	6 160 000	4 278 780	6 280 000	4 278 780	6 280 000
E	3 036 540	5 421 104	3 705 290	6 622 526	3 705 290	6 622 526
F	114 385	217 497	114 385	217 497	114 385	217 497
IRL	14 811	27 803	14 304	27 803	14 304	27 803
I	31 263 917	45 769 750	33 939 304	50 723 387	33 939 304	53 245 387
L	1 439 923	2 960 102	1 974 093	3 598 323	1 974 093	3 598 323
NL	50 687	73 159	52 592	80 365	53 097	107 088
A	286 454	613 753	286 454	613 753	315 672	757 519
P	2 461 200	6 809 600	2 461 200	6 809 600	2 461 200	6 809 600
FIN	111 072	153 912	122 778	186 189	126 472	189 770
S	156 000	181 800	168 000	193 800	174 000	199 800
UK (E/W)						
UK (NI)						
UK (SC)	12 147	21 954	12 147	21 954	12 147	21 954
EFTA/EEA						
IS	1 186 912	1 974 328	1 186 912	1 974 328	1 172 596	2 086 276
LI						
NO	192 123	248 673	196 285	254 654	200 324	262 839
Pre-accession countries						
BG						
CZ	105 137	157 494	108 034	159 669	117 750	188 447
EE	31 800	66 200	31 800	66 200	31 800	66 200
LV	818	1 016	818	1 016	818	1 016
LT	6 804	8 379	6 804	8 379	7 119	8 379
HU	436 800	786 500	436 800	786 500	513 500	924 300
PL	11 232	14 268	11 232	14 268	11 232	14 268
RO	8 756 292	13 081 668	9 078 456	16 359 84	9 463 920	16 359 840
SI	1 858 354	3 915 266	1 858 354	3 915 266	1 858 354	3 915 266
SK	77 040	119 460	77 040	119 460	85 500	119 460
CY	˙ 9 453	18 290	9 453	20 700	9 453	20 700

Source: Eurydice.

SPECIAL EDUCATION

NUMBER OF CHILDREN RECOGNIZED AS HAVING SPECIAL EDUCATIONAL NEEDS AND NUMBER OF CHILDREN WITH SPECIAL EDUCATIONAL NEEDS ATTENDING SPECIAL SCHOOLS (SEPARATE CLASSES AND SCHOOLS).
COMPULSORY PRIMARY AND SECONDARY EDUCATION, 1997/98

(FIGURE H5) (1 000)

	TOTAL NUMBER OF PUPILS	CHILDREN RECOGNIZED AS HAVING SPECIAL EDUCATIONAL NEEDS	PUPILS IN SPECIAL SCHOOLS OR CLASSES
European Union			
B	1934.8	67.2	66.3
DK	600.0	75.0	10.3
D			405.4
EL	1638.4	12.9	3.9
E	6805.8	113.3	20.1
F	11927.2		297.8
IRL	446.4		14.5
I			
L		1.7	1.2
NL	2344.8	127.8	121.4
A	685.2	25.6	16.6
P	1700.0	45.0	9.0
FIN	584.2	103.9	21.5
S	938.9		0.8
UK (E)	8260.7	242.3	98.5
UK (W)	510.2	16.6	3.7
UK (NI)	352.4	7.9	4.7
UK (SC)	758.5	15.3	11.7
EFTA/EEA			
IS			
LI			
NO	478.5	31.0	2.5
Pre-accession countries			
BG			
CZ	1098.5	89.6	59.1
EE	247.2	18.3	5.4
LV	30.8	14.2	10.2
LT	473.6	43.1	7.0
HU	1347.5	38.8	24.2
PL	4896.4	124.3	87.7
RO	2522.8	36.9	35.8
SI	195.5	3.4	3.4
SK	696.1	26.2	23.4
CY	113.3	2.7	0.2

Source: National statistics.

Additional notes

Belgium: 1995/96 for the French-speaking Community, 1996/97 for the Flemish Community.
Denmark and **France**: Estimate.
Germany: The above mentioned statistics do not include for all *Länder* the number of pupils with special educational needs in mainstream education.
Netherlands: Estimate for children recognized as having special educational needs.
Austria, Portugal and **Sweden**: 1995/96.
Finland: 1998/99. The vast majority of pupils recognized as having special educational needs receive part-time special education; they are given special support for their minor learning or adjustment problems in conjunction with regular education.
United Kingdom (E/W, NI): 1996/97 for Wales. The statistics only refer to children with statements of special educational needs; those children at earlier stages of the process of the identification and assessment of special educational needs are not included. The figures for children educated separately do not include those in special classes or units of mainstream schools.
Norway: 1995/96.
Czech Republic, Slovakia and **Cyprus**: 1995/96.
Lithuania, Poland, Romania and **Slovenia**: 1997/98.
Slovenia: The percentage of children with special educational needs following mainstream education is estimated to be 1 or 2%.

FOREIGN LANGUAGES

DISTRIBUTION OF PUPILS IN PRIMARY EDUCATION (ISCED 1)
ACCORDING TO THE NUMBER OF FOREIGN LANGUAGES LEARNED, 1996/97

(FIGURE I2)   (1 000)

	European Union							
	EU	**B**	**DK**	**D**	**EL**	**E**	**F**	**IRL**
0 LANGUAGES	5 798.9	(:)	236.9	(:)	341.9	721.6	2 269.8	358.8
1 LANGUAGE	5 766.5	(:)	109.6	(:)	304.3	1 981.0	1 709.7	-
2 LANGUAGES AND OVER	79.7	(:)	0	(:)	5.7	-	-	-

	I	**L***	**NL**	**A**	**P**	**FIN**	**S**	**UK**
0 LANGUAGES	1 575.1	-	1 141.8	168.8	(:)	126.1	(:)	(:)
1 LANGUAGE	1 235.1	28.4	380	217.5	(:)	204.2	(:)	(:)
2 LANGUAGES AND OVER	-	23.3	(:)	(:)	(:)	50.6	(:)	(:)

	EFTA/EEA				Pre-accession countries			
	IS*	**LI**	**NO**		**BG**	**CZ**	**EE**	**LV**
0 LANGUAGES	21.5	(:)	(:)		398.7	405.6	36.5	(:)
1 LANGUAGE	3.8	(:)	(:)		28.9	255.5	67.4	(:)
2 LANGUAGES AND OVER	4	(:)	(:)		4.2	(:)	22.9	(:)

	Pre-accession countries (continued)							
	LT	**HU**	**PL**	**RO**	**SI**	**SK**		**CY**
0 LANGUAGES	155.9	(:)	(:)	417.5	74.3	(:)		(:)
1 LANGUAGE	66.7	(:)	(:)	987.8	25.7	(:)		(:)
2 LANGUAGES AND OVER	0.1	(:)	(:)	-	(:)	(:)		(:)

Source: Eurostat, UOE.

Additional notes

Belgium (B de): In the German-speaking Community, all ISCED 1 pupils learn one foreign language.
France: 1997/98.
Netherlands and **Portugal**: 1995/96.
Austria: 1997/98; pupils learning two languages are included in those learning one.
Finland: The national language taught in schools where it is not the teaching language is counted as a foreign language.
Czech Republic and **Slovenia**: Pupils learning two languages are included in those learning one.
Estonia: The national language taught in schools where it is not the teaching language is counted as a foreign language.

NUMBER OF PUPILS IN PRIMARY (ISCED 1) EDUCATION LEARNING ENGLISH AND FRENCH – AND ADJUSTED NUMBER OF TOTAL PUPILS ENROLLED, 1996/97

(FIGURES I3 ET I4)   (1 000)

	European Union											
	EU	**B fr**	**B nl**	**DK**	**D**	**EL**	**E**	**F**	**IRL**	**I**	**L**	**NL**
ENGLISH	6 459.6	3.4	-	109.6	279.2	306.4	1 925.2	1 316.9	(–)	1 021.5	-	380
FRENCH	568.8	(–)	131.2	-	95.3	5.5	48.4	(–)	-	180.4	23.3	-
PUPILS ENROLLED	18 566.1	314.7	394.2	346.5	3 709.7	652	2 702.6	3 979.5	358.8	2 810.2	28.4	1 521.8

	European Union (continued)					EFTA/EEA			Pre-accession countries		
	A	**P**	**FIN**	**S**	**UK**	**IS**	**LI**	**NO**	**BG**	**CZ**	**EE**
ENGLISH	214.9	239.8	238.6	424.1	(–)	4	(:)	(:)	23.2	120.2	56.3
FRENCH	4.1	45.3	7	22.5	(:)	-	(:)	(:)	2	2.9	1.3
PUPILS ENROLLED	386.2	285.9	380.9	688.9	(:)	29.3	(:)	(:)	431.8	661.1	126.8

	Pre-accession countries (continued)								Other PHARE countries		
	LV	**LT**	**HU**	**PL**	**RO**	**SI**	**SK**		**CY**	**AL**	**BA**	**MK**
ENGLISH	42.2	47.5	103	1 098.9	292.5	18.6	12.7		23.4	35.6	(:)	(–)
FRENCH	0.4	3.9	2.4	90.6	605.6	-	0.4		(:)	1.9	(:)	(–)
PUPILS ENROLLED	146.7	222.7	502.6	5 021.4	1 405.3	98.9	331.8		64.8	303.6	191.8	133

Source: Eurostat, UOE.

Additional notes

Belgium (B de): In the German-speaking Community, English is not taught at ISCED 1; all pupils learn French from the first year of primary school.
France and **Austria**: 1997/98.
Netherlands and **Portugal**: 1995/96.
Poland: ISCED 2 students are also included.

NUMBER OF PUPILS LEARNING FOREIGN LANGUAGES IN GENERAL SECONDARY EDUCATION (ISCED 2 AND 3) – AND ADJUSTED NUMBER OF TOTAL PUPILS ENROLLED, 1996/97

(FIGURE I6)   (1 000)

	European Union								
	EU	B fr	B nl	DK	D	EL	E	F	IRL
PUPILS	28 284.2	297.3	501.2	612.1	7 478.2	1 041.1	3 516.9	7 329.1	346.9
PUPILS ENROLLED	20 680.6	209	262.4	308.7	6 055.9	682.2	2 946.2	4 545.3	351.5

	I	L*	NL	A	P	FIN	S	UK	
PUPILS	3 034.5	27.5	1 042.0	577.4	405.5	763.6	507.9	(:)	
PUPILS ENROLLED	2 642.5	9.5	698.8	482.6	405.9	310.2	295.3	(:)	

	EFTA/EEA				Pre-accession countries			
	IS	LI	NO		BG	CZ	EE	LV
PUPILS	53.2	(:)	(:)		717.6	709.6	204.3	378.3
PUPILS ENROLLED	30.7	(:)	(:)		526.8	613.7	95.9	207.8

	Pre-accession countries (continued)							
	LT	HU	PL	RO	SI	SK		CY
PUPILS	503.2	1 007.3	1 339.1	2 219.0	279.8	598.9		113.3
PUPILS ENROLLED	326.6	900.1	793.2	1 475.5	223.4	416.6		56.7

Source: Eurostat, UOE.

Additional notes

Belgium (B de): In the German-speaking Community, the average number is 1.4.
France: In ISCED 3, pupils from technological education are included in general education.
Ireland: Only full-time students are included.
Netherlands: 1995/96; only full-time students are included.
Austria: 1997/98.
Portugal: 1995/96; only ISCED2 students are included; including students from the vocational stream.
Finland: The national language taught in schools where it is not the teaching language is counted as a foreign language.
Sweden: Only ISCED2 students are included.
Iceland: In ISCED 3, students from the vocational stream are also included.
Czech Republic: Only full-time students are included.
Estonia, Hungary and **Latvia**: The national language thaught in schools where it is not the teaching language is counted as a foreign language.
Poland: Only ISCED 3 students are included.
Slovenia: In ISCED 3, students from the vocational stream are also included.
Slovakia: Only ISCED 3 students are included; the national language taught in schools where it is not the teaching language is counted as a foreign language.

NUMBER OF PUPILS LEARNING ENGLISH, FRENCH, GERMAN AND SPANISH IN GENERAL SECONDARY EDUCATION
(ISCED 2 AND 3) – AND ADJUSTED NUMBER OF TOTAL PUPILS ENROLLED, 1996/97

(FIGURES I7, I8, I9 AND I10)   (1 000)

	European Union										
	EU	B fr	B nl	DK	D	EL	E	F	IRL	I	L*	NL
ENGLISH	18 089.8	133.5	186.7	308.7	5 680.9	563.3	2 820.6	4 337.9	(–)	2 009.9	7.3	658
FRENCH	4 277.5	(–)	250.1	47.5	1 475.5	430	664.8	(–)	245	904.1	9.3	81
GERMAN	2 091.2	10.6	63.6	235.1	(–)	47.8	24.9	1 197.8	86.6	90.6	9.3	97
SPANISH	1 698.5	6	0.9	18.2	70.9	-	(–)	1 547.0	13.5	12.2	1.1	-
PUPILS ENROLLED	20 209.2	209	262.4	308.7	6 055.9	682.2	2 946.2	4 545.3	351.5	2 642.5	9.5	698.8

	European Union (continued)					EFTA/EEA			Pre-accession countries		
	A	P	FIN	S	UK	IS	LI	NO	BG	CZ	EE
ENGLISH	473.5	305.9	307.2	295.3	(–)	23.4	(:)	(:)	296.8	334.5	78.5
FRENCH	63.2	(:)	41.1	62.6	(:)	2.5	(:)	(:)	108	21	2.2
GERMAN	(–)	0.4	96.6	130.9	(:)	7	(:)	(:)	112.5	328.8	33.2
SPANISH	7.3	(:)	2.8	18.5	(:)	0.7	(:)	(:)	6.5	3.2	0.2
PUPILS ENROLLED	482.6	405.9	310.2	295.3	(:)	30.7	(:)	(:)	526.8	613.7	95.9

	Pre-accession countries (continued)							CY	Other PHARE countries		
	LV	LT	HU	PL	RO	SI	SK		AL	BA	MK
ENGLISH	150.7	211.6	426.5	578.7	759.3	179	253.3	56.7	165.5	(:)	132.9
FRENCH	3.2	25.1	37	127.2	1 097.1	3	19.8	56.7	87.7	(:)	72.4
GERMAN	64.9	99.7	431.7	420.3	132.4	82.4	259	(:)	0.9	(:)	10.4
SPANISH	3.3	-	3.3	4	8.6	0.2	1.5	(:)	(:)	(:)	(:)
PUPILS ENROLLED	207.8	326.6	900.1	793.2	1 475.5	223.4	416.6	56.7	333.5	(:)	211.6

Source: Eurostat, UOE.

Additional notes

Belgium (B de): In the German-speaking Community, 93 % students in general secondary education learn English; all pupils in general seconday education learn French.
France: In ISCED 3, pupils from technological education are included in general education.
Ireland: Only full-time pupils are included.
Netherlands:1995/96; only full-time students are included.
Austria: 1997/98.
Portugal: 1995/96; only ISCED2 students are included, including students from the vocational stream.
Sweden: Only ISCED2 students are included.
Iceland: In ISCED 3, students from the vocational stream are also included.
Czech Republic: Only full-time students are included.
Poland: Only ISCED 3 students are included.
Slovenia: In ISCED 3, students from the vocational stream are also included.
Former yugoslav Republic of Makedonia: In ISCED 3, students from the vocational stream are also included.

NUMBER OF PUPILS LEARNING ONE, TWO OR MORE FOREIGN LANGUAGES IN GENERAL (G) AND VOCATIONAL (V) SECONDARY EDUCATION (ISCED 2 AND 3), 1996/97

(FIGURE I12)   (1 000)

		European Union											
		EU	B	DK	D	EL	E	F	IRL	I	L	NL	A
1 LANGUAGE	G	(:)	(:)	10.2	(:)	317.2	2 375.5	1 895.3	251.2	1 556.8	-	(:)	477.6
	V	(:)	(:)	44.4	(:)	129.0	638.6	754.8	2.6	(–)	1.3	(:)	154.4
2 LANGUAGES	G	(:)	(:)	262.6	(:)	355.5	570.7	2 516.3	45.6	294.5	2.5	(:)	(:)
	V	(:)	(:)	7.5	(:)	-	-	64.48	0.60	(–)	7.1	(:)	(:)
3 LANGUAGES	G	(:)	(:)	34.5	(:)	-	-	133.72	1.11	-	5.4	(:)	(:)
	V	(:)	(:)	-	(:)	-	-	-	0.02	(–)	9.3	(:)	(:)
4 LANGUAGES	G	(:)	(:)	-	(:)	-	-	-	0.03	-	1.6	(:)	(:)
	V	(:)	(:)	-	(:)	-	-	-	-	(–)	-	(:)	(:)
PUPILS IN	G	(:)	(:)	308.7	(:)	682.2	2 946.2	4 545.3	351.5	2 642.5	9.5	(:)	482.6
ISCED 2, 3	V	(:)	(:)	119.1	(:)	135.4	905.9	853.9	19.7	1857.3	19.3	(:)	169.7
TOTAL		(:)	(:)	427.7	(:)	817.6	3 852.1	5 399.2	371.2	4 499.8	28.8	(:)	652.3

		European Union (continued)					EFTA/EEA				Pre-accession countries		
		P	FIN	S	UK		IS	LI	NO		BG	CZ	EE
1 LANGUAGE	G	(:)	2.2	0.7	(:)		3.6	(:)	(:)		453.1	457.4	20.1
	V	(:)	(:)	31.6	(:)		(:)	(:)	(:)		201.6	285.5	12.3
2 LANGUAGES	G	(:)	176.5	17.3	(:)		16 .8	(:)	(:)		73.7	126.1	45.6
	V	(:)	(:)	20.7	(:)		(:)	(:)	(:)		5.0	90.8	9.8
3 LANGUAGES	G	(:)	114.8	7.2	(:)		4.8	(:)	(:)		-	-	27.6
	V	(:)	(:)	3.3	(:)		(:)	(:)	(:)		-	-	0.5
4 LANGUAGES	G	(:)	16.0	3.0	(:)		0.3	(:)	(:)		-	-	2.5
	V	(:)	(:)	0.3	(:)		(:)	(:)	(:)		-	-	.
PUPILS IN	G	(:)	310.2	28.4	(:)		30.7	(:)	(:)		526.8	613.7	95.9
ISCED 2, 3	V	(:)	(:)	56.0	(:)		(:)	(:)	(:)		206.6	389.6	22.6
TOTAL		(:)	(:)	84.4	(:)		30.7	(:)	(:)		733.4	1 003.3	118.5

		Pre-accession countries (continued)								Other PHARE countries		
		LV	LT	HU	PL	RO	SI	SK	CY	AL	BA	MK
1 LANGUAGE	G	(:)	119.5	(:)	(:)	1 445.6	156.8	-	(:)	247.3	(:)	112.1
	V	(:)	11.7	(:)	(:)	525.0	(:)	(:)	(:)	14.4	(:)	-
2 LANGUAGES	G	(:)	191.8	(:)	(:)	-	50.0	62.0	(:)	11.2	(:)	15.2
	V	(:)	18.1	(:)	(:)	-	(:)	(:)	(:)	2.3	(:)	-
3 LANGUAGES	G	(:)	(:)	(:)	(:)	-	5.6	3.0	(:)	-	(:)	-
	V	(:)	(:)	(:)	(:)	-	(:)	(:)	(:)	-	(:)	-
4 LANGUAGES	G	(:)	(:)	(:)	(:)	-	-	-	(:)	-	(:)	-
	V	(:)	(:)	(:)	(:)	-	-	(:)	(:)	-	(:)	-
PUPILS IN	G	(:)	326.6	(:)	(:)	1 475.5	133.0	65.0	(:)	333.5	(:)	127.9
ISCED 2, 3	V	(:)	52.2	(:)	(:)	793.8	90.4	259.7	(:)	16.6	(:)	0.1
TOTAL		(:)	378.8	(:)	(:)	2 269.3	223.4	324.7	(:)	350.2	(:)	127.9

Source: Eurostat, UOE.

Additional notes

The vocational stream at ISCED level 2 exists only in Spain, France, Luxembourg and Austria.
France: In ISCED 3, students from the technological education are included in general education.
Italy: Only ISCED 2 students are included.
Netherlands and **Portugal**: 1995/96.
Austria:1997/98; the number of students learning two languages is included in those learning one.
Finland: The national language taught in schools where it is not the teaching language is counted as a foreign language.
Sweden: 1995/96; only ISCED 3 students are included.
Iceland: In ISCED 3, students from the vocational stream are included as well.
Czech Republic: Only full-time students are included.
Estonia: The national language taught in schools where it is not the teaching language is counted as a foreign language.
Poland: Only ISCED 3 students are included.
Slovenia: In ISCED 3, students from the vocational stream are also included.
Slovakia: Only ISCED 3 students are included; the national language taught in schools where it is not the teaching language is counted as foreign language.

TABLE OF FIGURES

Chapter A — Context   1

Figure A1:   Change in the numbers of young people in the 0-9, 10-19 and 20-29 age groups   1
             in the European Union, from 1975 to 1997

Figure A2:   Percentage of the population in the 0-9, 10-19 and 20-29 age groups,   1
             1997

Figure A3:   Percentage in the 0-29 age group by NUTS 1 and NUTS 2 regions,   2
             1997

Figure A4:   Percentage of people who do not have an upper secondary qualification,   3
             by age group, 1997

Figure A5:   Percentage of people in education or training among young people aged 15 to 24,   4
             1987 and 1997

Figure A6:   Pupils and students (in thousands),   4
             1996/97

Figure A7:   Proportion of pupils and students in the 0-29 age group,   5
             1996/97

Figure A8:   Pupils and students of compulsory school age, in thousands and   5
             as a proportion of the total number of pupils and students, 1996/97

Figure A9:   Change in the unemployment rates by age group,   6
             in the European Union, 1987-1997

Figure A10: Change in the unemployment rates   7
             by age group and Member State, 1987-1997

Figure A11: Unemployment rates in the 15-24 age group   8
             who have left school and in the 25-59 population, 1997

Figure A12: Percentage of employees with insecure jobs   9
             by age group, 1997

Figure A13: Unemployment rates in the 25-59 age band,   10
             by level of education, 1997

Figure A14: Unemployment rates among higher education graduates,   11
             by age group, 1997

Figure A15: Unemployment rates of the 25-59 year old population   12
             by education level and sex, 1997

Figure A16: Occupations of people with higher education qualifications   13
             by age groups, 1997

Figure A17: Percentage of employees aged 25-59 with insecure jobs,   14
             by education level, 1997

Figure A18: Average gross monthly earnings,   15
             by education level, in Euros, 1995

Chapter B — Structures and schools   17

Figure B1:   Structures of schools and tertiary education institutions,   18
             1997/98

Figure B2:   Distribution of pupils and students by level of education,   24
             as a percentage, 1996/97

Figure B3:   Distribution of primary and secondary students according to the type of school they   25
             attend, as a percentage, 1996/97

Figure B4:   Autonomy of public-sector primary schools,   27
             1997/98

Figure B5:   Autonomy of public-sector lower secondary schools,   28
             1997/98

Figure B6:   Range of dates of the return to school, primary and secondary education,   32
             1997/98

Figure B7:   Distribution of school holidays over the school year, primary and secondary education,   34
             1997/98

Figure B8:   Role of national-level bodies which include representatives of parents.   35
             Compulsory education, 1997/98

Figure B9:   Powers of school-level bodies which include parent representatives, in 5 areas.   37
             Compulsory education, 1997/98

Figure B10: Monitoring the education systems at the primary and/or secondary level.   39
             Compulsory preparation of a school plan, 1997/98

Figure B11: Monitoring the educational systems at the primary and/or secondary level.   41
             Publication of the overall results of external tests, 1997/98

Chapter C — Pre-primary education   43

Figure C1:   Participation rates of 4-year-olds in education-oriented pre-primary institutions,   43
             as a percentage, from 1960 to 1997

Figure C2:   Organization of pre-primary institutions,   44
             public and private sectors, 1997/98

Figure C3:   Participation rates in education-oriented pre-primary institutions and primary institutions,   47
             by age, as a percentage, 1996/97

Figure C4:   Distribution of children attending education-oriented pre-primary provision   48
             according to the type of institution they attend, as a percentage, 1996/97

Figure C5:   Participation rates of 3-year-olds in education-oriented pre-primary institutions,   49
             by NUTS 1 and NUTS 2 regions, as a percentage, 1996/97

Figure C6:   Enrolment of 3-year-olds in education-oriented pre-primary institutions, as a percentage, in   50
             comparison to percentage of mothers with a 3-year-old child and in employment, 1996/97

Figure C7:   Average duration of attendance by children aged 3-7 at an education-oriented pre-   51
             primary institution in comparison to duration of official provision, in years, 1996/97

Figure C8:   Principal methods of grouping children in education-oriented pre-primary institutions,   52
             1997/98

Figure C9:   Prescribed or recommended maximum numbers of 4-year-old children per adult   54
             in schools and other education-oriented pre-primary institutions, 1997/98

Figure C10:   Fee-paying/free admission to education-oriented pre-primary institutions and   55
              percentage of fee-paying children, 1997/98

Figure C11:   Levels of education covered by the official document setting out guidelines   56
              for education-oriented pre-primary provision, 1997/98

Figure C12:   Contents of the official guidelines, in schools and   57
              other education-oriented pre-primary institutions, 1997/98

Figure C13:   General and specific objectives stipulated in the official guidelines,   58
              education-oriented pre-primary institutions, 1997/98

Figure C14:   The five areas of activity selected are specified in the official guidelines, schools and   59
              other education-oriented pre-primary institutions, 1997/98

Figure C15:   Recommendations for pupil evaluation in the official guidelines, schols and   60
              other education-oriented pre-primary institutions, 1997/98

Figure C16:   Teaching approaches recommended by the official guidelines,   62
              education-oriented pre-primary institutions, 1997/98

Figure C17:   Age limits for the admission of children to compulsory primary education,   63
              1997/98

Chapter D — Primary education   65

Figure D1:   Organization of compulsory primary or single structure education,   65
              1997/98

Figure D2:   Class size regulations or recommendations,   67
              1997/98

Figure D3:   Main models for dividing teaching and subjects among the teachers (around age 7),   68
              1997/98

Figure D4:   Total annual taught hours at around age 7,   69
              1997/98

Figure D5:   Total annual taught hours at around age 10, 1997/98   70

Figure D6:   Minimum annual hours of taught time at around age 7 and age 10,   70
              1997/98

Figure D7:   Recommended allocation of annual hours of teaching of compulsory subjects   72
              at around age 7, 1997/98

Figure D8:   Recommended allocation of annual hours of teaching of compulsory subjects at around   73
              age 10, 1997/98

Figure D9:   Progression to the next year during primary education, 1997/98   74

Figure D10:   Conditions of admission to lower secondary education, public and private grant-aided   75
              sectors, 1997/98

Chapter E — Secondary education   77

Figure E1:   Organization of secondary education structures,   78
              1997/98

Figure E2:   Pupils' age of the end of compulsory full-time education and   82
              the organization of lower secondary education, 1997/98

Figure E3:   Distribution of pupils in general and   83
              vocational lower secondary education (ISCED 2), as a percentage, 1996/97

Figure E4:   Distribution of students in general and   84
             vocational upper secondary education (ISCED 3), as a percentage, 1996/97

Figure E5:   Distribution of students between general and vocational streams   85
             at upper secondary level (ISCED 3), by gender, as a percentage, 1996/97

Figure E6:   Percentage of upper secondary students (ISCED 3) in general education   86
             by NUTS 1 and NUTS 2 regions, 1996/97

Figure E7:   Annual number of hours of taught time   87
             in general lower secondary education, 1997/98

Figure E8:   Annual number of hours of taught time   88
             in general upper secondary education, 1997/98

Figure E9:   Minimum annual hours of taught time   88
             in secondary education, 1997/98

Figure E10: Percentages of minimum annual timetable allocated to compulsory subjects   89
             around age 13 in general lower secondary education, 1997/98

Figure E11: Percentages of minimum annual timetable allocated to compulsory subjects   91
             around age 16 in the science section of general upper secondary education, 1997/98

Figure E12: Percentage of those aged 22 who have successfully completed   92
             at least upper secondary education (ISCED 3), 1997

Figure E13: Number of girls per 100 boys obtaining   93
             a general upper secondary education qualification, 1996/97

Figure E14: Certification at the end of general lower secondary education   94
             or compulsory full-time education, 1997/98

Figure E15: Certification at the end of general lower secondary education   95
             or compulsory full-time education, 1997/98

Figure E16: Certification at the end of general upper secondary education,   97
             1997/98

Figure E17: Certification at the end of general upper secondary education,   98
             1997/98

Figure E18: Participation rates, overall and broken down by sex,   100
             at the end of compulsory education, as a percentage, 1996/97

Chapter F — Tertiary education 103

Figure F1: Proportion of students in tertiary education (ISCED 5, 6, 7),   103
in thousands and as a percentage of all pupils and students, 1996/97

Figure F2: Trends in the number of students in tertiary education (ISCED 5, 6, 7),   104
from 1975/76 to 1996/97

Figure F3: Tertiary education students (ISCED 5, 6, 7)   105
as a percentage of all pupils and students, by NUTS 1 and NUTS 2 regions, 1996/97

Figure F4: Limits on the number of places available in most branches of private, grant-aided and   107
public tertiary education, 1997/98

Figure F5: Increasing numbers of students selected to take part   108
in an Erasmus exchange programme, in thousands, from 1988/89 to 1998/99

Figure F6: The growth in the budgets allotted to Erasmus students,   109
in millions of ECU, from 1988/89 to 1998/99

Figure F7: Percentage of tertiary level students selected to go abroad and   109
be received within the Erasmus programme, 1997/98

Figure F8: Percentage of tertiary education students (ISCED 5, 6, 7) studying in   110
another EU Member State or EFTA/EEA country, 1996/97

Figure F9: Registration and tuition fees and other payments made by students on full-time   111
undergraduate courses, public sector, 1997/98

Figure F10: Components of grant and/or loan support to students on undergraduate courses,   113
1997/98

Figure F11: Participation rates in tertiary education (ISCED 5, 6, 7),   114
by age and by gender, as a percentage, 1996/97

Figure F12: Trends in the number of women per 100 men enrolled   116
in tertiary education (ISCED 5, 6, 7), from 1975 to 1996

Figure F13: Participation rate of students aged 19 to 24 (living with their parents) in tertiary   117
education (ISCED 5, 6, 7) by educational level of parents, as a percentage, 1997

Figure F14: Proportion of young people aged between 30 and 34   117
with tertiary education qualifications (ISCED 5, 6, 7), as a percentage, 1997

Figure F15: Proportion of people aged between 35 and 59   118
with tertiary education qualifications (ISCED 5, 6, 7), by age group, 1997

Figure F16: Women per 100 men graduating   119
from tertiary education (ISCED 5, 6, 7),1996/97

Figure F17: Distribution of graduates among the different fields of study (ISCED 5, 6, 7),   120
as a percentage, 1996/97

Figure F18: Proportion of females with tertiary education qualifications (ISCED 5, 6, 7),   121
by field of study, as a percentage, 1996/97

Chapter G — Teachers   123

Figure G1:   Duration and level of the initial education and training of   124
pre-primary teachers, 1997/98

Figure G2:   Duration and level of the initial education and training of   125
primary teachers, 1997/98

Figure G3:   Duration and level of initial education and training of teachers   126
for lower secondary schools (general education), 1997/98

Figure G4:   Duration and level of initial education and training of teachers   127
for upper secondary schools (general education), 1997/98

Figure G5:   Teachers as a percentage of the total active population. Primary and secondary   128
levels (ISCED 1, 2 and 3), public and private sectors combined, 1996/97

Figure G6:   Percentage of teachers working part-time, primary (ISCED 1) and   129
secondary (ISCED 2 and 3) levels, 1996/97

Figure G7:   Distribution of teachers by age band, as a percentage.   130
Primary education (ISCED 1), public and private sectors combined, 1996/97

Figure G8:   Distribution of teachers by age band, as a percentage. Secondary education   131
(ISCED 2 and 3), public and private sectors combined, 1996/97

Figure G9:   Age of retirement, primary and secondary education,   132
1997/98

Figure G10: Percentage of teachers within 10 years of retirement in primary (ISCED 1) and   134
secondary education (ISCED 2 and 3), 1996/97

Figure G11: Percentage of female teachers. Primary (ISCED 1) and secondary (ISCED 2 and 3)   135
education, public and private sectors combined, 1996/97

Figure G12: Minimum and maximum salaries of primary teachers relative to per capita GDP,   136
1997/98

Figure G13: Minimum and maximum salaries of lower secondary teachers relative to per capita   137
GDP, 1997/98

Figure G14: Minimum and maximum salaries of upper secondary teachers relative to per capita   137
GDP, 1997/98

Chapter H — Special education   139

Figure H1:   Development over this century of educational structures for children   140
with special educational needs

Figure H2:   Main patterns of provision for children   142
with special needs, 1997/98

Figure H3:   Initial training for special educational needs. Primary and secondary level teachers,   144
1997/98

Figure H4:   Organization of structures of special education in separate schools,   146
1997/98

Figure H5:   Percentage of children recognized as having special educational needs and   149
percentage of children with special needs educated separately (special classes
and schools). Compulsory primary and secondary education, 1997/98

Chapter I — Foreign languages · 151

Figure I1:	The availability of foreign languages at pre-primary, primary and general secondary levels, 1997/98	152
Figure I2:	Distribution of pupils in primary education (ISCED 1) according to the number of foreign languages learned, 1996/97	155
Figure I3:	Percentage of pupils in primary education (ISCED 1) learning English, 1996/97	156
Figure I4:	Percentage of pupils in primary education (ISCED 1) learning French, 1996/97	157
Figure I5:	Foreign languages most often learned at primary level (ISCED 1) and percentage of pupils learning them, by country, 1996/97	158
Figure I6:	Average number of foreign languages learned per pupil in general secondary education (ISCED 2 and 3), 1996/97	159
Figure I7:	Percentage of pupils learning English in general secondary education (ISCED 2 and 3), 1996/97	160
Figure I8:	Percentage of pupils learning French in general secondary education (ISCED 2 and 3), 1996/97	160
Figure I9:	Percentage of pupils learning German in general secondary education (ISCED 2 and 3), 1996/97	161
Figure I10:	Percentage of pupils learning Spanish in general secondary education (ISCED 2 and 3), 1996/97	161
Figure I11:	Foreign languages most learned at general secondary level (ISCED 2 and 3) and percentage of pupils learning them, by country, 1996/97	162
Figure I12:	Percentage of pupils in general and vocational secondary education (ISCED 2 and 3) learning foreign languages. Distribution according to the number of languages learned, 1996/97	163

Chapter J — Information and communication technology · 165

Figure J1:	Education levels covered by official documents on the use of ICT (in force during 1997/98)	165
Figure J2:	National or official bodies with a remit for ICT in education, 1997/98	166
Figure J3:	Implementation schedule for typical ICT projects. Primary and secondary education, 1980-2005	168
Figure J4:	Responsibility for the purchase and maintenance of hardware. Primary and secondary education. Projects under way in 1997/98	169
Figure J5:	Distribution of the specific budget between the purchase of equipment and expenditure on human resources. Primary education. Projects under way in 1997/98	170
Figure J6:	Distribution of the specific budget between the purchase of equipment and expenditure on human resources. Lower secondary education. Projects under way in 1997/98	171
Figure J7:	Distribution of the specific budget between the purchase of equipment and expenditure on human resources. General upper secondary education. Projects under way in 1997/98	171

Figure J8:   Objectives in ICT.   172
               Primary education. Projects under way in 1997/98

Figure J9:   Objectives in ICT.   173
               Lower secondary education. Projects under way in 1997/98

Figure J10:   Objectives in ICT.   173
               General upper secondary education. Projects under way in1997/98

Figure J11:   Inclusion of ICT in the curriculum.   174
               Primary education, 1997/98

Figure J12:   Approaches to ICT defined in the curriculum.   175
               Primary education, 1997/98

Figure J13:   Objectives defined in the curriculum for the teaching or the use of ICT.   176
               Primary education, 1997/98

Figure J14:   Inclusion of ICT in the curriculum.   177
               Lower secondary education, 1997/98

Figure J15:   Approaches to ICT defined in the curriculum.   178
               Lower secondary education, 1997/98

Figure J16:   Objectives defined in the curriculum for the teaching or the use of ICT.   179
               Lower secondary education, 1997/98

Figure J17:   Inclusion of ICT in the curriculum.   180
               General upper secondary education, 1997/98

Figure J18:   Approaches to ICT defined in the curriculum.   181
               General upper secondary education, 1997/98

Figure J19:   Objectives defined in the curriculum for the teaching or the use of ICT.   182
               General upper secondary education, 1997/98

Figure J20:   Specialist ICT teachers.   183
               Primary and secondary education, 1997/98

Figure J21:   ICT courses during initial training of general class teachers (or specialists in other   184
               subjects). Primary education, 1997/98

Figure J22:   ICT courses during initial training of general class teachers (or specialists in other   185
               subjects). Lower secondary education, 1997/98

Figure J23:   ICT courses during initial training of specialists in other subjects.   186
               General upper secondary education, 1997/98

ACKNOWLEDGEMENTS

AUTHORS

EURYDICE EUROPEAN UNIT

Arlette Delhaxhe

Annick Sacré

STATISTICAL OFFICE EUROSTAT

Claudia Casín

Laurent Freysson (chapter A)

Séverine Jacquemart

Anne-France Mossoux

Spyridon Pilos (coordination)

LAYOUT AND PREPARATION OF GRAPHICS

Patrice Brel, Eurydice European Unit

SECRETARIAL SUPPORT

EURYDICE EUROPEAN UNIT

Helga Stammherr

STATISTICAL OFFICE EUROSTAT

Claudine Greiveldinger

TRANSLATION AND REVISION OF ENGLISH VERSION

For the part of Eurydice, Judith Hague

For the part of Eurostat, Anne-France Mossoux

Original edition in French

Final edition, Eurydice European Unit

EURYDICE NETWORK

Eurydice European Unit
Rue d'Arlon 15
B-1050 Brussels
(http://www.eurydice.org)

National Units which have contributed to the preparation of the report

EUROPEAN UNION

BELGIQUE / BELGIË
Unité francophone d'Eurydice
Ministère de la Communauté française
Direction générale des Relations internationales
Bureau 6A/002
Boulevard Leopold II, 44
1080 Bruxelles
Contribution: joint responsibility

Vlaamse Eurydice-Eenheid
Ministerie van de Vlaamse Gemeenschap
Departement Onderwijs
Afdeling Beleidscoördinatie
Koning Albert II - laan 15
1210 Brussel
Contribution: Erwin Malfroy

Agentur Eurydice
Ministerium der deutschsprachigen Gemeinschaft
Agentur für Europäische Programme
Quartum Centre
Hütte 79 / Bk 28
4700 Eupen
Contribution: joint responsibility

DANMARK
Eurydice's Informationskontor i Danmark
Institutionsstyrelsen
Undervisningsministeriet
Frederiksholms Kanal 25D
1220 København K
Contribution: joint responsibility

BUNDESREPUBLIK DEUTSCHLAND
Eurydice - Informationsstelle beim
Bundesministerium für Bildung und Forschung
Heinemannstrasse 2
53175 Bonn
Contribution: joint responsibility

Eurydice - Informationsstelle der Länder
im Sekretariat der Kultusministerkonferenz
Lennéstrasse 6
53113 Bonn
Contribution: Dr. Gerdi Jone, Dr. Beatrix Sauter

ELLADA
Eurydice Unit
Ministry of National Education and Religious Affairs
Direction CEE / Section C
Mitropoleos 15
10185 Athens
Contribution: Antigoni Faragoulitaki, Elene Mathiopoulou,
Angela Methodiou, Evi Zigra

ESPAÑA
Unidad de Eurydice
Ministerio de Educación y Cultura
CIDE – Centro de Investigación y Documentación Educativa
c/General Oráa 55
28006 Madrid
Contribution: Carmen Morales Gálvez, Laura Ocaña Villuendas,
Irene Arrimadas Gómez, Begoña Arias González

FRANCE
Unité d'Eurydice
Ministère de l'Éducation nationale, de la Recherche et de la
Technologie
Délégation aux Relations internationales et à la Coopération
Sous-Direction des relations multilatérales
Bureau des affaires européennes
Rue de Grenelle 110
75357 Paris
Contribution: joint responsibility

IRELAND
Eurydice Unit
Department of Education and Science
International Section
Marlborough Street
Dublin 1
Contribution: joint responsibility

ITALIA
Unità di Eurydice
Ministero della Pubblica Istruzione
Biblioteca di Documentazione Pedagogica
Via M. Buonarroti 10
50122 Firenze
Contribution: joint responsibility

LUXEMBOURG
Unité d'Eurydice
Centre de Psychologie et d'Orientation Scolaires
Route de Longwy 280
1940 Luxembourg
Contribution: joint responsibility

NEDERLAND
Eurydice Eenheid Nederland
Afd. Informatiediensten D073
Ministerie van Onderwijs, Cultuur en Wetenschappen
Postbus 25000 – Europaweg 4
2700 LZ Zoetermeer
Contribution: joint responsibility (Ministry of Education, Culture and
Science); Anneke Van Dorp (co-ordination)

ÖSTERREICH
Eurydice - Informationsstelle
Bundesministerium für Unterricht und
kulturelle Angelegenheiten – Abt. I/6b
Minoritenplatz 5
1014 Wien
Contribution: joint responsibility

EUROPEAN UNION (continued)

PORTUGAL
Unidade de Eurydice
Ministério da Educação
Departamento de Avaliação, Prospectiva e Planeamento (DAPP)
Av. 24 de Julho 134
1350 Lisboa
Contribution: Filipe do Paulo (expert), Margarida Madureira (Eurydice Unit)

SUOMI / FINLAND
Eurydice Finland
National Board of Education
Hakaniemenkatu 2
00530 Helsinki
Contribution: joint responsibility

SVERIGE
Eurydice Unit
Ministry of Education and Science
Drottninggatan 16
10333 Stockholm
Contribution: joint responsibility

UNITED KINGDOM
Eurydice Unit for England, Wales and Northern Ireland
National Foundation for Educational Research
The Mere, Upton Park
Slough, Berkshire SL1 2DQ
Contribution: joint responsibility

Eurydice Unit Scotland
International Relations Branch
The Scottish Office Education and Industry Department
Floor 2 Area B Victoria Quay
Edinburgh EH6 6QQ
Contribution: joint responsibility

EFTA/EEA countries

ÍSLAND
Eurydice Unit
Ministry of Education, Science and Culture
Division of Evaluation and Supervision
Sölvholsgata 4
150 Reykjavik
Contribution: joint responsibility

LIECHTENSTEIN
National Unit of Eurydice
Schulamt
Herrengasse 2
9490 Vaduz
Contribution: joint responsibility

NORGE
Eurydice Unit
Royal Norwegian Ministry of Education,
Research and Church Affairs
P.O. Box 8119 Dep.
Akersgaten 42
0032 Oslo
Contribution: joint responsibility

PRE-ACCESSION COUNTRIES

BĂLGARIJA
Eurydice Unit
International Relations Department
Ministry of Education, Science and Technology
2A, Knjaz Dondukov Bld
1000 Sofia
Contribution: joint responsibility

ČESKÁ REPUBLIKA
Eurydice Unit
Institute for Information on Education – ÚIV/IIE
Senovážné nám. 26
Praha 1, 111 21
Contribution: joint responsibility

EESTI
Eurydice Unit
Estonian Ministry of Education
9/11 Tonismägi St.
5192 Tallinn
Contribution: joint responsibility

LATVIJA
Eurydice Unit
Ministry of Education and Science
Departement of Education and Strategy
Valnu 2
1050 Riga
Contribution: joint responsibility

LIETUVA
Eurydice Unit
Ministry of Education and Science
A. Volano 2/7
2691 Vilnius
Contribution: joint responsibility with Ministry officials and the Research and Higher Education Department as well as Centre of Information Technologies for Education

MAGYARORSZÁG
Eurydice Unit
Ministry of Education
Szalay u. 10-14
1054 Budapest
Contribution: joint responsibility

POLSKA
Eurydice Unit
Foundation for the Development of the Education System
Socrates Agency
Al. Szucha 25
00-918 Warszawa
Contribution: Anna Smoczyńska

ROMÂNIA
Eurydice Unit
Socrates National Agency
1 Schitu Magureanu – 2nd Floor
70626 Bucharest
Contribution: Alexandru Modrescu

PRE-ACCESSION COUNTRIES (continued)

SLOVENIJA
Eurydice Unit
Ministry of Education and Sport
Zupanciceva 6
1000 Ljubljana
Contribution: joint responsibility

SLOVENSKÁ REPUBLIKA
Eurydice Unit
Slovak Academic Association for International Cooperation
Staré grunty 52
842 44 Bratislava
Contribution: joint responsibility

KYPROS
Eurydice Unit
Ministry of Education and Culture
Pedagogical Institute
Latsia
P.O. Box 12720
2252 Nicosia
Contribution: joint responsibility

EUROSTAT CONTACT POINTS

Statistical Office of the European Communities
Bâtiment Jean Monnet
L-2920 Luxembourg

National contact points that have taken part in preparing this report

EUROPEAN UNION

BELGIQUE / BELGIË
Service des Statistiques
Communauté française de Belgique
Boulevard Pachéco 19 - Bte 0
1010 Bruxelles
Contribution: Jean-Claude Roucloux, Nathalie Jauniaux

Ministerie van de Vlaamse Gemeenschap
Departement Onderwijs
Hendrik Consciencegebouw, tower 5B
Koning Albert II-laan, 15
1210 Brussel
Contribution: Ann Van Driessche, Liselotte Van de Perre

DANMARK
Ministry of Education
National Authority for Institutional Affairs
Frederiksholms Kanal 25
1220 Kobenhavn OE
Contribution: Ken Thomassen

Danmarks Statistics
Sejrogade 11
Postboks 2550
2100 Kobenhavn OE
Contribution: Karsten Kühl

BUNDESREPUBLIK DEUTSCHLAND
Statistisches Bundesamt
Statistics of Education and Culture
Wittelsbacher Strasse 10
65180 Wiesbaden
Contribution: Walter Hörner, Christiane Krüger-Hemmer

ELLADA
Ministry of Education
Director of Planning and Operational
Mitropoleos Street 15
10185 Athens
Contribution: Christos P. Kitsos

ESPAÑA
Ministerio de Educación y Cultura
Oficina de planificación y estadistica
C/Alfonso XII, 3 - 5
28014 Madrid
Contribution: Mr Jesús Ibáñez Milla

FRANCE
Ministère de l'Education nationale
Boulevard du Lycée 58
92170 Vanves
Contribution: Pierre Fallourd

IRELAND
Department of Education
Statistics Section
Irish Life Center, Block 1
Lower Abbey Street
Dublin 1
Contribution: Mary Dunne

ITALIA
ISTAT - Istituto Nazionale di Statistica
Via Cesare Balbo, 16
00198 Roma
Contribution: Angela Silvestrini

LUXEMBOURG
Ministère de l'Education nationale et de la Formation
Professionnelle
29, rue Aldringen
2926 Luxembourg
Contribution: Jérôme Levy

NEDERLAND
Centraal Bureau voor de Statistiek
Prinses Beatrixlaan 428
2270 AZ Voorburg
Contribution: Max Van Herpen

EUROPEAN UNION (continued)

ÖSTERREICH
Österreichisches Statistisches Zentralamt
Hintere Zollamtstrasse 2b
1030 Wien
Contribution: Wolfgang Pauli

PORTUGAL
Ministerio da Educaçao
DEPGEF
Av. 24 de Julho 134
1350 Lisboa
Contribution: Joaquim Maia Gomes

SUOMI / FINLAND
Statistics Finland
Työpajakatu 13
00022 Helsinki
Contribution: Heikki Havén, Mika Tuononen

SVERIGE
Statistics Sweden
Department of Labour and Education
23 Klostergatan
701 89 Örebro
Contribution: Bengt Gref, Michael Karlsson, Mats Haglund

UNITED KINGDOM
Department for Education and Employment
Room 139B, Analytical Services HEES12
Mowden Hall
Staindrop Road
Darlington DL3 9BG
Contribution: Stephen Mowbray, John Canlin

EFTA/EEA COUNTRIES

ÍSLAND
Statistics Iceland
Education Statistics
Skuggasundi 3
150 Reykjavik
Contribution: Asta Urbacic

LIECHTENSTEIN
Schulamt
Education Statistics
Contribution: Hans Peter Walch

NORGE
Statistics Norway
2225 Kongsvinger
Norway
Contribution: Elisabetta Vassenden, Lise M. Styrk Hansen

PRE-ACCESSION COUNTRIES

BĂLGARIJA
National Statistical Office of Bulgaria
2, P. Volov Str.
1527 Sofia
Contribution: Stoyan BAEV

ČESKÁ REPUBLIKA
Institute for Information on Education – ÚIV/IIE
Senovážné nám. 26
Praha 1, 111 21
Contribution: Marie NĚMEČKOVÁ

EESTI
Statistical Office of Estonia
Endla 15,
15174 Tallinn
Contribution: Aavo HEINLO

LATVIJA
Central Statistical Bureau of Latvia
1, Lãčpleša Street
1301 Riga
Contribution: Maranda BEHMANE
Agnese GRŽIBOVSKA

LIETUVA
Statistics Lithuania
Gedimino av. 29
2746 Vilnius
Contribution: Gailė DAPŠIENĖ
Salvinija CHOMIČIENĖ

MAGYARORSZÁG
Hungarian Central Statistical Office
Keleti Karoly u. 5-7
1024 Budapest
Contribution: Katalin JANAK
Erzsebet VARGA

POLSKA
Central Statistical Office
Al.Niepodleglosci 208
00-925 Warszawa
Contribution: Alina Baran

ROMÂNIA
National Commission for Statistics of Romania
16 Libertatii Blvd.
Bucharest 5
Contribution: Daniela Stefanescu

SLOVENIJA
Statistical Office of the Republic of Slovenia
Vožarski pot 12
1000 Ljubljana
Contribution: Tatjana ŠKRBEC,
Breda LOŽAR

SLOVENSKÁ REPUBLIKA
Institute of Information Prognosis of Education
Staré grunty 52
842 44 Bratislava
Contribution: Alzbeta Ferencicova

Statistical Office of the Slovak Republic
Dúbravská 3
842 21 Bratislava
Contribution: Alexandra PETRÁŠOVÁ

KYPROS
Department of Statistics and Research
13 Andreas Araouzos Str.
1444 Nicosia
Contribution: Alekos Agathangelou

OTHER COUNTRIES TAKING PART IN THE PHARE PROGRAMME

ALBANIA
Institute of Statistics of Albania
Leke Dukagjini, Nr=5
Tirana

Ministry of Education and Science
Rruga e Durresit
Tirana
Contribution: Lili DODI,
Alma SHENA, Besa PEÇI

BOSNIA AND HERZEGOVINA
Institute of Statistics of the Republika Srpska
Jevrejska 28
78000 Banja Luka
Contribution: Jelena DOKIĆ

THE FORMER YUGOSLAV REPUBLIC OF MACEDONIA
Statistical Office of the Republic of Macedonia
Darne Gruev - 4
Skopje
Contribution: Mira TODOROVA

CONTACT POINTS

European Agency for Development in Special Needs Education

Teglgaardsparken 10
DK-5500 Middelfart

National contact points that have taken part in preparing this report

EUROPEAN UNION

BELGIQUE / BELGIË
EPESCF
Avenue Max Buset 24
7100 La Louvière
Contribution: Thérèse Simon

Ministerie van de Vlaamse Gemeenschap
Departement Onderwijs
Secretariaat-generaal
Hendrik Consciencegebouw, Toren B
Emiel Jacqmainlaan 165, 5de verdieping, lokaal 11
1210 Brussel
Contribution: Theo Mardulier

DANMARK
Undervisningsministeriet
H.C. Andersens Boulevard 43
1553 Kobenhavn V
Contribution: Poul Erik Pagaard

BUNDESREPUBLIK DEUTSCHLAND
IPTS 22 - Beratungsstelle für Integration
Schreberweg 5
24119 Kronshagen
Contribution: Anette Hausotter

ELLADA
Ministry of Education
Directorate of European Union
Section C - Eurydice
Mitropoleos Street 15
10185 Athens
Contribution: Antigoni Faragoulitaki

ESPAÑA
Ministerio de Educación y Cultura
Subdirección General de Educación Especial y
de Atención a la Diversidad
c/Los Madrazo 15-17
28071 Madrid
Contribution: Justino Rodriguez Esteban

FRANCE
Centre national de Suresnes
58-60, avenue des Landes
92150 Suresnes
Contribution: Nel Saumont

IRELAND
Offices of the Inspectorate
Department of Education
South Mail 1A
Cork
Contribution: Peadar McCann

ITALIA
Biblioteca di Documentazione
Pedagogica
Via Buonarroti 10
50122 Firenze
Contribution: Giovanni Biondi

LUXEMBOURG
Service ré-éducatif ambulatoire
Rue Charles Martel 64
2134 Luxembourg
Contribution: Pia Englaro

NEDERLAND
GION
Rijksuniversiteit Groningen
Westerhaven 15
9718 AW Groningen
Contribution: Dr. Sip Jan Pijl

ÖSTERREICH
Pädagogische Institut des Bundes
in Salzburg
Erzabt-Klotz-Strasse 11
5020 Salzburg
Contribution: Irene Moser

PORTUGAL
Department for basic education
Av. 24 de Julho 140
1391 Lisboa
Contribution: Vítor Morgado

SUOMI / FINLAND
Ministry of Education
Meritullinkatu 10
P.O. Box 293
00171 Helsinki
Contribution: Eero Nurminen

SVERIGE
SIH
Box 47611
117 94 Stockholm
Contribution: Lena Thorsson

UNITED KINGDOM
National Foundation for Educational
Research
The Mere,Upton Park
Slough
Berkshire SL1 2DQ
Contribution: Felicity Fletcher-Campbell

EFTA/EEA countries

ÍSLAND
Menntamálaráduneytid
Sölvhólsgata 4
140 Reykjavik
Contribution: Kolbrún Gunnarsdottír, Gudni Olgeirsson

NORGE
Nasjonalt læremiddelsenter
Boks 8194 Dep
0034 Oslo
Contribution: Vibeke Thue, Agnes Stubbe